Ethnic American Minorities

Ethnic American Minorities

A Guide to Media and Materials

Edited and Compiled by
HARRY A. JOHNSON

R. R. BOWKER COMPANY
New York & London, 1976

Published by R. R. Bowker Co.
1180 Avenue of the Americas, New York, N.Y. 10036

Printed and bound in the United States of America

Library of Congress Cataloging in Publication Data
Johnson, Harry Alleyn.
Ethnic American minorities.

Includes indexes.
1. Ethnic studies—Audio-visual aids—Catalogs.
2. Minorities—United States—Bibliography.
I. Title.
E184.A1J58 016.30145'0973 76-25038
ISBN 0-8352-0766-8

Contents

Preface ix

I THE AFRO-AMERICAN IN THE MELTING POT 1
Harry A. Johnson

A Historical Perspective 3
The Social and Psychological Needs of Afro American Youth on Entering Mainstream America. 7
Black Studies and the Curriculum 8
Multimedia and Telecommunications Technology 10
Notes 12
Bibliography. 12
Media and Materials—Annotated 17
Films (16mm) 17 · Filmstrips 41 · Slides 55 · Transparencies 57 · Audio Recordings and Audio Cassettes 61 · Video Cassettes 68 · Study Prints/ Pictures/Posters/Graphics 69

II ASIAN AMERICANS—QUIET AMERICANS? 71
Minako K. Maykovich

Prewar Period (–1945) 72
Chinese Immigration 72 · Japanese Immigration 73 · During the War 74 · Filipino Immigration 75 · Korean Immigration 76
Postwar Period 76
Rise of Economic Status 77 · Rise of Ethnic Pride 79
Cultural Heritage 80
Asian Social Structure 80 · Asian Religions 81 · Asian Family System 82 · Asian American Experience 83

Educational Needs 83
Language Education 84 · Broadening Curriculum Alternatives 85
Notes 87
Bibliography. 89
Media and Materials—Annotated 92
Films (16mm) 92 · Filmstrips 106 · Slides 120 · Transparencies 123 · Audio Recordings and Audio Cassettes 124 · Video Cassettes 130 · Study Prints/ Pictures/Posters/Graphics 131

III THE NATIVE INDIAN AMERICAN 133
S. Gabe Paxton, Jr.

Historical Milestones 135
Prehistorical Period 135 · Early Historical Period 136 · The Mission Period 136 · The Treaty Period 137 · The Allotment Period 138 · The Meriam Report and the New Deal Period 138 · The Termination Period 139 · The Beginning of the Pan-Indian Period 139 · Indian Awareness Period 139
Special Educational Needs of the Native Indian American 140
Learning Styles and Characteristics 141 · Criteria for Selection of Materials 141 · Implications for Research 143
Bibliography. 143
Media and Materials—Annotated 148
Films (16mm) 148 · Filmstrips 168 · Slides 176 · Transparencies 178 · Audio Recordings and Audio Cassettes 179 · Video Cassettes 185 · Study Prints/ Pictures/Posters/Graphics 186

IV THE SPANISH-SPEAKING AMERICAN 189
Lourdes Miranda King

The U.S. Experience 189
A Profile 191 · The Mexican American or Chicano 194 · The Puerto Ricans 195 · The Cubans 197
Cultural Needs 198
Style of Reasoning 199 · Relationships 200 · Family Structure 200 · Religion 201
Educational Needs—Bilingual Education 201
Notes 205

Media and Materials—Annotated 206
Films (16mm) 206 · Filmstrips 220 · Slides 229 · Transparencies 231 · Audio Recordings and Audio Cassettes 232 · Video Cassettes 237 · Study Prints/ Pictures/Posters/Graphics 238

V OTHER ETHNIC MINORITIES ON THE AMERICAN SCENE 241
Harry A. Johnson

Media and Materials—Annotated 242
Films (16mm) 242 · Filmstrips 251 · Slides 258 · Audio Recordings and Audio Cassettes 258 · Video Cassettes 261 · Study Prints/Pictures/Posters/Graphics 263

Directory of Producers and Distributors 265
Media Indexed by Title 279
Index 295

Preface

The recording of American history traditionally has omitted an effective coverage of the heritage and contributions of American ethnic minorities. The primary purpose of this book, therefore, is to provide an understanding and appreciation for American minorities and to present a highly documented, annotated source of instructional materials and media on four major minorities—Afro-Americans, Asian Americans, Native Indian Americans, and Spanish-speaking Americans. The roles of these minorities have been ignored or inaccurately portrayed in curriculum materials thus depriving them of their heritage, their history, and their heroes. The materials and writings presented in this book draw attention to those aspects of history, literature, and contributions that have been omitted or dealt with in a superficial manner at all educational levels.

The concept of cultural pluralism in American education is diametrically opposed to the principle of assimilation. Since our schools must prepare young people to live harmoniously in an industrialized nation, curriculum reform to accommodate ethnicity and cultural pluralism is essential. The recent policy statement by the American Association of Colleges for Teacher Education (AACTE) states it well and provides a thrust toward a reality in our society.

> To endorse cultural pluralism is to endorse the principle that there is no one model American. To endorse cultural pluralism is to understand and appreciate the differences that exist among the nation's citizens. It is to see these differences as a positive force in the continuing development of a society which professes a wholesome respect for the intrinsic worth of every individual. Cultural pluralism is more than a temporary accommodation to placate racial and ethnic minorities. It is a concept that aims toward a heightened sense of being and of wholeness of the entire society based on the unique strengths of each of its parts.*

This book is designed to assist librarians, administrators, teachers, and students in developing a more comprehensive coverage of the history and diverse cultures of America while focusing on the current social, economic, and political stresses and strains that affect their instructional plans and learning activities.

---

*AACTE Statement on Multicultural Education. "No One Model American." *Journal of Teacher Education* 24 (4): winter 1973, p. 264.

In the first chapter the author-editor focuses on Afro-Americans—their history, characteristics, and problems of identity. The second chapter is written by an outstanding American educator of Asian descent, Minako K. Maykovich, who sets forth the composition of Asian Americans and their problems as a minority. The third chapter, by S. Gabe Paxton, Jr., deals with the plight of Native Indian Americans and their aspirations and desires to rid America of their stereotyped image. In the fourth chapter, Lourdes Miranda King, an American of Puerto Rican ancestry, focuses on the commonalities of problems and characteristics of Spanish-speaking Americans including the Chicanos, Puerto Ricans, Cubans, and others of Spanish ancestry. The fifth chapter deals with a cross section of other minorities such as American Jews, migrant Americans, and young adults. These chapters lend authenticity and provide a rationale for understanding the social structure, cultural heritage, educational needs, and learning styles of America's major ethnic groups.

Bibliographies of publications are provided in some chapters to help the teacher and the research scholar seek out more detailed information on the ethnic groups.

The media and materials sections concluding each chapter include annotated entries for films (16mm), filmstrips, slides, transparencies, audio recordings and audio cassettes, video cassettes, and study prints/pictures/posters/graphics. In compiling these sections I initially analyzed some 1,000 multimedia sources during 1973 and 1974; final selection of entries was made in 1975 and 1976 from some 300 producers and distributors of standard and new materials. Such sources as university film libraries, producers, distributors, television inventories, tape and videotape libraries, the resources of ERIC (Educational Resources Information Center), and Stanford University were utilized.

Grade level, release date where possible, and other technical information provide the user with useful and necessary information. Purchase and rental prices changed drastically during the research. The annotations carry the latest figures available at this writing. However, users are cautioned to use the listed price only as a guide. Annotations and technical information differ in each of the media categories. Most films are available for rental and purchase. Filmstrips are available for purchase only, with rental practically impossible. This also holds true with other media, especially audio recordings, both cassettes and records; and reel-to-reel tape recordings. Producers tend to provide very sketchy and limited information on transparencies. Coded identification cataloging is not uniform with distributors. Smaller companies use no alphabetical or numerical identification but rely on the title of the item.

This is a selective list and the selection process was not an easy task. The entries were selected on the basis of availability, authenticity, suitability for children and youth, and relevance in today's world. Few entries were selected which predated this past decade nor were any entered which were condescending or degrading to any ethnic group. Ethnic educators were consulted in the selection process. The selection process for the fifth chapter differed from the in-depth evaluation of the other four. The items here were selected in some cases because they were the only ones available. Others were selected because they dealt with several ethnic groups and were, therefore, best suited to this chapter. There was a dearth of materials on most of the other minorities. An evaluation was inherent in the selection process. Whereas these evaluations are not stated with each entry, the selection process gives the user some background on the criteria for, and the process of, selection. In each annotation I attempted to give enough information so that the user could discard or select this information for further evaluation.

An effort has been made to provide at least one source for the user. In some instances only the producer is listed because that producer also distributes the productions. Often both producer and distributor are included and in others, a distributor only. However, every entry provides at least one source whose full address is listed in the complete directory at the end of this book.

Inclusion does not necessarily mean general endorsement. It is recommended that materials be further evaluated for their relevance and need in a given learning environment. The annotations are conveniently listed after each ethnic chapter to encourage the reader to use the chapter and the annotations together.

In general, the Afro-American and Native Indian American materials tend to deal with the indigenous cultures of those two ethnic groups, while the Asian American and Spanish-speaking American materials deal with the history, culture, and customs from the vantage point of their national origin rather than their experiences in this country.

It is hoped that the users of this guide will find it an effective selection and teaching tool as well as a source of enlightenment.

Harry A. Johnson
Virginia State College

CHAPTER I

The Afro-American in the Melting Pot

by Harry A. Johnson,
Professor of Education,
Virginia State College

The teaching of history and the social sciences is in a state of revolution in the United States. This unsettling curriculum revolution has begun to make an impact at all levels of education. One of the chief causes appears to be an unwillingness on the part of the youth of this generation to accept the values, practices, views, and educational priorities set by previous generations. Children and young adults are becoming increasingly aware that traditional history and social studies often reflect values and attitudes long considered outmoded and slanted.

The melting-pot concept of American unity is an ideal that has never come to fruition. Bayard Rustin states it quite simply: "There never was a melting pot, there is not now a melting pot, there never will be a melting pot, and if there was it would be such a tasteless soup that we would have to go back and start all over." The melting-pot theory has, to a degree, succeeded in bringing immigrants into the mainstream of economic productivity, but fortunately, it has had difficulty melting the cultural differences out of the immigrants or their descendants. Despite various assimilation efforts, ethnic groups have clung tenaciously to their cultural traditions and folkways.

Louis Adamic states that there are two ways of looking at American history:

> One is this: that the United States is an Anglo-Saxon country with a White-Protestant-Anglo-Saxon civilization struggling to preserve itself against infiltration and adulteration by other civilizations brought here by Negroes and hordes of foreigners.
>
> The second is this: that the pattern of the United States is not essentially Anglo-Saxon, although her language is English. Nor is the pattern Anglo-Saxon with a motley addition of darns and patches. The pattern of America is all of one piece; it is a blend of cultures from many lands, woven of threads from many corners of the world. Diversity is the pattern, is the stuff and color of the fabric.[1]

History can no longer reflect only the dominant beliefs and values of the majority subculture in society. It must clearly reflect the interpretations, values, and beliefs of the various ethnic groups within the culture. Members of all racial, religious, and ethnic groups are now demanding that their contributions to the development of this great nation be recorded in a fair and impartial manner. For too long, history in our textbooks has been parochial, chauvinistic, and indoctrinated with myths and half-truths, but worst of all, omissions.

For more than half of this century the history of the South was written largely by white Southerners or those who generally sympathized with the traditional views of white Southerners. Until some twenty years ago historians generally accepted the views of Ulrich B. Phillips; namely that slavery in the Old South was a relatively benign and largely unprofitable system of reciprocal relationships. Modern historians reject the Phillips interpretation of slavery as being too pro-slave owner and too anti-Black.

The contention of Stanley Elkins that the typical slave was a "Sambo" who had been brainwashed has been challenged by John W. Blassingame and others who deny that slavery infantilized Blacks. Indeed, the latest trend is to show how even as slaves "Black Americans struggled successfully to maintain their dignity, their competence, and the integrity of their family life." A recent study of slavery—Robert W. Fogel's and Stanley L. Engerman's *Time on the Cross* (1974)—stresses the record of black achievement under adversity. So does Eugene D. Genovese's new book, *Roll, Jordan, Roll* (1974).

Black leaders have been writing the history of black people since James W. C. Pennington, a fugitive slave, examined for the first time Africans in the new world with his ten volume *Text Book of the Origin and History of the Colored People* in 1841. The eminent scholar W. E. B. DuBois, first black Harvard graduate, gave to America his scholarly writing, "Suppression of the African Slave Trade." Another Harvard trained black man, Carter G. Woodson became the unofficial spokesman for Black history. He organized the prestigious Association for the Study of Negro Life and History in 1915. He began what may be termed the modern Black-history movement. Other scholars who researched and published during this century (A. A. Taylor, Horace Mann Bond, Charles H. Wesley, Luther P. Jackson, Lorenzo Green, Rayford W. Logan, and John Hope Franklin) sought for the truth. These men along with many others had a tremendous job trying to correct the false accounts of such writers as Thomas Dixon (*The Clansman*) and Charles Carroll (*The Negro a Beast*). Though their efforts were valiant, their works often were not fashionable and accepted in their time.

Although the Civil War emancipated Blacks from slavery and three Constitutional amendments were passed to ensure their civil rights, Blacks were not fully recognized as part of the American culture until many years later. They often felt that the South wanted to keep them enslaved while the North did not want them at all. It was not until the New Deal that Blacks could regard government as having a personal interest in their welfare, although discrimination from those entrusted with implementing government policies was not uncommon. Intelligent Americans would be the first to admit that the majority of white people acquiesced to the campaigns of terror made against Blacks down through the years. Even so, most white Americans would insist that the gains of the last thirty years indicate major progress toward racial equality. The political power of Northern Blacks and the liberalism of the federal courts were greatly responsible for these changes. But it took the snarling dogs and the fire hoses throughout the South to catapult the true condition of Blacks before the American conscience and to make the educated public and intellectuals realize what progress had not been made in the first half of this century.

The growing self-awareness of black Americans, especially among the young, had been unfolding as dramatically as our own ventures into space. It paralleled in the fifties and sixties the development of black nationhood on the African continent. Young Blacks became aware that there were close to 30 million of their people in America with a very special history, culture, and range of problems, and they began to insist that if major universities of the land could offer degrees and training in the culture of the classical Greeks and Romans, and other defunct civilizations, they could also provide the same treatment for the history and the contemporary issues of Africa and its descendants in America.

A HISTORICAL PERSPECTIVE

The history of Blacks in America is the history of the American racial dilemma. Blacks have for centuries seen themselves through the revelation and measurement of white people who have looked on them with sentiments ranging from amused contempt and pity to hard-core fear and hatred.

To the Romans, slaves were merely vulgar and conquered people who were not accorded the rights and privileges of Roman citizenship. The Greeks looked upon slaves as unfortunate citizens of their plundered lands who had failed to cultivate their minds and desires, and were thus reduced to that lowly but necessary state. But in America, slaves were considered property and were not even accorded recognition in the human race. They were sold from the auction blocks like animals and labeled as chattel in the American courts.

With the Emancipation Proclamation came the vain search for freedom. Like a bright but fleeting cloud, it was there, but not there. The holocaust of war, the terrors of the Ku-Klux-Klan, the deceits of the carpetbaggers, and the shattered promises of a young government left black men and women floundering like bewildered serfs still echoing the cry for freedom.

For three centuries on this continent black people's powers of body and mind have been wasted, unused, and forgotten. They have been denied access to education and economic security, and condemned to menial levels of work or joblessness which has resulted in poverty, disunion, and misery for countless millions.

Throughout their struggle Blacks have wanted to be Black *and* American with pride in both—therein lies their dilemma. Blacks have always felt that their African heritage had something to offer America, as have the European ethnic cultures. Blacks would not Africanize America, neither would they wish to bleach their blackness into a white Americanism. Blacks are unique and different and want to remain that way.

From amidst these complexities grew a generation of black leaders and a new perception of liberty. Power was the word. The goal of freedom demanded for its achievement powerful means, and these were forthcoming with the fifteenth amendment to the Constitution. Blacks now saw the ballot as the chief means for gaining and perfecting the liberty which the emancipation had promised. With a renewed zeal Blacks started to vote themselves into the mainstream of the nation, but the post-slavery decade soon faded into history and a new vision emerged, gradually replacing the dream of political power.

Booker T. Washington was without a doubt the spokesman for black people from the time of his famous Atlanta speech in 1895 until his death in 1915. He had caught the leadership mantle thrown by the established leader, ex-slave Frederick Douglass; however, their ideologies were poles apart. Washington labored for the economic preparation of Blacks through the "let down your bucket where you are" philosophy. Douglass, the predecessor, was a more militant leader, who had advised John Brown at Harper's Ferry and Abraham Lincoln to free the slaves. He had urged education as the channel to complete freedom.

Scholar, spokesman, and writer, William Edward Burghardt DuBois (1868-1963) catapulted into the role of the intellectual leader of Blacks. Few great men have become legends in their own times. DuBois was the proud, confident, and militant scholar who launched the Niagara Movement which advocated the immediate ending of racial discrimination and segregation in America. He disagreed violently with Booker T. Washington's emphasis on vocational education for black people. He believed that Blacks were entitled to develop all of their faculties and talents to the utmost. While Washington stressed vocational education and a "place" for Blacks in America, DuBois stressed training in the liberal arts and humanities. DuBois was to see many of his views implemented through teacher training at such prestigious institutions as Howard and Fisk universities.

The long, hard struggle for survival of the black man in America has always been based on poverty. For more than a century private charity, the federal government, and some state agencies have attempted to provide subsistance for the poor, but our economic system, precipitated by depression, discrimination, and lack of education, prohibited much progress in eliminating the problem.

The mobility of black workers in the American economy is best characterized by cycles of progression and retrogression. Blacks have made their strongest advances during periods of rapid economic growth and suffered setbacks during economic declines. World War I provided Blacks with widespread occupational opportunities. Because of the curtailment of European emigration during World War I and rapid industrial expansion, many Blacks were able to move into jobs that white native Americans or white foreign born workers did not want or had vacated as better opportunities turned up. Many Southern Blacks migrated to the North, therefore, and obtained unskilled, manual jobs in steel mills, auto plants, foundries, packing houses, highway construction, railroad maintenance, laundries, food industries, and some branches of the needle trades. Since World War I, the swift population growth, and the migration to the urban centers have combined to generate new generations of poor Blacks.

In 1919, a triumphant army of tacky soldiers passed in review up New York's Fifth Avenue to the cheers of countless citizens crowding the sidewalks and windows. It was generally agreed that one of the most thrilling sights and sounds was that of the 369th Colored Infantry, swinging up the avenue toward Harlem, marching to the syncopated beat of James Europe's blaring jazz band. These black soldiers, like those all over the country in the big cities and small towns, little realized that they would be returning to civilian life to defend their lives all over again. For by the summer of 1919, bloody rioting had taken place in Chicago, Omaha, Longview (Texas), Washington, D.C., and Arkansas. Black men were dragged from streetcars, beaten on the sidewalks or attacked in their homes. "The land of liberty is in danger of becoming the land of lynchers," warned Kelly Miller of Howard University. The Ku-Klux-Klan enjoyed a spectacular rise in membership and power during and after the war. By the time the war in Europe had ended, the Klan had extended its hate campaign to include Catholics, Jews, Orientals, and others.

Amidst this tragic period in American history, the Black Renaissance had been born; sociologists, philanthropists, and even black leaders were unable to account for the "new Negro." The vibrant young generation exhibited a new psychology and created a new spirit among the masses. The main change was the shifting of the black population into the large cities of the north and west where they became an integral part of the large industrial and social problems of that period. Better jobs and urban living rapidly introduced the process of class differentiation; there was no longer an en masse consideration of Blacks, but instead they were becoming identifiable in all strata of the society of the 1920s. No longer could the Booker T. Washingtons speak for the black people. Popular support was being shifted from the officially recognized orthodox spokesmen for the race, to those of the independent, popular, and often radical types of the new order.

By the late twenties a great many Blacks were going to high school and college and the experiences of a liberal education left their traces. The emergence of a black middle class was quite evident. The world of the professional man had opened up, and even the field of music had taken on a new dimension, for the big bands of the twenties and thirties were largely black middle-class enterprises. Men who had gone to college became the leaders in this period, including Duke Ellington, Coleman Hawkins, Jimmie Lunceford, Sy Oliver, and Don Redman. The greatest social gain of this period was that of releasing the talented and trainable minds of the black American from the arid fields of controversy and debate to the productive fields of creative expression and the professions. Blacks were beginning to demand a reevaluation in the thinking of white Americans—the keystone to any considerable improvement of race relations. They were beginning to "sit at the table" as so simply expressed by Langston Hughes in "I Too."

I TOO

I, too, sing America
I'm the darker brother.
They send me to eat in the
kitchen when company comes,
but I laugh and eat well,
and grow strong; tomorrow I will
sit at the table when company comes.
Nobody will dare say to me eat in

the kitchen then besides they will
know how beautiful I am and be
ashamed,–
I, too, am an American.[2]

While the 1920s represented a period of prosperity for Blacks in the North because of their relatively low unemployment rates, the depression of the 1930s returned many blacks to their pre-1900 impoverished status.

Three factors converged to make the depression of the 1930s particularly catastrophic for Blacks: the collapse of cotton agriculture in the South, the shrinking employment opportunities in the North, and the invasion by white workers into many of the jobs traditionally held by Blacks.

Much of the occupational progress made by Blacks was lost during the depression. For example, the number of Blacks in mechanical and mining occupations fell from 1,100,000 in 1930 to 738,000 in 1940, and the number in wholesale and retail trade declined from 398,000 to 288,000. The proportion of Blacks in manufacturing industries also declined, from 7.3 percent to 5.1 percent.[3]

The institution of work relief and other social welfare programs of the New Deal were particularly helpful to Blacks in their impoverished condition. The Federal Emergency Relief Administration reported in October 1933 that 27 percent of urban Blacks were on relief. They were represented to a lesser degree in southern areas.

The Harlem Renaissance passed into oblivion and so did the thirties and World War II. The new militants of the postwar period became outraged at being called extremists. They had long taken the position that the Constitution of the United States conferred complete equality on all of its citizens. They rested their case on the proposition that there is only one side, the constitutional side. Their impatient thrust for full citizenship and dignity and the eradication of segregation and discrimination gave them no rest. Every civil rights victory added to the black American's self-determination and drive for complete participation and acceptance in every phase of American life.

In 1954 *Brown* v. *Board of Education* paved the way for school desegregation, and less than a year later the Montgomery bus boycott started a trend of active civil rights movements aimed at ending "Jim Crow" segregation for all time. The late 1950s and early 1960s saw the passage of three new civil rights acts by Congress . With the impact of the movement led by Dr. Martin Luther King, Jr., the raising of the national consciousness seemed finally to be under way. Integration in housing, opening up of educational facilities and opportunities, social programs to improve economic conditions, and wide participation by Blacks in the political system have indeed made a different world for today's black youth.

The struggle is not yet over, however; mainstream America must still come to grips with the fact that black Americans, if they are to gain a sense of self-determination and dignity, must have the power to take initiative and action in their own behalf. It is far more important that things be done *by* black Americans than that they be done *for* them. Education is the tool that can make this need a reality. Every effort must be made to stimulate indigenous leadership and activities among black Americans, so that they will gain economic and political power which will broaden their perspectives on life and relieve them from exploitation and oppression by the white majority.

THE SOCIAL AND PSYCHOLOGICAL NEEDS OF AFRO-AMERICAN YOUTH ON ENTERING MAINSTREAM AMERICA

The basic psychological need of black youth is that of developing a positive self-image and an identity with which they are proud, or at least comfortable. They need, both in and out of the nation's schools, models available for patterning their behavior. Black youths need to realize rewards for their efforts, and their teachers must seek ways to reward them, to further motivate them, and to provide constant encouragement to enhance their growth and development.

Schools and colleges need to get on with the job of providing alternative instructional strategies and a wide variety of instructional resources, which reach outside of the narrow Anglo-Saxon heritage and history. The need is urgent for expanding ethnically oriented curriculum for our pluralistic student bodies. Dr. Jacquelyne Jackson of the Duke University Medical School points out the need for black behavioral scientists who can fill the gap that white researchers have reported on in such studies as "The Kerner Report," "The Coleman Report," and "The Moynihan Report." Dr. Jackson says:

> Perhaps one of the most important of the social and psychological needs of ghetto youth at this decisive point in our current history is that of the need for more informed and more courageous social and behavioral scientists who (usually federally funded) continue to amass datum after datum, interpretation after interpretation, conclusion after conclusion, implication after implication about them. . . .
>
> A basic social and psychological need, once again, is for the development of more black, ghetto youth as competent social and behavioral scientists, who, given sufficient insights into and experiences in the black ghetto, and provided with sufficient scientific and humanistic training, will help close the present gaps in our knowledge and our understanding of the black ghetto in general, and ghetto youth in particular.[4]

Perhaps the most urgent social need of black youth is that of social acceptance as first class citizens and first-class human beings with access to a guaranteed job with an annual income sufficient enough for a moderate standard of living; with access to improved employment, at equal wages, with adequate retirement benefits; and with easy access to education and provisions for occupational mobility in an upward direction.

There is an urgent need for drastic educational reforms so that black youth will learn and will be motivated to continue to learn. There is a need for teachers who are trained to teach, for those who have been trained in human growth and development, psychology, and techniques of teaching based on proven theories of learning. Every effort must be made to effectively teach these children.

The basic psychological needs include those developing positive self-images or identities, or having adequate models available for behavioral patterning, of being able to realize the reward of success for their efforts. Consistent failure breeds more failure, and finally the effort to achieve dies right there in the classroom. Youths need to receive continuous motivation and encouragement to enhance their growth and development. Black youth have a right to schools where administrators and teachers are aware of literature and information pertaining to such factors as achievement, black self-images, measurement of ability, effects of deprivation upon perception, development of logical thinking, environmental effects on attitude and learning, and certain effects of segregation.

The educational advances of Blacks, however, has been one of continuous progress. It is most clearly reflected in the sharp reduction in the dropout rates of black youngsters. Between 1963 and 1972, the high school dropout rate for black youth declined from 33 percent to 19 percent over the decade.

Not only are more black youths completing high school, they are also going on to college in increasing numbers. In 1962, about half (51 percent) of the white students who graduated from high school that year were enrolled in college by fall 1962. Yet only one-third (34 percent) of the black high school graduates in 1962 were enrolled in college by that fall. But ten years later, the proportion of black high school graduates going on to college was about equal to that of white graduates. In 1972, 49 percent of the white high school graduates were enrolled in college by the fall, while 48 percent of the black high school graduates that year were enrolled in college by fall 1972. This upward mobility of Blacks being educated must be considered by teachers and counselors as they deal with the design of relevant curriculums.

BLACK STUDIES AND THE CURRICULUM

Structured curriculum not meeting the needs of learners is observed in the best and the poorest schools. Irrelevant instructional materials, obsolete teaching methods, rote learning, and traditional strategies inflicted on Blacks and the economically deprived prevent progress, hamper achievement, and make a mockery of effective and valued education. Formal education is not responsive enough to the needs of youth of the seventies and eighties. It takes little account of what is known about the process of human learning, particularly of the range of individual differences and different learning styles of children and young adults.

Individuals differ in the way they learn, in their motivation to learn, and even their desire to learn. Researchers have proved this to us over and over again. Yet, most institutions are locked into conventional patterns of grade structure, time span, and subject divisions that fail to exploit each student's individual interests, abilities, capacities, and personality traits.

This is particularly relevant to the black youth. This systematic failure to develop autonomy, relevance, individuality, and the pressure of conformity to middle-class standards have done more to crush the creativity children possess and push black youths out of school than any other force in the black community.

Designing a curriculum in a changing society is a task that educators must face squarely as they prepare for education in the eighties and beyond. This need has reached crisis proportion in the black community. The verbatim transfer of suburban middle-class curriculum to black children and the poor and culturally deprived has proven to be a failure. A need exists for curriculums to be designed which accommodate Afro-American youths and their heritage. Therefore, black studies must be added to the curriculums. Dr. Deborah Partridge Wolfe defines black studies as follows:

> "Black studies" is the organizing of knowledge around the experiences of people of Africa and African descent. It is both historical and contemporary since it *must* deal with the experience itself with its *real issues* and problems as lived in the past and present. It utilizes the content, methodology, and skills of the separate disciplines of history, sociology, anthropology, psychology, literature, language, linguistics, political science, biology, geography, social welfare, economics, law, theology, music, art, and drama but it is also interdisciplinary since the Black Experience is interdisciplinary. Certainly, there is sufficient evidence to demonstrate that the traditional disciplines have not been adequate to the task of understanding Blacks.[5]

A well designed program of black studies should build an understanding of the history of African civilizations with special focus on Africa below the Sahara. Such a focus should be on the study of government, family and community structure, music and art, literature and language, drama, laws, education, customs, religion, occupations, and other aspects of African culture. Such a curriculum should heighten awareness of the effect of the migration of black Africans to the Americas. It would deepen the appreciation of the student for the contributions of Africa and black people to the development of other civilizations. It would foster an understanding of the black experience in the United States as it is reflected in the Afro-American's social and political institutions, modes of cultural expression, and developments within the cultural, social, and economic life as a whole in the United States. Finally, a black studies curriculum would give attention to the problems which Afro-Americans face in American communities today and seek broad long-term solutions to these problems.

Experiences which develop a pride and understanding of one's self are extremely important. If curriculum planners and other experts believe that schools must develop a better understanding of the importance of the social and psychological dynamics of cultural differences and translate this into sound educational programs, then the curriculum must reflect this view.

The development of skill in concept formation and language must extend from young children through to the youths in upper grades. Every black child should be provided in school an opportunity to read poetry of such Blacks as Countee Cullen, Margaret Williams, Phillis Wheatley, James Weldon Johnson, LeRoi Jones, Claude McKay, and other Afro-Americans. Through reading relevant materials black children will learn about America's cultural diversity, reject stereotype thinking about the black man, and develop a better understanding of society. Therefore, teachers and librarians must insist on books by and about black men and women. No activity in the school curriculum lends itself more to the development of improved human relations and understanding of the democratic process than reading.

Even today, after the turmoil of the last decade, adequate provisions for the inclusion of instruction about Blacks and about other American minorities is still conspicuously absent in the vast majority of curriculums on all grade levels and in higher education. Thus, a moral obligation still exists for the schools and colleges of America to review and change their instructional programs.

MULTIMEDIA AND TELECOMMUNICATIONS TECHNOLOGY

The learning environment needs an arrangement of resources whereby the Afro-American student responds and learns to the unlimited extent of his curiosity. Implicit in such an environment, if it is to be effective, is the teacher who is aware of the role of technology in developing a spirit of inquiry, self-motivation, and achievement for Afro-American children.

Educational technology in particular is providing increased learning through a wide range of instructional strategies. Teachers and curriculum specialists are, in an increasing number, showing a growing concern for nonbook materials. They are beginning to advocate the expansion of instructional resources to include not only books but a wide variety of nonbook materials such as instructional 8mm single-concept films, teaching machines, programmed materials, recordings, audio tapes, models, filmstrips, learning kits, and video tapes. Lately we have seen the inclusion of such far-reaching and innovative facilities as dial access information retrieval systems, decentralized content zones, carrels, and other information-holding devices in our libraries and instructional media centers. These are essential resources for many Afro-American children and youth.

Programmed materials allow black youth to learn at their own rate of speed. They build their limited vocabulary with programmed materials, solve simple mathematical problems, learn the principles of combustion engines, or the process of local city government all at their own pace—and with no frustrating failures, no competition, no sarcasm from a teacher tired of repeating, and no threats of failure. Properly programmed materials paint for them a total picture in sequences small enough for them to handle. Immediate feedback gives them a sense of confidence and accomplishment.

Study carrels and independent learning facilities equipped with single-concept 8mm film, record players, filmstrips, and color slides with earphones, lend a person-to-person excitement to learning. These materials can reinforce an inspiring teacher's introduction to almost any type of study. A system employing self-study facilities has vast resources for repetitive, stimulating, and creative activities.

Tape teaching, programming for flexible groupings, redeploying the teacher for more personal assistance, and programming learners into sequences utilizing audiotapes could be one of the most profitable features of educational technology. Such tapes, used individually in a tutorial arrangement, are often better planned and sequenced than many live lectures. A classroom or a laboratory wired to a tape recorder frees youngsters to move about as instructions are given. These and other resources and teaching strategies help guarantee black youth the relevant materials and alternative learning channels that will insure their success.

Television can do much toward helping black youngsters identify and develop a pride in race and cultural heritage. Educational television has not begun to tap the potential it has for minority and ghetto children. Television resources give slow children an opportunity to deal with the vast, never-ending flow of information. Unlike middle-class suburban youth, the ghetto youth, in order to even survive in the mainstream competition, must play catch up!

Perhaps the greatest breakthrough in technology for individualizing learning is the computer. The computer is capable of serving a large group of learners simultaneously, dealing with the same problems. It therefore becomes a tool for problem solving; far more resourceful than a teacher in a much shorter time. Before the student can make the computer solve a mathematical problem, the problem must be analyzed and its solution explicitly formulated as a series of discrete, operationally defined steps corresponding to the computer's repertoire of operations.

Modern educational technology can be the greatest boon to bridging the cultural and educational gap for black ghetto youth in this century. The complexity of educational problems requires redesigning the curriculum, retraining educational personnel, and proper utilization of educational media experts and supporting staff—all within an instructional systems approach to educating ghetto youth.

In developing programs for minority youths, curriculum specialists and educational media specialists must develop a greater respect for each other as fellow educators in recognizing the school's curriculum needs and the significance that technology can bring to the process of education. Advances in educational technology and its potential in individualizing instruction have placed new and increasingly complicated demands on curriculum developers. The new emphasis on instructional development as a way of curriculum changes and the selection and utilization of newer media demand a new kind of curriculum expertise for instructional improvement through use of applied technology.

The knowledge of curriculum, learning theory, instructional strategies, and child development which curriculum specialists possess must be put to work in this environment. They not only continue to work with teachers on these matters, but they begin dialogues with the technologists—the computer programmer, the media specialist, and the television producer. This relationship is a new one, but it is vital if technology is going to serve our purposes; that of making education meaningful and relevant to black American youth.

Educational technology provides no panaceas. Perhaps its failure, where it has failed, came from expecting too much from it. Yet a careful assessment of its potential within the framework of a systematized approach to instruction focusing on the individual holds promises far beyond our most optimistic dreams for the twenty-first century.

It must be remembered, however, that there is a point at which a black child needs a teacher rather than a machine or a program to confer with and relate to. This relationship between teacher and student should not be eliminated. The values that accrue from the intellectual interactions and social relationships with other students should not be rejected. Black students need all the help they can get in this great melting pot.

NOTES

1. Louis Adamic, *A Nation of Nations* (New York and London: Harper and Bros., 1945), p. 6.
2. Langston Hughes, *Selected Poems* (New York: Alfred A. Knopf, Inc., 1959). Copyright 1926 by Alfred A. Knopf, Inc., and renewed 1954 by Langston Hughes from *Selected Poems*. Reprinted by permission of the publisher.
3. Andrew F. Brimmer, "The Negro in the National Economy," in *The American Negro Reference Book*, ed. by John P. Davis, vol. 2 (Englewood Cliffs, N.J.: Prentice-Hall, 1973), p. 251.
4. Jacquelyne Jackson, "A Black Sociologist Crystallizes Sociological and Psychological Needs to the Characteristics and Special Problems of Ghetto Youth," in *Multimedia Materials for Afro-American Studies*, ed. by Harry Alleyn Johnson (New York and London: R. R. Bowker Company, 1971), pp. 38, 41.
5. Deborah Partridge Wolfe, "Integrating Black Studies into the Curriculum of Today's Schools," in *Multimedia Materials for Afro-American Studies*, p. 60.

BIBLIOGRAPHY

Social and Psychological Needs

Baldwin, James. *The Fire Next Time*. New York: Dial Press, 1963.

Batchelder, Alan. *Poverty: The Special Case of the Negro*. In *Poverty in America: A Book of Readings*, ed. by Louis A. Ferman, Joyce L. Kornbluh, and Alan Haber. Ann Arbor: The University of Michigan Press, 1965.

Baughman, E. Earl and Dahlstrom, Grant W. *Negro and White Children: A Psychological Study in the Rural South*. New York: Academic Press, 1968.

Bennett, Lerone, Jr. "*The Black Worker.*" *Ebony* 27 (July 1972): 9.

Billingsley, Andrew. *Black Families in White America*. Englewood Cliffs. N.J.: Prentice-Hall, 1968.

Boskin, Joseph. "The Revolt of the Urban Ghettos, 1964-1967." *The Annals of the American Academy* 382 (1969): 1-14.

Bullock, Henry A. *A History of Negro Education in the South: From 1619 to the Present*. Cambridge, Mass.: Harvard University Press, 1967.

Clark, Kenneth B. "A Charade of Power: Black Students at White Colleges." *Antioch Review* 29 (1969): 145-148.

Cruse, Harold. *Rebellion or Revolution*? New York: Morrow, 1972.

Deutsch, Martin. "Happenings on the Way Back to the Forum." *Harvard Educational Review* 39 (1969): 523-557.

Deutsch, Martin; Katz, I.; and Jensen, A. R. eds. *Social Class, Race, and Psychological Development*. New York: Holt, Rinehart and Winston, 1968.

DuBois, William E. B. "Education and Work." *The Journal of Negro Education* 1 (1932): 60-74.

DuBois, William E. B. *The Souls of Black Folk*. New York: Blue Heron Press, 1953.

Duncan, Beverly and Duncan, Otis D. "Family Stability and Occupational Success." *Social Problems* 16 (1969): 273-285.

Fairchild, Henry P. ed. *Dictionary of Sociology*. Totowa, New Jersey: Littlefield, Adams and Co., 1970.

Ferman, Louis A.; Kornbluh, Joyce L.; and Haber, Alan eds. *Poverty in America: A Book of Readings*. Ann Arbor: The University of Michigan Press, 1968.

Finney, Joseph C. ed. *Culture Change, Mental Health, and Poverty*. Lexington: University of Kentucky Press, 1969.

Fogel, Robert W. and Engerman, Stanley L. *Time on the Cross*. Boston: Little, Brown, 1974.

Frazier, E. Franklin. *E. Franklin Frazier on Race Relations*. G. Franklin Edwards ed. Chicago: The University of Chicago Press, 1968.

Frazier, E. Franklin. *The Negro Family in the United States*, rev. ed. Chicago: The University of Chicago Press, 1966.

Freeman, Donald; Kimbrough, Rollie; and Brother Zolili. "The Meaning of Education." *The Journal of Negro Education* 37 (1968): 432-434.

Genovese, Eugene D. *Roll, Jordan, Roll*. New York: Pantheon, 1974.

Grier, William H. and Cobbs, Price M. *Black Rage*. New York: Basic Books, 1968.

Grossack, Martin M. Book review of Thomas F. Pettigrew, "A Profile of the Negro American." *Journal of Negro Education* 34 (1965): 78-79.

Harrison, E. C. "Working at Improving the Motivational and Achievement Levels of the Deprived." *The Journal of Negro Education* 32 (1963): 301-307.

Jackson, Jacquelyne J. "Black Women in a Racist Society. " In *Racism and Mental Health*, ed. by Charles V. Willie, Bernard M. Kramer, and Bertram S. Brown. Pittsburgh: University of Pittsburgh Press, 1974.

Katz, Irwin and Gurin, Patricia eds. *Race and the Social Sciences*. New York: Basic Books, 1969.

Kerner, Otto (Chairman). Report of the National Advisory Commission on Civil Disorders. Washington, D.C.: U.S. Government Printing Office, 1968.

Kozol, Jonathan. *Death at an Early Age*. New York: Houghton Mifflin, 1967.

Meier, August. "Negro Protest Movements and Organizations." *The Journal of Negro Education* 32 (1963): 437-450.

Moynihan, Daniel P. "The Negro Family: The Case for National Action." United States Department of Labor, Washington, D.C.: U.S. Government Printing Office, 1965.

Pickens, William G. "Teaching Negro Culture in High Schools—Is It Worthwhile?" *The Journal of Negro Education* 34 (1965): 106-113.

Ransford, H. Edward. "Isolation, Powerlessness, and Violence: A Study of Attitudes and Participation in the Watts Riot." *American Journal of Sociology* 73 (1968): 581-591.

Robinson, Armstead L.; Foster, Craig C.; and Ogilvie, Donald H. eds. *Black Studies in the University: A Symposium.* New Haven: Yale University Press, 1969.

Smythe, H. and Chase, L. "Current Research on the Negro: A Critique." *Sociology and Social Research* 42 (1957-1958): 199-202.

The Social and Economic Status of Negroes in the United States, 1969. BLS Report No. 375. Current Population Reports, Series P-23, No. 29. Washington, D.C.: U.S. Government Printing Office, 1969.

Trubowitz, Sidney. *A Handbook for Teaching in the Ghetto School.* New York: Quadrangle Books, 1968.

Wright, Nathan. *Let's Work Together.* New York: Hawthorn Books, 1968.

Introduction to Afro-American History

Ashmore, Harry S. *The Negro and the Schools,* rev. ed. Chapel Hill: University of North Carolina Press, 1970.

Bouma, Donald H. and Hoffman, James. *The Dynamics of School Integration.* Grand Rapids: Eerdmans, 1968.

Broderick, Francis L.; Meier, August; and Rudwick, Elliott. *Black Protest Thought in the Twentieth Century.* 2nd ed. Indianapolis: Bobbs, 1971.

Cook, Mercer and Henderson, Stephen E. *The Militant Black Writer in Africa and the United States.* Madison: University of Wisconsin Press, 1969.

DuBois, W. E. B. *The Negro Church.* Atlanta University Report No. 8, 1903 (reprinted by Arno Press and the *New York Times*, 1969), for a compilation of statistics relative to these matters.

Harding, Vincent. *Beyond Chaos: Black History and the Search for the New Land.* Atlanta: 1970.

Henderson, Vivian W. "The Role of the Predominantly Negro Institutions." *The Journal of Negro Education* 36 (1967): 266-273.

Lacy, Leslie A. *Cheer the Lonesome Traveler: The Life of W. E. B. DuBois.* New York: Dial Press, 1970.

Lester, Julius ed. *The Seventh Son: The Thoughts and Writings of W. E. B. DuBois.* 2 vols. New York: Random House, 1971.

Lewis, David L. *King: A Critical Biography.* New York: Praeger, 1970.

Meier, August and Rudwick, Elliott M. *From Plantation to Ghetto,* rev. ed. New York: Hill and Wang, 1970.

Styron, William. *The Confessions of Nat Turner.* New York: Random House, 1967.

Black Studies

Bethune, Lebert. "Afro-American Studies: Perspectives Toward a Definition." *IRCD Bulletin* 5,3 (Summer 1969): 9.

City College of San Francisco General Catalogue, 1969-1970.

Coleman, James B. et al. "Equality of Educational Opportunity." Washington, D.C.: Office of Education, U.S. Department of Health, Education, and Welfare, 1966.

Faculty-Student Committee, State University of New York at Buffalo. "Proposal for a Black Studies Program Offering an Undergraduate Major." Mimeographed report, 1969, pp. 1-2.

Gasberro et al. "Solutions to History in Crisis: American History in the High School." Mimeographed by Atlantic City Public School, Atlantic City, New Jersey, August 2, 1968.

Guban, Larry. "Not Whether, But Why? and How? Instructional Materials on the Negro in Public Schools." *The Journal of Negro Education* 36 (1967): 434-436.

Hamilton, Charles V. "The Question of Black Studies." *Phi Delta Kappan* 51, 7 (March 1970).

Havighurst, Robert J. "The Neighborhood School: Status and Prospects. A Curriculum for Children." Alexander Frazier, ed. Washington, D.C.: Association for Supervision and Curriculum Development, 1969.

Howard, Lawrence C. Comments on a paper by W. Todd Furniss on "Racial Minorities and Curriculum Change." Mimeographed paper presented at 52nd Annual Meeting of American Council on Education, October 9, 1969, p. 2.

Jablonsky, Adelaide. "Toward Curriculum Relevance for Minority Group Children." *IRED Bulletin* 5, 3 (Summer 1969).

Oberlin College Bulletin, 1969-1970, May 1969.

Riessman, Frank. *The Strategy of Style, Education of the Disadvantaged*, A. Harry Passow et al., eds. New York: Holt, Rinehart and Winston, 1967.

School District of the City of Pontiac, Michigan. "An Outline of Content and Concepts for Teaching the Contributions and Participation of Afro-Americans in the Elementary Grades." Mimeographed, Pontiac, Michigan, 1968.

Walton, Hanes, Jr. "African and Afro-American Courses in Negro Colleges." *The Quarterly Review of Higher Education Among Negroes* 36, 4 (October 1968): 188-189.

Educational Media and Technology

Commission on Instructional Technology. *To Improve Learning: A Report to the President and the Congress of the United States (The McMurrin Report).* Washington, D.C.: U.S. Government Printing Office, March 1970.

Dale, Edgar. *Audiovisual Methods in Teaching.* 3d ed. New York: Dryden Press, 1969.

Edling, Jack V. *Individualized Instruction* 15 (February 1970): 13-18.

Ely, Donald P. ed. "The Field of Educational Technology: A Statement of Definition." *Audiovisual Instruction* (October 1972): 36-43.

Engler, David. "Instructional Technology and the Curriculum." *Phi Delta Kappan* 51, 7 (March 1970).

Erickson, Carlton W. H. and Curl, David H. *Fundamentals of Teaching with Audiovisual Technology*. 2d ed. New York: Macmillan, 1972.

Fransecky, Roger B. and Ferguson, Roy. "New Ways of Seeing: The Milford Visual Communications Project." *Audiovisual Instruction* (April 1973): 44-49; (May 1973): 56-65; (June/July 1973): 47-49.

Gerlach, Vernon S. and Ely, Donald P. *Teaching and Media: A Systematic Approach*, Englewood Cliffs, N.J.: Prentice-Hall, 1971.

Guidelines for Two-Year College Learning Resources Programs. Washington, D.C.: Association for Educational Communications and Technology and Chicago: American Library Association, 1972.

Heinich, Robert. "Technology and Teacher Productivity." *Audiovisual Instruction* 16 (January 1971): 79-82.

Johnson, Harry Alleyn. *Multimedia Materials for Afro-American Studies*. New York and London: R. R. Bowker Company, 1971.

Johnson, Stuart R. and Johnson, Rita B. *Developing Individualized Instructional Material: A Self-Instructional Material in Itself*. Palo Alto: Westinghouse Learning Press, 1970.

Kemp, Jerrold E. *Instructional Design*. Belmont, Calif.: Fearon Publishers, 1971.

Kemp, Jerrold E. *Planning and Producing Audiovisual Materials*. San Francisco: Chandler, 1968.

Marien, Michael. *Alternative Futures for Learning: An Annotated Bibliography of Trends, Forecasts, and Proposals*. Syracuse: Syracuse University Research Corporation, 1971.

Minor, E. O. and Frye, Harvey R. *Techniques for Producing Visual Instructional Media*, New York: McGraw-Hill, 1970.

Toffler, Alvin. *Future Shock*. New York: Random House, 1970.

Weisgerber, Robert A. "Individualized Learning." The ERIC Clearinghouse on Educational Media and Technology. Stanford, Calif: Stanford University, February, 1972.

Wigren, Harold E. "What Is Here in Educational Technology." *A Curriculum for Children*. Alexander Frazier, ed. Washington, D.C.: Association for Supervision and Curriculum Development, 1963.

Wiman, Raymond V. *Instructional Materials*. Worthington, Ohio: Charles A. Jones Publishing Co., 1972.

Wiman, Raymond V. and Mieerhenry, Wesley C. eds. *Educational Media: Theory into Practice*. Columbus, Ohio: Merrill, 1969.

Wing, Richard L. "The Relation of Computer-Based Instruction and Other Media to Individualized Education." DAVI Conference, Atlantic City, N.J., April 4, 1967.

Wittich, Walter A. and Schuller, Charles F. *Instructional Technology: Its Nature and Use*. 5th ed. New York: Harper & Row, 1973.

MEDIA AND MATERIALS—ANNOTATED

Films (16mm)

AFRICA: AN INTRODUCTION. BFA 1968. P-El-J. 18 min col. Rental $12.50; purchase $179.

An overview of Africa and its many different peoples, concentrating on the major differences between the desert, grassland, and the tropics. Explains how and why the lives of the people of Africa differ between areas.

AFRICANS ALL. IFF/EALING 1963. P-El-J. 23 min col. Rental $10; purchase $150.

A portrayal of the real Africa in all its diversity and color. The animation by Philip Stapp parodies popular misconceptions about Africa. Included are authentic African music and sounds recorded on the spot. A good film to use for discussions of the real Africa vs. the stereotyped ideas still harbored by many Americans.

AIN'T WE GOT A RIGHT? MMM 1972. J-S-A. 4 min b&w. Rental $25; purchase $250.

A morality play of the entire ministry of Martin Luther King, Jr., from the beginning of his residence in Montgomery until his assassination in Memphis. Music and dialogue are the fundamental elements in this film with King intermittently struggling with his own doubts and torments in monologue.

A MAN NAMED CHARLIE SMITH. CCMS. J-S-A. 26 min b&w. Rental $12.50; purchase $165.

This film recounts the history of slavery and the black man through the memories of a man named Charlie Smith, who was 120 years old at the time the film was made. In 1854, Mr. Smith was captured in Liberia and brought to America on a slave ship. Through humor and wisdom, Charlie Smith tells of his experiences, adventures, and misfortunes.

AMERICA, HOME OF THE FREE, LAND OF THE BRAVE. CFS 1969. S-A. 7 min col. Rental $10; purchase $125.

This is a satirical underground film modeled after the famous "Oh Dem Watermelons." The film shows scenes of violence, crime, and lust from old Holly wood movies, and scenes of black people being beaten and repeatedly arrested. Some brief nudity.

AMERICAN NEGRO SINGS, THE. MLA 1969. J-S-C-A. 26 min col. Rental $15.

Traces the history of the American Black through the medium of song, dance, and art. Includes examples of Negro spirituals, work songs, blues, jazz, and contemporary music.

AMERICAN REVOLUTION OF '63. NBC 1963. S-C-A. 180 min col.

Examines the origins, philosophy, and impact of the Black American's struggle for equality. Describes the goals of the civil rights movement in different parts of the country; voter registration in the South; equal job opportunities; open housing in the North; and everywhere, the fight for school desegregation. Includes scenes of demonstrations and violence in numerous cities.

AN AFRO-AMERICAN THING. FRITH 1968. El-S-A. 25 min b&w. Rental $12.50; purchase $150.

This film presents the similarities and contrast of African and American cultures. Soul music and primitive dance provide the principle background based on the premise that the performing arts is an important part of black culture. From the similarities presented, the viewer can draw conclusions about the African heritage of black culture in the United States.

ANCIENT AFRICANS, THE. NET/IFF 1969. J-S-A. 27 min col. Rental $14; purchase $380.

In an attempt to answer the question "Who were the ancient Africans?" this film studies the life of this ancient civilization as shown by their arts, their trade, their architecture and monuments, and their religions. Drawings and maps locate ancient territories in relation to today's countries, and photographic sequences show the ruins of Kush and Axum, and Ethiopia and Sudan.

ANDERSON PLATOON, THE. MGH 1969. S-A. 65 min b&w. Rental $35; purchase $520.

This documentary about a black lieutenant, Joseph B. Anderson, in Vietnam explores his feelings and those of his men as they fight and live together. The viewer learns what it is like to be ready to give the supreme sacrifice for one's country and the misgivings a black soldier can feel.

ANGELA: LIKE IT IS. ADF 1970. S-C-A. 60 min b&w. Rental $65; purchase $250.

Angela Davis speaks from prison after her arrest in December 1970, answering thirteen questions asked through a survey of the people of Harlem. It also includes a panel discussion including attorney Margaret Burnham, editor Joe Walker of "Mohammed Speaks," and Charlene Mitchell of the Angela Davis defense committee.

A RAISIN IN THE SUN. AUDIOF 1961. El-J-S-C. 127 min col. Rental $42.50.

Lorraine Hansberry wrote the screenplay for this drama adapted from her own Drama Critics Circle Award winning Broadway production. The principal characters are played by Sidney Poitier, Diana Sands, Ruby Dee, and Claudia McNeil—all from the original cast of the play. The story is one of humor, turmoil, and pathos revolving around the Youngers, a black family in the throes of deciding how to spend the $10,000 insurance left to them by the death of Mr. Younger.

music

ARETHA FRANKLIN, SOUL SINGER. MGH 1974. J-S-C-A. 25 min col. Rental $20; purchase $370.

This film goes behind the scenes for a close-up profile of this renowned singer whose vocal magnetism has brought her packed performances throughout the world and a string of smashing record successes as well as the Grammy Award and "female vocalist of the year" awards by leading trade magazines. Miss Franklin began her career in the choir of her father's church, and her gospel style comes through in her rhythm and blues recordings. The viewer sees Miss Franklin in rehearsals; at intimate skull sessions with her friends and advisers; on stage before jammed audiences; and at home relaxing. Based on the ABC News special "The Singers: Two Profiles."

A SLAVE'S STORY: RUNNING A THOUSAND MILES TO FREEDOM. LCA 1972. J-S-A. 29 min col. Rental $30; purchase $369.

The dramatization of the Craft's actual escape from slavery in 1848 follows their journey from the Deep South to Philadelphia. A careful plan, devised by William, was made possible by the fact that he was sufficiently light-skinned to masquerade as white. So with Ellen, his wife, he disguised himself as a man traveling north, with his slave, and the young couple set out on the thousand mile trip. They eventually crossed the Mason-Dixon line to freedom.

A TRIBUTE TO MALCOLM X. NET/IU 1969. S-C-A. 15 min b&w. Rental $5; purchase $100.

The influence of Malcolm X on the present black liberation movement is reported in this film. His life is recollected through an interview with his widow, Betty Shabazz. Malcolm X, whose father was killed and whose mother was committed to a mental institution when he was a child, became a minister of Islam and a leader of the black struggle until his assassination. This film is one of a group of NET Productions by black filmmakers to acquaint all people with black America.

AUTOBIOGRAPHY OF MISS JANE PITTMAN, THE. MGH 1974. P-El-J-S-C-A. 110 min col. Rental $100.

This is an award-winning saga of a true American heroine. The fictional Miss Pittman's 110 years encompass a segment of our country's history from slavery to the civil rights movement of the early sixties. Her story is not so much that of one remarkable woman as it is an enthralling portrait of the people and times around her. Cicely Tyson, who rose to fame as the mother in the movie *Sounder*, gives a stunning performance as the courageous ex-slave.

BATTLE OF EAST ST. LOUIS, THE. CBSTV/CAROUF 1970. J-S-C-A. 46 min b&w. Purchase $250.

In the spring of 1969, East St. Louis was a racial bomb waiting to detonate. Fear prompted the city to get opposing groups together to discuss their grievances in order to avoid mass violence. The catalyst used was an encounter and sensitivity-training marathon with black militants and white policemen. The results provide hope for all the cities of this country. Highly recommended for use by police-community action groups, management-personnel relations groups, church, and other adult organizations.

BERNIE CASEY: BLACK ARTIST. ACI 1971. S-C-A. 21 min col. Rental $25; purchase $240.

Casey, a former football player, is a painter with a growing reputation. This film follows him as he wanders through woods and fields, gathering impressions and images, and then in his studio at work, where he speaks of his feelings about being an artist. Finally, in a setting among the grass and trees which he loves, he shows a number of his finished paintings.

BLACK ACHIEVERS IN THE NORTH 1790-1860, THE. WCBSTV/HRW 1969. J-S-A. 30 min col. Purchase $300.

Professor E. A. Toppin discusses achievements of many noteworthy black Americans. Included are such historical figures as James Foster, Paul Cuffee, Dr. James Smith, and other writers, artists, and athletes.

BLACK AMERICAN DREAM, THE. BBCTV 1973. J-S-C-A. 65 min col. Rental $65; purchase $610.

Presents a contrast of two black American leaders and the different approaches they advocate for change. The African based Stokely Carmichael and the non-violent Jesse Jackson each has his own idea of what black people are.

BLACK AND WHITE: UPTIGHT. BFA 1969. J-S. 35 min col. Rental $15; purchase $420.

The initial integration of Riverside, California, provides the background of this film. Conflicting positions are expressed in interviews to fully explore the meaning of the Fourteenth Amendment. This film focuses special attention on the area of conflicts between minority and white groups. Viewers are encouraged to closely examine their attitudes toward injustice and prejudice.

BLACK ATHLETES. CI 1970. S-C-A. 40 min b&w. Purchase $55.

This film presents portraits and action shots of black athletes in football, basketball, baseball, track, boxing, and wrestling. Audio tape accompanies the film. Although in black and white the film can be an inspiration to young people. Its authentic feature is a strong point.

BLACK COP, THE. NET/IU 1969. S-C-A. 16 min b&w. Rental $7; purchase $110.

Explores the relationship of the black policeman to other Blacks by interviewing those on both sides in New York City and Los Angeles. Points out that some see black police officers as representing a white system badly in need of change while other Blacks accuse the black cop of seeking only the instant authority that comes with a badge. From the "Black Journal Film" series.

BLACK DIMENSIONS IN AMERICAN ART. AIMS 1971. El-S-C-A. 15 min col. Rental $15; purchase $150.

Features 50 black artists and their paintings. Shows every major style in painting today, from the African influence, through the struggle for freedom to pure abstract art. The film is an introduction to well-known and some not so well-known artists. It offers interesting contrasts of their works.

BLACK FRONTIER. GPN 1970. J-S-A. 60 min each col. Rental $84; purchase $480.

A series of four films financed by a Ford Foundation grant and produced by University of Nebraska Television focuses on several of the black men whose distinguished contributions to settling the Great Plains have largely been overlooked. Great Plains National has been appointed distributor of this series. Titles: New Americans, Cowherders, Buffalo Soldiers, and Exodusters.

BLACK HERITAGE: A HISTORY OF AFRO-AMERICANS. HRW 1969. El-S-C. 27 min b&w. Purchase $165.

This series of 108 filmed lectures, supplemented with visual effects, is a comprehensive and professionally compiled film study of black history. All the material was developed by a Black Heritage Advisory Board. Leading black scholars, writers, artists, and activists, including Lerone Bennett, Charles Hamilton, St. Clair Drake, James Farmer, Straughton Lynd, James Boggs, and LeRoi Jones, examine in detail the black American experience from its beginning in Africa to 1969.

BLACK HEROES OF AMERICAN HISTORY. CI 1970. J-S. 40 min b&w. Purchase $55.

This film re-creates the lives and activities of black people prominent in American history. Audio tape lecture accompanies film.

BLACK HISTORY. ADF 1971. C-A. 120 min col. Rental $25.

The history of black America is presented, from Africa through the years of slavery to the Civil War, black Reconstruction, the civil rights movement, black power, black liberation, the Black Panther Party, and the Third World revolution. Four parts; in production.

BLACK HISTORY: LOST, STOLEN, OR STRAYED. CBS/BFA 1968. J-S-A. 54 min b&w. Rental $35; purchase $575.

This film is a Bill Cosby guided tour through a history of attitudes—black and white—and their effects on the black American. It is a portrayal of some of the things that happen to an American if he is black. Cosby reviews black American achievements omitted from American history texts, the absence of recognition of Africa's contributions to Western culture, and the changing Hollywood stereotype of the black American. Two parts.

BLACK MUSIC IN AMERICA: FROM THEN TILL NOW. SCREEN GEMS/ USC 1971. S-C-A. 28 min col. Rental $12.15; purchase $390.

The history of the black American's contribution to American music is traced in unforgettable filmed performances of great black musicians. Louis Armstrong, Mahalia Jackson, B. B. King, "Leadbelly," Count Basie, Nina Simone, and the only film ever recorded of the great Bessie Smith, to name only a few, show impressive accomplishments of black artists. Interspersed with the performances are woodcuts showing the history of the music which is in effect the history of Blacks in America.

BLACK MUSLIMS SPEAK FROM AMERICA. TIMELI 1969. S-C-A. 33 min b&w. Rental $25; purchase $250.

Who are the Black Muslims? What do they believe in? How do they fit into the social structure of America? These and many more questions are answered as Malcolm Muggeridge interviews a group of seven young Black Muslims about their discontent and their beliefs which include the need for total destruction of America. A highly controversial but informative film.

BLACK POWER: WE'RE GOING TO SURVIVE AMERICA. MMM 1968. S-C-A. 15 min b&w/col. Rental $20 (col); purchase $200 (col).

A speech concerning survival by Stokely Carmichael at a rally on the birthday of the imprisoned Huey Newton. His theme is the preservation of the black race along with recognition of its culture and ancestral roots. He warns the black race to stay conscious of their nobility and not to become prey to the white man's racism.

BLACK RECONSTRUCTION. WCBSTV/HRW 1969. J-S. 30 min b&w. Purchase $175.

William Strickland discusses the American tradition which created a myth regarding the inferiority and lack of accomplishment of black people as a means of supporting the racist nature of society. Clips from *Birth of a Nation* are included.

BLACK RESISTANCE, THE. WCBSTV/HRW 1969. S-C-A. 30 min b&w. Purchase $175.

Dr. Earl E. Thorpe describes the efforts of W. E. B. DuBois and other Blacks to form progressive movements and work for their rights as Americans during the early years of the century as evidenced by the formation of such groups as the NAACP, the National Negro Business League, and the Negro Movement. Describes the conflict between DuBois and Booker T. Washington.

BLACK ROOTS. ADF 1970. J-S-C-A. 61 min col. Purchase $135.

Through the faces and experience of black Americans this film shows the beauty, anger, and pride of the black communities in U.S. musical selections by "Leadbelly," Ray Charles, John Coltrane, Memphis Slim, Jimi Hendrix, and James Brown. Viewers are presented with some commonalities and contrasts among these well-known black personalities.

BLACK SOLDIER. CBSTV/BFA 1968. El-J-C-A. 25 min b&w. Rental $5; purchase $170.

Surveys the history of the black American's participation in the armed forces of the United States, from the Revolutionary War to the war in Vietnam. Bill Cosby narrates the film using battle scenes from films of wars in this century. Film clips include some rare silent footage depicting the role played by many black Americans in the defense of their country.

BLACK VIEWS ON RACE. TIMELI 1970. J-S-C. 80 min col. Rental $7.50; purchase $600.

A series of 20 four-minute color sequences presenting statements by 20 prominent Blacks of their positions on the race issue in America. The 20 contemporary figures are: Ralph Abernathy, Julian Bond, H. Rap Brown, Jim Brown,

Shirley Chisholm, Eldridge Cleaver, Coretta King, Sidney Poitier, Jackie Robinson, Bayard Rustin, Harry Belafonte, Edward Brooke, James Brown, Stokely Carmichael, Mohammed Ali, Dick Gregory, Martin Luther King, Jr., Adam Clayton Powell, Carl Stokes, and Malcolm X.

BLACK WORLD. CBSTV/BFA 1968. El–J–S–A. 53 min b&w/col. Rental $35; purchase $300 (b&w), $575 (col).

In an international round-robin conversation moderated by Mike Wallace, the position of blacks in the world today is examined. Panelists, Rep. John Conyers, Jr., in Washington, D.C.; the Hon. Thomas Mboya of Kenya in Nairobi; Floyd McKissick of the Congress of Racial Equality in New York; and Dr. Alex Kwapong, Vice-Chancellor of the University of Ghana, discuss the civil rights movement in America and how it looks to Africans. From the "Black Americans" series.

BOOKER T. WASHINGTON. BFA 1967. El–J–S. 11 min col. Rental $6.50; purchase $130.

This film covers the early years of Booker T. Washington, who was born a slave in 1856, and who later built Tuskegee Institute, which has become a monument to education. Traces and documents his achievements and explains the important contributions of Dr. Washington to his people and to mankind.

BOYHOOD OF GEORGE WASHINGTON CARVER, THE. NFBC/IU 1973. J–S. 13 min col. Rental $4.75; purchase $170.

Presents incidents of George Washington Carver's early years in Missouri. Tells of his experience with his brother Lawrence, and follows him as he works, travels, and learns. Film fills in the often omitted portion of the life of this great scientist.

BRIAN'S SONG. LCA 1972. J–C–A. 76 min col. Rental $150; purchase $1,195.

The story of the friendship between Brian Piccolo and Gayle Sayers when they were teammates together with the Chicago Bears. It starts from the beginning at the Bears' training camp in 1965 and ends with Brian's tragic death from cancer in 1970 at the age of 26.

BROTHER JOHN. MACMAB 1971. J–S–C. 94 min col. Rental $35.

John Kane (played by Sidney Poitier) unexpectedly returns to his home town in Alabama. The assassination of a black labor leader shortly after Kane's arrival in town makes him suspect of engineering the crisis. Originally made as a full-length feature film, this release is designed for use in educational institutions.

CHARLES LLOYD—JOURNEY WITHIN. MACMAB 1968. J–C–A. 60 min b&w. Rental $45.

Eric Sherman produced this jazz documentary on the personal and professional world of Charles Lloyd. The film records Lloyd and his musical background in the Memphis ghettos to his concert triumphs from the Fullmore Auditorium to Warsaw's Congress Hall.

CIVIL RIGHTS MOVEMENT: HISTORIC ROOTS. NBCTV/FI 1966. J-S-C. 16 min b&w. Rental $8.50; purchase $102.50.

This film presents and reviews the origin of the civil rights movement, starting with the slave trade, slavery, abolitionism, and ending with the Emancipation Proclamation.

CIVIL RIGHTS MOVEMENT: MISSISSIPPI SUMMER PROJECT. NBCTV/FI 1966. J-S-C. 17 min b&w. Rental $8.50; purchase $102.50.

This film discusses the civil rights project that began when hundreds of people gathered in Oxford, Ohio, for nonviolent resistance training to prepare for a massive attack on the problems of Blacks in Mississippi.

CIVIL RIGHTS MOVEMENT: THE ANGRY VOICES OF WATTS. NBCTV/FI 1968. J-S-C. 52 min b&w. Rental $25; purchase $250.

This film documents the anger of Blacks who witnessed days and nights of riots; the frustration and disappointment of people forced into unsatisfactory existence, and the hostilities which could fuel a black revolution.

CIVIL RIGHTS MOVEMENT: THE NORTH. NBCTV/FI 1966. J-S-C. 23 min b&w. Rental $15.50; purchase $151.

The tense atmosphere of race relations in many northern cities is depicted. The film discusses integration attempts in Chicago; unemployment problems in Elizabeth, New Jersey; and education problems in Englewood, New Jersey. Inadequate educational facilities and de facto segregation in northern slums are also included.

CIVIL RIGHTS MOVEMENT: THE PERSONAL VIEW. NBCTV/FI 1966. J-S-C-A. 25 min b&w. Rental $15.50; purchase $151.

The story of a well-to-do black professional family living in a white neighborhood is the basis for an exploration of the problem of community race relations. A presentation of black stereotypes in fiction and films demonstrates the distortion of the image of Blacks.

CIVIL RIGHTS MOVEMENT: THE SOUTH. NBCTV/FI 1966. J-S-C. 28 min b&w. Rental $15.50; purchase $167.50.

This film discusses the civil rights movement in the South after the Supreme Court desegregation decision, and recalls Little Rock in 1957, the 1955 Montgomery bus boycott, the 1960 Greensboro sit-ins, and the 1963 registration day at the University of Alabama. The principle of civil disobedience is traced from Thoreau to Gandhi to Martin Luther King, Jr.

COLOR US BLACK. NET/IU 1967. S-C-A. 60 min b&w. Rental $15.25; purchase $265.

This film shows the black man's struggle in his search for his own identity over and above the white "norm." It is covered from the point of view of black students at predominantly black Howard University in Washington, D.C. A four day take-over of the administration building is shown, including the successful ending of the rebellion.

CONSIDER THE ZEBRA. PAULP 1969. J–S–A. 28 min b&w. Rental $12.95; purchase $160.

This film is about a parish council being formed in a neighborhood rapidly going black. A progressive parish priest, a black nun, a Chicano merchant, and three old-time white parishioners form a parish council. They agree to begin a black community center of black culture. There is a showdown and the viewer is left with an important question: Despite years of church attendance, were these members really Christians?

CONVERSATIONS IN BLACK. HRW. S–C–A. 30 min b&w. Purchase $175.

This series of six 30 min films examines the major problems faced by Blacks in America today. Presents distinguished figures in the black community including Shirley Chisholm, Ralph Abernathy, Whitney Young, and Bayard Rustin. Includes Community Involvement Pts. 1 and 2: Employment, Higher Education, Politics, Urban Education.

CORNER, THE. BRAN 1963. C–A. 26 min b&w. Rental $15; purchase $165.

An exploration of the problem of juvenile delinquency through an understanding of the way juvenile gang members understand themselves. A documentary filmed on the streets of Chicago at night. This film is intended to be neither a defense nor an incrimination, but rather a subjective statement in the words of members of a black gang called "The Vice Lords" describing their world.

CREATION, THE. OXF 1972. El–S. 12 min col. Rental $15; purchase $156.

The Creation is the story of Genesis told simply and poetically in the language of the black culture. One of seven sermons in verse of God's Trombones by James Weldon Johnson, presenting the gentle warmth, humor, and deepness of feeling within the black culture. The poem is recited by the well-known black actor, Raymond St. Jacques; the poem is then reread by Margaret O'Brien with words superimposed on the screen. An added excitement is provided by the beautiful original musical score.

CRISIS IN LEVITTOWN. MSU 1963. J–S–C–A. 30 min b&w. Rental $9; purchase $150.

When a black family moved into all-white Levittown, Pennsylvania, the drama of complex forces released by the event made national headlines. This film records on-the-spot interviews with residents. The attitudes revealed, both enlightened and unenlightened, are searchingly analyzed by Dr. Dan W. Dodson, director, Center for Human Relations and Community Studies, School of Education, New York University.

CRY, THE BELOVED COUNTRY. AUDIOF 1952. J–S. 105 min b&w. Rental $65.

The late Canada Lee portrays a simple country priest drawn to the city in search of his son. There, amid the squalor and evil atmosphere, he finds human misery and tragedy in the discovery that his son has been sentenced to death for murder. The setting is South Africa, and the film is based on the best selling novel and hit play by the same title.

DEATH OF SIMON JACKSON, THE. PAULP 1969. J-S-C-A. 28 min b&w/col. Rental $12.95 (b&w), $18.95 (col); purchase $160 (b&w), $325 (col).
This is a story of a black poet's passionate involvement in his race's struggle for equal rights. Through his poetry he preaches nonviolence and brotherhood. His work is rejected by the Uncle Tom magazines as controversial, and by the black militants. A riot occurs and he warns the crowd against violence, trying to convince his brothers that they will succeed in their fight for dignity through love and nonviolence.

DISCOVERING JAZZ. CBS/BFA 1969. El-J-S-C-A. 21 1/2 min col. Rental $15; purchase $265.
The history of jazz is traced from its roots in nineteenth-century black America. The black American added rhythmic and melodic freedom to the harmony and structure of European music and contributed such techniques as note blending and call and response. Jazz is traced from Dixieland and blues through such styles as swing, bop, cool jazz, and free improvisation.

FAMILIES GET ANGRY. OXF 1972. El-S. 9 min col. Rental $15; purchase $125.
An approach to important personal feelings, the film permits children to gain insight into frustrations that arise from family quarrels. The quarrel depicted begins as the father in a black, low-income family is trying to stretch too little money to pay too many bills. Equally frustrated, the mother sharply defends her spending as absolutely minimal. Though not directly involved in the friction, their two children are strongly affected by the conflict.

FAT BLACK MACK. CCMS 1973. P-El. 5 min col. Rental $7.50; purchase $75.
An animated film of a fat black cat named Mack who wants to be blue like all the other cats. He tries to be like the majority but never succeeds. A film for self-development and pride for the young, especially young black children.

FAYETTE STORY, THE. SCHLAT 1970. S-C. 54 min col. Rental $65; purchase $550.
This film examines the social forces working in today's South. In the film we meet Charles Evers, the first black mayor of a bi-racial southern community since reconstruction. Focuses on Fayette, Mississippi, and provides a brief history of Mississippi. Film presents views of white community and history of the political milestones in that state.

FELICIA. ROE/IU 1965. J-S-A. 13 min b&w. Rental $5.
A 15-year-old black girl's quiet inquiry into her life in a segregated community. *Felicia* was filmed in Felicia's home, school, and neighborhood in Watts, California, in the spring of 1965, shortly before the area was devastated by rioting. The

film has gained importance as an introduction to discussions of the origins of racial tensions and the general frustrations of the black population as a whole.

FOR ALL MY STUDENTS. EMCC/UCEMC 1968. C–A. 36 min b&w. Rental $13; purchase $175.

Filmed at Ravenwood High School in East Palo Alto, California, this film reveals the particular problems and rewards of teaching black high school students. The students reveal their discouragement about school, their teachers, and themselves. The teachers express their doubts and convictions and talk about their feelings of frustration and their failures and small successes.

FREDERICK DOUGLASS: HOUSE ON CEDAR HILL. MGH 1951. J–S–A. 17 min b&w. Rental $12.50; purchase $130.

Portrays the life of Frederick Douglass with historical documents, period drawings, photographs and memorabilia found in the Douglass home in Washington, D.C. Presents Douglass alongside such figures as Abraham Lincoln, John Branch, and Susan B. Anthony.

FREDERICK DOUGLASS: PROFILES IN COURAGE. SAUDEK 1964. J–S–A. 50 min b&w. Rental $9; purchase $350.

This film shows how Douglass' revelation of his true identity as an escaped slave, in order to work openly for the Abolitionist Movement, made him subject to recapture under the Fugitive Slave Act and forced him to live in exile until he could raise money to purchase his freedom.

FREE AT LAST. NET/IU 1965. S–C–A. 30 min b&w. Rental $6.75.

Dramatic readings from the works of Frederick Douglass, Booker T. Washington, W. E. B. DuBois, and Marcus Garvey are used to trace the history of the American Black from emancipation to the end of World War II. Shows that, immediately after the Civil War, black and white children went to the same schools and that both black and white Congressmen sat in Congress. Discusses the influence of Washington, DuBois, and Garvey on the present black-white position in the United States.

GEORGE WASHINGTON CARVER. ART 1959. El–S. 12 min col. Purchase $130.

This documentary film is a sensitive, penetrating study of Dr. George Washington Carver. It presents his philosophy, his work, and his contributions to the field of science. Although an older film, it captures inspiring features of the boyhood and schooling of this great American.

GEORGE WASHINGTON CARVER. VIGNET/BFA 1967. El–J–S. 11 min b&w. Rental $5; purchase $70.

Using historic footage of Dr. Carver at work in his laboratory during the early 1930s, this film provides a documented account of the achievements of this great black American who was born a slave in 1864. His many important contributions toward agricultural research in this country are presented. Stresses his achievements through experimentation with the peanut plant.

GRAMBLING COLLEGE—100 YARDS TO GLORY. WABCTV 1968. S-C-A. 60 min col. Rental, free.

Grambling College, one of the largest predominantly black institutions of higher education in the Deep South, has been famous for producing outstanding athletes. This film relates how two men helped combat discrimination against Blacks on professional football teams.

GUESS WHO'S COMING TO DINNER. MACMAB 1967. J-S. 108 min col. Rental $65.

A social conscience film which portrays a young white woman from a prominent family. She surprises her parents by bringing home a brilliant black doctor whom she intends to marry. The parents are forced to test lifelong liberal beliefs. Stars: Spencer Tracy, Katherine Hepburn, Sidney Poitier, and Katherine Houghton.

HARLEM IN THE TWENTIES. EBEC 1971. S-C-A. 10 min col. Rental $6; purchase $95.

Traces the development of Harlem from a fashionable white suburb in the 1800s to the largest and most squalid slum in the United States. Describes the new black culture which began in the 1920s and shows its impact on American life.

HARLEM-RENAISSANCE: THE BLACK POETS. CAROUF 1970. J-S-A. 20 min col. Purchase $250.

This film dramatizes the poetry of Countee Cullen and Waring Cuney, and presents the works from Georgia Douglas Johnson, Fenton Johnson, W. E. B. DuBois, and Langston Hughes. The film captures the black experience in the 1920s and 1930s from childhood to old age.

HARLEM—THE MAKING OF A COMMUNITY. HRW. S-C-A. 30 min b&w. Purchase $175.

Presents John Henrik Clarke lecturing on the black American in New York, the role of Harlem in the black revolution, and the contributions of such leaders as DuBois, Garvey, Malcolm X, Adam Clayton Powell, Jr., and Father Divine.

HARRIET TUBMAN AND THE UNDERGROUND RAILROAD. CBSTV/MGH 1964. S-C-A. 54 min b&w. Rental $29; purchase $325.

This film describes the first nineteen trips Mrs. Tubman, a conductor on the Underground Railroad, made into slave territory between 1850 and 1860. Filmed with a notable cast that includes Ethel Waters, Ruby Dee, and Ossie Davis. From the Great Adventure Series. In two parts.

HERITAGE IN BLACK. EBEC 1969. S-A. 27 min col. Rental $11.50; purchase $380.

This film traces the black experience in America from the American Revolution (and the first rebel casualty, a black man) to the dream of Martin Luther King, Jr., to be "free at last." Scene after scene documents the Blacks' intense participation in American life, the vital role played in the nation's growth, and the contributions made in every area of society.

HERITAGE OF SLAVERY, THE. CBSTV/BFA 1968. El-J-S-C-A. 53 min b&w/col. Rental $20 (b&w), $35 (col); purchase $300 (b&w), $575 (col).

Examines slavery and the attitudes established during slavery which still persist today. Interviews with descendants of plantation owners and present-day black activists, by CBS News reporter Geo Joster, demonstrate the parallels between attitudes under slavery and now. Film emphasizes that oppression breeds rebellion, pointing out the more than 250 slave revolts in America.

HERITAGE OF THE NEGRO. NET/IU 1965. S-A. 30 min b&w. Rental $9.50; purchase $165.

Examines the civilization and achievements of ancient Africa and their significance to the American Blacks today. Emphasizes that African history as recorded by white historians has traditionally ignored the old civilizations of Africa below the Sahara. Explores the art, sculpture, and present-day pageantry which reflect the old cultures.

HEY DOC. CAROUF 1970. S-A. 25 min col. Purchase $300.

A film about Ethan Allen, a black physician who works in the North Philadelphia ghetto. *Hey Doc* presents the slum streets and the vicious urban environment, spotlighting the lives of the addicted, the aged, and the angry.

HIGHER EDUCATION. HRW 1972. S-C-A. 30 min b&w. Purchase $175.

Presents Shirley Chisholm, Martin Kilson, Patricia Harris, and Samuel Proctor who probe the question of whether there is a different function for black students than there is for other students in higher education and whether black colleges are valid institutions for higher learning. From the "Conversations in Black" series.

HITCH. IFB 1970. S-A. 90 min col. Purchase $900.

An exploration of ghetto life, focusing on Hitch, a black teenager and migrant from a small town in the South. Photographed in the streets, alleyways, rooftops, empty lots, and schools of Harlem. The senseless waste of young people is the pervasive theme of this film.

HOW COME WHEN IT'S THUNDERIN . . . YOU DON'T SEE THE MOON? CCMS. C-A. 13 min col. Rental $15; purchase $145.

The eighth and ninth grade students from Junior High School 43 in Harlem show their view of the city through their art. A sense of hope and promise for the future emerges from their work on art projects. Steve Gordon, their teacher, describes how he tried to trace the children's reactions to their world through art and indicates how we must consider the problems of directing and guiding such children to make the transition between their present life and their potential future.

HUEY. ADF 1968. S-C-A. 33 min b&w. Rental $40; purchase $200.

This film is an historical document defining the position of the Black Panther party in 1968. It is a celebration of the imprisoned Huey P. Newton's birthday. There are speeches by the leaders of black liberation including Eldridge Cleaver, Stokely Carmichael, Rap Brown, James Foreman, and Bobby Seale.

I (AM, BE) SPEAKING ENGLISH. GREAVES. S-C-A. 24 min col. Rental $75; purchase $225.

This film addresses itself to the sensitivity and special skills required in teaching textbook English to dialect-speaking children. Produced by Dillard University under a grant from the Department of Health, Education and Welfare.

I AM SOMEBODY. MGH 1970. S-A. 18 min col. Rental $30; purchase $415.

This documentary record of the Charleston, South Carolina, black hospital workers strike portrays what can be accomplished by a civil rights organized labor coalition. Compiled of film footage taken during the marches, parades, and meetings which took place during the 113-day strike, the film shows how organized labor and the civil rights movement combined to crack the resistance to both in the deep south.

IF THERE WEREN'T ANY BLACKS, YOU'D HAVE TO INVENT THEM. MMM 1969. El-S-A. 58 min b&w. Rental $30; purchase $300.

This is a dramatic morality play set in a cemetery. The central character is a young man who, upon joining society for the first time, is accused of being black and inferior. His accuser is a bigoted, blind man who enlists others, such as an army officer, a priest, a doctor, an undertaker, and a sexton in the young man's destruction. The film recognizes the conspiracy that prevails when there is bigotry, hypocrisy, unenlightened self-interest, fear, and indifference. The human potential for evil; evil performed in the name of the good, and at the expense of the weak is also explored.

IMAGES IN BLACK. UEVA. J-S-A. 20 min col. Purchase $245.

The actor, James McEaclin, portrays black humor and pathos in several story vignettes of everyday life and world events. A good basis for discussion of stereotyping and prejudice in our daily lives.

I'M A MAN. MGH 1970. S-A. 20 min col. Rental $24; purchase $275.

The comments of John Barber and those of his family, friends, and enemies are used to show his personal ideological struggle for freedom and manhood.

IMMIGRANTS IN CHAINS. FI 1972. El-S-A. 11 min b&w. Rental $15; purchase $70.

A depiction of the capture and trading of Africans who were brought to the United States as slaves. A saga of the African immigrants, continuing with the story of black Americans struggling for their civil rights. From the "Americans, a Nation of Immigrants" series.

IN SEARCH OF A PAST. CBSTV/BFA 1968. J-S-C-A. 53 min col. Rental $35; purchase $575.

Part 1—A six-week visit to Ghana by three black Washington, D.C. high school students was filmed by CBS News. An effort was made to discover how pertinent Africa is to today's black American. Through the eyes of these three young people, African civilization is examined. The students conclude that their heritage is, after all, in the country that their forebears helped to build and defend. Part 2—A continuation of the visit of these students as they search for their identity and African heritage.

IVANHOE DONALDSON. BRAN/CCMS 1964. S-C-A. 57 min b&w. Rental $35; purchase $350.

Full-length documentary on the civil rights workers in crucial areas of the Deep South, showing the actual experiences of a field secretary of SNCC and his colleagues during three months in 1963 in Danville, Virginia; Selma, Alabama; and the Mississippi Delta. This film is of permanent interest as a background for understanding the emergence of the 1964 Civil Rights Act, the 1965 Voting Rights Act, and the national effort to achieve full implementation of the laws.

JACKIE ROBINSON. WOLPER/SF 1965. J-S. 26 min b&w. Rental $15.

Presents the life story and deeds of baseball player Jackie Robinson. Although made in the mid-sixties, the film is a good source for historical facts and provides inspiration for young people.

JACK JOHNSON. MACMAB 1970. S-A. 90 min b&w. Rental $55; purchase $650.

This documentary portrays Johnson, the first heavyweight champion of the world, as an unforgettable individualist. It features his career and the picturesque era in which he lived. Racial relations and the achievements of Johnson in that era provide an excellent contrast to the situation of improved racial understanding of the seventies.

JAMES WELDON JOHNSON. OXF 1972. El-S-C. 12 min col. Rental $20; purchase $165.

This is a story of a black man dedicated to his people and country; a man whose multifaceted career included music, poetry, and teaching. He served as American consul to Nicaragua and Venezuela. James Weldon Johnson was a fighter for Blacks' rights long before it became a popular issue of the day and serves as Executive Secretary of the NAACP. Johnson's poem, "The Creation," comes alive on the screen. Film is good for teaching poetry.

JEFFRIES—JOHNSON 1910. MGH 1971. S-A. 21 min b&w. Rental $16; purchase $165.

The film reveals personal glimpses of Johnson and traces the racist sports campaign which brought Jeffries out of retirement. The film is compiled from rare photographs and old newsreels on the legendary Jack Johnson, the first black heavyweight champion of the world.

JESSE OWENS RETURNS TO BERLIN. MGH 1970. S-A. 51 min b&w. Rental $28; purchase $385.

This film takes the renowned Jesse Owens back to Berlin's Olympic Stadium for a re-creation of his four-medal sweep in 1936. This athlete recalls the pomp and ceremony, the strong friendship between Olympians, and the thrill of competition. The film offers a good view of the Olympics of the thirties and also offers an excellent overview of an ex-athlete's days of greatness.

JOE LOUIS STORY, THE. ABFI 1953. El–S. 87 min b&w. Rental $27; purchase $500.

This is the story of a ghetto boy who traded in his violin for boxing gloves and went on to become the world's champion. It is highlighted by actual scenes of his memorable battles with Braddock, Baer, Carnera, and others.

JOHN OUTERBRIDGE: BLACK ARTIST. ACI 1971. P–El–J–S. 21 min col. Purchase $240.

Outerbridge sculpts in metal and he is shown at various stages in the formation of a major piece of work. He speaks of his background and its influence on his work; of the efforts of all artists to express their ideas through their art. Outerbridge discusses his approach and his philosophy and what it means to be a black artist in America.

JUSTICE? ADF 1971. J–S–C–A. 60 min b&w. Rental $40.

The cases of Angela Davis, the Soledad brothers, Bobby Seale, and other black prisoners in America are discussed among black prisoners at San Quentin. The film focuses on the growing feeling that all Blacks in prison are social and political hostages of the dominant white society. Provides background for group discussions on justice and its value to a democratic society.

LEARNING TREE, THE. FSR/MACMAB 1969. El–J–S. 107 min col. Rental $50.

Directed, produced, and written by Gordon Parks, based on his autobiographical novel, the story is a series of episodes and incidents in the lives of black teenagers growing up in Kansas in the 1920s.

LEGEND OF JOHN HENRY, THE. PFP 1973. P–El–J. 11 min col. Rental $15; purchase $160.

This beautiful film tells the story and legend of John Henry, the "Black Steel-drivin' Man"; it is a symbol of laboring Americans who built the railroads. Roberta Flack, rhythm and blues singer, adds an emotional dimension to the film. A CINE prize-winning film.

LEOPOLD SEDAR SENGHOR. IU 1967. El–J–S. 30 min b&w. Rental $9.50; purchase $165.

An introduction to Leopold Sedar Senghor, the poet and president of the Republic of Senegal. His poetry and his philosophy concerning the blending of the African and Western cultural traditions are presented through a reading of his works, focusing mainly on the beauty of the concept of Négritude.

MALCOLM X. WCAUTV/CAROUF 1971. El–J–S. 23 min col. Purchase $275.

This film biography spans the life of Malcolm X from the eighth grade when he was an honor student through his days as a con man, hustler, Black Muslim, and leader, to February 1965, when he fell to an assassin's bullet. From the "Tell It Like It Is" series.

MALCOLM X SPEAKS. GROVE 1970. El-J-S-A. 44 min b&w. Rental $12.
Documents the life and thoughts of Malcolm X. Includes his most important speeches, interviews, and dialogues with those who knew him best. Film provides his views on nonviolence, human rights, ballots or bullets, black nationalism, and the Birmingham Sunday School bombings.

MALCOLM X–STRUGGLE FOR FREEDOM. GROVE 1966. J-S-C-A 22 min b&w. Rental $12.
Film presents the great leader Malcolm X at a time when his views were changing to include world problems as related to race relations. Includes interviews with him during his visits to Europe and Africa shortly before his assassination in the United States.

MAN, THE. MACMAB 1972. El-J-S-A. 93 min col. Rental $45.
Adapted from the novel written by Irving Wallace, this film is about the first black president of the United States. James Earl Jones plays the black senator who accedes to the presidency—through succession, unelected by the people and unknown to them—during a crisis period. He emerges to become a president of strength and determination in spite of the contempt around him and the fierce prejudice of the nation.

MARIAN ANDERSON. LES/MSU 1953. El-S-C. 30 min b&w. Rental $4.75.
Vignettes of the great singer's life, from her early years through her Town Hall recital, where she presents a program of favorites, including such traditional spirituals as "O What a Beautiful City," "He's Got the Whole World in His Hand," "Crucifixion," and "Deep River." An older film but age does not diminish its purpose.

MARTIN LUTHER KING. TIMELI 1967. S-A. 30 min b&w. Rental $25; purchase $250.
This is a filmed interview with Martin Luther King, Jr., a big, quiet-voiced man who was modest, stoic, and above all, honest and dedicated. He believed: "It's not important how long you live, but how well you live." This was the creed by which the Nobel Peace Prize winner lived.

MARTIN LUTHER KING: A MAN OF PEACE. JOU 1968. J-S-C-A. 30 min b&w. Rental $15; purchase $200.
This film shows portions of sermons, speeches, and interviews with Martin Luther King, Jr., giving an insight on his ethic of love and its power against injustice. He describes his philosophy of nonviolence and its pacifist roots in both the Old and New Testaments of the Bible and in Gandhi and his methods. This film also shows him accepting the Nobel Peace Prize.

MARTIN LUTHER KING: THE MAN AND THE MARCH. NET/IU 1967. El-S-A. 83 min b&w. Rental $17; purchase $325.
This documentary records the preparations for the "Poor People's March" and Dr. Martin Luther King's role in it. Dr. King is shown soliciting support at

rallies, schools, and from people he met during his travels. The picture also shows his aides working for support from other ethnic groups.

MARTIN LUTHER KING, JR. EBEC 1971. El-J-S-A. 10 min col. Purchase $200.

Traces the career of Dr. King from the first boycotts in Alabama, through the years of the sit-ins, voter registration drives, and Freedom Rides, to his assassination in 1968. Describes his role as spokesman for millions of black Americans.

MARTIN LUTHER KING, JR.: FROM MONTGOMERY TO MEMPHIS. BFA 1969. J-S-C-A. 27 min b&w. Rental $15; purchase $175.

A biography of the life of Dr. Martin Luther King, Jr., from the time he first rose to national prominence as a result of his courageous leadership in the struggle against segregation in Montgomery, Alabama. Influenced by his example, and often under his active guidance, a mass movement developed to oppose the pervasive system of segregation in the South. The civil rights campaigns in Albany, Georgia, and Birmingham, Alabama; and the massive march in Washington, D.C., which helped bring about meaningful civil rights legislation, are recorded. The story continues through 1961, when Dr. King was awarded the Nobel Peace Prize, up to April 4, 1968, when he was assassinated in Memphis, Tennessee.

MATTER WITH ME, THE. OXF 1972. El-J-S-A. 15 min col. Rental $25; purchase $220.

The film follows the movement of a 12-year-old black boy through two worlds—one white, one black. Through the camera, the viewer sees the boy in various places in these two worlds and sees both worlds through the boy's eyes. The contrasts are many.

MISSING PAGES. FISKU/PEI 1972. El-J-S-C-A. 14 min col. Rental $15; purchase $150.

An historical account of the Underground Railroad as told to a Fisk University social scientist by ex-slaves in the 1930s. The importance of the storyteller is stressed through the art work of students.

NEGRO KINGDOMS OF AFRICA'S GOLDEN AGE. ATLAP 1968. J-S-A. 17 min col. Rental $15.

Shows the changing climate of Africa. Discusses the trans-Sahara transportation and emergence of several prosperous and mighty empires in tropical Africa.

NEW SOUTH, THE. NET/IU 1972. S-A. 58 min col. Rental $5.25; purchase $265.

Author Pat Watters gathers opinions of black and white Georgia citizens in this documentary examining changing social and economic conditions in the South. Topics covered include racism, pollution, education, black electoral struggles, and poverty. Watters finds the South experiencing many problems typically thought of as "northern."

NO JAIL CAN CHANGE ME. UC 1968. C–A. 30 min b&w. Rental $13; purchase $180.

This film is an interview of a 21-year-old black man who, since the age of ten, has spent all but a few scattered months in correctional institutions. It deals with his childhood and his experiences in penal institutions, problems with his wife, his search for masculine identity, and his attempts to control his life.

NOVEL, THE: RALPH ELLISON ON WORK IN PROGRESS. NET/IU 1966. El–J–S. 30 min b&w. Rental $6.75; purchase $125.

This film presents an interview with Mr. Ralph Ellison during which he discusses his philosophy concerning writers, American novels, the unity of the American spirit, and the genesis of his first novel, *The Invisible Man*. Further insight into the personality of Mr. Ellison is provided by a brief synopsis of his life and views of the interior of his apartment are shown.

OF BLACK AMERICA: BODY AND SOUL (Part 1). CBS/BFA 1968. El–J–S–C–A. 24 min b&w/col. Rental $20; purchase $170 (b&w), $300 (col).

Harry Reasoner presents an examination of the black American's contribution to sports in America. Harry Edwards, leader of the Olympic Games boycott, is interviewed along with leading black athletes Tommie Smith, Lee Evans, Charlie Green, Jim Hines, and Ralph Boston.

OF BLACK AMERICA: BODY AND SOUL (Part 2). CBS/BFA 1968. El–J–S–C–A. 28 min b&w/col. Rental $20; purchase $170 (b&w), $300 (col).

Soul music is discussed in detail by singer Ray Charles. Mr. Charles explains that because of isolation and the misery and humiliation suffered by the American Blacks, they developed their own music and dance forms. Only through this outlet of rhythm and sound have the Blacks been able to release some of their frustration and grief. Singers Mahalia Jackson, Billie Holiday, and Aretha Franklin are presented.

OH FREEDOM. NYT/IU 1972. J–S–C–A. 26 min col. Rental $12; purchase $250.

An emotional but factual and sequential history of the civil rights movement in America during the last two decades. Focuses particularly on the work of Martin Luther King, Jr., and the nonviolent efforts to desegregate the South up to the beginning of the Black Panther movement.

OSCAR ROBERTSON. OXF 1973. El–J–S–A. 22 min col. Rental $30; purchase $275.

Success and admiration have followed Oscar Robertson, all-pro guard of the Milwaukee Bucks, throughout his illustrious career. Robertson is described by his opponents as "the man who knows what to do with the basketball." This is evidenced through isolated camera shots taken during two exhausting battles with the Chicago Bulls.

OUR COUNTRY! TOO. NET/IU 1965. S–C–A. 30 min b&w. Rental $9.50; purchase $165.

Explores the inner world of the black American's attitudes and impressions of life. Interviews held at various places include an African rite in Harlem, a debutante ball, the office of a black newspaper, and a black-owned radio station.

PANOLA. ADF 1970. J-S-C-A. 21 min b&w. Rental $30; purchase $175.
A portrait of a black man in Mississippi who with his family is supported through the charity of a local white church. He views with frustration the continued manipulation of his life by the black community and the white friends who provide his support.

PAUL LAWRENCE DUNBAR—AMERICAN POET. BFA 1966. P-El-J-S. 14 min col. Rental $8; purchase $165.
This film portrays the life of the black American poet Paul Lawrence Dunbar whose poems reflect pride in his race and heritage. It relates his struggles from the age of 13 when his father, an escaped slave who fought in the Civil War, died, to his time of worldwide fame. When he died at 33 years of age, he had already fashioned out of his rich heritage a wealth of poems, songs, plays, and novels.

PETER'S CHAIR. WWSI 1971. P-El. 5:38 min col. Rental $6 (per day).
Peter, a little black boy, is upset that his family is planning to paint his old cradle for the new baby. Then they want to paint Peter's chair. He and his dog decide to run away and, when they do, Peter finds he has grown up in more ways than one.

PORTRAIT IN BLACK AND WHITE (Parts 1 and 2). CBSTV/BFA 1968. El-J-S-A. 54 min b&w. Rental $25; purchase $300.
Produced by CBS News, this film examines various facets of historical and contemporary history of the black man in America. It includes filming in America and Africa and makes use of such personalities as Congressman John Conyers and comedian Bill Cosby. This examination of black attitudes toward the white community and white attitudes toward the black community was produced with the use of a nationwide poll. CBS News prepared a 45 minute questionnaire and interviewed some 1,500 people. The results of these interviews showed people's attitudes and feelings on the race question to be both subtle and complex.

RED, WHITE AND BLUE AND BLACK. CBSTV/CAROUF 1970. S-A. 19 min b&w. Rental $15 (approx); purchase $125.
In this documentary CBS News examines the racial violence among U.S. troops. The film focuses on the incendiary situation in Germany with both factions given a chance to express their views. Reveals yet another area of governmental indifference to the problems and needs of all the people.

RIGHT ON BE FREE. LFR 1971. El-J-S. 15 min col. Rental $15; purchase $190.
This film shows the energy, vitality, and strong sense of identity of the black American artists, presenting the black mood and temperament in music, poetry,

painting, and dance. Shows the effects of the black experience in America on the art of these American artists.

ROBERTA FLACK. WGBHTV/IU 1971. S-C-A. 30 min col. Rental $12.50; purchase $315.

Shows Roberta Flack, a contemporary black singer and pianist, in appearances at the Newport Jazz Festival and elsewhere. She discusses problems of mixed marriage and dual careers. From the "Artists in America" series.

RON LYLE. OXF 1973. S-A. 22 min col. Rental $30; purchase $275.

Heavyweight boxer Ron Lyle offers a place in his corner at his victory over the Canadian fighter Bill Drover. Hearing the encouragement and advice of his trainer during the fight, and following Lyle through training and workouts, the viewer has a close look at boxing's unusually important trainer-athlete relationship. The film gives a personal look at a man who served a prison sentence and drew dedication and maturity from the experience.

SIGNIFICANCE OF MALCOLM X. HRW 1970. S-C-A. 30 min b&w. Rental $6; purchase $175.

A biography of Malcolm X with special emphasis on his influence as a black leader after he became a follower of Elijah Mohammed. The early years of his leadership and his philosophy are focused on. The impact of his message on civil rights struggle today provides interesting parallels.

SLAVERY. NET/IU 1965. S-C-A. 30 min b&w. Rental $9.50; purchase $165.

Based on actual testimony of former slaves, this film tells of the tragic but sometimes humorous nature of life in the Old South. Small incidents in the lives of many slaves are depicted. The liberation of slaves by the Yankee troops is seen, with Negro spirituals helping to tell the story.

SNOWY DAY, THE. WWSI 1964. P. 6 min col. Rental $5.

The story portrays a little black boy, Peter, in a snowy city. The film is done with collages; the film contrasts the qualities of snow with the warmth of home and family.

SOUTH AFRICAN ESSAY: FRUIT OF FEAR. NET/IU 1965. S-C-A. 60 min b&w. Rental $15.25; purchase $265.

Documents and contrasts the two societies existing in South Africa today—the black majority and the ruling white minority. Interviews leaders of both factions to present their views of the apartheid doctrine. Contrasts social and economic privileges of the two groups.

SOUTH AFRICAN ESSAY: ONE NATION TWO NATIONALISMS. NET/IU 1965. S-C-A. 60 min b&w. Rental $15.25; purchase $265.

Uses documentary film footage to examine the country's Nationalist Party and the policy of strict separation of people according to racial and tribal origins. Features interviews with leaders from the several groups concerned. Focuses on the power of the white Nationalist Party.

SPORTRAITS IN EBONY. NBC/ROE 1963. El–J–S–A. 30 min col. Purchase $275.

Depicts outstanding black American athletes in action in baseball, basketball, football, and track. Narration is in sports jargon. Although not a new film, it is relevant for viewers to see black sports personalities as they developed up to and including the early 1960s.

STILL A BROTHER: INSIDE THE NEGRO MIDDLE CLASS. MGH 1968. J–S–C–A. 90 min b&w. Rental $40; purchase $400.

This is a picture of the progress of the black middle class. This group which parallels the white middle class economically, but is virtually separate socially, comprises around 5 million people. They are shown at work, play, and at home. The huge black consumer market is contrasted with the limited black ownership. Such concepts as black nationalism, black American culture, religion, and soul are explored. In three parts.

STORY OF A THREE-DAY PASS. SIGMAT/MACMAB 1967. S–C–A. 87 min b&w. Rental $70.

Directed and written by Melvin Van Peebles, this is an impressionistic life story. Turner, a black G.I. stationed in France, gets a three-day pass and spends an idyllic weekend with Mariam. The couple express love for each other, but Turner is later demoted and restricted to the base. Later, Turner learns that Mariam has lost interest in him.

STRANGERS IN THEIR OWN LAND: THE BLACKS. ABC/XEROX 1971. J–S–A. 12 min col. Purchase $195.

This film discusses the general nature of prejudice and the specific problems and potentials of one ethnic group—the Blacks. The focus is on black art and culture as a means of establishing "identity" as well as on difficulties facing the blacks who are for many reasons "strangers in their own land." Film shows the development of a new source of pride in their search for African roots.

TAKE A GIANT STEP. RTBL 1968. El–J–S–A. 25 min col. Rental $27.50; purchase $185.

Filmed on location in the riot-torn Watts area of Los Angeles, this film follows the progress of a former black rioter, Lester Johnson, through his development until he becomes a productive and valuable employee. This film sheds light on hiring practices, developing the potential of unskilled workers, changing attitudes, and solving knotty supervisory problems.

TELLING IT LIKE IT IS AND HOW IT OUGHT TO BE. CCMS. C–A. 30 min b&w. Rental $15; purchase $145.

Frank Robinson of the Baltimore Orioles and Joe Garagiola of NBC discuss the problems related to being a black American in a white dominated society. A good discussion film to inspire black youngsters and provide others with an insight into the struggle and problems of minorities as they attempt to achieve.

THINKING SEVENTEEN. UC 1969. J-S-C-A. 16 min col. Rental $12.

This is an interesting sociological study of a 17-year-old black teenager, Dennis Johnson. In an interview he discusses his views of life, black militants, racism, college, jobs, and his hopes and suspicions. Dennis seems bitter, yet is likeable and perceptive.

THREE BLACK WRITERS. CBSTV/HRW 1969. S-C-A. 30 min b&w. Purchase $175.

Larry Neal acts as moderator as Addison Gayle, Toni Cade, and Charlie Russell discuss the changes in black culture since the 1950s as revealed in the writings of Ralph Ellison, James Baldwin, and Richard Wright.

TO BE BLACK. ABC/MGH 1970. J-S-C-A. 54 min b&w. Rental $29; purchase $350.

This documentary depicts the plight of the black man in America. Several black people discuss the frustrations they encounter living in America. The film tries to explore the psyche of black people so that some solutions can be formed.

TO BE YOUNG, GIFTED AND BLACK. NET/IU 1972. El-J-S-C-A. 90 min col. Rental $27; purchase $665.

A cast comprised of Ruby Dee, Al Freeman, Jr., Claudia McNeil, Barbara Barrie, Lauren Jones, Roy Scheider, and Blythe Danner pays tribute to Lorraine Hansberry in this play depicting the life and works of the late black playwright. In this film, much of the script is in Lorraine Hansberry's own words drawn from her plays, letters, and diaries written prior to her premature death from cancer at the age of 34.

TO SIR WITH LOVE. MACMAB 1967. J-S. 105 min col. Rental $50.

Here is a story of a tenacious teacher who clashes with his unruly pupils in a rough London school. He wins their respect only after throwing away the rulebook and relating to his students, not as delinquents but as adults.

TRIAL—THE CITY AND COUNTY OF DENVER VS. LAUREN R. WATSON. NET/IU 1970. S-C-A. 90 min b&w. Rental $21; purchase $360.

This film is an actual courtroom trial. The defendant, a Black Panther, is charged with resisting a police officer. He claims the arrest is police harassment; the prosecution believes otherwise. This film has far-reaching significance for it shows the importance in resolving social conflicts in the courts instead of in the streets. One of five films in a series.

TRIAL—THE FIRST DAY. NET/IU 1970. S-C-A. 90 min b&w. Rental $21; purchase $360.

A jury of six is selected to try defendant Lauren R. Watson. The jury selected is white and middle class. A motion by the defendant's lawyer to quash the jury is denied. As a result, questions concerning what is meant by a jury of one's peers are discussed by James Vorenburg, professor of law at Harvard.

TRIAL—THE SECOND DAY. NET/IU 1970. S-C-A. 90 min b&w. Rental $21; purchase $360.

Through the cross-examination of the arresting officer and others, the prosecution tries to prove that Lauren R. Watson both resisted arrest and interfered with a police officer. Leonard Davies, the defense attorney, finds some conflicting statements in the two officers' testimony and tries to show that Watson was not resisting because he twice stopped his car and talked with the police prior to arrest. Professor Vorenburg, professor of law at Harvard, sums up the day's proceedings and discusses the amount of force police have a right to use during apprehension.

TRIAL—THE THIRD DAY. NET/IU 1970. S-C-A. 90 min b&w. Rental $21; purchase $360.

The prosecution rests its case against Lauren R. Watson and the defense, after making a motion for a judgment of acquittal, presents its witnesses. The interference charges are dropped for lack of evidence. Davies tries to show that the defendant was being harassed and did not resist arrest. Professor Vorenburg discusses the value of public trials which allow the present trial system to be criticized.

TRIAL—THE FOURTH AND FINAL DAY. NET/IU 1970. S-C-A. 90 min b&w. Rental $21; purchase $360.

Both sides have rested their cases. Instructions are given to the jury and they spend two hours deliberating. Interviews are given by the judge, arresting officer, the defendant, both attorneys, and some of the jury after deliberation. Lauren R. Watson believes, win or lose, it was not a fair trial because it was not a jury of his peers and if he wins it was only because he had access to a good lawyer, an advantage beyond the resources of most poor people.

WALK IN MY SHOES. MGH 1973. J-S-C. 54 min col. Rental $29; purchase $375.

Who speaks for the black Americans? Despite a commonality of experience, no single spokesman can incorporate the diversity of views within the black community. In this powerful exploration of the black experience, many voices are heard: A New York taxi driver, Dick Gregory at San Francisco's "Hungry i," the Black Muslims, city people and country people, northerners and southerners, and Percy Sutton, Harlem political leader and Manhattan Borough President. They speak for and against moderation and radicalism. But one point is agreed upon—the black man is not yet accepted in the mainstream of American life. Produced by ABC News.

W. C. HANDY. VIGNET/BFA 1967. J-S-A. 14 min col. Rental $6.50; purchase $165.

The film reflects the political, economic, and sociological conditions in America during the period 1890-1950. It depicts the cultural contribution of an outstanding black composer, William Christopher Handy, the "Father of the Blues." The experiences which demanded Handy's simple philosophies and uncomplaining acceptance of the blows of fate show that work, determination, and talent can help in achieving one's goals.

WEAPONS OF GORDON PARKS, THE. UC/EMCC 1966. C–A. 17 min b&w. Rental $6; purchase $100.

This story of Gordon Parks, ex-photographer for *Life* magazine, shows a constructive way of dealing with the race problem. He voices the hope that his children and grandchildren in their struggle for success will take the path of love, not hatred. In recounting his own struggle, he notes that his mother did not allow him to take refuge in the excuse that he had been born black.

WHISTLE FOR WILLIE. WWSI 1965. P–El. 5:30 min col. Rental $5; purchase $90.

This is a story of a black boy, Peter, who wants to be able to whistle for his dog. He tries very hard to learn how. The story of his trying is told in such lovely, simple words and beautiful, glowing pictures that learning to whistle seems to be the happiest thing any boy could possibly do.

WILLIAM FROM GEORGIA TO HARLEM. LCA 1971. J–S–A. 15 min col. Rental $15; purchase $195.

How does a southern farm boy cope with life in a big city ghetto? They call him Willie, and he is just up from a Georgia farm. His big city cousin calls him a hick. It is not easy for Willie to face the adjustment to a totally different way of life, and he finds he has a lot to learn about the reality of Harlem. The film offers contrasts between urban and rural life-styles of youth.

WORLD OF JULIAN BOND, THE. NET/IU 1969. S–C–A. 8 min col. Rental $5.25; purchase $85.

This film is a candid study of the young Georgia state legislator in which he explains why, as an integrationist, he would still adopt some black separatist policies. The recent career of Julian Bond is reviewed in light of his having been the first black man to be nominated for the vice-presidency at a Democratic National Convention. Bond believes that segregation in the South is causing black capitalism and community control. Scenes show him campaigning in New York for Paul O'Dwyer, a white liberal, and then returning to his own political duties in Atlanta.

YOU DIG IT. FRITH 1968. J–S–C–A. 28 min b&w. Rental $12.50; purchase $170.

Largely an autobiographical account of a ghetto teenager and the environment in which he grew up. It portrays the hardships and harsh realities of New York's Lower East Side; its poverty, broken home life, and its rumbles. Written by Leon Williams at the age of 16.

Filmstrips

AFRICAN ABC. TA. col. 42 frs, captioned only $7.

Children will enjoy this entertaining introduction to Africa. Against the colorful backdrop of Africa's people, places, and animals, children learn the alphabet. Captions contain alliterative key words to help reinforce letter sounds.

AFRICAN ART AND CULTURE. SCHLAT 1968. J-S-C. col. No. T306: 3 sound filmstrips, program guide, 65 frs. Avg 17 min each. With discs $63; with cassettes $72.

Introduces the western student to the mystery and beauty of seven centuries of art and culture of the African nations. Using authentic artifacts, the program illustrates the influence on western art from African artists and explores the traditions, religions, livelihoods, and tribal customs of these fascinating nations. Offers a source of study of African history and art.

AFRICAN HERITAGE. PPC 1970. El-J-S. col. LC 79-739430. 73 frs and 95 frs, 2 parts with discs.

The roots of modern Afro-Americans are traced in this colorfully illustrated sound filmstrip portraying the history and culture of Africa. Colored photographs, illustrations, dramatizations, authentic music and sounds beautifully illustrate the heritage that is Africa. Set contains student guide and teacher's manual including scripts. Also, an LP record with narration by James Earl Jones. From the "Eyewitness Afro-American History" series.

AFRICAN PAST, THE. UEVA 1969. J-S-C. col. LC 76-734846. 42 frs with audio tape $6.

This history includes the recent anthropologists' discoveries that indicate Africa as the starting point of the human race. Discusses items isolated by archaeological discoveries of ancient African kingdoms.

AFRO-AMERICAN HISTORY. EBEC 1972. El-J-S. col. Nos. 3004, 3071, 3073, 3075, 3079, and 3081: 10 min each. With discs $95; with cassettes $115.

Heritage, culture, achievements, and problems are explored in this series documenting black Americans' struggle for identity and equality. Films trace African origins, life in Southern slavery and urban ghettos, the development of black nationalism, and individual contributions in many fields. From EBEC's "Afro-American History" series.

AFRO-AMERICAN LITERATURE: AN OVERVIEW. EDC 1968. J-S-C. col. No. 302: 2 sound filmstrips, 80 frs, 18 min each. 2 LP records $41; 2 cassettes $45.

Traces the development of Afro-American literature from the early folktales of plantation slaves to modern writings from the depression to present times. Stresses the part blacks have played in the total scheme of American literature.

AFRO-AMERICANS SPEAK FOR THEMSELVES. EDC 1969. J-S-C. col. No. 304: 3 sound filmstrips, 80 frs, 18 min each. 3 LP records $61.50; 3 cassettes $67.50.

Provides an insight into the "Black Experience" through the voices of black Americans, including Malcolm X and Eldridge Cleaver. Series provides an in-depth look into the thinking of black people.

A HISTORY OF BLACK AMERICA. UEVA 1969. J-S. col. 45 frs, with cassettes $6.

Examines the plantation system from 1800 to 1830, pointing out its effects on the slave families. The revolts resulting from the slavery system are described, including those led by Gabriel Prosser, Denmark Vesey, and Nat Turner.

A HISTORY OF BLACK AMERICA (FIREBRANDS AND FREEDOM FIGHTERS). UEVA 1969. J-S. col. 41 frs, with cassettes $6.
Presents the politics and personalities involved in the abolitionist movement, the Underground Railroad, the Fugitive Slave Law, John Brown's raid at Harper's Ferry, and the election of Abraham Lincoln.

A HISTORY OF BLACK AMERICA (FROM FREEDOM TO DISAPPOINTMENT). UEVA 1969. J-S. col. 41 frs, with cassettes $6.
Traces the events and activities which followed the Civil War, including the establishment of the Freedman's Bureau, the battle against illiteracy, the political successes of Robert Elliot and R. B. S. Pinchback, the entrenchment of the 'separate but equal' doctrine, Booker T. Washington's advocation of vocational education for Blacks, and the resultant opposition from white labor unions at the turn of the century.

A HISTORY OF BLACK AMERICA (HOPE, DISILLUSIONMENT AND SACRIFICE). UEVA 1969. J-S. col. 46 frs, with cassettes $6.
Chronicles the advances made against segregation during the 1940s and 1950s, the accomplishments of Blacks in the Korean conflict, the beginnings of nonviolent protest and boycotts, the achievements under the Kennedy administration, the rise of militant groups, and the assassination of Martin Luther King, Jr.

A HISTORY OF BLACK AMERICA—NEW LEADERSHIP AND THE TURNING TIDE. UEVA 1969. J-S. col. 41 frs, with cassettes $6.
Contrasts the opposing philosophies of Booker T. Washington and W. E. B. DuBois and discusses the establishment of the NAACP, the national recognition of black musicians, the black role in World War I, the beginnings of progress in the Civil Rights struggle, and Marcus Garvey's failure to provide the leadership so sorely needed for Blacks during this crucial period.

A HISTORY OF BLACK AMERICA—PROGRESS, DEPRESSION AND GLOBAL WAR. UEVA 1969. J-S. col. 38 frs, with cassettes $6.
Points out the accomplishments of Blacks such as Louis Armstrong in jazz; Langston Hughes in drama; James Weldon Johnson in poetry; and Oscar DePriest, Thurgood Marshall, and Asa Phillip Randolph in politics and civil rights movements. Gives reasons for the resurgence of the Ku Klux Klan, segregation and discrimination in World War II, and some favorable Supreme Court rulings.

A HISTORY OF BLACK AMERICA—SLAVERY AND FREEDOM IN THE ENGLISH COLONIES. UEVA 1969. J-S. col. 40 frs, with cassettes $6.
Attributes the colonial acceptance of outright Negro slavery to the establishment of indentured immigrants. Conflicting opinions about slavery and its importance to the economy of the colonies are presented, culminating in the large-scale liberation of slaves after the American Revolution and the reasons for the resurgence of slavery and the emergence of the plantation system.

A HISTORY OF BLACK AMERICA (THE AFRICAN PAST). UEVA 1969. J-S. col. 42 frs with cassettes $6.

An eclectic view of ancient Africa, including the findings of recent archaeological studies by Dr. Louis Leaky and writing from the histories of Greece, Rome, Egypt, and Israel to outline the black Sudanese empires such as Ghana and Songhay. Ends with the fifteenth century beginnings of the slave trade.

AMERICAN NEGROES. TRA 1969. P-El. col. Complete unit 8 filmstrips $56.

This unit provides children with an important introduction to the history of the black American, exploring the lives and times of men and women dedicated to justice and freedom. Here is the story of inspired leaders, each fighting for the cause of freedom in his own individual way; each playing a major role in American history and contributing to the cultural heritage of his people. Includes: Harriet Tubman, Frederick Douglass, Sojourner Truth, Booker T. Washington, George Washington Carver, Mary McLeod Bethune, Martin Luther King, Jr., and Jackie Robinson.

AMERICAN NEGRO PATHFINDERS. BFA 1967. J-S-A. b&w. No. VO 1000: 6 filmstrips with captions $48.

This series depicts the outstanding contributions to American society of six prominent black leaders. Using constructive action instead of violence, each person furthered the cause of human dignity, individual freedom, and social justice. Titles: Dr. Ralph Bunche: Missionary of Peace; Justice Thurgood Marshall: Mr. Civil Rights; Gen. Benjamin O. Davis, Jr.: American Guardian; A. Phillip Randolph: Elder Statesman; Dr. Mary McLeod Bethune: Courageous Educator; Dr. Martin Luther King, Jr.: Nonviolent Crusader.

A PEOPLE UPROOTED (1500-1800). EBEC 1969. El-J-S. col. No. 11860: 7 filmstrips, 55 frs each $50.40; individually $8.

The series traces the roots of Afro-Americans, beginning in sixteenth century Africa; compares African art to Western art; traces the development of slavery in the United States and its effect on tobacco production in Virginia. Presents the Blacks' role in the Revolutionary War, a strong role based on their belief in the principle of freedom. Titles: Africa: Historical Heritage; Africa: Artistic Heritage; The Slave Trade; Slavery in Plantation Virginia; Black People in the Revolution; Benjamin Banneker, Man of Science; and Richard Allen, Man of God.

BLACK AMERICAN CIVIL RIGHTS LEADERS. MGH 1971. El-J-S. col. Complete series 5 sound filmstrips with guides, avg 22 min each. Individually: filmstrip with record $21; filmstrip with cassette $21. Individual filmstrip $15; record $8; cassette $8. Five filmstrips with 5 records $90; 5 filmstrips with 5 cassettes $90.

The evolution of the black struggle is clearly seen in the lives and achievements of five major figures. Each illuminates a different approach to the problems confronting black Americans. Included are excerpts from actual speeches. Titles: W. E. B. DuBois, Marcus Garvey, Martin Luther King, Jr., Malcolm X, and Stokely Carmichael.

BLACK AMERICAN HISTORY. RMIF. P-El-J. col. Nos. 1515 and 1625: Approx 53 frs, 15 min each. $15 and $20 respectively.

No. 1515: The Negro Cowboys. Following the Civil War over 5,000 Blacks drifted into the American Southwest, became cowhands, and conducted many great cattle drives.

No. 1625: *George Washington Carver: A Study in Genius.* A visit to Dr. Carver's boyhood home near Diamond, Mo., shows the trails he wandered through as a child collecting his beloved flowers. Tuskegee Institute and the laboratory where Dr. Carver started his long day's work are also shown.

BLACK AMERICANS AT WORK. CORF 1970. J-S-C-A. col. Avg 52 frs, 11 min. No. S187: 6 filmstrips, 3 records $55. No. M187: 6 filmstrips, 6 cassettes $70.

These documentary interviews provide insights into the daily lives, occupations, backgrounds, and hopes of six black Americans. Through candid views of their work, their families, and the society in which they live, they give new perspectives on how black people see themselves and their opportunities. Produced for Coronet by Gary Stallings Productions. Titles: George Bruno: Hospital Administrator; Betty Belcher: Office Worker; John Claiborne: Butcher; Jonathan Lanier: Student; Gaddis Rathel: Storekeeper; Shelvin Hall: Minister.

BLACK AMERICANS IN GOVERNMENT. MGH 1969. El-J-S. col. Complete series 5 sound filmstrips with guides, 22 min each. Individually: Filmstrip with record $21; filmstrip with cassette $21. Individual filmstrip $15; record $8; cassette $8. Five filmstrips with 5 records $90; 5 filmstrips with 5 cassettes $90.

Within the political framework the black struggle takes on a different dimension. The contributions of five outstanding black political leaders are examined in respect to civil rights legislation, urban problems, and the need for black studies programs. With candid interviews. Titles: Thurgood Marshall, Robert Weaver, Edward Brooke, Shirley Chisholm, and Patricia Harris.

BLACK EXPERIENCE IN ARTS. SCHLAT 1971. J-S-A. col. No. T322: complete set of 4 filmstrips with discs and cassettes. 15 min each. Each set with discs $70; with cassettes $85.

This series presents four distinguished artists. Charles Gordone, Pulitzer prizewinner, discusses his life and work in the theater. Dean Dixon discusses his work as a leading American musician and symphony conductor. Jacob Lawrence, painter, discusses his background in Harlem during the depression and its influence on his paintings. James Earl Jones, actor, discusses his early reasons for going into the theater, his experiences, and his hopes. Titles: Charles Gordone: Playwright; Dean Dixon: Conductor; Jacob Lawrence: Painter; and James Earl Jones: Actor.

BLACK FOLK MUSIC IN AMERICA. SVE 1970. J-S. col. No. 682-SAR: set of 4 filmstrips, 2 records, 4 guides $32.50. No. 682-SATC: set of 4 filmstrips, 2 cassettes, 4 guides $36.50. Each filmstrip with teacher's guide $7. No. 682-1RR: record for No. 682-1 and No. 682-2 $4. No. 682-2 RR: record for

No 682-3 and No. 682-4 $4. No. 682-1 TC: cassette for No. 682-1 and No. 682-2 $6. No. 682-2 TC: cassettes for No. 682-3 and No. 682-4 $6.

This series of filmstrips chronicles the history of black music in America from early Jamestown to today. Artwork, compelling narrations, and songs performed by Brother John Sellers combine to create a powerful portrayal of the black musical heritage. The filmstrips include the following titles: *Songs of Slavery*. Describes first African slaves brought to America; the "new" black way of life. Songs include "Sometimes I Feel Like A Motherless Child" and "Michael Row the Boat Ashore" (58 frs, 19 min). *Black Songs of the Civil War.* Uncle Tom's cabin gives Americans a true look at slave conditions. Blacks prove themselves as Civil War soldiers. Songs include "Oh, Freedom" and "Slavery's Chain Done Broke At Last" (56 frs, 19 min). *Black Songs After the Civil War.* Black Americans head west; blues introduced in the South. Songs include "When I Was A Cowboy" and "Lift Every Voice and Sing" (57 frs, 19 min). *Black Songs of Modern Times.* Courts help bring Blacks new freedoms. Civil rights movement evolves. Songs include "Hallelujah," "I'm A-Travelin'," and "We Shall Overcome" (59 frs, 19 min).

BLACK LEADERS OF THE TWENTIETH CENTURY. LLL/IBC 1969. P-El-J-S. col. 55 frs each, with cassettes $90.

The biographies of ten black leaders of twentieth-century America are presented in terms of their personal achievements and their contributions to American life. Included are leaders in politics, the arts, science, labor, and education. Because they were drawn from several generations, although all within the twentieth century, a study of all ten is desirable. They are: Carl Stokes, Charles Drew, Edward Brooke, Langston Hughes, Lorraine Hansberry, Malcolm X, Martin Luther King, Jr., Mary M. Bethune, Percy Julian, and A. Phillip Randolph.

BLACK MEN IN BLUE. RMIF 1969. El-J-S. col. LC 77-737177. 74 frs, 23 min, with discs $20.

A discussion of the bravery, endurance, problems, and accomplishments of the Ninth and Tenth Negro Cavalry Regiments after the Civil War. Stresses the success of their work despite racial prejudice encountered from white settlers and army men. These "Buffalo Soldiers" were a major force in maintaining peace and furthering civilization in the Southwest. Peter Hirsch, writer consultant.

BLACK MUSIC. SCHMAG/FRSC 1973. J-S-A. col. 2 pt series. With audio tape $42. Kit 1: 91 frs. Kit 2: 79 frs.

Two entertaining and educational filmstrips trace the development of black American music from its roots in Africa through the rhythm and blues of today, using great personalities such as Louis Armstrong, John Coltrane, and Fletcher Henderson. A supplementary record or cassette is included in each kit.

BLACK PEOPLE IN THE NEW SOUTH. SVE 1972. El-J-S-C. col. LC 72-736324. 88 frs with audio tape $67.50.

Describes recent changes in the economic, social, and political life of southern black people. Gives viewpoints of students, a dentist, and a rural Alabama sheriff. Traces the development of the civil rights movement in the South over the 1950s and 1960s. From the "Focus on America—The South" series.

BLACK POEMS, BLACK IMAGES. SCHLAT 1971. J-S-C-A. col. 6 filmstrips, 10 min each, with discs $120; with cassettes $138; individually $23.
This series presents unique and interesting discourses on the black experience. Shows the moods of childhood, impressions and views of the South, cities, and the United States. The six filmstrips are: Childhood, 87 frs; Manhood, 81 frs; The Past, 101 frs; Place, 103 frs; The Present, 98 frs; and Womanhood, 83 frs.

BLACK POETRY. SCHMAG/FRSC 1973. El-J. col. 2 pt series with audio tape $36. Kit 1: 101 frs. Kit 2: 87 frs.
A presentation of the poetry of noted young black poets of the 1970s. Included are: Don L. Lee, Mari Evans, Nikki Giovanni, Amini Baraka, Julia Fields, Arthur Pfister, and others whose writings explore the fundamental ambivalence of the black experience.

BLACK RABBITS AND THE WHITE RABBITS, THE: AN ALLEGORY. SP. P-El. col. No. G305: 1 sound filmstrip, program guide, 41 frs, 7 min. With discs $22.50; with cassettes $25.50.
Two adjacent and peaceful communities of rabbits, one populated with black rabbits, one populated with white rabbits, clash when the white community decides to exploit the black community for selfish gain. The white rabbits view the black ones as inferior and subject them to hard and menial work. The black rabbits finally overthrow the white rabbits and the reverse process begins, leaving several thought-provoking questions for the students to debate.

BLACK RELIGION. SCHMAG/FRSC 1973. J-S-C-A. col. 2 pt series with audio tape $36. Kit 1: 79 frs. Kit 2: 88 frs.
A study of religion is presented in two filmstrips: "The Church," its history in America and its special role in the community in which it has long served as a framework for survival of Blacks; "The Preacher," portrays his important role in the community as spiritual head, politician, civil rights advocate, teacher, and economist.

BLACK REVOLUTION. VEC 1969. El-J-S. col. 2 pts with record, 40 frs each, $15.45.
Part I, "Slavery to 1965," is a history of slavery in America from the year 1619 to 1965, documented with photographs and illustrations. Part II, "1965 to Present," deals with the new leaders of the late 1960s and early 1970s; analyzes their goals and methods.

CHAINS OF SLAVERY (1800-1865). EBEC 1969. J-S-C. col. LC76-738009. No. 11700: 6 captioned filmstrips, $43.20; individually $8.
Focusing on the way black people lived in the past and the actions of specific historic figures, this series helps students understand the role of black people in American history, 1800 to 1965. Race relations are explored in terms of such concepts as abolition, Jim Crow, and the Dred Scott Decision. Black participa-

tion in the Civil War and the "military necessity" for the Emancipation Proclamation are illustrated. The series documents social injustice in the North and formation of a closed society in the South. Brilliant full-color artwork created especially for the series provides an accurate picture of the times. Captions are short, and factual in content. Average length 53 frs. Titles: Harriet Tubman; Frederick Douglass; Black People in the Free North, 1850; Black People in the Slave South, 1850; Nat Turner's Rebellion; and Black People in the Civil War.

CLASSROOM APPROACHES TO THE TEACHING OF BLACK HISTORY AND LITERATURE. EDR 1972. C-A. col. 2 pts with discs and guides, 140 frs, $39.

Authored by William Katz, Judy Klugmann, and Warren Halliburton, the two filmstrips in the series define and put into perspective black history in America. They discuss teaching approaches, context source, information, student activities, and special notations. The program also contains a record component which treats black literature in the same manner.

CONTEMPORARY AFRO-AMERICAN ART. EDDIM 1970. J-S-C. col. No. 306: 2 sound filmstrips, 15 min each. With 2 LP records $41; with 2 cassettes $45.

An examination of the creative works of black painters and sculptors and their place in contemporary America.

CONTEMPORARY BLACK PAINTERS AND SCULPTORS. EDDIM 1971. J-S-C-A. col. LC 72-733329: with script.

Presents paintings and sculptures of various styles that were executed in the last decade by black artists of America.

DREAM AWAKE, THE—THE BLACK EXPERIENCE IN AMERICA. SPA 1970. J-S-A. col. LC 70-735572. No. SA2006: complete set with LP record $179; No. SAC2006: complete set with cassettes $197.95.

Written by Owen Dodson, the renowned poet and dramatist, *The Dream Awake* recounts the history of Blacks from Africa through the long struggle for freedom in America before, during, and after the Civil War, up to the present day. The filmstrips include: Africa, The Amistad-Crispus Attucks-Harriet Tubman and The Emancipation Proclamation, The Black Cowboy, The Black Quartet, The Martyrs, Resurrection City and the Children, and The Black Arts. The program is dramatically performed by James Earl Jones, Josephine Premice, Josh White, Jr., Esther Rolle, and an outstanding cast.

FAYETTE MISSISSIPPI: A STUDY IN BLACK AND WHITE. SCHLAT 1970. J-S-C. col. No. T319: 2 sound filmstrips with program guide. Avg 90 frs, 14 min each. With discs $42; with cassettes $48.

This filmstrip presents the town's population showing their feelings about the black and white situation of the South. The mayor, Charles Evers, talks about events that have happened during his term of office. Marie Walker, editor of the local newspaper, acts as spokeswoman for the whole community.

FIGHT FOR OUR RIGHTS. SCHLAT 1968. P-El-J. col. Part 1: No. T309: 4 sound filmstrips with program guide. Avg 70 frs, 12 min each. With discs $80;

with cassettes $92. Part 2: No. T310: 4 sound filmstrips with program guide. Avg 65 frs, 15 min each. With discs $80; with cassettes $92.

These filmstrips describe the right to attend school as guaranteed by our Bill of Rights. Illustrations from the 1954 Supreme Court decision in the case of student Linda Brown and from the 1957 attempt of the governor of Arkansas to keep black students from entering the white high school in Little Rock. Titles, Part I: Freedom of the Press, Freedom of Religion, The Right of Peaceful Assembly, and The Right to Go to School. Part II: The Right to Counsel, Freedom of Speech, The Right to Bear Arms, and The Right to Vote.

FIVE BLACK AMERICANS AND THEIR FIGHT FOR FREEDOM. BFA 1974. J-S-C-A. col. No. VV9000: 6 sound filmstrips with 6 cassettes $102. No. VV8000: 6 sound filmstrips with 6 records $84.

This series examines the lives of five political activists with similar ideas and goals but different methods in fighting prejudice and injustice. Instead of following a strict biographical format, each strip incorporates a behavioral objective which leads students to further discussion and investigation of a particular philosophy or point of view. Titles: Denmark Vessey: Armed Revolt; George T. Downing: The Politics of Lobbying; Marcus Garvey: Black Nationalism; Malcolm X, Part 1—Violence and Self-Defense; Malcolm X, Part 2—The Roots of Racism; and Shirley Chisholm: Political Representation.

X FOLK SONGS AND FREDERICK DOUGLASS. SCHLAT 1969. J-S-A. col. No. T501: 6 sound filmstrips, with program guide. Avg 44 frs, 14 min each. With discs $120; with cassettes $138.

Covers the history of American slavery including slave ships and auctions, Dred Scott Decision and Fugitive Slave Law. Shows Douglass' early life as a slave, his escape to the North and early association with abolitionist movement. Follows his flight to England, return to America, activities during the Civil War, and his eventual appointment as minister of Haiti. Presented against a background of Negro spirituals and ballads. In two parts.

400 YEARS: BLACK HISTORY IN AMERICA. EDR 1971. El-J. col. 2 pt series. 1 sound filmstrip, 52 frs, 13 min $21 each; with disc $18.50 each.

A series of biographical data of famous people and organizations. Titles include: The Era of Black Slavery, The Black Man in the Late 19th Century, The Black Man in the Early 20th Century, and The Black Revolution.

GHETTOS OF AMERICA. SCHLAT 1969. El-J-S-A. col. Part 1: 136 frs, 14 min, Part 2: 120 frs, 14 min. With discs $70 each; with cassettes $85 each.

Life in America's two largest ghettos as seen through the eyes of two young inhabitants of each, "Jerry Lives in Harlem" and "Anthony Lives in Watts." Each youngster is accompanied through his daily routine in overcrowded dwellings, filthy street playgrounds, and substandard schools. This vivid program gives students an understanding of how ghettos are created and sustained.

GROWING UP BLACK. SCHLAT 1968. El-J. col. No. G307: 4 sound filmstrips with program guide, 60 frs, 10 min each. With discs $70; with cassettes $85.

Young black adults discuss the spectrum of problems which they are confronted with daily. Contains interviews with young men and women who record their bitter experiences as they search for success.

HARLEM RENAISSANCE AND BEYOND, THE. GA 1969. J-S-C-A. col. No. 514 586: 2 filmstrips with two 12″ LP records $48.50. No. 514 636: 2 filmstrips with 2 cassettes $48.50. LC 72-735353: discussion guide.

Black poetry and prose offer students valuable insights into the black experience in America, as photos and art reflect the social conditions of Harlem. Part 1 portrays Harlem as a post-World War I "race capital," a new center of white literary interest. Langston Hughes' Jesse B. Simple personifies new concern for ordinary black people as opposed to the "talented tenth." Gripping poetry by Hughes, Countee Cullen, and Claude McKay captures Harlem's early hopes and cruel disillusionment during the twenties. Part 2 begins with Richard Wright's "Native Son" and its vivid portrait of black life in the thirties.

HARLEM RENAISSANCE: THE HISTORY OF THE BLACK MAN IN THE UNITED STATES. EAV 1970. J-S-C. col. 52 frs. No. 91RF345: 8 filmstrips with 4 LP records $88. No. 99KF457: 8 filmstrips with 8 cassettes $120.

Reviews the revival of a distinct black culture in the post-World War I period, Harlem in the 1920s, and black artists and the dual existence of the black intellectual in a white world.

HERITAGE OF AFRO-AMERICAN HISTORY. TRA. El-J-S. col. Complete unit 9 filmstrips $63; individually $7.

These filmstrips trace the history and heritage of Afro-Americans, and demonstrate how black history is deeply entwined with American history. From African origins to the struggle for equality, Afro-American history is filled with noble leaders, important events, and the great challenge of freedom and justice for all citizens living in America. Titles: From Africa to the New World, 1000-1713; Life in the New American Colonies, 1713-1792; The Plantation System, 1790-1850; From Abolition Movements to Civil War, 1850-1865; From Reconstruction to Jim Crow, 1865-1898; The Long Hard Struggle, 1898-1942; Changing Currents of Civil Rights, 1942-1960; Years of Challenge, 1960-present; and Leaders Who Left Their Mark.

HISTORY OF THE AMERICAN NEGRO, THE. MGH 1965. El-J-S. col. No. 405360-4: Complete series © 1965, 8 captioned filmstrips, guide, and catalog cards $65. Individually $9.

A history of the black American from the beginning of slavery to the mid-1960s. The series contains scenes depicting each period of Afro-American history. Titles: From Africa to America, Slavery in the Young American Republic, Slavery in "A House Divided," The Negro in the Civil War and Reconstruction, The Negro in the Gilded Age, The Negro Faces the 20th Century, The Negro Fights for the "Four Freedoms," and The Threshold of Equality.

HISTORY OF THE BLACK MAN IN THE UNITED STATES, THE. EAV 1970. J-S-C-A. col. 8 frs. With records $84; with cassettes $116.

This sound filmstrip set traces the history of the black man in the United States from Colonial times to the present. The visuals are presented in paintings, cartoons, photographs, and other forms of illustration contemporary to the times discussed. The correlated narration incorporates quotations from people involved in the events described, excerpts from literature and music. A teacher's manual includes a full text of the narration. Titles: The Colonial Period, The Abolitionists, The Civil War, Reconstruction, Harlem Renaissance, The Black Man in the Depression, Racism and the Kerner Commission Report, and Black Protest Movements.

JAZZ: THE MUSIC OF BLACK AMERICANS. EDC 1972. J-S-C. col. No. 308: 4 sound filmstrips, 80 frs, 12 min each. With 4 LP records $82, with 4 cassettes $90.

Classic sounds are combined with original music to demonstrate jazz forms and provide an exciting background for the history of black music in America. The series is in four parts beginning with work songs of the American South to the evolution of blues.

JUSTICE THURGOOD MARSHALL—MR. CIVIL RIGHTS. BFA 1969. P-El-J-S-C-A. col. 31 frs with captions.

In his fight for civil rights, Justice Marshall carried his arguments to the Supreme Court, the highest court in the United States. As a result of Marshall's work the Supreme Court eventually ruled against segregation in public facilities.

LEADING AMERICAN NEGROES. SVE 1970. J-S-A. col. No. 242-SAR: 6 filmstrips with 6 teacher's guides and 3 records $49.50; with cassettes $59.50.

Biographies depict significant contributions of black Americans to American culture. Each researched biography relates personal achievements to the growth of our nation. Full-color artwork is synchronized with factual narration. Author: Russell L. Adams. Titles: Mary McLeod Bethune (1875-1955), George Washington Carver (1864-1943), Benjamin Banneker (1731-1806), Robert Smalls (1839-1915), Frederick Douglass (1817-1895), and Harriet Tubman (1820-1913).

LEARN, BABY, LEARN. SCHLAT 1971. J-S-C-A. Approx 90 frs each $40.

Adapted from the program, "They Have Overcome." Affords slower readers the opportunity to become aware of the inspiring accomplishments of five prominent black leaders. The dialogue, made up in the words of these five people, appears in large, easy-to-read captions on the screen. The five personalities interviewed are: Gordon Parks, author, photographer, and filmmaker; Claude Brown, author; Dr. James Comer, psychiatrist; Dr. Dorothy Brown, educator and surgeon; and Charles Lloyd, composer, jazz great.

LIVING IN HARLEM. FH 1965. P-El-J. col. 38 frs with discs $15.

This filmstrip shows a black family at home in Harlem with the slums, vacant lots, and new housing projects. Shows the role of the various agencies and a black construction worker.

MARTIN LUTHER KING, JR. MGH 1970. El-J-S. col. No. 101805: with discs $21. No. 102214: with cassettes $21. Teacher's guide $2.50.

Presents Martin Luther King, Jr., the apostle of nonviolence. Shows his direct action, civil disobedience, and massive nonviolent protest.

MODERN AMERICAN DRAMA: A RAISIN IN THE SUN. EDC 1975. S-C-A. col. No. 750: 1 sound filmstrip, 18 min with cassette $22.50.

One of the greatest social protest plays ever written, this classic by Lorraine Hansberry is a passionate plea for social justice and human understanding. This filmstrip program treats the play both as a dramatic experience and as a depiction of black ghetto life.

MODERN AMERICAN DRAMA: THE EMPEROR JONES. EDC 1975. S-C-A. col. No. 742: 1 sound filmstrip, 18 min with cassette $22.50.

Nobel Prize-winner Eugene O'Neill creates in *The Emperor Jones* a brilliant and bluntly honest "tragi-comedy." The play deals with man's ruthlessness, particularly to the black experience.

NAT TURNER'S REBELLION. EBEC 1969. J-S-C. col. 62 frs with discs $10.

Filmstrip discusses the Nat Turner rebellion in Virginia in August 1831, one of a series of slave insurrections in the South. From the "Chains of Slavery—1800-1865" series.

NEGRO COWBOYS. RMIF 1968. P-El-J. col. LC 73-73776: 59 frs with disc.

Describes how freed Negroes found employment after the Civil War as trail herders who drove steer north and west from Texas. From the "America History" series.

NEGROES IN AMERICA. NYT/TRF 1968. J-S. b&w. 72 frs with discs $10.

From slavery to freedom to civil rights, the focus is not only on black problems but also on black strengths.

NEGROES, THE. SCHLAT 1973. S-C-A. col. LC 73-732753. No. T330: 2 sound filmstrips with program guide. Avg 50 frs, 15 min each. With discs $44; with cassettes $50.

A section revised and taken from "Minorities Have Made America Great." Outlines black history in the United States with emphasis on individual contributions and the struggles for civil rights. From colonial times to present, viewers see the historical achievements of such famous leaders as Booker T. Washington, W. E. B. DuBois, Ralph Bunche, George Washington Carver, and others.

NEW GOALS FOR BLACK AMERICANS. CURAF 1971. P-El-J. col. LC 74-738168. 63 frs with discs $22.

This filmstrip describes the evolution of the black revolution since the end of World War II; the legal phase, the nonviolent direct action phase for integration, and the massive demonstration phase; the insurrection phase and the black power phase. Shows that during the 1960s black Americans made significant strides, yet discrimination and inequality still exist in America.

OUR FAMILY IS BLACK. CORF 1970. P-El. col. Avg 50 frs, 10 min each. No. S163: 6 filmstrips with 3 records $69. No. M163: 6 filmstrips with 6 cassettes $77.

This series studies problems, hopes, and goals of a black urban family. Camera follows each member through daily activities—six-year-old son, teenage son and daughter, working mother and filling-station attendant father. Titles: The Family Together; Father at Work; Mother Works Hard, Too; Jerry's First Day at School; Rose Is Sixteen; and Charles and His Friends.

POETIC VOICE OF BLACK EXPERIENCE, THE. EDC 1971. El-S. col. No. 307: 2 sound filmstrips, 15 min each with 2 LP records $41; with 2 cassettes $45.

A study of the work of black poets from various periods. Includes the works of Paul Lawrence Dunbar, Langston Hughes, Countee Cullen, Waring Cuney, and Georgia Douglas Johnson. The black poet rages and pleads to an alien society while praising nature and brotherly love. A perfect introduction to the voices of black experience.

QUEST FOR EQUALITY. EBEC 1969. J-S-C. col. No. 11870. 6 captioned filmstrips $43.20; individually $8.

Leaders and events in the Blacks' bid for full equality include W. E. B. DuBois, exponent of direct action and symbol of civil rights and the Pan-African movement; and Martin Luther King, Jr., the "conscience" of civil rights and the inspiration of student sit-ins and freedom rides.

REVEREND DR. MARTIN LUTHER KING, JR., THE. SVE 1968. P-El-J. col. LC FIA68-4770. 43 frs with disc $12.50.

Objective, pictorial biography of Dr. Martin Luther King, Jr. Very appropriate photos from news services, excerpts from speeches, plus narrations tell how his devotion shaped his method of operation in attempting to gain equal rights for all Americans. Consultant: David L. Ross, Jr. Narrator: Wendell Smith.

ROBERT AND HIS FAMILY. SVE 1967. P-El. col. No. 208: 4 filmstrips 34 to 43 frs, 8 mins. each with 2 discs $39.

Robert Anderson is a black boy living in an urban area. Full-color, on-site photography, with accompanying story-type narration on records or cassettes, portrays Robert and his family in their various daily activities. The story is told with humor and simplicity, and is helpful in promoting better understanding among racial and ethnic groups, in providing a sense of identification for black children, and in developing desirable attitudes toward work, family, school, and community. Titles: No. 208-1: Robert's Family at Home; No. 208-2: Robert's Family and Their Neighbors; No. 208-3: Robert Goes Shopping; No. 208-4: Robert and Father Visit the Zoo.

RUSH TOWARD FREEDOM. SCHLAT 1970. El-J-S-C. col. No. T308: 8 sound filmstrips with program guide. Avg 115 frs, 15 min each. With discs $120; with cassettes $146.

This series portrays the meaning, direction, and effects of the struggle for freedom among black people in America. First-hand accounts of events and conflicts are presented by Dr. Martin Luther King, Jr., John F. Kennedy, George Wallace, Medgar Evers, Orval Faubus, James Meredith, and others. Titles: States against the Nation; Supreme Court Decision 1954; Birth of Direct Action; The Non-Violent Creed; Give Us the Ballot; To Make Things Better; Over the Edge; Will It End?; Black Is Beautiful.

SEPARATE AND UNEQUAL (1865). EBEC 1969. J-S-C. col. No. 11640: 6 captioned filmstrips $43.20; individually $8.

Organized in terms of key men, events, and places, this series objectively examines the history of Afro-Americans from 1865 to 1910. Details of major events and the people associated with them are illustrated: the passage of the black code which subordinated black people in Southern society and the Supreme Court's decision (*Plessy* v *Ferguson*) which upheld the validity of separate-but-equal laws. Illustrations of social conditions, both north and south, shed light on many of today's racial problems. Journalistic prints of the day and original art compatible with these prints are an ideal means to create an accurate picture of the times from the point of view both of black and white Americans. Titles: Booker T. Washington: National Leader; Bishop Turner: Black Nationalist; Black People in the North, 1900; Black People in the South, 1877–1900; The Black Codes, "Separate But Equal."

THEY HAVE OVERCOME. SCHLAT 1967. El-C-A. col. No. T301: 5 sound filmstrips with program guide. Avg 90 frs, 15 min. each. With discs $85; with cassettes $100.

Five famous black Americans tell how they overcame great odds to attain their present lifestyles: Gordon Parks, Claude Brown, Dr. Dorothy Brown, James Comer, and Charles Lloyd. Drawing on the words of such noted experts as Ashley Montagu, Gordon Allport, and Oscar Handlin, this program transmits an understanding of the inner workings of prejudice and prejudicial decision-making; can assist students in evaluating their own thoughts and feelings. Winner of Blue Ribbon award, American Film Festival.

UNDERSTANDING CONTEMPORARY AFRO-AMERICAN ART. EDS 1973. J-S-C. col. No. 306: 2 sound filmstrips, 15 min each. With 2 LP records $35; with 2 cassettes $39.

The creative works of today's black painters and sculptors are presented within a format that examines their aesthetic values as well as their place in the political and racial polarization that grips the country today. The works of Hunt, Lawrence, and many others have been collected into the largest group exhibition ever made available.

WHISTLE FOR WILLIE. WWSI 1965. P-El. col. LC FIA67-3032: 29 frs. No. 65: with 7″ LP $9.20. No. 65C: with tape $12.75. Booklet $7.25.

This filmstrip is written and illustrated by Ezra Jack Keats and concerns a little black boy who wants to learn how to whistle for his dog. Simply told with beautiful illustrations. From the Weston Woods Set 16 series.

WILLIAM F. BUCKLEY'S "FIRING LINE," THE BLACK REVOLUTION. SCHLAT. S–C–A. col. No. T314: 8 sound filmstrips with program guide. Avg 70 frs, 15 min each. With discs $120; with cassettes $146.

Taped from Buckley's nationally syndicated television forum, this unique, eight-part program presents debates on black separatism, the Black Panther movement, the ghetto, and black power. Guests include Milton Henry, Eldridge Cleaver, Dr. Kenneth Clark, and Nat Hentoff.

Slides

AFRICAN ART. UCSC. J–S–C. col. Art of Africa, 50 slides, $24.50. African Art, 25 slides, $10.95; 50 slides $24.50. African and Oceanic Art, 50 slides, $24.50; 100 slides, $47.50. Oceanic Art, 50 slides, $24.50. African Tribal Sculpture, 2 booklets with 64 slides, $18.95. African Rock Art, 22 slides, $9.95. Contemporary African Art, 25 slides, $12.50. African Art (In Institute of Ethnography—Leningrad), 50 slides, $24.50. African Art (Its Background and Traditions), 24 slides, $12.50.

Each set of slides may be purchased with an accompanying book. Books written by well-known authorities on African and black American art.

AFRICAN SCULPTURE. ACA. J–S–C. 41 slides and commentary $49.

This series presents examples of sculptures in wood, metal, clay, and ivory, with figures, masks, panels, and utilitarian objects shown. The art-style ranges from naturalism to the ultra abstract.

AFRICAN SCULPTURE—FROM PRIVATE COLLECTIONS. SAN. J–S–C. col. 55 slides $71.50.

This slide set presents selections of nineteenth-century African art from the six major regions of the west central part of the continent. The regions included are: Western Sudan, the Atlantic Coast and Forest Belt, the Guinea Coast, Nigeria, the Gabon region, and the Congo.

AFRICAN TEXTILES AND DECORATIVE ARTS. SAN. S–C–A. 40 slides (plastic and glass mounted), $52; 40 slides (cardboard mounted), $34.

In October 1972 the Museum of Modern Art exhibited an extensive survey of African textiles and decorative arts. Included in the exhibition were approximately 250 examples of African textiles, jewelry, ornaments, and personal accoutrements which have remained largely unknown in the Western world to all but collectors and museum curators.

AFRO-AMERICAN STUDIES MATERIALS. PROTHA 1969. P–El–J–S. col. Avg 27 frs per set $20.

The set includes: Afro-American Artists; Religious Paintings—Wm. Johnson; Summary of Wm. Johnson; Survey of Wm. Johnson; Survey of fifteen contemporary Afro-Americans; and Twenty-six Afro-American Artists.

ART OF AFRICA. SVE. J–S–C. Each set of 20 slides with guide and display folder $8.50.

Designed to develop an appreciation of African art, this program focuses on the traditional and contemporary art of Africa. Titles: No. SG-29S: Treasures and Traditions of African Art; No. SG-30S: African Dress and Design; No. SG-31S: African Art Today; No. SG-32S: Modern African Carvings.

BLACK AFRICA. EDDIM 1972. J-S-C. col. 20 slides, 2″ × 2″ with captions $17.

Ceremonial masks and objects from sub-Sahara Africa exemplify the diverse techniques and styles prevalent in the history of African art and crafts.

BLACK AMERICANS: A HISTORICAL PORTFOLIO. EDR 1971. J-S. col. No. ERI 435: 150 slides with annotated guide $98.75.

Based on the William Loren Katz collection of rare prints and photographs, this portfolio documents a full range of people and events: the roots of slavery in West Africa; Jean Baptiste Du Sable, "Founder" of Chicago; Peter Salem, black patriot at Bunker Hill; the surrender of Nat Turner; Seminole Negro warriors; black men in action in the Civil War; and many others.

BLACK EXPERIENCE, THE. SAN 1973. J-S-A. col. No. 730: 60 slides (plastic and glass mounted), $78; No. 731: 60 slides (cardboard mounted), $56.

The works graphically illustrate such themes as the slave trade, slave revolts, the Underground Railroad, the abolitionists, the Civil War, Reconstruction and continuing violence, life in the rural South, life in the big city, the black Renaissance, social conscious art, and the continuing struggle. The accompanying text for set No. 731 was written by Dr. Phillip S. Foner and Romane Bearden.

BLACK MAN IN THE MODERN WORLD, THE. EDR 1971. J-S-A. col. 30 slides with teacher's guide $30.

These slides include such subjects and personages as: Dr. Ossian Sweer and Clarence Darrow, NAACP Lynchburg flag, CIO pickets, Father Divine, Jesse Owens, Marian Anderson at Lincoln Memorial, World War II soldiers, Charles Drew, A. Phillip Randolph, Adam Clayton Powell, Ralph Bunche, demonstrators attacked by police dogs, march on Washington, Selma, Alabama, James Meredith, Malcolm X, H. Rap Brown, Eldridge Cleaver, and Shirley Chisholm. From "Black Americans: A Historical Portfolio" series.

CONTEMPORARY BLACK ARTISTS. SAN. S-C-A. No. 673: 47 slides $61.10.

An exhibition of "Thirty Contemporary Black Artists" was shown at the Minneapolis Institute of Arts in October 1968. The exhibition, organized in collaboration with Ruder and Finn, Inc., N.Y., then toured major museums throughout the country. Biographical and critical commentaries prepared by Dr. Fishwick of Lincoln University are included free with the purchase of this set.

CONTEMPORARY BLACK PAINTERS AND SCULPTORS. EDDIM 1971. J-S-C. col. 20 slides $15.

A balanced collection of the best Afro-American paintings and sculptures being produced today, covering a full range from representation to total abstraction.

MASKS OF AFRICA. ACA. J-S-C. No. ACA-2: 34 slides with commentary $41.

Here are 34 masks, photographed to show details of carving, color, and character, from 21 tribes of west and central Africa with location shown on the map slide.

STRUGGLE TO END SLAVERY, THE. EDR. J-C-A. col. 30 slides with teacher's guide $30.

Covers such subjects as the cotton gin, plantation slave, house slave, notice of slave raffle, Dred Scott, Seminole Negroes, Nat Turner, Cinques, James Beckwood, Delany Garrison, and Henson. Included as well are etchings, prints, and documents. From "Black Americans: A Historical Portfolio" series.

SURVEY OF FIFTEEN CONTEMPORARY AFRO-AMERICAN ARTISTS. PROTHA 1969. J-S-C-A. col. 40 slides $25.

Surveys the works of 15 American artists selected from the collection at Fish University, Nashville, Tenn. Shows how the racial identity of each artist is reflected in his work.

YORUBA RITUAL ART. ACA 1969. El-S. col. No. ACA-43: 33 slides with commentary $39.50.

Series shows examples of masks, statues, and other ceremonial art reflecting the life of the Yoruba people.

Transparencies

AFRICA. EBEC 1963. El-J. col. 16 overviews 10″ × 10″ transparencies with 3 teacher's guide unit envelopes $50.

Three units illustrate basic facts about the African continent including Madagascar. Sequential build-ups cover agricultural and mineral resources, size and terrain, peoples—diversity of population and languages, the status of African religions, economic role of emerging African regions, transition from colonialism to independence, influence of European colonial policies, and significance of African power in the UN. Unit 1: The Land. Unit 2: The People. Unit 3: Africa, Past and Present.

AFRO-AMERICAN HISTORY. AEVAC 1969. El-J-S-C. col. No. AF-41: 18 8½″ × 11″ transparencies with 49 overlays $126.50.

Provides a comprehensive overview of the Black in America from pre-Colonial explorer times through Martin Luther King's dream. . .with emphasis on the Afro-American's influence on, and contributions to, American trends and developments.

A HISTORY OF AFRO-AMERICANS. SCOTT 1970. J-S. col. No. 71012: 3 sets of transparencies $65.

Presents in three parts the history of Afro-Americans in the United States. Part 1: The African Heritage; Part 2: Jamestown Through Reconstruction; Part 3: Reconstruction to the Present.

BIOGRAPHIES OF OUTSTANDING NEGRO AMERICANS. CREATV 1967. El-J-S-C. LC 72-735492. No. 920. AO-SR: 56 sepia transparencies $257.60.

Five volumes showing portraits of outstanding figures and events in black history. Printed materials offer good chronological program for black studies.

BLACK AMERICAN, THE: PAST AND PRESENT. HSPC 1972. J-S. No. 9212: transparencies with masters $5.00; spirit master only $3.50.

Traces the struggles and accomplishments from African heritage to the present. Includes highlights of the history of black Americans.

BLACK AMERICANS, THE. BTC. P-El-J. 24 transparencies $105.84; individually $4.90.

Presents the heritage, contributions, and life of the black American, including From Africa to America, The Bonds of Slavery, The Southern Slave, The Northern Slave, Freedom-Citizenship, The Negro and Education, Southern Segregation, Early Black Politics, Early Black Economy, Black Capitalism, Modern Black Politics, The New Black Image, New Black Leaders, and The Black Man's Future.

BLACK EXPERIENCE. MILLIKEN 1971. J-S. 2 pts. Pt. 1: 12 trs. Pt. 2: 13 trs.

Includes: Carvings of Modern Africa; Black Historians; Black Legislators; Blacks in World Wars I and II; King's Audience; Liberia and Sierra Leone; Map Study of Africa; Map Study of Ghana, Mali, Songhay; and the People of Egypt.

BLACK MAN'S STRUGGLE, THE. BTC 1968. P-El-J. 16 transparencies $70; with cassettes $70; with records $52.

Reviews the history of the black protest and white reaction to it in America from 1619 through the present. Includes situation before the Mayflower, life on a cotton plantation, Nat Turner's slave revolt, the Underground Railroad, Frederick Douglass, the Civil War, the Ku Klux Klan, Reconstruction, blacks in the armed forces, civil rights movement, and black power. Written by Janice Wagner.

CONTEMPORARY AFRO-AMERICAN, THE. TWEEDY/BTC. El-J-S. col. No. 1874-24/1874-31: 8 transparencies with 16 overlays $46.50.

Illustrates the civil rights movement, identification with Africa, nationalism, and integration. Time charts and review.

EMPLOYMENT STATUS OF THE NEGRO IN AMERICA. LANSFD 1970. J-S-C. LC 73-734105. 8″ × 10″ transparencies $55.

Changes in occupation; labor force participation; life expectancy; employment; black legislators; black officers; percent of all workers; and self-employment.

FREE AND SLAVE STATES. HAMMOND 1969. P-El. col. Transparencies with 4 overlays $7.96.

Traces the history of the U.S. slave states.

GREAT AMERICAN NEGROES. SVE. El-J. No. OT-105: 6 transparencies with teacher's guide $9.95.

Two-color artwork presents portraits of great American Negroes. Set of six transparencies in vinyl case includes pictures of Mary McLeod Bethune, George Washington Carver, Benjamin Banneker, Harriet Tubman, Robert Smalls, and Frederick A. Douglass. Interesting biographical notes in accompanying teacher's guide. (Afro-AM Publishing Company, Inc.)

HISTORY AND CULTURE OF AFRICA. AEVAC 1972. P-El-J-S. No. AF-44: Parts 1 and 2, 10 transparencies, 31 overlays, $65 each. Complete set $126.50.

Examines the complex historical and cultural development of Africa from the emergence of the earliest tool-making man. Africa is revealed as the dynamic cradle of human life and civilization on this planet. Casting aside confusion which often surrounds African history, this new program traces the rise of such important empires as Egypt, Kush, Ethiopia, Sudan, ancient Ghana, and Mali. It emphasizes the heights achieved by these various civilizations, and describes the accomplishments of their great kings, scientists, and artists.

*KEY SUPREME COURT DECISIONS. AEVAC 1967. J-S-C. b&w. LC 72-734109.

Part 1: Describes landmark Supreme Court decisions reached between 1803-1905, from the Dred Scott Decision to the Wabush Case. Part 2: Emphasizes the social revolution begun in the 1930s. Examines cases from 1911 to 1966 including the civil rights cases.

NEGRO AND THE CIVIL WAR. CREATV 1971. J-S-C. LC 72-735583. No. 973.71 AO-SR: 8 8″ X 10″ sepia transparencies with teacher's guide $36.80.

Series includes: Combat, Emancipation Proclamation, First into Richmond, Negro Officers, the Negro Soldier, Northern View, Recruiting, Southern View.

NEGRO AND THE NEW ORDER, THE, 1946-1954 (NEGRO-AMERICAN CITIZEN). BTC. J-S-C. 6 transparencies $34.80, 6 cassettes $34.80, individually $6.20.

The Search for Justice; The Quest for Equal Educational Opportunity; Equality and Access; Employment Opportunities and Job-Training; Negro Breakthrough in Sports; Supreme Court Decision and Rights Theory. Classroom World.

NEGROES—AMERICAN TOO (NEGRO-AMERICAN CITIZEN). BTC. J-S-A. No. 632: 6 transparencies $34.80.

Titles: In the Political World, In Education and Religion, In the American Economy, In the Living Arts, In Organizations, and In Athletics. Classroom World.

NEGRO FAMILY. LANSFD 1971. J-S-C. LC 73-734337.

Presents U.S. Department of Labor's study of the Negro family. It discusses percentages dealing with divorces, illegitimacy, use of narcotics, and unemployment.

NEGRO FROM 450 B.C. to 1865, THE. BTC. J-S-A. No. 626: 6 transparencies $34.80.

Prehistoric Africa (450 B.C. to 1400); From Native Land to American Shores (1400-1619); Into Bondage and Slavery (1619-1776); The Negro in the North Under Slavery (1776-1860); The Abolitionist Movement. Classroom World.

NEGRO HISTORY: 1800-1865. CES 1969. El-J-S. 15 transparencies $45.

Relates Negro history to men of the period including Paul Cuffee of Massachusetts; Ira Aldridge, the great dramatist; Nat Turner, Frederick Douglass, and many others.

NEGRO HISTORY 1865-1919. BTC. J-S. col. 25 transparencies with teacher's guide $65.

Negro History 1865-1919 illustrates adjustments to freedom, rise in education, the NAACP, discrimination, music, literature, and many prominent personalities. A Civic Education Service.

NEGRO HISTORY: 1920-1945. BTC. J-S. col. 19 transparencies with teacher's guide $50.

Pictures such black Americans as Marcus Garvey, A. Phillip Randolph, Joe Louis, Jesse Owens, Marian Anderson, and others. Also shows Harlem, race riots, the black soldier, literature, and art. A Civic Education Service.

NEGRO IN AMERICA. LANSFD 1969. El-J-S. No. T-40: a series of 10 transparencies with charts $49.95.

Shows the differences between black and white Americans based on authoritative data. It deals with distribution of family income, live-birth rates, political participation, population, family types, employment, and education.

NEGRO IN POST CIVIL WAR AMERICA, THE (THE AFRO-AMERICAN). BTC. J-S. col. No. 1874-16/1874-23: 8 transparencies with 14 overlays $42.75.

Illustrates life during the Reconstruction and post-Reconstruction periods.

PHYSICAL, SOCIAL AND ECONOMIC GEOGRAPHY OF AFRICA. AEVAC. P-El-J-S. No. AF-42: 13 transparencies with 44 overlays $109.

Examines the awesome physical features, virtually unlimited natural resources, and the remarkably varied peoples of Africa. From the towering mountain ranges to the expansive rain forest and grasslands; from the great rivers Nile, Congo, and Niger to the broad deserts and stories-high jungle growths north and south of the equator—region-by-region tour of this breathtaking continent.

RECONSTRUCTION TO DISFRANCHISEMENT, 1860-1900 (NEGRO-AMERICAN CITIZEN). BTC. J-S-C. No. 627: 6 transparencies $34.80.

Titles: Out of the Depths of Slavery, Freedom and Paper Citizenship, The Negro and the Law, The Negro and Industrial Expansion, The Negro and Educational Advancement, and The Negro and Disfranchisement. Classroom World.

SLAVERY IN THE AMERICAS. TWEEDY. J-S. col. No. 1874-7/1874-15: 9 transparencies with 18 overlays $55.

Illustrates the history of slavery from arrival in the Americas to the Civil War period.

Audio Recordings and Audio Cassettes

AFRICAN VILLAGE FOLKTALES (Vol. 3). CAED. El. 12″ record, 33⅓ rpm, 2 sides.

Features Brock Peters and Diana Sands reading African village folktales. The Mighty Warrior in Hare's House (Masai); A Lot of Silence Makes a Great Noise (Swahili), The Light in The House (Galla), Lion and the Woman (Ambara), and The Wise Old Camel (Egyptian).

AFRICA, SOUTH OF THE SAHARA. FRSC 1958. J-S. No. FE 4503: $17.90.

A serious effort toward presenting a true picture of this vast segment of the earth and the people inhabiting what is known as black Africa.

AFRO-AMERICAN HISTORY (IN SONG AND STORY). EBEC. 4 LP records $22.90; individually $7.

Four records give expression to the soul of America's black people. Tribal chants, dramatic recitations, and songs give students still another picture of the black man's life and times. Spiritual songs from the plantation fields, the sound of Harlem jazz, the angry protests of Blacks rioting in Watts. Performed by a black cast. Titles: A People Uprooted, Chains of Slavery, Separate and Unequal, and Quest for Equality.

AMERICAN NEGRO FOLK AND WORK SONG RHYTHMS. FRSC 1966. El-J. No. 7654: 12″ record $5.95.

Ella Jenkins and the Goodwill Spiritual Choir of Chicago celebrate the musical heritage of the black American. Simple work songs, rhythmic chants, and inspiring spirituals voice their suffering and aspirations for freedom and equality. Special section on the spirituals.

ANTHOLOGY OF NEGRO POETS. FRSC 1960. J-S-C-A. No. 9791: 12″ record, 33⅓ rpm, 2 sides $6.50.

Six distinguished Negro poets read from their own works. Voices of Langston Hughes, Sterling Brown, Claude McKay, Margaret Walker, Countee Cullen, and Gwendolyn Brooks give added power to the musical and intellectual appeal of their poetry. Booklet has biographical notes by the editor Arna Bontemps.

AUTOBIOGRAPHY OF FREDERICK DOUGLASS. FRSC 1970. J-S. No. 5526: two 33⅓ rpm records, 4 sides $5.95.

Narrated by Ossie Davis, describes Douglass' years as newspaper publisher, association with John Brown, flight to England, Civil War years, and after.

BLACK AMERICA: THE SOUNDS OF HISTORY. BTC. El-J-S. No. 430020: 15 records $79.

Rise of Blacks seeking to attain civil rights. Among the titles are: African Heritage, Black Cargoes, Separate and Unequal, Harlem Renaissance, and others.

BLACK AMERICANS. BTC/EDUCDE. El-J-S. No. 455.15: 1 cassette. side A, 18:40 min; side b, 15:00 min $11.50.

Contents treat forced migration, slavery, Crispus Attucks, Benjamin Banneker, slave rebellions, Ku Klux Klan, Jim Crow, the Way West, The NAACP, and so on. From the "Ethnic Studies: The People of America" series.

*BLACK CONTRIBUTIONS TO AMERICAN CULTURE. SVE 1970. El–J–S. col. No. IC–105: $1^7/_8$ ips audio cassettes $62.

Features historical biographies that dramatize the contributions of black Americans to the culture of their country from colonial times to present day—Black men and women in arts and letters, music, science, and government.

BLACK EXPERIENCE, THE. SPA/BIGSUR 1969. S–C–A. No 6010: $1^7/_8$ ips tape, 180 min $9.

Presents an example of vitality and openness and describes the unifying bond of vulnerability and humanism of the black experience.

*BLACK HERITAGE. IMPRL. El–J. With cassettes.

Presents the dramatized biographies of black men and women who have made important contributions to American life and culture: Althea Gibson, Benjamin O. Davis, Thurgood Marshall, Louis Armstrong, and twenty-four others.

BLACK LIKE ME. XEROX. J–S. No. CBC 308: cassette, 60 min $16.95.

A talk by John Howard Griffin, the Texas-born white man who, in the chronicle "Black Like Me," told of his experiences while living as a Black in the United States. In this talk, he discusses racial conditions and attitudes as they exist ten years after his book was written, with particular reference to the role of the church.

BLACK MAN IN AMERICA. EDRECS 1972. El–J. 12" record, $33^1/_3$ rpm $6.95.

James Baldwin interviewed by Studs Turkel. Baldwin's opinions about America and his experiences as a black man are stimulating and thought provoking. Interview reveals much of Mr. Baldwin's thoughts that interlace his well-known writings.

BLACK MAN'S STRUGGLE, THE. SVE. El–J–S. No. S7-R: set of 8 records $52; No. S7–CT: set of 8 tape cassettes $70.

A presentation of the black man's efforts to win equal rights and opportunities throughout American history from 1619 to present. Includes: Before the Mayflower, 1619; Life on a Cotton Plantation; Myth and Reality: The Years before Emancipation; Nat Turner's Slave Revolt; Frederick Douglass: Black Abolitionist; Black Power in the 1870s; Reconstruction; Life in the South after Reconstruction.

BLACK PATHFINDERS OF ANCIENT TIMES. LLI 1971. J–S. Record, $33^1/_3$ rpm, 2 sides, cassette available $7.95.

Features R. Ethel Dennis, black author/educator, who provides bibliographic notes on black pathfinders of ancient times. Recording presents some highlights of Blacks in an age infrequently discussed with black people as a part of it.

BLACK PIONEERS IN AMERICAN HISTORY (Vol. 1). CAED. S-C. LC R68-3710. 12″ LP record $6.98; cassette $7.95.

Eartha Kitt and Moses Gunn read the autobiographies of Frederick Douglass, Charlotte Forten, Susie King Taylor, and Nat Love.

BLACK PIONEERS IN AMERICAN HISTORY (Vol. 2). CAED. P-El-J-S. LC 68-3710. 12″ LP record $6.98; cassette $7.92.

Diana Sands and Moses Gunn read the autobiographies of Mary Church Terrell, W. E. B. DuBois, Josiah Henson, and William Parker.

BLACK PROGRESS: THE HISTORY OF THE AFRO-AMERICAN. BTC. S-C. 24 cassettes $90.

An overview of the black American showing how different opinions encourage critical thinking. Correlated with the Progress of the Afro-American (Benefic Press).

BLACKS IN ART. SVE. El-J. No. IR-33: album of 2 records $13.50; No. IC-33: album of 2 cassettes $17.50.

Album 33: Blacks in Art—Henry Ossawa Tanner (painter of religious subjects), Charles White (modern painter), Richmond Barthe (realistic sculptor), Ira Aldridge (black tragedian), Langston Hughes (a poetic voice), and three others. From "Black Contributions to American Culture" series.

BLACKS IN GOVERNMENT AND HUMAN RIGHTS. SVE 1970. El-J. No. IR-31: album of 2 records $13.50; No. IC-31: album of 2 cassettes $17.50.

Album 31: Blacks in Government and Human Rights—Robert C. Weaver (first black cabinet member), Thurgood Marshall (Mr. Civil Rights), Mary C. Terrell (champion of women's rights), Whitney Young (leader of National Urban League), and four others. From "Black Contributions to American Culture" series.

BLACKS IN MUSIC. SVE. El-J. No. IR-32: album of 2 records $13.50; No. IC-32: album of 2 cassettes $17.50.

Album 32: Blacks in Music—Harry T. Burleigh (the Negro spiritual), W. C. Handy (father of the blues), Marian Anderson (contralto of the century), William Grant Still (modern composer), and two others. From "Black Contributions to American Culture" series.

BLACKS IN SCIENCE. SVE 1970. El-J. No. IR-30: album of 2 records $13.50; No. IC-30: album of 2 cassettes $17.50.

Album 30: Blacks in Science—Charles Drew (pioneer in blood plasma), Elijah McCoy (the real McCoy), Mathew A. Henson (polar explorer), Daniel H. Williams (first successful heart surgeon), and four others. From "Black Contributions to American Culture" series.

BLACK SOLDIERS AND SETTLERS IN THE OLD WEST. EDUCDE. J-S. No. 480.03: side A, 13 min; side B, 12 min $11.50.

Black businessmen, legislators, army units and other settlers and their accomplishments are featured in this album. Side B deals with black cowboys and outlaw personalities such as Bill Pickett and Deadwood Dick.

CHOICE OF WEAPONS. FRSC 1970. J-S-C-A. LC 11010. No. R-79-751021. 33⅓ record $6.98.

Gordon Parks, one of America's top photographers, describes his long, painful struggle for recognition as a photographer and as a man. Excerpted from his autobiography. Portfolio of photos included.

COUNTEE CULLEN—THE POETRY OF COUNTEE CULLEN. CAED. S-C-A. LC 79-752656. 12″ LP record $6.98; cassette $7.95.

The poetry of this early black writer is brought to life through the talents of Ruby Dee and Ossie Davis.

DISCRIMINATION IN THE NORTH 1780-1860 and BLACK BUSINESSMEN AND PROFESSIONALS 1780-1860. EDR. J-S. Cassette, side A, 9 min; side B, 11 min $11.50.

Includes quotes by Gerritt Smith, Daniel Webster, and the story by Prudence Crandall plus an explanation of the emerging patterns of discrimination. Side B deals with tapes of black professionals.

DREAM AWAKE, THE. SPA/BTC. J-S-C. No. SA-1095: record $6.50.

Traces the history of the black man from his beginnings in Africa through his struggles in America in the Civil War up to the present day. Based on a poem by Owen Dodson.

EMANCIPATION (Side A)—**THE AFTERMATH OF THE CIVIL WAR** (Side B). EDR. J-S. No. 480.08: record, 10 min $11.50.

From mid-1862 to the end of the war. Includes changes in Union policy, exploits of Harriet Tubman, the Emancipation Proclamation and Emancipation Day, successes of black troops. Side B deals with Lincoln's assassination, Freedman's Bureau, and the Black Codes.

FAMOUS NEGRO LEADERS. TRA 1971. Complete unit 10 cassettes $49; individually $4.90.

The lives and achievements of outstanding black leaders, from the colonial mathematician, Benjamin Banneker, to the twentieth century leader Martin Luther King, Jr. Professional narration and sound effects present an authentic portrait of the men and their times, and reveal the driving forces behind their contributions to American history.

GREAT AFRICAN CIVILIZATIONS IN THE WORLD, THE (Side A)—**BLACK EXPLORERS** (Side B). EDR 1973. J-S. No. 480.01: cassette $11.50.

Deals with the African roots of black Americans and the accomplishments of Esteranico and other black explorers in the service of Columbus, Cortez, Balboa, and others.

GREAT DEPRESSION, THE (NEGRO-AMERICAN CITIZEN). CLSWP/BTC. J-S. No. 629: 6 cassettes $34.80; No. 629: 6 cassettes, album $36.80; No. 629: 6 reel-to-reel tapes $34.80; individual cassette $6.20.

The Negro and the New Deal Era; Back to Africa Movement; New Religious Influences; New Horizons in Culture Attainment; The Negro and Public Education; The Negro Competitor in Sports.

GWENDOLYN BROOKS—GWENDOLYN BROOKS READING HER POETRY. CAED. S-C-A. LC 77-75036. 12″ LP record $6.98; cassette $7.95.

Miss Brooks reads poems from *A Street in Bronzeville; Annie Allen; The Bean Eaters*; *Black Expression*, Vol. 1; and *In Mecca.*

HISTORY OF BLACK AMERICANS, THE. ESP. No. 1400: complete set of 24 lessons on 12 cassettes $72.

A dramatic presentation of the heritage, contributions, struggles, and heartaches of black Americans which emphasizes their efforts to win equal rights and a place in America's future. This well-written set of cassettes will stretch the imagination of every student in the classroom. This series was conceived, written, and produced by a racially mixed panel of educators working to get well-balanced programs.

LANGSTON HUGHES. SIMPLE STORIES. CAED. J-S. LC R68-2578: 12″ LP record $6.98; cassette $7.95.

Sample of Indian Blood, A Toast to Harlem, Last Whipping, Golden Gate, and others. All poems by Langston Hughes, read by actor Ossie Davis.

LANGSTON HUGHES. SELECTED POETRY. CAED. J-S. LC R68-3573. No. CDL 5172.

America's great black poet, whose humor transcends his bitterness; and humanity his blackness. Read by two well-known black dramatists, Ruby Dee and Ossie Davis.

LANGSTON HUGHES. THE POETRY OF LANGSTON HUGHES. CAED. J-S. LC R68-3573. 12″ LP record $6.96; cassette $7.95.

Poems from The Panther and the Lash, One Way Ticket, Ask Your Mama. Selected poems are read by actress Ruby Dee.

LIFE AND WORDS OF MARTIN LUTHER KING, JR. FRSC 1970. J-S. LC 79-75-1738. No. R0723: 7″ book $2.25.

Ira Peck and children describe highlights of King's life and read from his speeches. Electronic music background.

LORRAINE HANSBERRY AND ROBERT NEMIROFF—TO BE YOUNG, GIFTED AND BLACK. CAED. J-S. 12″ LP record $6.98; cassette $7.95.

James Earl Jones, Barbara Baxley, Claudia McNeil, Diana Sands, and cast. Lorraine Hansberry's posthumous work, adapted by Robert Nemiroff and read by a group of distinguished black actors.

LORRAINE HANSBERRY. A RAISIN IN THE SUN. CAED. J-S. LC 70-542884. 12″ LP record $6.98; cassette $7.95.

Ossie Davis, Ruby Dee, Claudia McNeil, Diana Sands, and cast read the famous work of a distinguished black writer.

MUSIC, THEATRE, AND SPORTS 1885-1929 (Side A)—**THE WORLD WAR ERA** (Side B). EDR. J-S. No. 480.14: record, Side A, 10 min; Side B, 8 min $11.50.

The birth of the Niagra Movement, the NAACP, the Urban League; the policies of Washington and DuBois. Side B shows exploits of black troops in the war, the silent protest march in New York, and the wave of anti-black violence that swept the nation after the war.

NEGRO, THE—AMERICAN CITIZEN. CLSWP 1961. El-J-S. No. 625: Cassette series, complete program $229.50; unit price $37.

A chronology of the American Black—his struggle to attain "first-class citizenship" and to find his rightful place in our society. This series provides a dimension of relevant understanding which might otherwise be lacking, to the many problems and challenges which the Black has faced from prehistoric Africa to current times.

NEGRO IN AMERICA, THE. XEROX. J-S-C-A. 35 min 12″ LP record $14.95.

"The tragedy of discrimination," in the words of Robert C. Weaver, "is that it provides an excuse for failure while erecting barriers to success." Mr. Weaver himself surmounted the obstacles and became an administrator and Cabinet member, but he hasn't forgotten the struggle of his people who remain trapped on the other side. Here he gives a moving account of the disabilities suffered by Blacks who want to be successful in our society. A program from the Center for the Study of Democratic Institutions.

NEGRO WOMAN, THE. FRSC 1972. J-S. No. FH 5523: 12″ LP record, 2 sides $14.50.

Speeches and writings of Phillis Wheatley, Harriet Tubman, Sojourner Truth, Mary McLeod Bethune, Frances Harper, Ida Wells, and others. Read by Dorothy Washington.

NONVIOLENT APPROACH TO CIVIL RIGHTS 1925-1963, THE (Side A)—**MILITANCY AND UPHEAVAL 1964-Present** (Side B). EDR 1972. J-S-C-A. No. 480.18: cassette, Side A 12 min; Side B 18 min, $11.50.

Side A: From the Montgomery bus boycott to the 1963 march on Washington including freedom riders, sit-ins. Side B: Formation of Black Panthers and other militant black groups; ghetto riots, Selma; assassinations of Martin Luther King, Jr., Malcolm X, and Robert Kennedy.

PATRIOT SOLDIERS (THE QUEST FOR FREEDOM). BTC. El-J. No. 4404: cassette $7.50.

Surveys black participation in the Revolutionary War, Civil War, the Buffalo Soldiers, World War I, and World War II, B. O. Davis, Jr., and others.

RICHARD WRIGHT, BLACK BOY. CAED. J-S-C-A. LC 77-751034. 2 12" LP records $13.96; 2 cassettes $15.90.

Brock Peters, black American actor, reads the well-known work of Mr. Wright in a condensation of the autobiographical account conveying the turbulence of growing up in the pre-Civil Rights Act era of the South.

"SATCHMO" BY LOUIS ARMSTRONG. KR. El-J-S. No. KC-91: cassette only $7.

In an interview the great Louis Armstrong tells the story of his rise from abject poverty to the top of his profession. The beloved "Satchmo" lived with every indignity, faced every challenge ever confronted by any black human being in America. But he built himself into a peerless professional success and a top international good-will ambassador for his nation. A magnificently inspiring message.

SILHOUETTES IN COURAGE. BTC. J-S-A. No. CS 532: 8 records $52.

A history of the black man from 500 B.C. to modern times, with special emphasis on his role in the political, industrial, social, and cultural development of America. Narrated by Ossie Davis, Brock Peters, Frederick O'Neal, and Ruby Dee.

SLAVERY, CIVIL WAR AND RECONSTRUCTION. FRSC. El-J-S. 7 pt audio cassette program, 10 to 15 min, 7 teacher's guides $71.

Arna Bontemps, Ann Petry, Irene Hunt, and Milton Meltzer reexamine their own views in seven exciting panel discussions about the Civil War period. A personal tone is set through the panelists' tales of their own family experiences, letters, and poetry as they reflect various racial, regional, and political differences. Their reexamination of the period will help students to see it more critically.

SOCIAL PROGRESS IN THE LATE 1940'S (Side A)—THE EISENHOWER YEARS AND SCHOOL DESEGREGATION (Side B). EDR. El-J-S. No. 480.17: record, side A, 11 min; side B, 10 min $11.50.

The Truman administration's concern with civil rights; the integration of the armed services, baseball, and football. The accomplishments of Ralph Bunche, Charles Drew, and others. Side B covers the Korean War, how Eisenhower helped integrate Washington, D.C., the McCarthy era, and the 1954 Supreme Court decision.

STORY OF JAZZ, THE. FRSC. J-S-C. No. 7312: record 33⅓ rpm $4.50.

Development of jazz from African drum rhythms and field hollers of slavery days to cool sounds of modern jazz. Written and narrated by Langston Hughes especially for young people. Excerpts from documentary: Armstrong and Ma Rainey, blues; Meade Lux Lewis, boogie woogie; Dizzy Gillespie, be-bop; Lennie Tristano, modern jazz.

W. E. B. DuBOIS. FRSC 1961. J-S-C. No. FH 5511: $5.95.

Moses Asch interviews the great black historian, educator, and civil rights leader; covers early college years, founding of NAACP.

Video Cassettes

AMERICANS FROM AFRICA: A HISTORY WITH EDGAR TOPPIN. GPITVL. J-S. b&w. Thirty 30 min lessons, $72.50 each.

This series is aimed at developing better understanding among students by increasing their awareness of the part that all Americans have played in the making of this nation. By emphasizing the historical role of the American Negro, generally omitted from schoolbooks, the series seeks to contribute to an easing of the tensions and an understanding of the present-day crises. The television teacher is Dr. Edgar Allan Toppin, professor of history at Virginia State College in Petersburg.

BLACK AMERICAN DREAM, THE. BBCTV/TIMELI. S-C-A. col. 2 pts, 65 min $430; 16mm $610; rental $40.

In exclusive meetings with black leaders, this film reveals that today Black Power appears to mean all things to all men. The revolutionary Panther, the African-based Stokely Carmichael, the nonviolent Jesse Jackson; each has his own idea of what Black Power is.

BLACK FRONTIER, THE. GPITVL. El-J-S. Four 60 min lessons. Set $1,750; individually $480; individual rental $84.

A focus on the hundreds of black men rarely given credit for helping to carve civilization out of raw country. Concentrates on several of those black men who contributed to settling the Great Plains.

BLACK WEALTH. NET 1974. J-S-A. No. 05010: 20 min. Video $150; 16mm $230.

A spiritual richness has emerged in the work of black writers who stress the common striving of blacks for freedom and recognition. This program presents the recollections of writer and photographer Gordon Parks, and Margo Barnett's dramatic re-creation of nineteenth-century crusader Sojourner Truth. Miss Barnett also reads from the works of several black poets. From the "A Matter of Fact" series.

ODYSSEY IN BLACK. GPITVL 1971. J-S-A. Fourteen 30 min lessons, $72 each.

This interesting and extremely well-produced series (on monochrome video tape only) takes the viewer from the African origins of the black race through the American Civil War to today's black revolution.

RHYTHMS FROM AFRICA. NET 1971. P-El. No. 01502: 15 min. Video $125; 16mm $180.

This program specifically concerns Americans of African descent who in the 1970s are engaged in an active search for an expression of their historical past. Instruments of the African orchestra are introduced and set in motion. Children everywhere are invited to blend their hands, feet, and voices into the musical mix. From the "Ripples" series.

Study Prints/Pictures/Posters/Graphics

AFRICAN SCULPTURE. DPA. El-J. No. P.C.-108: col 30″ X 40″ chart with teaching notes $2.50.

Explaining that exaggerated body forms give shape to abstract ideas, the chart shows a bronze head from Benin, Yoruba door panels, an Ashanti cleansing vessel, a headcrest from the Congo, a Dogan ancestral couple, and masks from Mali and the Cameroons.

BLACK ABC'S. SVE. P. No. PPSSP-120: 26 picture story prints $26.

The set, with its emphasis on black, instills appreciation of black culture in children and spurs learning for black youngsters.

BLACK AMERICAN ACHIEVEMENT POSTERS. HSPC 1972. El-J. col. No. VC 194: 20 posters 12″ X 18″ on glossy paper $3.

Colorful photographs depicting past and present achievements in science, government, medicine, inventions, sports, and so on. Designed for bulletin boards, hall, or classroom.

BLACK AMERICAN WALL POSTERS. CES/BTC. J-S. Twelve col 2′ X 3′ posters with teacher's guide $17.40.

Shows many black leaders in various fields including such personages as Dr. Daniel Hale Williams, Joe Louis, Althea Gibson, Malcolm X, Harriet Tubman, Martin Luther King, Jr., and others.

BLACK AMERICA—YESTERDAY AND TODAY. DCC 1969. El. No. A1865: Twenty col 11″ X 14″ pictures with teacher's manual $3.95.

Presents an overview of black American history and contributions of Blacks to America. Background information, stories, quotations, discussion guidelines, and poetry by black writers are included.

CONTEMPORARY ART BY AFRO-AMERICANS. UPMPD. J-S. col. 10 art prints of selected Afro-American artists in wall-designed portfolio with resource sheet and biographical notes $12.50.

CONTEMPORARY BLACK BIOGRAPHIES. SSSS. El-J-S. 32 posters and text, 12½″ X 16″ charts with teacher's guide $4.95.

Illustrates the lines and accomplishments of prominent blacks: Ralph Bunche, Louis Armstrong, Joe Louis, Althea Gibson, Thurgood Marshall, Jackie Robinson, and others.

EDUCATION AND RELIGION. AAPC 1969. J-S-A. Twenty-four 11″ X 14″ prints $4.95.

Latter-day religious figures and early minister/educators contributed to the social and civic welfare of black people: John Hope, Charles S. Johnson, Alaine Locke, Robert Moton, William Scarborough, Arthur Schomburg, Richard Allen, James A. Healy, Daniel Payne, Mordecai Johnson, Benjamin Mays, and others.

FAMOUS BLACK AMERICANS. AVMC 1970. El-J-S. No. 20600: twelve col 15″ × 11½″ pictures.

Outstanding men and women have emerged in the black American's historic struggle for equality and individuality. The portraits included in this series of prints are: Frederick Douglass, Booker T. Washington, George Washington Carver, Benjamin Oliver Davis, Jr., Thurgood Marshall, Charles Drew, M.D., Martin Luther King, Jr., Willie Mays, Marian Anderson, S. B. Fuller, W. C. Handy, and Sidney Poitier.

GREAT NEGROES (Picture Display Portfolios). SVE. El-J-S. Each packet contains 24 two-col plastic coated prints 11″ × 14″, $14.95 a set.

A series of attractive prints with short biographical sketches pointing out the contributions of black Americans. Titles: (P 43 B) Negroes in Our History, (P 43 C) Modern Negro Contributions, (P 43 D) Negroes of Achievement, (P 43 E) Science and Invention, (P 43 F) Business and Professions, (P 43 G) Education and Religion, (P 43 H) Fighters for Freedom, (P 43 J) Champions of Human Rights, and (P 43 K) Government and Judicial. Afro-American Publishing Co.

HISTORICAL BLACK BIOGRAPHIES. SSSS. El-J-S. 32 posters with 48 page teacher's guide $4.95.

Presents line of prominent black Americans from every period of American history. Each poster summarizes the highlights of a great personality: Frederick Douglass, Phillis Wheatley, Benjamin Banneker, and others.

ILLUSTRATED BLACK HISTORY. SSSS. El-J-S. Twenty 12½″ × 16″ posters with 64 page teacher's guide $4.95.

Features personalities and events of the history of American Blacks, from Africa to the American civil rights movement, African art, slave ship, Reconstruction politics, World War II, and others.

NAT TURNER'S SLAVE REVOLT. JACK. El-J. SBN 670-50505: 12 exhibits, 5 broadsheets, contents brochure $3.95.

Examines the now-famous slave uprising of 1831 as the events and conditions of life affected both black and white people. Exhibits include a list of the white men who were killed, the governor's proclamation of a reward, the record of the trials of Nat Turner, and a draft of a bill for stricter control of Blacks.

NEGRO EXPERIENCE IN AMERICA, THE. DPA 1971. J-S. Set of forty-eight 11″ × 14″ pictures with teacher's guide $27.

This set delivers an unparalleled look at the roots of white-black interaction, emphasizing the salient events of the past three centuries. Pictures include slavery, plantations, black Union soldiers, KKK, Black Panthers, riots, poverty, demonstrations, and so on.

SEARCH, THE. SCH. J. No. 2474: set of 10 posters $7.50; with discs $5.25.
Poems, short stories, nonfiction, drama by Langston Hughes, Julian Bond, Countee Cullen, Gwendolyn Brooks, and dozens more.

CHAPTER II

Asian Americans – Quiet Americans?

by Minako K. Maykovich,
Professor of Sociology,
California State University, Sacramento

Sexy Susy Wong, inscrutable Charlie Chan, Johnny Sakko and his giant robot, Toshiro Mifune and his samurai—these are some of the images of Asian Americans in American mass media. Until a few years ago Asian Americans seldom appeared on television, on the movie screen, or in school textbooks. When they did, they played only minor roles such as those of servants, clever technicians, sweet and obedient oriental girls, or treacherous soldiers.[1] They were perceived as accommodating and adaptable to the dominant American society.

The term "Asian American" encompasses distinct ethnic groups composed of immigrants and their descendants from a number of East Asian countries, including China, Japan, the Philippines, and Korea. Migrants from the first two arrived, primarily, during the periods of 1850-1882 and 1890-1924, respectively, while those from the latter two were more recent newcomers.

Through adherence to traditional norms and values that closely resembled those embodied in the Protestant ethic, they gradually made progress in terms of education, occupation, and income. The basic strategy used was one of accommodation to obstacles and of hard work. Today, by conventional indicators of income and style of life, Asian Americans are being touted as "model" minorities to be imitated by other minorities. Thus, experience of Asian Americans are quite different from those of any other racial and ethnic group in the United States, and should be studied separately.

This chapter is divided into three parts. The first part presents a history of the Asian American experience and its contribution to this country. The second part deals with cultural heritage, characteristics, and experience. The third part deals with educational needs.

PREWAR PERIOD (-1945)

Chinese Immigration

Cultural contribution by the Chinese antedates their immigration to this country by more than half a century. The chinoiserie style which became popular in Europe in the sixteenth century reached America by the end of the eighteenth century, leaving Chinese bric-a-brac and tapestries in colonial homes and frontier cabins. Interest in Chinese art, architecture, and government was not, however, accompanied by much knowledge of, or deep compassion for, the Chinese people.

From 1787 until 1848 few Chinese visited the United States. These early visitors were received with a mixture of curiosity and amazement. Chinese equestrians and jugglers were employed as stage performers in New York City.[2] In addition to the queue and foot binding there were other traits and customs which puzzled Americans throughout the nineteenth century—the yellow complexion, slanted eyes, strange clothes, strange language, absence of wives, and opium smoking.

Chinese immigration to America effectively began in 1847, when the news reached Hong Kong that gold had been discovered in California. During more than thirty years of free immigration, the decade of 1868 to 1877 witnessed the largest continuous influx of Chinese, with more than 130,000 arrivals against fewer than 60,000 departures.[3] The gold rush and the resulting demand for labor in California were the economic pulling forces making Chinese seek employment in the United States. Perhaps more forceful was the ruin and resulting poverty in the southern portion of China; the aftermath of the Taipin Rebellion.

For the first few years at least, the arrival of Chinese laborers was hailed, and they were warmly welcomed both by the people of California and by state and county officials.[4] The Chinese were seen to be reticent, industrious, thrifty, and adaptable to various kinds of employment—ready and willing to perform labor uncongenial to the Caucasian. They were satisfied with low wages and were cooperative with their employers. With the acute scarcity of unskilled labor and with the Chinese totaling about 25 percent of the foreign-born population of California (1860-1880), the Chinese soon filled in as general laborers, domestic servants, cooks, and gardeners. The majority went into the mines; several thousand went into the construction of the Central Pacific Railroad. Thus the contribution of the Chinese pioneers to the economic development of American society was significant.

Although the Chinese were openly praised and were in many quarters considered to be desirable, as early as 1852 they found opposition in the mining camps, when white laborers found themselves unable to compete with the more industrious Chinese workers. The fact that employers such as railroads, transportation companies, and landholders all used Chinese workers to their advantage made for the antagonism of native laborers. While prosperity prevailed and demand exceeded supply, all was well in the community. However with a depression setting in and the consequent lack of employment, employees thrown out of work blamed their hardship on the foreigners.

Newspapers of the time frequently mentioned the mob riots against the Chinese.[5] There were various kinds of agitation and attacks against the Chinese. The organized opposition to the Chinese by Dennis Kearney and his Workingmen's Party, and sensationally unfavorable newspaper reports about Chinatown brought forth antagonistic political platforms. Although the causes of the anti-Chinese movement were many, in reality organized labor and political parties were the main instruments responsible for the eventual Chinese restriction.[6] The extensive efforts of the state of California to deal with the Chinese question were chiefly constitutional, legislative, or municipal enactments,[7] resulting in the final passage of the Chinese Exclusion Act in 1882.

Not only seen as economic invaders, the Chinese were also viewed as unassimilable and immoral. The sociocultural behavior of the Chinese facilitated this racial stereotype. Their style of life was different from that of white Americans. They wore different clothes, ate different food, and lived in seclusion. Also, the lonely Chinese men without wives were sometimes found gambling, smoking opium, or using prostitutes. In snort, the Chinese were thought of as a Yellow Peril.

The contribution of the Chinese to American society is not limited to their economic activities. Their suffering and perseverance should be added as an important phase of American history because the understanding of such experiences provided the strength to persevere in adversity, and the determination to fight against social injustice.

Japanese Immigration

Japan embarked on a policy of isolation which lasted for more than two centuries until its forcible rupture by Commodore Matthew Perry in 1853. Emigration did not become legal until 1886. Despite the fact that California was, by the end of the 1860s, already anti-Chinese, these early migrants from Japan were received with great favor.

After the passage of the Chinese Exclusion Act in 1882, a vacuum was created for agricultural labor, since California agriculture had always been dependent upon large numbers of seasonal workers.[8] In the decade after 1880, the whole pattern of Japanese immigration changed because of (1) the shortage of labor in California; (2) the need of Hawaiian sugar planters for cheap labor; and (3) the socioeconomic dislocation of many Japanese brought about by westernization during the Meiji Restoration. More than 30,000 Japanese were brought to Hawaii during 1885-1894.

Responses to Japanese immigrants in the United States have followed much the same pattern as those to Chinese immigration. At first they were welcomed, but by 1900 there were demands that the Japanese be excluded, and these demands grew more and more insistent. Because of the high degree of unionization in northern California and the anti-Oriental agitation which had been prevalent since the 1860s, no significant number of Japanese were hired by white firms, factories, or offices. The Alien Land Bill (1913) reduced the number of Japanese in agriculture. Many Japanese went into small businesses catering to the Japanese, or into gardening.

In 1907 a Gentleman's Agreement was reached between the U.S. and the Japanese governments, by which the latter would voluntarily restrict Japanese emigration. Although the number of Japanese entering the United States was decreased drastically, agitation against the Japanese was such that a national law was passed in 1924 allowing no further Japanese immigration.

Through traditional values of hard work and social conformity, both the Japanese and Chinese made similar contributions to the history of the United States in the spheres of national economic development and character formation. However, prior to World War II, the Japanese were more effective than the Chinese in reinforcing their cultural heritage to defend themselves against discrimination, and also to improve their status in this country.

In Japan and China, traditional values were transmitted through the family system. Among immigrants, the Chinese were less successful than the Japanese in maintaining the family, which would serve as a vehicle for cultural heritage. According to custom, Chinese men sojourned abroad without their wives. A man's return to hearth and village was thus secured, and he labored overseas in order to return home. When in 1882, America's restrictive legislation unwittingly converted Chinese custom into legal prohibition by prohibiting the immigration of wives of Chinese laborers, it exaggerated and lengthened the separation of husbands from wives.[9] Also it delayed for nearly two generations the birth of a substantial second generation. In the case of the Japanese, neither custom nor law barred them from bringing wives to the United States. Within two decades of their arrival, the Japanese had brought over enough women to guarantee the birth of the second generation. And, it was through this generation that the Japanese began to become acculturated into the dominant white society. The first channel of acculturation was their educational achievement which was motivated through their family system.

The Japanese came from a society which, even during the feudal period, emphasized education. Upon arrival in the United States, the Japanese confirmed their belief in the importance of education. Because of language and other handicaps, the Japanese immigrants were unable to attain a higher education, but acted as a gyroscope in directing their children toward educational achievement.

The emphasis on educational achievement operated within the context of competing with the white majority.[10] This became a pragmatic pursuit to demonstrate the superiority of the Japanese. This also fitted with the Issei reminder that being Japanese meant something special. The statement often made by the parents in time of stress "You are a Japanese" was not simply a reference to an ethnic identification but rather to one endowed with spirit and purpose and one who could overcome great obstacles.

During the War

World War II reversed the positions of the Japanese and Chinese in the United States. There was little doubt that the increasing unpopularity of the Japanese was not without advantage to the Chinese. Chinese participation in World War

II and their previous resistance against the Japanese in the Sino-Japanese War aroused vast pro-Chinese sentiment in the United States.

In addition to these changing power relations, there were demographic factors. The contrast between the position of the Japanese, who were allowed to consolidate their population gains despite the Gentleman's Agreement, and that of the Chinese, who were denied similar facilities, was striking. Because of the favorable sex and age structure of the Japanese population in the United States, their number increased, while the number of Chinese was decreasing because of the imbalance in sex ratio. These trends tended to justify the acceptance of the Chinese. In 1943 the Chinese Exclusion Act was repealed, and they could now bring their wives and unmarried children to the United States.

After Pearl Harbor the groups that had long agitated against the Japanese lost no time in telling the federal government that the presence of the Japanese on the West Coast was a grave threat to the safety of the country. During 1942 more than 110,000 West-Coast Japanese, regardless of their citizenship, were evacuated to the war relocation centers.

Whatever the role of economic factors in causing the evacuation of Americans of Japanese descent, the economic results were clearcut and severe for the people involved.[11] Nevertheless, the evacuation was rapid, smooth, and efficient, primarily because of the cooperation of the Japanese. With few exceptions, the majority of Japanese-American Youths were invited to join the military, and many of them volunteered to show their loyalty to the United States.

There are several factors accounting for this Japanese nonresistance. First of all, prewar Japanese in the United States were politically powerless—the immigrants were denied citizenship and their children were just reaching voting age. Further, there were no prominent Japanese public figures on the political scene or elsewhere.

Economic considerations also help to explain the behavior of the Japanese. There was a short period prior to the evacuation when the Japanese could have migrated to the Midwest and the East, but few did. Most were so poor that the financial risk of moving to other parts of the country was overwhelming.

Although there was an interdependence among all of the reasons, the sociopsychological explanations of Japanese behavior appear to be the most relevant. Norms and values of traditional culture emphasizing conformity and obedience meant that those in power, such as the U.S. military, were able to use this position to gain the cooperation of the evacuated population.[12]

Filipino Immigration

The Filipino immigration problem was a peculiar one. There was a major difference between the Filipino and Japanese or Chinese immigration to the United States. While the Immigration Act of 1924 definitely and specifically excluded the Chinese and Japanese because of their ineligibility for citizenship, Filipinos were neither considered aliens nor citizens. They were "subjects" of the U.S. government and could therefore permeate the American frontier unchecked. However, with no official proclamation against them by the government, Filipinos were left in an unstable situation, having inherited the already organized attitudes against the Oriental.[13]

Filipino immigration to the United States did not begin until after the military occupation by the United States in the Philippines was ended in 1901. The Gentleman's Agreement in 1907, excluding Japanese, caused a drastic upheaval in labor forces. The Hawaiian planters were forced to find another source of cheap labor and the Filipinos filled the vacuum.

The Filipinos, like the Japanese, were used largely in agriculture, employed as "stoop" laborers. Because of their small stature, they were highly adaptable to picking berries, tomatoes, grapes, lettuce, and so forth. They worked for low wages. It can be argued that even during the depression the inclusion of Filipinos in agriculture actually aided America.[14]

Because the Japanese and Chinese were economically more settled and socially established on the West Coast, they tended to frown upon the Filipinos who were starting at the bottom of the ladder. Also, competition for jobs among Orientals resulted in hostility toward the newcomers, the Filipinos. In an atmosphere of hostility, the Filipinos, being young, male, and largely without families, found themselves social outcasts.

Korean Immigration

Until 1945, Koreans in America constituted a very small and isolated minority. While their color and ethnic heritage set them apart from white society, their distinct social organization and outlook set them apart from other racial and ethnic minorities.[15]

Korean immigration to the United States began in 1902, when representatives from Hawaiian plantations went to Korea for agricultural laborers. In 1904 American railway companies sent representatives to Honolulu to recruit Korean and Japanese workers.

After 1910 the Japanese annexation of Korea cut many Koreans from their homeland and increased their sense of isolation. Although largely quiescent during the 1920s, the independence movement was revitalized with the Japanese seizure of Manchuria in 1931 and especially after the outbreak of the Sino-Japanese War in 1937. Ideology and activities of the Korean independence movement among Koreans in America were highly important in maintaining the separateness of the Korean community.

In contrast to the Chinese communities abroad and to some extent to the Japanese as well, Korean society in the United States was largely lacking in traditional clan association, merchant guilds, district or regional association, and lodges and gentry-type benevolent associations. In their absence, many of the social functions and services were performed by Korean Christian churches.

POSTWAR PERIOD

Just as in the prewar period, the legislative changes in the postwar years were the most important and vital sources for the acquisition of power by the Asian

Americans. The postwar U.S. government lifted restrictive legislations from Asians slowly but steadily.

The Walter-McCarren Act of 1952 brought Japan into the American immigration quota system. However, the quota system and the quantitative limit based on racial distinctions were essentially retained, except that Asian countries were now assigned their appropriate quotas. Resident aliens from the Orient, formerly ineligible for citizenship, were granted naturalization rights.

Under the 1965 Immigration Law, national quotas were eliminated and replaced by two international quotas: 170,000 per year for the Eastern Hemisphere, with a maximum of 20,000 from any one country; and 120,000 for the Western Hemisphere, without specific national limitations. Preference was given to relatives of U.S. citizens or of resident aliens, and to persons with occupational skills.

Postwar Asian immigrants are quite different from their prewar counterparts. They are emigrating from independent and/or industrialized rather than subordinate and/or rural Asian countries of prewar days.

Present day Asian immigrants are more heterogeneous than their prewar counterparts, including professionally trained people who are given preferential treatment under the new immigration law, and those who have illegally fled from communism.

Rise of Economic Status

As soon as legal restrictions were relieved, the Japanese and Chinese began to show a remarkable economic upward mobility. They knew that the main key to material success was education.

By 1940 the Japanese had passed the whites in the median school year completed (see Table 1). In contrast, the Chinese in 1940 ranked as low as the Blacks and other minority groups with a completion level below the sixth grade. Many of the older Chinese immigrants had little or no education, 23.3 percent of males 25 years old and over having had no schooling.[16]

By 1950 the Japanese median school year was 12.2, which was almost three years higher than the whites' median school year. More than half of the Japanese males, 25 years old and over, had completed college, while their white counterpart finished only a high school education. Between 1940 and 1950,

TABLE 1. MEDIAN SCHOOL YEAR COMPLETED FOR MALES, 25 YEARS OLD AND OVER

Race	*1940*	*1950*	*1960*	*1970*
White	8.1	9.3	10.7	12.1
Black	5.3	6.3	7.4	9.4
Japanese	8.8	12.2	12.5	12.5+
Chinese	5.5	7.0	9.2	12.4+
Filipino	7.4	7.3	8.8	12.2+

Sources: 1940–1960, Schmid and Nobbe (1965), p. 914 (excluding Hawaii and Alaska); 1970, U.S. Census (including Hawaii and Alaska).

that is, the decade between the prewar and postwar periods, the Japanese raised their median school year by three years. Through 1970 the Japanese had more schooling than any other ethnic group in America.

The Chinese and the Filipinos, who until 1960 had kept their levels higher than the Blacks but lower than the white and Japanese students, made significant leaps over the white Americans by 1970.

By 1970 differences in median school years among Asian Americans were very small. Across the nation, more than half of the Japanese, Chinese, and Filipino Americans, 25 years old and over, had attained above college level education, while the median school year completed by Blacks was still low.

Despite whatever discrimination remained after the war, large numbers of Japanese and Chinese succeeded in moving up to middle class positions. By 1960 both the Japanese and Chinese were more likely to be found in professional and technical positions than any of the ethnic groups including white Americans.[17]

According to the 1970 census, Japanese, Chinese, and Filipinos were all more likely to be found in the professional and technical occupations than white Americans or Blacks (see Table 2). It is surprising to find a larger proportion of Filipino professionals than their white counterpart. This is due partly to the fact that professionals are given first preference to enter the United States under the 1965 Immigration Law. The majority of Filipino immigrants are doctors, lawyers, engineers, teachers, nurses, and other professionals who have very few opportunities for employment at home. Despite their training, however, they are having difficulty in getting jobs because their credentials are not accepted in this country. So, some Filipino doctors work as laboratory aides; teachers as secretaries; lawyers as clerks; and many professionals also work as laborers.

TABLE 2. OCCUPATIONAL DISTRIBUTION, MALES, 14 YEARS OLD AND OVER, 1970 (IN PERCENTAGES)

Occupation	*White*	*Black*	*Japanese*	*Chinese*	*Filipino*
(Total)	43,501,103	4,091,390	148,162	115,396	79,088
White collar					
Professional and technical	14.2	5.2	21.2	28.7	18.1
Managerial	11.4	2.7	11.6	11.3	3.1
Clerical, sales	14.5	9.0	15.2	13.9	11.2
Manual work					
Craftsmen, foremen	20.4	13.2	19.6	7.2	13.0
Operative	17.5	26.0	10.3	10.4	14.3
Service	6.9	13.8	6.3	23.6	19.8
Labor	5.4	13.6	10.0	3.4	8.3
Farming					
Manager	2.9	0.7	3.0	0.4	0.7
Labor	1.5	3.1	2.1	0.3	11.1

Source: 1970, U.S. Census.

Filipinos are more likely than Japanese or Chinese but less likely than Blacks to be found in manual works. Among manual workers, while Blacks are predominantly in operative positions, Japanese are likely to be craftsmen or foremen, and Chinese and Filipinos are in service works. Most of the Japanese and Chinese had left farming by 1970 and Filipinos, the newcomers, are more likely to be found in agriculture than other Asians.

By 1959 the Japanese had not achieved parity in income with white Americans in spite of their advances in education and occupational status. Thus, until 1959 it was argued that Japanese and Chinese were still discriminated against since they were excluded from the top, high-paying positions monopolized by white Americans within each occupational category including professional work.

By 1969, however, the situation was quite different. The Japanese median income ($7,472) was higher than that of any other group including white Americans ($6,773). However, Chinese who have attained a similar educational and occupational status to Japanese and white Americans earn much less ($5,120) than the latter. Filipinos were making much less ($4,989) than Japanese or Chinese but more than Blacks ($4,069).

In many ways, the Filipino has fared more similarly to the Blacks, Chicanos, and Indians than to the Japanese or Chinese. This is true of income and occupational status, although not of educational attainment.

The success story Asian American style is not applicable to all the Asians. In spite of romantic descriptions of Chinatowns and Filipino sections, these ghettos are plagued with unemployment, crime and delinquency, mental illness, and other social pathologies.[18]

Rise of Ethnic Pride

Japanese and Chinese have been cited as model minorities who have attained middle-class status through hard work and conformity to social order. Recently, however, the validity of this quiet, conforming image has been challenged by the Asian American youth. The major issue raised by the activist youth is the need to replace the image of quiet Americans with that of a new self-determining Asian American identity.

Several factors may account for this rising militancy. First, there is an increased awareness of prejudice and discrimination against Asian Americans. The traditionally held idea that Asian Americans are well accepted and acculturated into the mainstream of American society has been openly challenged.[19] Second, a great impact was felt because of the recent Black and Chicano movements. The imitation of Blacks and Chicanos by Asian American youth is seen in the style of Yellow Power militancy. Finally, there is a generation gap. The youths are unable to accept parental values of conformity and passivity and are in search of new values and identity.

One of the main activities of the Asian Americans has been to establish ethnic study programs. Without any precedence, they had to initiate everything. They have negotiated with the universities to institute such programs, made curriculums, selected instructors, compiled bibliographies on Asian American materials, written textbooks, and taught Asian American children.[20]

Some Asian American militants accept violence as necessary to realize their goals.[21] They demonstrate, join strikes, and sometimes participate in destructive movements, which are reproached by older generations. Although some of the immediate consequences of violence by the militant youth are negatively perceived by the public, and their rhetoric is ineffective, it is high time that quiet Americans spoke their minds. Not only white Americans but also Asian Americans are to blame for the maintenance of white racism if the latter do not begin to take the course toward self-determination.

CULTURAL HERITAGE

The cultural heritage of Asian Americans is noted in their patterns of racial structure, religion, and family system. Of particular significance however are the Asian cultural characteristics of:

1. *Collective orientation*: individuality sacrificed for the general being of some higher authority or universe.
2. *Hierarchical relation*: authority based on position and status which cannot be challenged.
3. *Character management*: inhibition of expression was a positively upheld virtue.
4. *Share culture*: individual behavior controlled by perception of the collectivity rather than by internalized standards.

The emergence and development of these characteristics throughout the years have contributed to a distinct Asian American character. The impact of these characteristics can be more deeply appreciated after an analysis of their emergence within the Asian culture.

Asian Social Structure

Collective orientation and the individual's social conformity date back in the traditional political system of ancient China. Originally developed by the Han dynasty (206 B.C.–A.D. 220), the system divided society into three layers: monarchy (the emperor), administrative bureacracy (the scholar-officials), and everyone else (the small landowners, merchants, craftsmen, and the majority peasantry), with power and privileges concentrated in the first two.[22]

A hierarchical social structure was established in Japan, too, in 1603 by the Tokugawa Shogunate. To combat social mobility and rioting, the Tokugawa Shogunate widened the gaps between each class, and within each social position, inserted a still more minutely graded ranking system, all linked by lord-retainer or master-servant relationships. Each individual was responsible to some particular individual higher than himself in the social hierarchy. The Japanese individual learned that to stay in the proper station in life, was to be safe and secure.

Korea was originally settled by various families, but it was the Chinese who most influenced the Koreans' language, culture, and customs. Korean immigrants had experienced direct contact with the culture of the Yi dynasty (1392–

1910). The long duration of the Confucian Yi dynasty allowed a very firm consolidation of cultural patterns.

The Filipino society was not dominated by Confucianism, but its social structure under Spanish control shows some similarities to oriental despotism. Pre-Spanish Philippine society was structured into a small upper and governing class of nobles, a larger class of freemen, and a still larger servile, dependent class whom the Spaniards misleadingly called slaves. Three centuries of Spanish rule added little to the traditional bases of class structure, occupation, education, and racial origin. Filipino society during the Spanish regime actually consisted of two different societies: the Filipino and the Spanish.

The immigrants from Asia came from the bottom layers of horizontal societies, oppressed by the power elite. Generations of rulers had made certain that the social structure would be maintained by means of meticulous status differentiation, formal and ritualized role requirements, and espionage systems.

Asian Religions

Confucianism: The hierarchical social structure was made possible by an ideology based on the moralistic and worldly ethic of Confucius. It stressed character management in achieving a harmonious society run by morally perfect men.

Because China was frequently plagued by limitations on or scarcities of resources, the Confucianists felt that the only way to solve the problem and to maintain social order was to make social positions distinct and definite, that is, unequal, and to distribute wealth and power according to status.[23] In later times, the philosophy of Confucius was exploited as a rationale for political obedience and given supernatural sanctions. Originally intended as a check on an absolute monarchy and aristocracy, the doctrine eventually defended the literati's possession of land and the power of the state. Thus, the precursor of the meek, inscrutable, and nonaggressive Chinaman was the model of the Confucian gentleman.

In Japan the Tokugawa Shogunate made use of the deeply ingrained ethical and religious systems of Confucianism. In Korea, too, the Yi dynasty made it one of its major preoccupations to see that the doctrines and especially the behavioral pattern of Confucianism were spread and enforced throughout the country.

Buddhism: While Confucianism teaches individuals to stay in their own place in the social structure, Buddhism preaches the negation of self in the world of infinity. Thus, it was shameful for individuals to wish to pursue self-interests over the interests of others. The greatest obstacle to the emancipation and deliverance of the mind, proclaimed Buddha, is the self.[24]

The determinate, differentiated portion of all things, both personal selves as well as natural objects, is seen as transitory. It is precisely because these transitory factors in man and nature are in the center of the consciousness that man is naturally attached to them. But since all these things are transitory, man inevitably must suffer and be unable to obtain peace of mind. To these suffering individuals, Buddha offers salvation, stating that the conventional pattern of referring to a self has no real basis in the process of existence. Salvation means disengagement from ego-centered and social drives.

Duty to one's superiors was a direct reflection of the Buddhist concept of indebtedness, and expressed a deep sense of devotion to one's lord. Self-control was stressed so that one might not develop desires or covetousness. Showing one's feelings was considered weakness. Buddhism furnished a sense of calm trust in fate, a quiet submission to the inevitable, a stoic composure in the face of danger or hardship.

Catholicism: While oriental societies were ingrained with Confucianism and Buddhism, the Filipinos were indoctrinated with Roman Catholicism by the Spanish conquerors. Under the Spanish rule, church and state were united, with the state providing financial and other forms of support to the Catholic church. Some similarities are found between oriental and Filipino religions. First, in both cases there is a strong tie between religion and state. The governments made certain to convert all the people into the state religion. Religion was not to meet the individual psychological needs but to meet the needs of society as a whole, and the ruling class in particular. Second, all these religions tend to emphasize the importance of the social group rather than the individual. Although Christianity does not negate the existence of self as Confucianism and Buddhism do, Catholicism is more oriented toward tradition and collectivity than Protestantism.

Thus, in the Philippines, Catholicism was effective in subjugating the mass peasantry to the authority of the church united with the government. As in the oriental societies, religion gave ethical and moral legitimacy to the power of the ruling class.

Asian Family System

The basic unit of social action in all of the four societies was the family system. In the oriental societies the family system was based on Confucian ideologies.

The perfect embodiment of Confucianism was the well-structured patriarchal family, the microcosm of the order that should prevail in the state and in society. Sons were to show filial piety; young brothers, respect; wives, obedience; younger men, deference; and subjects, loyalty. These deferential roles were to be matched with appropriate reciprocation from above: fathers were to show kindness; elder brothers, nobility; elders, humaneness; and rulers, benevolence. Such were the requirements for attainment of general harmony and true human welfare. Hence, we can appreciate the derivation of the notion of "taking care of one's own," for by stabilizing one's own immediate relationships, one does something toward the eventual reform and harmonization of society at large.

The kinship group became the most immediate manifestation of an enormous amount of total institutional power that impinged upon the life of an individual. Under such a system individual interests were sacrificed for the needs and well-being of the family. Moreover, family needs were sacrificed for the interests and well being of the ruler and state.

Asian American Experience

Such was the general cultural heritage the Asians brought to the United States. However, some variations should be noted.

Many people have regarded Chinese American heritage to be synonymous with Great Traditions of Cathay. Chinese Americans, being perpetual aliens who have somehow managed to enjoy an unbroken connection with a centuries-old golden culture, are supposed to be interpreters of the oriental mind.

The truth of the matter is that the majority of Chinese Americans descended from the peasant stratum of Kwangtung, a class which certainly was not the repository of thousands of years of sophisticated civilization. They were uneducated and knew very little about the finer aspects of classical Chinese culture. Their cultural heritage was not that of the scholar-official class but was of the peasant-laborer mentality. Their Confucian heritage included taking care of oneself, working hard, and not being concerned with anyone else's affairs. The Chinese migrated from a state that was not a nation, and they conceived of themselves primarily as members of local extended kin units and only secondarily as citizens of the Chinese empire.

The Japanese emigrant departed from a different type of society. Japan was a nation as well as a state. The Japanese were products of a culture that was undergoing vast social changes from a feudal system to an urban and industrial society. After 1868 emigration was sometimes sponsored by the government and certainly encouraged. Although the majority of Japanese emigrants were from the farming class, they were different from the peasants. Although often poor, farmers belonged to a respectable class in the Japanese feudal system. The majority of them had the equivalent of an eighth grade education and were ambitious and intelligent. Their cultural heritage included not only the Tokugawa Confucian conformity but also a certain amount of self-determination.

Korean emigrants were relatively unorganized in traditional social groups. The majority of the Korean migrants came from northern Korea which was lacking in clan and other traditional forms of social organization.

As for the Filipinos, it is difficult to delineate their cultural heritage. They carry traces of Asian, Spanish, and American cultures. When Filipinos started emigrating, their country was under American control and exposed to American culture.

Characteristics of Asians attributable to their cultural heritage helped them survive in the strange land to which they immigrated. Through experience these characteristics were validated and reinforced instead of being modified and eradicated.

EDUCATIONAL NEEDS

Because of a high educational attainment and a large proportion of professional and technical workers, Asian Americans in general are viewed as free from educational problems. The American public tends to consider Asian Americans as financially capable of sending their children to school, and that these children are highly motivated toward education and do not need any help or counseling.

This does not mean that educational needs of the Asian Americans are satisfactorily met. Rather, it suggests peculiarities in their needs derived from their cultural heritage and the necessity of dealing with them separately.

Given the cultural heritage and the experiences which have formed the characteristics of Asian Americans, two educational needs seem apparent. The first is to provide an adequate language education program which enhances the ability of Asian American children to communicate effectively in their society. The second is to modify the existing curriculum to meet the special education needs of Asian American children, who appear to be "doing well at school," yet suffer from serious problems caused by having poor self-concepts.

Language Education

Due to the constant influx of immigrants, evidence has shown that there are a number of Asian children who are unable to communicate in English. They are unable to understand what transpires in the classroom. Therefore there is a need for the non-English-speaking Asian child to acquire a basic fluency in English as quickly as possible. However, one must not ignore or deny the child's knowledge and skill in a native language and culture in attaining this fluency. Language is a cultural phenomenon. The Asian child has internalized a language system within a social and cultural context that is implicitly different from that of the United States. In effect, this child is not merely involved in the process of substituting one language for another, but also in developing another conceptual system as well. The child's native conceptual system, then, must be used as a resource.

Children are not motivated to learn when their surroundings are totally foreign and even hostile to them. Providing relevant experiences for children will facilitate the acquiring of a new language and develop positive attitudes toward their native and adopted culture. Therefore, the goal is twofold: to develop the basic academic and the basic social skills needed for a child to function effectively in school and community.

One educational approach would be for all schools to identify non-English-speaking students as early as possible. The bilingual teachers would assess each child in order to ascertain oral and reading skills. In teaching, stress would be placed on comprehension of listening and speaking skills prior to reading and writing readiness. Idioms would be introduced almost immediately. For example, a child is not taught "It is I" but "It's me," or "It is a book" but rather "It's a book." This would avoid the typical problem experienced by many Asian students who have learned English for several years in their home countries and still cannot comprehend nor be comprehended by Americans upon arrival in this country. In Asian countries English is frequently taught through grammar and writing rather than speaking. Idiomatic and colloquial expressions are the last thing learned. So we encounter Japanese college students trying to communicate in English with a Japanese intonation.

In the beginning stages of learning English, the native Asian language will have to be used to facilitate translations whenever necessary. However, after these students begin to learn English and gain competency, less and less old language would be used. Bilingualism is successful in some situations, but not always. The Spanish language, for instance, has some similarities to English and therefore might be used as a bridge to learning English. Chinese, Japanese, and Korean, on the other hand, have little, if any, transference value into English since their tones, grammars, and structures are often quite different. If anything, the oriental language probably ultimately acts as a barrier to the proper acquisition of English.

Broadening Curriculum Alternatives

One of the Asian American characteristics—lack of individuality—takes various forms. One manifestation is the limited selection of career fields. Many Asian Americans go to college, but their degrees are almost never in the liberal arts, but rather in business administration, optometry, engineering, or other professional fields. Thus, education is considered as a means of acquiring a saleable skill rather than a means of developing a critical mind.

This is due in part to the past experience of Asian Americans. First they went into low-level clerical and technical work in order to avoid direct competition with white Americans. Once they performed well in these areas, the positive stereotype was created. These areas then became established as fields in which the Asian American was expected to excel naturally. Parents pushed their offspring into accounting, engineering, drafting, and clerical work until they became "math and science freaks, eating their meals with slide rules."

Another reason for their concentration in science is that it requires less human interaction than other fields. Asian Americans are not good at verbal skills and social interaction because of their cultural heritage and their subordinate position in America. Traditionally they have been taught not to express their feelings freely, which makes social interaction with white Americans difficult because the latter are used to more spontaneous expression. Often a feeling of inferiority toward white Americans makes the Asian Americans timid and inadequate when in direct contact with them. Asian Americans feel much more at ease dealing with numbers or machines than with people.

The lack of individuality is also manifested in their learning style. Dating back to the Confucian literati, learning for Asian Americans means understanding and memorizing what is taught rather than exploring or criticizing. Most often Asian American students get high grades on multiple choice or true-or-false examinations but do poorly in essays.

A lower grade teacher may consider Asian American children who are sitting quietly in the back of the classroom as well behaved. However, the lack of high verbal functioning and emotional aggressiveness stifles the development of one's mental capacities. Fear of appearing aggressive and a lack of confidence usually interfere with critical thinking. Timidity in voicing ideas can prevent organizing them sufficiently to arrive at intelligent conclusions. Any personality trait that hampers the use of mental capacities tends to limit the functioning of intelligence.

The Asian American education curriculum needs to cultivate ethnic pride and self-determination. Acceptance of white Americans' stereotypical descriptions has led Asian Americans to feel that they cannot speak for themselves. Their experiences are valid only if they are validated by white Americans.

Younger generations of Asian Americans are realizing that they should stop seeking acceptance by white Americans and that they should develop pride in their own physical and cultural heritage. They advocate self-acceptance as the first step toward strengthening the personality of Asian Americans. The content of a typical ethnic study program has three areas of emphasis: education, research, and action. The study includes Asian culture, society, and history to acquaint students with the Asian heritage and the experiences of Asian Americans.

The Confucian idea of taking care of oneself has been replaced by the ideology of social concern and a united front. Unlike the traditional Asian American students whose sole concern was to get high grades, today's activist youths show interest and concern for other people. They are engaged in research on Asian communities and on the needs of other less successful Asians. Their action includes offering legal aid to recent immigrants, teaching English to immigrant children, or writing textbooks for Asian Americans.

The important thing is the participation itself rather than the outcome of these activities. Through taking care of others, they are discovering their potential for self-determination. In order to create new programs, they have to use their own minds because they cannot find a ready-made answer in the Confucian texts. At one American university when ethnic study programs were not given to students by the university, the students proposed the program forcibly to the university. Through the experience of negotiating with the university, Asian American students broke the stereotypical image of quiet Americans—to themselves and to others.

The subject matter of ethnic group experiences and contributions has long been absent from the educational process, or it has been presented in a cursory and stereotypical manner. Whether this is due to oversight or some form of racism is still debatable. What is clear and important is that this subject matter is seen as significant, not just to those with a personal interest but as part of the total American experience and, in a broader sense, the experience of man. It, therefore, deserves to be part of the educational process.

In order to develop an understanding of minority groups, it is essential that we have some knowledge of the unique features of people's cultures. As one gains this knowledge, one is better able to understand or assess objectively the fundamental characteristics of each group that will transcend the superficial differences. This understanding should enable one to place every member of mankind in an equalizing category—that of human being.

The study of Asian Americans should attempt to develop a positive self-concept in students of oriental backgrounds. To assist in this development a wide variety of teaching strategies and media should be employed. Moreover, diversified instructional materials such as bibliographies of books, articles, and documents on Asian Americans should be made available for student use.

Until several years ago very few resources were available on Asian Americans but now there is an emergence of materials and a necessity to establish selection criteria and utilization procedures. The first criterion should be the authenticity of the material. As far as the Asian cultural heritage is concerned, there are many ways to examine the authenticity of the audiovisual materials against already validated written documents in the native language of each Asian country. White Americans have tended to view Asians in a prejudiced and biased manner in past years, so careful review and evaluation of instructional materials must be made before using them in the classroom.

Objectivity must also be maintained. Prejudice against ethnic minorities has been sufficiently emphasized, but reverse racism has to be watched. The story of Yellow Peril told by white people has been damaging to the image of Asian Americans, but so is the slogan of Yellow Power by Asian American radicals who condemn white Americans for every historical event. Some of the audiovisual materials produced by radical Asian American youth may have this inclination. While presenting such a film, the teacher should point out the discrepancies between ideological fervor and objective facts. For instance, the power struggle among Asian Americans themselves and the exploitation by more successful Asian Americans of their fellowmen should be noted along with the discussion of exploitation of the Asians.

Finally, relevance of ethnicity to human experience must be considered. There are poor white Americans, rich Chinese, and middle-class Blacks. Asian American's cry "I am Yellow and I am beautiful, long live the emperor" is important in raising racial consciousness. However, race or ethnicity is only one of the sources of social identity among other sources such as age, occupation, religion, or any combination thereof. While viewing audiovisual materials one should remember that one is primarily a human being more than a white, black, or Asian American.

NOTES

1. Minako K. Maykovich, "Reciprocity in Racial Stereotypes: White, Black, and Yellow," *American Journal of Sociology* 77 (1972): 876-897.
2. J. Milton Mackie, "The Chinaman," *Putman's Monthly* (1857): 337-350.
3. Elmer C. Sandmeyer, *The Anti-Chinese Movement in California* (Urbana: University of Illinois Press, 1939).
4. S. W. Kung, *Chinese American Life* (Seattle: University of Washington Press, 1962), chap. 3.
5. Chester P. Dorland, "The Chinese Massacre at Los Angeles in 1871," Annual Publications, Historical Society of Southern California, III, pt. 2 (1894): 22-26, and Mildred Welborn, "The Events Leading to the Chinese Exclusion Acts," Annual Publications, Historical Society of Southern California, IX (1914): 49-58.
6. L. Eaves, *A History of California Labor Legislation* (Berkeley: University of California Press, 1910).
7. Elmer C. Sandmeyer, "California Anti-Chinese Legislation and the Federal Courts: A Study in Federal Relation," *Pacific Historical Review*, vol. 5, no. 3 (1936): 211.

8. Varden Fuller, "The Study of Agricultural Labor as a Factor in the Evolution of Farm Organization in California," Hearings before a Subcommittee of the Committee on Education and Labor, U.S. Senate, 76th Cong., Third Session pursuant to S. Res. 266 (74th Congress), Washington.
9. Stanford Lyman, *The Asians in the West* (Reno and Las Vegas: Desert Institute, University of Nevada System, 1971).
10. William Caudill and George De Vos, "Achievement, Culture and Personality: The Case of Japanese Americans," *American Anthropologist* 58 (1956): 1102-1126.
11. Jacobus tenBroek et al., *Prejudice, War and the Constitution* (Berkeley: University of California Press, 1954); Edward H. Spicer et al., *Impounded People* (Tucson: University of Arizona Press, 1969); and Allan R. Bosworth, *America's Concentration Camps* (New York: Norton, 1967).
12. Caudill and De Vos, "Achievement, Culture and Personality," pp. 1102-1126.
13. Violet Rabaya, "Filipino Immigration: The Creation of a New Social Problem," in *Roots: An Asian American Reader*, ed. by Amy Tachiki et al. (Los Angeles: Continental Graphics, 1971), pp. 188-200.
14. Sonia Emily Wallovits, *The Filipinos in California* (Los Angeles: University of Southern California, 1966).
15. Linda Shin, "Koreans in America: 1903-1945," in *Roots: An Asian American Reader*, ed. by Amy Tachiki et al., pp. 200-206.
16. Calvin F. Schmid and Charles E. Nobbe, "Socioeconomic Differentials among Nonwhite Races," *American Sociological Review* 30 (1965): 909-922.
17. Ibid.
18. *Kalayaan International*, "Filipinos: A Fast Growing U.S. Minority—Philippines Revolution," 1971, and Rocky Chin, "New York Chinatown Today: Community in Crisis," in *Roots: An Asian American Reader*, ed. by Amy Tachiki et al., pp. 282-295.
19. Amy Tachiki et al., *Roots: An Asian American Reader.*
20. Russel Endo, "Whither Ethnic Studies: A Re-examination of some Issues," in *Asian-American Psychological Perspectives*, ed. by Stanley Sue and Nathaniel N. Wagner (Palo Alto: Science and Behavior Books, 1973), pp. 281-294.
21. Minako K. Maykovich, "Political Activation of Japanese American Youth," *Journal of Social Issues* 29 (1973): 167-186; Neil Gotanda, "Interview with Alex Hing: Minister of Information, Red Guard Party," *Aion* 1 (1970): 32-43; and Amy Uyematsu, "The Emergence of Yellow Power in America," *Gidra* (October 1969).
22. Hsiao-tung Fei, *China's Gentry* (Chicago: University of Chicago Press, 1953); Ch'u Chai and Winberg Chai, *The Changing Society of China* (New York: New American Library, 1969); and Franz Schurmann and Orville Schell, *Imperial China: The Decline of the Last Dynasty and the Origins of Modern China, 18th and 19th Centuries* (New York: Vintage, 1967).

23. Alfred Doebbin, "Virtue and Leadership," in *Confucianism and Taoism*, ed. by A. Jeff Tudisco (Palo Alto: Field Educational Publications, 1969), p. 10.
24. Tyusaku Tsunoda et al., eds., *Sources of Japanese Tradition* (New York: Columbia University Press, 1958).

BIBLIOGRAPHY

Bell, Reginald. *Public School Education of Second Generation Japanese in California.* Palo Alto: Stanford University Press, 1935.

Bellah, Robert N. *Tokugawa Religion.* Glencoe: Free Press, 1959.

Benedict, Ruth. *The Chrysanthemum and the Sword.* Boston: Houghton Mifflin, 1946.

Bonacichi, Edna. "A Theory of Middleman Minorites." *American Sociological Review* 38 (1973): 583-594.

Bosworth, Allan R. *America's Concentration Camps.* New York: Norton, 1967.

Cady, John F. *Southeast Asia: Its Historical Development.* New York: McGraw-Hill, 1964.

Caudill, William. "Japanese-American Personality and Acculturation." *Genetic Psychology Monograph* 15 (1952): 3-102.

Caudill, William, and De Vos, George. "Achievement, Culture and Personality: The Case of Japanese Americans." *American Anthropologist* 58 (1956): 1102-1126.

Chai, Ch'u, and Chai, Winberg. *The Changing Society of China.* New York: New American Library, 1969.

Chin, Rocky. "New York Chinatown Today: Community in Crisis." In *Roots: An Asian American Reader*, ed. by Amy Tachiki et al. Los Angeles: Continental Graphics, 1971, pp. 188-200.

Confucius. "The Doctrine of the Mean." In *The Four Books*, trans. by James Legge. Shanghai: Commercial Press, n.d.

DeBary, William T., ed. *Sources of Japanese Tradition.* New York: Columbia University Press, 1958.

Doebbin, Alfred. "Virtue and Leadership." In *Confucianism and Taoism*, ed. by A. Jeff Tudisco. Palo Alto: Field Educational Publications, 1969.

Dorland, Chester P. "The Chinese Massacre at Los Angeles in 1871." Annual Publications, Historical Society of Southern California, III, Part 2 (1894): 22-26.

Duff, Donald F., and Arthur, Ransom A. "Between Two Worlds: Filipinos in the U.S. Navy." In *Asian-American Psychological Perspectives*, ed. by Stanley Sue and Nathaniel N. Wagner. Palo Alto: Science and Behavior Books, 1973, pp. 202-211.

Eaves, L. *A History of California Labor Legislation.* New York: Johnson Reprint Corp., 1910.

Eggan, Frederick, ed. *Human Relations Area Files: Area Handbook on the Philippines.* vols. 1 and 2. Chicago: University of Chicago for Human Relations Area Files, 1956.

Endo, Russell. "Whither Ethnic Studies: A Re-examination of Some Issues." In *Asian-American Psychological Perspectives*, ed. by Stanley Sue and Nathaniel N. Wagner. Palo Alto: Science and Behavior Books, 1973, pp. 281-294.

Fei, Hsiao-tung. *China's Gentry: Essays on Rural-Urban Relations.* Rev. and ed. by Margaret Park Redfield. Chicago: University of Chicago Press, 1953.

Feng, Yu-lan. *The Spirit of Chinese Philosophy.* Trans. by E. R. Hughes. Routledge, 1947.

Fuller, Varden. "The Study of Agricultural Labor as a Factor in the Evolution of Farm Organization in California." Hearings before a Subcommittee of the Committee on Education and Labor, U.S. Senate, 76th Cong., Third Session pursuant to S. Res. 266 (74th Cong.), Washington.

Glick, Carl. *Shake Hands with the Dragon.* New York: Whittlesey House, 1941.

Gotanda, Neil. "Interview with Alex Hing: Minister of Information, Red Guard Party." *Aion* 1 (1970): 32-43.

Guthrie, G. M. *Filipino Child and Philippine Society.* Manila: Philippine Normal College Press, 1961.

Henderson, Gregory. *Korea: The Politics of the Vortex.* Cambridge: Harvard University Press, 1968.

Hosokawa, Bill. *Nisei: The Quiet Americans.* New York: William Morrow, 1969.

Hsu, Francis. "Chinese Mind." In *Asian Psychology*, ed. by Gardener Murphy and Lois B. Murphy. New York: Basic Books, 1968, pp. 169-177.

Jacobson, Nolan P. *Buddhism: The Religion of Analysis.* Carbondale, Ill.: Southern Illinois University Press, 1970.

Kalayyan International, 1 (1971). "Filipinos: A Fast Growing U.S. Minority—Philippines Revolution."

Karlins, Marvin et al. "On the Fading of Social Stereotypes: Studies in Three Generations of College Students." *Journal of Personality and Social Psychology* 13 (1969): 1-16.

Katz, Daniel and Braly, Kenneth W. "Racial Stereotypes of 100 College Students." *Journal of Abnormal and Social Psychology* 28 (1933): 280-290.

Kirk, Grayson L. *Philippine Independence.* New York: Farrar & Rinehart, 1936.

Kitagawa, Daisuke. *Issei and Nisei.* New York: Seabury Press, 1974.

Kitano, Harry. *Japanese Americans: The Evolution of a Subculture.* Englewood Cliffs: Prentice-Hall, 1969.

Kung, S. W. *Chinese in American Life.* Seattle: University of Washington Press, 1962.

Lasker, Bruno. *Filipino Immigration to the Continental United States and to Hawaii.* Chicago: University of Chicago Press, 1931.

Lyman, Stanford. *The Asians in the West.* Reno and Las Vegas: Desert Research Institute, University of Nevada System, 1971.

Mackie, J. Milton. "The Chinaman." *Putman's Monthly* (1857): 337-350.

McWilliams, Carey. *Brothers Under the Skin.* Rev. ed. Boston: Little, Brown, 1951.

Maykovich, Minako K. *Japanese American Identity Dilemma.* Tokyo: Waseda University Press, 1972.

—— "Political Activation of Japanese American Youth." *Journal of Social Issues* 29 (1973): 167-168.

—— "Reciprocity in Racial Stereotypes: White, Black, and Yellow." *American Journal of Sociology* 77 (1972): 876-897.

Miller, Stuart C. *The Unwelcome Immigrant: The American Image of the Chinese: 1785-1882.* Berkeley: University of California Press, 1969.

Nivison, David S. and Wright, Arthur F. eds. *Confucianism in Action.* Palo Alto: Stanford University Press, 1959.

Northrop, F. S. C. *The Meeting of East and West.* New York: Macmillan, 1960.

Paik, L. G. *The History of Protestant Missions in Korea.* Pyongyang, 1929; repr. Seoul, 1969.

Palmer, Albert W. *Orientals in American Life.* New York: Friendship Press, 1934.

Petersen, William. "Success Story, Japanese-American Style." The *New York Times*, January 9, 1966.

Rabaya, Violet. "Filipino Immigration: The Creation of a New Social Problem." In *Roots: An Asian American Reader*, ed. by Amy Tachiki et al. Los Angeles: Continental Graphics, 1971.

Sandmeyer, Elmer C. *The Anti-Chinese Movement in California.* Urbana: University of Illinois Press, 1939.

— "California Anti-Chinese Legislation and the Federal Courts: A Study in Federal Relation." *Pacific Historical Review* 5, 3 (1936).

Schmid, Calvin F., and Nobbe, Charles E. "Socioeconomic Differentials among Nonwhite Races." *American Sociological Review* 30 (1965): 909-922.

Schurmann, Franz, and Schell, Orville. *The China Reader (Vol. 1)—Imperial China: The Decline of the Last Dynasty and the Origins of Modern China, 18th and 19th Centuries.* New York: Vintage, 1967.

Shin, Linda. "Koreans in America: 1903-1945." In *Roots: An Asian American Reader*, ed by. Amy Tachiki et al. Los Angeles: Continental Graphics, 1971.

Spicer, Edward H.; Hansen, Asael T.; Luomala, Katherine; and Opler, Marvin K. *Impounded People: Japanese-Americans in the Relocation Centers.* Tucson: University of Arizona Press, 1969.

tenBroek, Jacobus et al. *Prejudice, War and the Constitution: Causes and Consequences of the Evacuation of the Japanese Americans in World War II.* Berkeley: University of California Press, 1954.

Uyematsu, Amy. "The Emergence of Yellow Power in America." *Gidra* (October 1969).

Wallovits, Sonia Emily. *The Filipinos in California.* Los Angeles: R&E Research Associates, 1972.

Welborn, Mildred. "The Events Leading to the Chinese Exclusion Acts." Annual Publications, Historical Society of Southern California, IX (1914): 49-58.

MEDIA AND MATERIALS—ANNOTATED

Films (16mm)

AFGHANISTAN. ACI 1972. P-El-J. 15 min col. Rental $15; purchase $210.

This film presents an overview of exotic and remote Afghanistan. Authentic Eastern music accents striking visuals of remote tribesmen traveling by camel, skilled horsemen playing violent games (including the traditional *buzkachi*), farmers gathering their crops, and city dwellers bustling about in Kabul.

ALAHU AKBAR: FAITH OF FOUR HUNDRED MILLION. ACI 1970. J-S-A. 10 min col. Rental $15; purchase $130.

"Alahu Akbar" (the Moslem call to prayer meaning "Allah is great"), is a portrait of the Islamic faith which is practiced by 400 million Moslems and follows the teaching of the Prophet Mohammed. It claims to be the youngest of the world's major religions and the fastest growing in Africa and Asia.

ANCIENT CHINESE, THE: AN INTRODUCTION. IFF 1974. J-S-C-A. 24 min col. Purchase $360.

Scenes today in Peking's forbidden city, on a silk plantation, and of an artist practicing calligraphy—the ancient art of Chinese writing—help show that China's history and deep-rooted traditions have continued longer than those of other civilizations.

ANCIENT ORIENT: THE FAR EAST. CORF/IU 1957. El-J-S. 14 min b&w/col. Rental $6.75 (b&w), $8.50 (col); purchase $164.

Traces through reenactments and authentic locales the growth of early oriental civilizations in India, China, and Japan. Uses early manuscripts, paintings, sculptures, and architecture to show the heritage and ideas that have shaped oriental life and thought from ancient times to the present day. Merrill R. Goodall, Ph. D., Cornell University, Consultant.

ASIA: A CONTINENTAL OVERVIEW. CORF/USC 1964. J-S. 14 min col. Rental $7.50; purchase $208.

Gives a picture of the wide range of living conditions on this largest and most populous of the continents and the many changes taking place. Treats principal physical regions of Asia and examines each in terms of its natural resources and human use. Joseph E. Spencer, Ph. D., University of California at Los Angeles, Consultant.

BORN CHINESE. ROBECK 1967. J-S. 57 min b&w. Rental $40; purchase $300.

Hong Kong has been chosen as the site for this study which throws a new light on the Chinese by studying their human traits rather than their politics. This film presents a story of the daily life of the Lung family. There are no English words spoken in the film other than those of Anthony Lawrence, Far East Correspondent.

BURMA, PEOPLE OF THE RIVER. EBEC/IU 1958. J-S. 14 min b&w/col. Rental $8.50; purchase $95 (b&w), $185 (col).

Explores the varied regions and life in Burma. The film shows: rice fields, rivers which serve as highways, jungles of bamboo and teakwood, and village and city (Rangoon) life.

CAVE PEOPLE OF THE PHILIPPINES, THE. NBCTV/BCMI 1972. J-S-C-A. 39 min col. Rental $20; purchase by rental only.

The life-style of the Tasaday, gentle Stone Age tribe, is documented in an "NBC Report" which was premiered on television on October 10, 1972. The film reveals how these almost isolated people exist in a kind of paradise, completely satisfied with their existence and, apparently, devoid of violence or hostility. There are glimpses of their daily routines, family relationships, and social life. They and their ancestors have lived more than 400 years in the caves of the rain forest, undisturbed by civilization.

CHINA: AN END TO ISOLATION. ACI 1972. P-El-J-S. 23 min col. Rental $25; purchase $300.

"Live simply, work hard." The effect of Mao's doctrine is examined in this look at China today—its economic, agricultural, and industrial accomplishments. The film offers a clear impression of Maoist thought and delineates the dynamics of the culture in which this theory flourishes. Unique visuals explore stores in Tsientsin, a commune near Shanghai; the Nanking bridge; and the Canton Trade Fair.

CHINA: A PORTRAIT OF THE LAND. EBEC 1967. J-S. 18 min b&w/col. Rental $7 (b&w), $11 (col); purchase $130 (b&w), $255 (col).

A look at six major regions—Manchuria, North China, South China, Inner Mongolia, Sinkiang Province, and Tibet—whose economic progress is to a great extent determined by the land. The film points particularly to Manchuria as a key to the nation's agricultural and industrial progress, showing what has been done in lumber and steel.

CHINA BY THE GOLDEN GATE. STOC 1952. El-J-S-A. 22 min col. Rental, free.

This film is the story of San Francisco's "Chinatown," the largest Chinese settlement outside of the Orient. Although an older film, it deals with a subject that is relevant today and reveals much of the daily life-styles of this Chinese ghetto.

CHINA IN THE 20TH CENTURY–THE TWO-HEADED DRAGON. HEARST 1971. J-S. 17 min col.

A review of the history of China since the Revolution of 1911. Shows the conflict between the Communists led by Mao Tse-tung and the Nationalists led by Chiang Kai-shek.

CHINA'S INDUSTRIAL REVOLUTION. MGH/IU 1967. J-S-A. 15 min b&w/col. Rental $15; purchase $115 (b&w), $220 (col).

Shows how the Communists are trying to change a land of artisans and peasants into a modern industrial nation with world power. The film reveals the difficulties and lag in modernized agriculture—untrained manpower, lack of machines and workers for industrial growth.

CHINA'S VILLAGE IN CHANGE. EBEC/IU 1967. J-S-C-A. 20 min b&w/col. Rental $10.75; purchase $150 (b&w), $290 (col).

A cameraman's visit to three villages in South China, North China, and Inner Mongolia shows the Communist's attempts to change centuries-old tradition with the introduction of modern improvements. The film shows how state ownership of land conflicts with the peasants' desire to work and own their property.

CHINA–THE AWAKENING GIANT. MGH 1967. J-S-A. 16 min col. Rental $9.75; purchase $215.

Contrasts the traditions of ancient China with the cultural innovations which are taking place today in language, education, religion, music and art, transportation, health care, recreation, housing, and status of women. The new trends in China are most revealing for those who know China from its old setting.

CHINA–THE PAST IS PROLOGUE. OXF 1973. S-C-A. 20 min col. Rental $30; purchase $275.

Presents an insight into the major internal struggles of China, including the Civil War between the Nationalists and the Communists and the role of the Red Guard in the Great Proletarian cultural revolution.

CHINA: THE SOCIAL REVOLUTION. MGH/IU 1967. S-C-A. 17 min col. Rental $7.50; purchase $225.

Gives a brief historical account of ancient China and relates its past history to China in the 1960s. Discusses the Japanese and Chinese war of the 1930s which was followed by two years of civil war in China. Describes the conditions which made China ripe for Communist takeover in 1949 and points out reforms taking place under Communist rule in agriculture, industry, and education.

CHINA UNDER COMMUNISM (Revised Edition). EBEC 1963. S-C-A. 22 min b&w/col. Rental $9 (b&w), $13.50 (col); purchase $150 (b&w), $290 (col).

John Strohm, foreign correspondent, first visited China in 1937. He returned in 1958 and traveled 7,500 miles observing and photographing phases of Chinese life. His film footage reveals the Communist regime's methods of forcing radical departures from traditional patterns of living. An interesting look into the "new" China.

CHINESE AMERICAN, THE: THE EARLY IMMIGRANTS. HFC 1973. El-J-S-A. 20 min col. Rental $27; purchase $270.

This history of the first Chinese to come to the United States, their role in the gold rush and the building of the transcontinental railroad, and their savage persecution and eventual unjust exclusion. Discussion topics: Reasons for early immigration, contribution to the building of the transcontinental railroad, reasons for the persecution of the Chinese in the late 1880s, and the Exclusion Act.

CHINESE AMERICAN, THE: THE TWENTIETH CENTURY. HFC 1973. El-J-S-A. 20 min col. Rental $27; purchase $270.

The development of San Francisco's Chinatown following the earthquake. Included are important Chinese personalities, President Nixon's visit to China, and the unique position and problems of the Chinese American who finds himself on the crossroads of two political systems. Interviews with a Chinese American student, a banker, and a judge. Discussion topics: Famous Chinese communities in the United States, the Nixon visit to China, Chinese achievers, and the unique position of the Chinese American minority.

CHINESE IN DISPERSION. UPMPD 1962. J-S-C-A. 40 min col. Rental $5.

The political, social, economic, and religious problems of Chinese migrants from the mainland to Hong Kong, Singapore, Burma, Thailand, Malay Peninsula, Taiwan, and so on. Shows the status of the Christian mission and the outcome for the future.

CHINESE, KOREAN, AND JAPANESE DANCE. NYCBED/AS 1965. P-El-S-A. 28 min col. Rental $11.20; purchase $200.

This film shows the dances of three ethnic groups—the Chinese, Korean, and Japanese. Viewer sees the common elements and the contrasts. Each group's dances are demonstrated step by step and interpreted by the narrator.

CITIZEN CHANG. REYP 1961. El-J-S. 25 min b&w. Rental $15; purchase $175.

A human relations training film leads the viewer—without lecturing or moralizing on human weakness—to examine his interpersonal conflicts through the unusual experiences of a small Chinese American boy and his encounters with the "adult" world.

COMMUNIST CHINA. MGH 1965. J-S-C. 23 min b&w. Rental $9; purchase $140.

Reports on the progress of communism in China and discusses China's potential power. Pictures efforts to unify the Chinese people through the life and discipline of the communes. Shows the building of industrial plants and attempts to update the methods of farming. Points out the use of education as a unifying factor.

CONFUCIUS. MCI 1975. J-S-C. 28 min col.

A brief history of Confucius and his era sets the stage for a depiction of Confucian morality. Scenes from an ancient ceremony honoring his birthday, interviews with Confucian scholars and students, and actual quotations complete the portrayal.

CULINARY ART OF JAPAN. CGJ 1964. El-J-S-A. 29 min col. Rental, free.

Depicts food and cooking in the land of the rising sun. The essence of Japanese cuisine lies in offering one's warmest hospitality through careful choice of specific foods at the peak of their season. To the Japanese, the preparation and serving of food has become refined to an art for good living, and great care is given to offer dishes which appeal to both the palate and eye of the diner. Thus, the food is arranged artistically on the most functional and attractive china in order to enhance the full enjoyment of the repast. Housewives shop daily in specialty stores to ensure absolute freshness of the fruits, vegetables, meats, and fish in season.

DISCOVERING THE MUSIC OF JAPAN. BFA 1967. El-J-S-A. 22 min col. Rental $15; purchase $250.

Japan's three major musical instruments, the koto, shamisen, and shakuhachi, are played, and their history and current use are explained. Traditional Japanese singing and dancing are depicted in a traditional teahouse setting. Explains some historical background of instruments and the way they are used.

FACE OF RED CHINA, THE. MGH 1962. J-S-C-A. 56 min b&w. Rental $8.75; purchase $275.

CBS News reports how the Communists work toward a modern society and reports on the conditions in Red China in 1958. Covers the communes by which Red China is mobilizing its vast human resources. In two parts, the film describes the after-hours labor that city dwellers contribute to home production.

FACES OF CHINATOWN. UCEM 1963. El-J-S. 27 min col. Rental $7.

This film presents a moving story of Chinese immigrants in San Francisco during 1877 to 1911. Hundreds of rare historical photographs help relate the story of early Chinatown during bonanza days. Dennis Kearney who demanded "The Chinese Must Go" and Gong Ching, a tong chief who was virtually king of Chinatown, are depicted. Also included are the San Quentin "mug shots" of the famous hatchet man, Little Pet; and Donalina Cameron, crusading woman who was devoted to the single-handed destruction of the slave trade.

FAMOUS TEMPLES OF THAILAND, THE. ACI 1974. P-El-J-S. 10 min col. Rental $15; purchase $160.

A brief view of Thailand's history and culture, and an introduction to the exotic architecture and sculpture of its temples and palaces.

FIVE CHINESE BROTHERS. SCHLAT 1958. P-El-J. 10 min col. Rental $5; purchase $120.

Five identical-looking brothers outwit the townspeople and save themselves from a tragic demise. This film is a folktale using original drawings from the children's book by Bishop and Wiese.

FLOATING MARKET, BANGKOK. ACI 1970. P-El-J-S. 11 min col. Rental $15; purchase $170.

This film, while focusing on a nineteen-year-old Thai girl, who spends her days traveling up and down the river in a small boat selling fruit to natives and tourists, provides an overall view of the city of Bangkok and its people.

FOOD OF SOUTHEAST ASIA. BFA 1966. J-S. 18 min col. Rental $12.50 (3 days); purchase $200.

Shows how the people of densely populated Southeast Asia subsist on a diet of fish, rice, and vegetables and how these foods are produced.

GEMS FROM A RICE PADDY. ACI 1970. J-S-A. 11 min col. Rental $15; purchase $135.

Although Ceylon is a modern country, the mining and processing of the buried treasures of this country—sapphires, rubies, topazes, and moonstones—have remained unchanged for thousands of years and reflect the country's ancient cultural heritage. They are found below vegetable gardens and rice paddies when the water is drained and the sand lifted out and washed. The film also provides an overview of life in modern Ceylon.

GUILTY BY REASON OF RACE. NBC/EE 1973. J-S-C-A. 51 min col. Rental $19.75; purchase $500.

This film, an NBC documentary in which the American conscience looks back at the internment of Japanese Americans during World War II, has attracted a great deal of attention. Beautiful photography and candid interviews sustain interest.

HAWAII—POLYNESIA IN THE U.S.A. CCM 1972. P-El. 17 min col. Purchase $250.

Explores the contrasting life in Hawaii today; set against the historical past of its discovery by Captain Cook, the reign of Kamehemehan, and the early missionaries who played an important role in changing the lives of the people.

HAWAII'S ASIAN HERITAGE. NEW/PEI 1966. El-J-S-C. 21 min col. Rental $24; purchase $240.

This film provides its audiences with some of the flavor of the various Asian cultures—Japanese, Korean, Filipino—from which half of Hawaii's present population has sprung. *Hawaii's Asian Heritage* is designed to show in vivid and authentic detail some of the surviving practices and ceremonials—the dances, the religious rites, the home and public ceremonies, and the athletic and recreational activities.

HAWAII'S HISTORY: KINGDOM TO STATEHOOD. BCB/USC-ISC 1960. El-J-S. 13 min col. Rental $8.

A history of our Island State. The gradual changes in ways of living from the days of natural kingdom to today's modern American community are shown. The culture from contact with New England whalers and missionaries, the growth of large plantations, and the United States' need for naval bases are also included.

HIRAM FONG. MGH 1970. P-El. 15 min col. Rental $15; purchase $225.

Hiram Fong, the son of a poor Chinese immigrant, grew up with poverty and a lack of education. Starting to work as a shoe-shine boy, Fong vowed to himself that he would get an education and advance in the world. His decision and the challenges it presented took Fong through Harvard School of Law to a successful business and eventually to his election to the U.S. Senate, the first Oriental to occupy that position.

HO CHI MINH. CBSTV/CCM 1968. S-C-A. 26 min b&w. Purchase $300.

Shows Ho Chi Minh as the mystery man of Asia who seems to hold the future to world peace in his hands. The film traces the growth in power of this Chinese leader and gives insight into his potential for securing or eliminating world peace.

HONG KONG—CROSSROADS OF THE ORIENT. UW/UEVA 1964. El-J-S. 17 min col. Purchase $190.

Gives an insight into the only city remaining open to traffic between the Western world and Communist China and presents the numerous problems arising from the flood of refugees who have come to Hong Kong to escape through the Bamboo Curtain.

INDIA: CRAFTS AND THE CRAFTSMAN. ACI 1968. P-El-J-S. 15 min col. Rental $15; purchase $190.

Depicts the role of the craftsman in India's society and emphasizes the importance of the craft tradition in Indian culture. The film documents a number of ancient and modern crafts techniques, and at the same time interweaves the influences of tradition—religious, aesthetic, and sociological—with the changing nature of Indian life.

INDONESIA—A NEW NATION OF ASIA. EBEC 1959. J-S-A. 16 min b&w/col. Rental $7 (b&w), $11 (col); purchase $115 (b&w), $220 (col).

Traces the history of Indonesia from Dutch rule through independence. Shows life in the cities, families in villages, and examines the natural resources, religion, and art. Describes the way people live, work, think, and feel. Combines authentic settings, indigenous sound and music, and the artistry and skill of many individual craftsmen in numerous locations throughout Indonesia.

INDONESIA—THE LAND AND THE PEOPLE. CORF 1966. El-J-S. 13 min col. Rental $15; purchase $172.

This film surveys the geography and history of the islands and shows how the people are working toward building a new nation. The overview includes the climate, terrain, density of population, the traditions, the islands as a "treasure house" of crops and mineral resources, and their transition to independence.

ISLAND IN THE CHINA SEA. UK 1974. S-A. 33 min col. Rental $14 (per day), $22.40 (per week).

Tai a Chau is home for both fishermen and farmers, who live aboard small junks and use the island as a permanent harbor. The daily routines of Mr. Wong, a fisherman, and Mr. Ng, a farmer, are representative of their respective problems of survival and hopes for the future.

ISLANDS OF THE SOUTH PACIFIC. BARR/IU 1959. El-J-S. 15 min col. Rental $15; purchase $165.

An overall presentation of the physical and cultural geography of the South Pacific Islands. Origin and characteristic features of the island are explained. Film locates and identifies the continental islands of Fiji, the New Caledonia, New Zealand, Australia, and New Guinea; describes their geologic origins.

JAPAN: A NATION OF GROWING CITIES. MGH 1967. J-S-A. 17 min col. Rental $12.50; purchase $210.

This film shows Japan today—a blend of the traditional and the modern—where ancient Japanese customs are still practiced. Buddhist shrines, the tea ceremony, Sanisan music, and stylized dancing that tell of Japan's past are also shown. But Japan is also a bustling industrial country. It ranks near the top in world trade, and is, therefore, the world's number one shipbuilder. The film points out that higher wages and availability of consumer products have revolutionized Japanese life.

JAPAN: AN HISTORICAL OVERVIEW. CORF 1964. J-S. 14 min b&w/col. Rental $6.75 (b&w), $8.50 (col); purchase $82 (b&w), $164 (col).

This film traces the major events in this nation's long history, from the clan society of about 800 B.C. to today's parliamentary government; emphasizes the twin themes of traditional and modern Japan; traces the influence of Buddhism and other cultural elements from Asia; and views the impact of Western culture and technology.

JAPAN—AN INTRODUCTION. BFA 1968. El-J-S-A. 17 min col. Rental $12.50; purchase $195.

Presents Japan as a highly industrialized nation against the background of centuries-old cultural traditions. Shows the development of industry from the available resources to modern shipbuilding and manufacturing enterprises. Film emphasizes the maximum use the Japanese people make of all resources, especially electricity.

JAPAN: EAST IS WEST. MGH 1963. J-S-A. 23 min col. Rental $12.50; purchase $270.

This film shows the ferment created by the impact of Western culture on Japan. Rapid economic changes have accompanied the social and cultural upheaval in modern Japan. Industry is expanding and changing in a way that no one could foresee, and mechanization has spread to agriculture. In contrast with the Westernization of the large cities, we see examples of the country's traditional culture in Kyoto, the ancient capital; its gardens, the Noh drama, and the puppet theatre.

JAPANESE AMERICAN, THE. HFC 1970. El-S-C-A. 30 min col. Rental $30; purchase $375.

Narrated by Ken Kashwahara, this film traces the Japanese Empire's two hundred years of isolation until Commodore Perry came to Japan. This film relates the migration of the Japanese to Hawaii and the U.S. mainland. The anti-Japanese laws passed in Congress, the Pearl Harbor period, and the contributions of Japanese Americans to American culture are presented.

JAPANESE BOY—THE STORY OF TARO. EBEC 1963. El-J. 20 min b&w/col. Rental $9 (b&w), $13.50 (col); purchase $150 (b&w), $290 (col).

The story of a Japanese child who loses a friend, gains a treasured possession, and learns that growing up often means sacrificing one end to gain another. The film shows a Japanese home and school, revealing the attitudes, customs, and problems of a farm family.

JAPANESE VILLAGE. HOLCOMB/HOL 1965. P-El-J-S. 17 min col. Rental $25; purchase $235.

This handsomely photographed film provides an interesting and perceptive analysis of a Japanese village. It explores the environment, the lives, the traditions, and the interfamily relationships of the people living there.

JAPAN—HARVESTING THE LAND AND SEA. EBEC 1963. El-J-S. 28 min col. Rental $12.50; purchase $360.

The fate of the Japanese people on the restricted land area of Japan is largely tied to the proficiency with which they extract food from the sea, as well as the land. This film portrays a typical day in a small fishing village through the life of one Japanese family.

JAPAN: MIRACLE IN ASIA. EBEC/IU 1963. El-J-S-A. 29 min b&w/col. Rental $10 (b&w), $17 (col); purchase $185 (b&w), $360 (col).

Documents the industrial revolution in Japan following the close of World War II to the present as a direct result of the change to a democratic form of government and their development of world trade. Shows sequences in several factories and industries to illustrate the highly modernized methods of mechanism, and the adoption of Western methods and customs.

JAPAN: PACIFIC NEIGHBOR. BFA 1972. El-J-S-A. 16 min col. Rental $10; purchase $170.

Discusses Japan's transportation, education, religion, industries, city and farm life. Shows that Japan faces a challenge because of her climate and growing population. Japan is shown as a land of mountains surrounded by sea and how the Japanese have adapted to their environment.

JAPAN'S GEOGRAPHY—HUMAN AND ECONOMIC. HRW/SF 1962. P-El-J-S. 14 min col. Purchase $165.

Japan is pictured in a panorama that highlights its age-old topography and modern, changing economy. From the Green Boso Peninsula to the hubbub of the congested railway confluence in urban Tokyo, the country is pictured in all its unique beauty.

JAPAN'S NEW FAMILY PATTERNS. SF/IU 1962. P-El-J-S. 16 min col. Rental $8; purchase $190.

This film shows a middle-class family as they go about their tasks at home and at work, living a life which daily demands adjustments from the old to the new. The modern life and new life-style for this Kyoto, Japanese family calls for adjustments from the old life.

KYUDO: JAPANESE CEREMONIAL ARCHERY. ACI 1970. J-S-A. 10 min col. Rental $15; purchase $130.

A study of archery as a discipline of mind and body, as taught in the classes of Kyonobu Ogasawara. Kyudo is a vigorous discipline, heavily dependent on the mastery of controlled breathing that sets the rhythm of the bow and arrow. This film is designed to further the appreciation of oriental culture.

LAST TRIBES OF MINDANAO, THE. BEE/FI 1972. J-S-C-A. 52 min col. Rental $25; purchase $260.

This is the National Geographic television special which describes the plight of the millions of almost forgotten people who, for centuries, were peaceful family farmers, but who are now being pushed aside, from their footholds in the rugged mountains and ignored by landgrabbers, and mining and lumbering interests.

LIFE OF A PHILIPPINE FAMILY. BEE 1957. P-El. 11 min col. Rental $4.50.

A Philippine family of a farm village illustrates the simple means by which these people meet their needs. The father tells of the daily life of the family as seen through his eyes; his work in the rice fields; his children's chores, schooling, and games; and finally, a birthday celebration for his son, Ramon.

MALAYA, LAND OF TIN AND RUBBER. EBEC 1957. J-S. 14 min b&w/col. Rental $6 (b&w), $9 (col); purchase $95 (b&w), $185 (col).

Presents a survey of life in the rain forests of the Malayan Peninsula; production of latex, mining and processing of tin ore are illustrated. Activities on the island of Singapore show reasons why this country is important to world trade.

MAO TSE-TUNG. MGM 1964. S-C-A. 26 min b&w. Rental $5.30; purchase $235.

Introduces Mao Tse-tung as head of the Chinese Communist Party which joined the Kumintang government of Sun Yat-sen. Mao joins forces briefly with anti-Communist government leader Chiang Kai-shek to fight against the anti-Communist government. In 1949 Mao Tse-tung's Communists control all of China and form an uneasy alliance with the Soviet Union.

MARCO POLO'S TRAVELS. EBEC 1955. P-El-J-S. 19 min b&w/col. Rental $9; purchase $95 (b&w), $185 (col).

Portrays the life of Marco Polo. Describes his famous adventure to the East and life in China under Kublai Khan. This film may be considered somewhat of a classic even though it is an older film.

MASUO IKEDA: PRINTMAKER. ACI 1973. J-S-A. 14 min col. Rental $15; purchase $190.

A modern Japanese artist living in New York creates a color print from copper plates as he explains how he finds ideas and how he creates his prints. His procedure and tools are shown in close-up detail as he makes the plates. A montage of many of his prints demonstrates the work of a master of contemporary art. Awards: CINE GOLDEN EAGLE, fall 1973; first runner-up, Seventh Annual Brooklyn Film Festival, 1974.

MUSIC AND DANCE OF THE BAGOBO AND MANOBO PEOPLES OF MINDANAO. UW 1971. S–A. 12 min col. Rental $6; purchase $175.

These Bagobo and Manobo peoples live on the west coast of the Gulf of Davao. They are among those who were not converted to Islam, as were the people of many other parts of Mindanao; and they have preserved earlier styles of music and dance in their culture. Their gong ensemble consists of a large gong, used for keeping rhythm, while a number of smaller gongs, fixed in a network of ropes hanging from trees or posts, are played melodically.

MUSIC AND DANCE OF THE HILL PEOPLE OF THE NORTHERN PHILIPPINES. UW 1971. S–A. 29 min col. Rental $15; purchase $275.

In the mountains of northern Luzon there are great numbers of different people who did not succumb to the waves of Hispanic culture that influenced the lowland and coastal people of the Philippines. In this region, a number of different types of gong playing, singing, and dancing have survived, of which this film features eleven performances. A solo on a bamboo tube zither is also presented.

NEPAL HIMALAYAN KINGDOM. HOLCOMB/HOL 1960. El–J–S. 18 min col. Rental $25; purchase $250.

Filmed in the mighty Himalayas, this film captures the essential factors which make the Nepalese culture what it is. Very fine photography reveals the character and beauty of the Nepalese and their remote medieval world. Excellent content and technical quality; highly recommended.

NEW AGE IN JAPAN. UPMPD 1968. S–C. 20 min col. Rental $5.

A series of visual and auditory images of modern Japan. Traditional Buddhism and Shinto coexist with Christianity and neo-Buddhist groups. Religious and political ideologies claim the devotion and energies of the Japanese people while guiding their destinies.

NISEI, THE: THE PRIDE AND THE SHAME. ABFI 1965. S–C–A. 26 min b&w. Rental $11.50; purchase $150.

An account of the Japanese American citizens who, on a wave of war hysteria, were herded into detention camps. This film centers on a part of World War II history of which some Americans are ashamed. It is treated in a factual and objective manner.

ORIENTAL BRUSHWORK. EBEC/IU 1956. S–C. 16 min col. Rental $7.15; purchase $220.

Features the brushwork by Tyrus Wong and Chura Obata and paintings from the Freer Gallery of Art, Washington, D.C.—The Eliot O'Hara series. Includes comment on oriental contributions to art.

ORIENT, THE—PEOPLES OF ASIAN LAND. UEVA/UW 1964. El-J-S. 17 min b&w/col. Rental $24; purchase $310.

Discusses the physical and cultural features of Asian lands. Contrasts Japan with the Philippines. Also pictures the crown colony of Hong Kong.

ORIENT, THE: TOWARDS A BETTER LIFE. MGH 1969. P-El-J-S. 19 min col. Rental $24; purchase $310.

A broad-based view of the Orient and the problems which are facing its ever-increasing population. The area suffers from three main deficiencies: lack of food, industry, and education. As a result, the populations of such nations as China and India spiral, while the inability to feed and clothe people remains unchanged. Oriental leaders hope that education will produce a generation which will be able to employ the Orient's vast natural resources to overcome their problems.

PEARL S. BUCK. NBCTV/FI 1960. S-A. 10 min b&w. Purchase $150.

Miss Buck describes her childhood in China, pointing out the basic differences between the Western and oriental approaches to living. She discusses the changes that have been taking place under the Communist regime in China and considers ways in which America may recover the goodwill which has been lost in Asia during recent years.

PEOPLE OF MALAYSIA. AVED 1964. S-C. 15 min col. Rental $10.

Emphasizes the social, economic, and religious backgrounds of the ten million East Asians in this new parliamentary democracy. Changes in recent years make this film somewhat outdated, but it is sufficiently accurate in its historical content.

PEOPLE OF PEOPLE'S CHINA, THE. ABC/XEROX 1975. S-C-A. 52 min col. Purchase $500.

This film presents interviews with representative Chinese in city and countryside and affords rare, penetrating views of the world's most populous nation. Distinguishes between official propaganda and actualities of life in China today.

PEOPLE OF THE ISLAND WORLD. HOE 1967. P-El-J-S. 17 min col. Purchase $280.

Describes how the islands of the South and Central Pacific were originally populated by three major groups of native people—the Melanesians, the Micronesians, and the Polynesians. Shows their movement to Australia from Asia and their migrating in fragile canoes to the islands to the north, east, and south.

PEOPLE OF THE PHILIPPINES. CFD/BEE 1964. P-El-J-S. 20 min col. Rental $8.

Depicts life in the Philippines among the three distinctive cultural minority groups: the Negritos, the Ifugaos, and the Muslim Moros. Contrasts old with new industrial methods in the Philippines. Shows chief crops of abaca, pineapple, and rice.

PHILIPPINES: GATEWAY TO THE FAR EAST. CORF/BEE 1957. P-El-J-C. 11 min col. Rental $4.50; purchase $500.

The past history, present activities, and direction of future growth in the Philippines form a picture of a young republic with many interests similar to those of the United States. Views of farm and city life show a wealth of raw materials, expanding production, and increased education.

PHILIPPINES: LAND AND PEOPLE. EBEC. P-El-J. 14 min b&w/col. Rental $6 (b&w), $9 (col); purchase $95 (b&w), $185 (col).

Reviews the history of the Philippine islands under Spanish and American rule, and shows the country today—almost entirely agricultural—with sequences of the people in their rural villages.

PHILIPPINES, THE: ISLAND REPUBLIC. MGH 1967. P-El-J-S. 16 min col. Rental $12.50; purchase $225.

Introduces viewers to the physical characteristics of the Philippine islands. It presents the Philippines as a relatively new country, successfully governing itself and achieving a stable economy, one of the richest in Southeast Asia, while still retaining its ties with America and American goods.

RED CHINA—A SERIES. ASAHIA/ICF 1969. P-El-J-S. 15 min (each) col. Rental $20; purchase $927.

A series of five films. Titles: China—Art and Leisure, China—Cities in the Transition, China—Life on the Land, China—Modernization through Human Power, China—The East Is Red.

RED CHINA DIARY WITH MORLEY SAFER. CBS 1968. S-A. 54 min b&w/col.

This film takes a first-hand look at the cultural revolution of chairman Mao Tse-tung, examines the impact of "Maoism," and covers the five principal cities in Red China. Interviews students, factory workers, and aggressive members of the Red Guard.

RICE. IU/MGH 1965. S-C. 30 min col. Rental $18; purchase $325.

This film shows how rice is cultivated in some of those countries where it is of prime importance as a staple and a commodity; includes scenes in the Philippines. Explains how the International Rice Research Institute hopes, through science and education, to point the way to a better life for the people of rice-producing countries.

RICE IN TODAY'S WORLD. CORF/IU 1958. J-S-C. 11 min b&w/col. Rental $3.15 (b&w), $4.75 (col); purchase $65 (b&w), $130 (col).

Discusses the importance of rice as a major food crop of the world and shows the rice-producing areas around the globe, with particular attention to the Orient. Factors contributing to rice growing are explained such as proper climate, water supply, and terrain.

SAMPAN FAMILY. IFF 1949. P-El-S-A. 16 min b&w. Rental $16; purchase $160.

Presents the daily activities of the Ling family who navigate the Min River in Fukien Province. Shows how Chinese families live and make a living aboard sampans. Presents the family's daily fishing activities, the housekeeping chores, preparation of food, and the entire family rowing the boat to the night's anchorage.

SAN FRANCISCO. EKC 1970. El-J-S. 31 min col. Rental $6.
Panorama of life in San Francisco. This film emphasizes the exotic aspects of cultural mixtures including the Chinese elements. Includes a brief historical sketch and shows the role of modern San Francisco in relation to the Chinese populace.

SHINTOISM. ICF 1968. J-S-C. 15 min col. Rental $22; purchase $240.50.
Studies the Shinto religion in Japan, explaining its division into two sects. Shows the results of the division in their religious practices. (A new edition entitled *Buddhism and Shintoism* is now available—1975 release.)

SIAM: THE PEOPLE OF THAILAND. DISNEY 1958. J-S-A. 31 min col. Rental $10.
A comprehensive survey of the people of Siam (Thailand). Their work, play, government, and customs are presented. The viewer gains an understanding of the problems of Siam as they see the people in their day-to-day chores.

"SIU MEI WONG—WHO SHALL I BE." LCA. P-El. 18 min col. Rental $20; purchase $220.
The story of a young Chinese girl from Hong Kong who has been in America for three years. She wants to be a ballerina but the question "Am I Chinese or Am I American?" causes her problems as she finds herself in conflict with her father who clings to the traditions of his heritage. From "The Many Americans" series.

SOUTHEAST ASIA FAMILY. BFA 1966. P-El-J. 15 min col. Rental $10; purchase $170.
This film shows the Sen family of Thailand at work, school, and church. Shows how hot, humid climate helps produce rice and other crops which are important to the livelihood of the people.

SOUTHEAST ASIA GEOGRAPHY. BFA 1967. P-El-J-S. 21 min col. Rental $10; purchase $225.
Shows how the land and climatic features of Southeast Asia affect its people by determining the crops that can be grown and the natural resources that are available. Describes the political importance of the city of Singapore and the countries of Burma, Thailand, Cambodia, and Malaya.

SOUTHERN ASIA—PROBLEMS OF TRANSITION. BARR 1969. J-S-A. 16 min col. Rental $15; purchase $180.
Shows how the culture of southern Asia differs from the Western world. Explores the traditions, attitudes, and conditions which affect modernization and reveals the complex problems of Asia.

SUMI ARTIST. LP 1955. J-S. 12 min col. Purchase $190.

Chuira Obata is one of the few Sumi artists in the United States. Dressed in native costume and painted in typical Japanese fashion, Mr. Obata creates scenes of memorable beauty with his flashing brushes. He reveals the various strokes and exhibits the different kinds of brushes used. Finished examples of his paintings are displayed.

THAILAND, LAND OF RICE. EBEC 1957. 14 min b&w. Purchase $95 (b&w), $185 (col).

Presents Thailand from the city of Bangkok—center of commerce, government, and the spiritual life of the nation—to the fertile river valley in which abundant rice crops are produced. Shows rice farming, the life-style of a typical farm family, the floating market on Bangkok canals, and the busy traffic in Bangkok harbor.

THREE ISLAND WOMEN. UK 1974. S-A. 17 min col. Rental $10 (per day), $16 (per week).

A young, middle-aged, and an old woman all agree that life on a small Chinese island in Hong Kong waters is better for them now than in the past. Participating fully in the island's decision making and economic life, they also share equally with men the rigors of manual labor.

TROUBLE WITH CHINATOWN. NBCTV 1970. El-J-S. 26 min col. Purchase $200.

Discusses the massive wave of immigration and a restless, younger generation among the Chinese, who are beginning to examine their traditional isolation. Presents ways to deal with new problems of a rapidly changing social structure through such solutions as bilingual professional groups to deal with the problems of housing, employment, family counseling, and legal assistance.

WATER PEOPLE OF HONG KONG. UW/UEVA 1959. P-El. 10 min b&w. Purchase $130.

Shows how the people living on sampans have dealt with the tasks of providing food, clothing, and shelter for their families amid the crowded harbor of Hong Kong. Shows one family fishing, performing daily chores, and going to a wedding.

Filmstrips

AGRICULTURE AND RURAL LIFE. MARSH 1972. El-J-S-A. col. LC FIA66-2521: 64 frs.

Shows photos taken from behind the Great Wall of China in 1971. Illustrates life in the People's Republic of China today and shows the similarities and differences between their way of life and the American way of life.

ARTS IN EVERYDAY LIFE IN JAPAN SERIES, AN ANTHROPOLOGICAL STUDY IN DEPTH. SCHLAT 1968. P-El-J. col. 49 frs. With record $116.50; with cassettes $142.

This in-depth anthropological study uses sound with pictures to show the origin and definition of art in Japan.

ASIAN FOLK TALES. LLL/IBC 1969. K-P. col. LO 78-73320, 50 frs each.
Presents Asian folktales with morals; emphasizes the similarities among cultures; and introduces the Asian character and culture. Titles: Kantjil the Mouse Deer (Indonesia); Koolookata (India); The Magic Leaf (Vietnam); The Man Who Cut the Cinnamon Tree (China); One-Inch Fellow (Japan); and The Sandalmaker (Japan).

ASIAN WORLD GEOGRAPHY. MGH 1969. J-S-C-A. col. Set 1— No. 633610-7: 5 captioned filmstrips with guide and catalog cards $40.50; Set 2— No. 633616-6: 5 captioned filmstrips with catalog cards $40.50; individually $9.
A view of life in seven Asian countries, presented in the form of open-ended questions which encourage students to draw their own conclusions. Emphasis is on traditional and modern cultural factors involved in the social changes taking place in each of the countries. Information concerning each nation is presented topically, so that basic concepts of society, geography, and culture can be fully developed. Titles (Set 1): Thailand: The Beginnings of Progress; A Look at India Today; Japan: Feeding the People; Japan: A Nation of Cities; and Japan: An Industrial Giant. Titles (Set 2): Pakistan: The Dry West; Pakistan: The Humid East; Malaysia; Afghanistan: Progress Amid Tradition, and Philippine Republic.

ASIA'S ECONOMIC SUPERPOWER. CA 1974. J-S-A. b&w/col. Purchase $20; $22.
Japan has become an economic power of first magnitude exerting great influence on international developments. Japanese firms are investing in American and European industries, and Japanese products are competing in world markets.

ASIA'S FIRST SUPERPOWER. CA 1974. J-S-A. b&w/col. Purchase $20; $22.
China's impact on the international scene is not commensurate with her huge population. Is she a helpless giant? Or is she on her way to becoming a superpower? This filmstrip attempts to explore these questions.

BANGKOK—CITY OF THE KLONGS. AIM 1966. El-J-S. LO FIA68-4761: 46 frs $5.
Presents photographs of the city of Bangkok, including views of modern streets and buildings, ancient means of transportation, the Royal Palace and temples, the emerald Buddha, and the Temple of Wat Arun. Pictures the life of Buddhist monks as well as life on the Klongs.

BOYS AND GIRLS OF BURMA. ABF/FRPR, revised 1969. P-El-J. col. 68 frs with discs $6.
Presents a view of Burma through the eyes of children.

CHANGING SKYLINES IN ASIA. YALEDV. El-J. col. 87 frs with discs and teacher's guide. Rental $6.

Shows involvement of church people in cultural, political, and religious changes along the east rim of East Asia, including Korea, Taiwan, Quemoy, and Hong Kong.

CHILDREN OF ASIA. SCHLAT 1969. P-El. col. LC 70-732845: 52 frs with discs.
Uses UNICEF art to illustrate various customs and cultures of the different peoples of Asia.

CHINA, CONTRASTS AND CONTINUITIES. UPMPD. J-S-C. col. 141 frs with discs and teacher's guide $7.50.
Shows life and landscape of China in a mosaic of harshness and beauty. Much of China is shown as it always has been. Most of what moves is moved by muscle—even in coal and steel production the handcart and the bicycle predominate.

CHINA IN PERSPECTIVE: ROOTS OF CIVILIZATION. GA 1970. J-S-C. col. LC 76-737584. 2 filmstrips with discussion guide. No. 3D-403 391: with two 12″ LP records $41.50; No. 3D-403 509: with 2 cassettes $46.50.
Traces history from early dynasties through twentieth century; stresses central role of peasant; reviews demography, geography, culture, art, and events leading to Communist rule. Produced in cooperation with the Associated Press.

CHINA IN THE MODERN WORLD. EAV. 4 filmstrips. No. 99RF 467: with 4 LP records $60; No. 99KF 468: with 4 cassettes $68.
This filmstrip describes and analyzes the changes that have taken place in China during the past 150 years, the period that began with the Western "invasion" of China's previously isolated society. Focusing on political history, the set traces the evolution of the Chinese nation from the fall of the Manchu dynasty, through the protracted struggle that brought the Communists to power in 1949, to the present day with a detailed look at the People's Republic.

CHINA JOINS THE WORLD. NYT 1972. J-S-A. b&w. Discs.
Examines Communist China as the third power in world diplomacy; discusses why China has abandoned its policy of isolation; and considers the implications of its new policy for world peace. From "Filmstrip On Current Affairs" series.

CHINA NOW. DISNEY 1973. S-C-A. col. 4 filmstrips. Avg 62 frs, 15 min each. With 4 records or 4 cassettes, 4 paperback books, source book, political map, and teacher's guide $84.
Covering all major aspects of life today on the Chinese mainland with special emphasis on the impact of Mao Tse-tung's leadership, this program traces the rise of communism in China over the past twenty years and contrasts life today wih life before Mao's regime. Titles: The Long March to Unity; The Human Side; Meeting the People's Needs; and Ideas in Action.

CHINA: PEOPLE, PLACES, AND PROGRESS. SED 1974. El-J-S. col. Each 62 frs $79.
Each filmstrip follows a boy, girl, or family through one or more days of their lives in modern China and Hong Kong. They are seen at home, work, school, play, and in special places dictated by the locale of the filmstrip. Titles: Peking:

The Capital City; Dahli Commune: A Communal Farm and Fish Nursery; Kwangchow: A River Port; Tientsin: A Suburb of the City; Shanghai: An Industrial City; and Hong Kong: The Floating Population.

CHINA REGIONAL GEOGRAPHY SERIES. MGH 1968. J–S. col. No. 633650-6: complete series, 6 captioned filmstrips with guide and catalog cards $49; individually $9.

Emphasizing the changes which have occurred in China during the twentieth century, these filmstrips compare the major physical and sociological differences between South China and West China. The various methods of farming in each region are discussed, and questions about the industrial future of China are raised. The significance of rivers, art, and architecture in development of the culture is also presented. Titles: China: Rivers and Canals; China: Industry; China: Its People; China: Art and Architecture; China: An Overview of South, North, and West; and China: Farming.

CHINA'S NEW LOOK. NYT/TERF 1974. El–J–S. col. 10 filmstrips, 55 frs each with teacher's guide. With 5 LP records $129; with 5 tape cassettes $129.

Based on recent material that has become available through the news-gathering resources of the *New York Times*, this comprehensive new look at the People's Republic of China offers students firsthand appraisals of China today. Through this researched ten-unit filmstrip program, a total picture of modern China emerges that captures its dynamism, ambition, dedication, and complexity. Titles: Cultural Heritage; Peasantry: A Way of Life; Years of Revolution; Geographic Diversity; City Scenes and Sights; Progress Through Industry; Agricultural Challenges; Educational Goals; Life-Styles in the Cities; and Peking and the Forbidden City.

CHINA TODAY: AS SEEN THROUGH THE EYES OF A TYPICAL CHINESE FAMILY. SPA 1973. C–A. col. No. SA 2019: with 6 LP records $110; No. SAC 2019: with 6 cassettes $120.

Part 1: China's Yesterdays. A survey of China's four-thousand-year history based on photographs of temple carvings, tomb furnishings, archeological finds, and precious artifacts. Part 2: The Revolution. How the People's Republic of China emerged from a war-torn feudal society. The roles played by the Red Army, Mao Tse-tung, and Chou En-lai. Part 3: China's Communes. The story of the unique collective farms as told firsthand by a young agricultural worker. Part 4: Transportation and Flood Control. A look at the amazing contrasts in Chinese transportation from square-sailed sampans and water buffalo to jet planes and diesel locomotives. How the Chinese rivers untamed for 4,000 years are tamed, and are now the servants of the new Chinese agriculture. Part 5: City Life in the People's Republic. How people work and live in the cities; the role of women; the care of children; schools; and the new housing projects. Part 6: Culture and Sports. How the people spend their leisure time. A survey of the Chinese theater, dance, and dynamic program of athletics.

CHINATOWN. SCHMAG 1972. K–P. col. LO 74-732898: 66 frs with audio tape.

Presents an account of family life in Chinatown, U.S.A. From "Five Families" series.

CHINA: TWENTY YEARS OF REVOLUTION. EBEC 1974. J-S-C. col. 5 sound filmstrips with teacher's guide. No. 64321: with records $58.50, individually $13; No. 6432K: with cassettes $67.28, individually $14.95.

This unique film series was shot in China by permission of the Chinese government. The colorful photography keynotes the revolutionary changes in China today in the areas of art, education, industry, use of the land, and the people themselves. Authentic music from the People's Republic of China adds a definitive note which accompanies the narration about "Mao's China." Students see a country on the move; an insular state dramatically emerging into a potential world power. Titles: China: The Revolution and the People; China: The Revolution and the Arts; China: The Revolution in the Schools; China: The Revolution on the Land; and China: The Revolution in Industry.

CHINESE AND JAPANESE ART. RAINAGE/FILMST 1967. S-A. col. 63 frs.

Portrays Chinese and Japanese art through the works of K. O. Jan, Chi Pai-Shih, Jui, Yao, Hodusai, Sharaku, Gyokundo, and many others. From "Book of Art" filmstrip series No. 9.

CHINESE ART. SCHLAT 1973. S-C-A. col. No. T240: 3 sound filmstrips with program guide. Avg 80 frs, 16 min each. With cassettes $72; with discs $63.

Traces the art and culture of China from her most ancient dynasties to today's People's Republic, illustrating how the religions and philosophies of the Chinese are interwoven in the development of her artistic creations. Part 1: European discovery of China, early development, religious influence, animal symbolism, and unification of China. Part 2: Han dynasty, Shang dynasty, Buddhism, Tai-Ping Rebellion, "Great Period," and the Communist takeover. Part 3: Painting styles and techniques, Taoist influence, Tang and Sung dynasty paintings, and the synthesis of old and new styles in painting.

CHINESE FOLKTALES. CORF 1973. P-El. col. 6 filmstrips, avg 49 frs, 9 min each. No. S 267: with 3 records $69; No. M 267: with 6 cassettes $77.

Animated characters, authentic Chinese music, and sound effects blend realism with fantasy to help children discover the beauty of the Orient. Age-old themes and subjects include greed, selfishness, generosity, and courage. Titles: The Heavenly Flower Man; The Magic Brocade; The Three Hairs of the Buddha; A Strange Case of Gems; Lo-Sun; The Blind Boy and the Clear Man and The Landlord.

CHINESE POETRY. SCHLAT 1966. El-J-S. col. No. T241: 2 sound filmstrips with program guide. Avg 95 frs, 14 min each. With discs $44; with cassettes $50.

A presentation of the literature and culture of the People's Republic of China reflecting the thoughts and true feelings of an ancient yet ever-changing society. Part 1: Folk song origins of Chinese poetry; recurrent themes and devices; excerpts from "East Gate Willow," "Spirit of the Mountain," and "Book of Songs"; selections from works of Li Shang-yin, Tu Fu, Wang Wei, Li Po, Li

Ch'ing-chao, and Pai Ch'iu. Part 2: Western discovery of China; parallels between literary and social revolution; selections from the works of Dr. Hu Shih, Hsu Chih-mo, Kuo Mo-jo, Mao Tse-tung, Ai Ching, and Yu Kwang-chung.

CHINESE TALES. SCHLAT 1973. P. col. Avg 73 frs.

Presents Chinese tales followed by postscripts which concern some cultural aspects of China. Titles: Clever Girl and the Marvelous Wedding Jacket; The Great Quest of Yenkang; Kan-Han and the Evil Dragon; and The Magic Brush of Po Ling.

CIVILIZATIONS OF THE EAST. EDC 1973. S-C-A. col. No. 1022: 2 sound filmstrips, 18 min each. With 2 LP records $41; with 2 cassettes $45.

An introduction to major Asian cultures: Islam, India, China, and Japan. Examines art, architecture, literature, and social institutions, with special emphasis on differences and similarities between each civilization.

COUNTRIES OF SOUTHEAST ASIA—BURMA—MALAYSIA AND THAILAND. EGH 1963. P-El-J-S. col. Avg 52 frs. With cassette $80; with disc $79.

Presents the basic factors of life, including social and economic conditions of each country. Titles: Burma, Industries and Transportation; Burma, the Land; Burma, the People and Their Cities; Malaysia, Singapore; Malaysia, the Land and the People; Thailand, Industries; Thailand, the Land and the Cities; and Thailand, the People.

DISCOVERING TODAY'S CHINA. NYT 1973. J-S-C. col. 2 filmstrips. Avg 87 frs, 14 min each. With 2 records or 2 cassettes, 4 paperback books, political map, and teacher's guide with spirit duplicator masters $54.

Program focuses on three major concepts—change, culture, and environment. The color photos for the filmstrips and books were taken on the Chinese mainland by photo correspondents for the *Toronto Globe and Mail.* Titles: Challenge and Change; and Building a New Society.

EVERYDAY LIFE IN JAPAN. IFB 1965. P-El-J-S. col. 35 frs.

Depicts everyday life in Japan. Shows how this nation is dependent on the exchange of manufacturing services for its imports of raw materials and foods for its people.

EVERYDAY LIFE OF THE CHINESE—HONG KONG. HUL 1970. J-S-A. col. 23 frs.

Pictures life in Hong Kong, including views of rice fields, growing grain, Buddhist monasteries, villages, a funeral , and a wedding.

FAMILY LIFE IN JAPAN. DOUBLE/SCHLAT 1972. J-S-A. col. 49 frs with discs $13.50 and $15.50.

This filmstrip describes Japanese homes, family life, etiquette, food, clothing, and various customs such as removing one's shoes before entering a home, flower arrangement, the tea ceremony, and respect for one's elders.

FAMILY OF CENTRAL ASIA. EBEC 1966. P-El. col. 49 frs $10.

This filmstrip gives an interesting view of the way people live in Central Asia. It is narrated in captions by a child of that area whose family helps to explain what is seen. From "Families of Other Lands" series.

FOUR FAMILIES OF JAPAN. BFA 1972. El. col. 4 sound filmstrips. Avg 85 frs each. No. VN 200: with cassettes $68; No. VN 1000: with discs $56.

Four children and their families are the means of comparing differences and similarities in food, clothing, shelter, family life, and socioeconomic conditions in Japan. Although the families' social and economic conditions are diverse, they stem from a common culture and history, and their life-styles reflect today's Japan. Titles: Rice Farm Family; Factory Town Family; Tokyo Suburb Family; and Fishing Community Family.

FROM UPPER ROOM TO CROWDED STREET. ABF/FP 1968. S-C-A. col. 70 frs with record $10.

Depicts the crowded streets of Hong Kong and the complex needs of the Chinese refugees. Shows how the Christian workers are helping with refugee problems. Buddhists are shown at a center which serves as a place of meditation and renewal for missionaries in Hong Kong.

FUNNY LITTLE WOMAN, THE. WWSI 1973. El. col. 38 frs. With disc $9.20; with cassette $12.75.

Long ago in old Japan lived a funny little woman who liked nothing better than to make rice dumplings and to laugh. When her dumpling rolled through a hole in the floor, she discovered a strange land inhabited by wicked and fearful Oni. The little woman's adventure with these creatures is based on a tale by Lafcadio Hearn.

HONG KONG—AN HISTORIC PORT. AF 1966. El-J. col. 46 frs.

Views Hong Kong, showing shops, rickshas, Tiger Balm Gardens, upper-class homes, life in the harbor, the walled town of Kam-Tin, the shore line, farms, and the Chinese frontier. Pictures the poverty of Hong Kong, with views of refugee apartments, primitive sanitation, shack city, and squatters.

IFUGAO TRIBE OF THE PHILIPPINES, THE. BEE. El-J. col. 124 frs, 2 filmstrips with 2 cassettes and guide $43.

In Ifugao Province in the mountains of northern Luzon live a people who have reshaped their mountainsides with remarkable terraces to provide fields for growing their rice. Part 1: Customs and Rituals describes ritual feasts, spirit-world beliefs, marriage, and funeral customs. Part 2: Subsistence Economy documents the life-style of these people showing their dependence on water and their inventive way of retaining this precious resource for the growth of their principal food, rice.

INDONESIA. POPSCI 1965. El-J-S. col. 41 frs.

Discusses the geography and history of Indonesia; explains the diversity in customs and traditions; the presence of vast underdeveloped resources; and the influence of education in developing national unity.

IN THE LAND OF FUJISAN. UPMPD 1968. P-El-J. col. Sound filmstrip, 92 frs. Filmstrip with record $10; with script only $7.50.

Today's Japan springs into colorful reality through the vivid contrasts between traditional life and Japan's phenomenal modernization.

INTRODUCTION TO JAPAN. DOUBLE 1963. J-S-C. col. 107 frs with 33⅓ rpm disc (audible tone and inaudible tone for automatic changer).

In this sound filmstrip are seen miniature gardens, doll-like girls in delicate kimonos, bright parasols, cherry blossoms, a tea ceremony, flower arrangements, old temples and shrines, and the majestic cone of Mount Fuji. Beside these aspects of Japan exists a jet-age nation—massive traffic jams, the active harbor, and always the pressure of the vast population. The faces of the factory worker and craftsman, the fisherman and farmer, the pretty children, a city secretary and her boss, the bank manager, a lovely geisha and a Kabuki actor, and the non-Japanese "Hairy Ainu" of Hokkaido are shown as representative of this nation of 94 million people.

INTRODUCTION TO SOUTH VIETNAM. DOUBLE 1969. J-S-C. col. 56 frs with 33⅓ rpm disc (audible tone and inaudible tone for automatic changer).

This is a pictorial study of the people of this Asian country and the war-torn land in which they live—the Mekong Delta area, the Coastal Plain, and the Highland Plateau. Here is the backbone of the population, the families who till the soil and who are ready to fight for that soil. The filmstrip covers Saigon, the capital of South Vietnam, and the people who live and work there. In contrast to this metropolis is the life in a Montagnard mountain village and a town in the Delta.

INTRODUCTION TO SOVIET CENTRAL ASIA. DOUBLEDAY MULTIMEDIA 1957. J-S-C. col. No. 78231: 70 frs with record $8.50.

Surveys the three countries that comprise Soviet Central Asia with emphasis on ancient art and architecture, modern machinery, collective farming, and education.

INTRODUCTION TO THE PHILIPPINES. BEE 1969. J-S. col. New, revised, 70 frs with sound and new study guide. With disc $9; with cassette $11.

Views the culture and life of the Philippine people.

JAPAN. DOUBLE 1971. P-El-J. col. 6 filmstrips. Avg 71 frs. $73.50; $85.50.

A series of six filmstrips which considers such varied aspects of Japanese culture as food, clothing, shelter, religion, customs, and traditions. The geography, industry, agriculture, transportation, communications, recreational activities, and art of Japan are also explored. Titles: Art and Recreation in Japan; The Geography and Climate of Japan; Festivals and Religious Customs in Japan; The Industries of Japan; Transportation and Communication in Japan; and Family Life in Japan.

JAPAN: A CHANGING NATION. NYT/TERF 1974. P-El-J-S. col. 6 filmstrips, 50 frs each, with teacher's guide. No. 410320: with 3 LP records $78; No. 410321: with 3 tape cassettes $78.

This filmstrip tour vividly captures the vitality of Japan. The new Japan remains in many ways the old Japan of the Buddhist and Shinto rituals, the emperor and the geisha girl; however, sweeping changes in all areas of Japanese life have permanently altered the traditional face of Japan. Through this penetrating appraisal of its people, cities, social structures and social concerns, economy, religions, and art, the total Japan becomes comprehensible to the viewer. Titles: The Japanese Way of Life; Farmers, Fishermen and Craftsmen of Japan; Japan Becomes a World Power; Young People of Japan; Cities of Japan; and Art and Religion in Everyday Life.

JAPAN: ASIA'S ECONOMIC SUPERPOWER. SSSS. J–S–C. col. 1 filmstrip with teacher's guide. No CA366R: with 1 LP record $20; No. CA366C: with 1 cassette $22.

An examination of Japan's drive to influence international development through economic power. Studies Japan's economic growth and Japanese investments in European and American industries. Considering Japan's rapprochement with China and its increase in defense spending, the filmstrip questions how American and Soviet influence in Asia may be affected.

JAPAN: ASIA'S MODERN POWER. BFA 1966. J. col. No. V 2 9000: 8 filmstrips. Avg 54 frs each $64.

The islands of Japan form part of the same huge sunken mountain range that creates the Aleutians and the Philippines. This overview of the geography, life, industry, and commerce of Japan covers such widely diverse areas as the volcanic growth of the islands, a day in a typical elementary school, a visit to a modern electronics factory, and the teeming traffic of downtown Tokyo.

JAPAN: A STUDY OF DEPTH. SCHLAT 1969. S–C–A. col. No. T400: sound filmstrips with program guide. Avg 50 frs, 10 min each. With discs $136; with cassettes $160.

An entertaining yet comprehensive visual essay depicting this unique nation through historical prints, engravings, silk screens, ancient paintings, and on-location photographs. The program is in eight individual sections enabling students to digest the wealth of information at their own rate. Titles: The History of Japan; The People of Japan; Social Classes in Japan; How People Earn Their Living in Japan; Family Life in Japan; Everyday Life in Japan. By Dr. Ethel J. Alpenfels, Honors Award, American Film Festival.

JAPAN: ECONOMIC MIRACLE. EBEC. P–El–J. col. No. 6907: $69.95.

The miracle which is modern Japan is explored through its geography, its history, its temperament, and the character of its people. Titles: The Physical Base; The Industrial Revolution; The Urban Explosion; Revolution in Food Supply; and Industry and Trade.

JAPAN: EMERGENCE OF A MODERN NATION (Parts 1, 2, 3). GA 1968. J–S–C. col. LC FIA-68-3723. 3 filmstrips with discussion guide. No. D-410017: with three 12″ LP records $49.50; No. 3D-410 058: with 3 cassettes $57.

Discusses ancient and modern-day life in Japan; describes the economic, political, and social life of Japan today, showing its emergence as a modern nation. American Film Festival Award.

JAPANESE—AMERICAN RELOCATION 1942. EAV. J-S-C. b&w. Kit no. 99AK 567: 2 filmstrips with LP record, 24 copies of a student booklet "Relocation Readings," 28 spirit masters, cards for use in simulation, headline cards, and catalog card kit, $70.

A multimedia unit actively involves students in a case study of one of the most extraordinary episodes in American history. It explores the causes, consequences, and implications of the evacuation and detention by the U.S. government during World War II of 110,000 residents—citizens and aliens—on the basis of their ancestry. A detailed teacher's guide provides teaching strategies for varying ability levels, background material, an annotated bibliography, and a final examination, as well as suggested research projects.

JAPANESE AMERICANS AND CHINESE AMERICANS. SCHLAT 1968. J-S-C. 70 frs. With disc $120; with cassette $138.

Tells of the lives and struggles of Japanese and Chinese families in America.

JAPANESE AMERICANS, THE: PREJUDICE IN AMERICA. SSSS. J-S-C. col. No. MM7011R: 4 filmstrips with teacher's guide. With 2 LP records $29.90; No. MM7011C: with 2 cassettes $33.90.

An examination of the American dream as seen by the Japanese immigrants and their descendants. Four units cover Asian Western immigrants, the relationship of native-born Japanese Americans to institutionalized discrimination, the chain of events that led to the evacuation camps, and the reactions of the contemporary Japanese American community to the camps and the postwar experiences. Produced in cooperation with the Japanese American Curriculum Project. A teacher's manual includes an outline and structure of the program, lesson materials, discussion questions, and an extensive bibliography. Multi-Media Productions.

JAPAN—OLD AND NEW. EGH. J-S. col. 8 filmstrips. No. TX227: with 4 cassettes $72, individually $5.95; No. DX227: with 4 records $71.25, individually $5.75; individual filmstrip $6.50.

Designed to convey information about Japan, both traditional and contemporary; to help children understand the similarities and differences of the Japanese and American civilizations; to stimulate children's interest in learning about and getting to know other cultures and peoples; and to understand their own way of life by comparing it to one that is different. Titles: Hiroshima—The Rebuilding of Japan's Cities; Economic Life; Recreation; Religion; Education: Daily Life; Old Japan; and The Countryside.

JAPAN: SPIRIT OF LEMOTO. EBEC 1969. P-El-J-S. col. No. 6908: $69.95.

The unique blend of personality traits, temperament, and respect for tradition typified by the word "Japanese" and the life-style it evokes are the subjects of these colorful filmstrips. Viewers are introduced to a typical rural Japanese family with its well-defined place in the group for each family member. Later, Japanese workers are seen in a large corporation. Titles: The Japanese Family; The Japanese at Work; The Spirit of Japan; and The Japanese at Play Lemoto.

LIVING IN CHINA TODAY. SVE 1966. El–J. col. 4 filmstrips with teacher's guide. Avg 53 frs, 13 min each. No. 288 SR: with 2 records $37.75, individually $5; No. 288 STC: with 2 cassettes, individually $6.50; individual filmstrip with teacher's guide $8.

This series depicts main aspects of life in China today. Students get an understanding of this important Asian power from on-site photos portraying current conditions. Review material following each filmstrip reinforces major topics, and recordings contain narration with background sound effects taped in China. Titles: No. 288-1: Agriculture and Rural Life. Geographic features, agricultural practices, and rural life under commune system; No. 288-2: Cities and City Life. Overview of urban life-styles, public buildings, housing, slums, products, medicine, arts, and recreation; No. 288-3; Resources, Industries, Transportation, and Communication; No. 288-4: Land of Change and Growth. Ancient and modern China, structure and functions of Communist government, aspects of "Cultural Revolution."

LIVING IN SOUTH VIETNAM. SINGER 1968. J–S. col. No. 287–SAR: 2 filmstrips with 1 record and 2 guides $18 each; filmstrip with teacher's guide $7.

Full-color photographs, specially adapted maps, and accompanying narration provide a comprehensive study of this vital world area. No. 287-1: South Vietnam: Historical Background and Modern Problems. Chinese influence on Vietnam's religious, political, and cultural development, and events leading to division of Vietnam into North and South. No. 287-2: provides an up-to-date view of present-day Vietnam and the twentieth-century influences.

MODERN EASTERN AND SOUTHEASTERN ASIA. SVE 1967. J. col. No. 290–SD: 4 captioned filmstrips. Avg 52 frs each. $22.50; individually $6.50.

Full-color photographs and specially adapted Rand McNally maps familiarize students with the countries and peoples of Eastern and Southeastern Asia. Questions at the end of each filmstrip are designed for discussion and test comprehension. Vernon W. Brockmann, Ph.D., Illinois Teacher's College, Chicago, Consultant. Titles: Modern Formosa and South Korea. Effects of dense populations, environment, and government. Modern Japan. What life is like in both city and rural areas; changes in ways of living; effects and problems of increased population. Modern Southeastern Asia. Burma, Thailand, Laos, South Vietnam, Cambodia, Malaysia, and Singapore. Importance of rivers, industries. Indonesia and the Philippines.

MUSIC OF THE EAST. EDC. S–C–A. col. No. 310: 4 sound filmstrips with 4 LP records $82; with 4 cassettes $90.

Culture and life-styles of the Eastern world are explored in music, photographs, and a rich accompanying narrative. Includes varied selections from the intriguing musical forms of both Near and Far Eastern lands.

NATIONALISM AS A FORCE IN ASIA. ABC/POPSCI 1969. S-C-A. col. LC FIA 68-4653. 43 frs.

Studies the rise of nationalism in Asia in nations which have become world trouble spots; examines colonialism and subsequent development of new colonialism by independent Asian states as a form of nationalism; and briefly discusses the commitment of the United States in Asia. From "Secondary Social Studies" series.

NEW JAPAN, THE. NYT 1973. P-El. col. 6 filmstrips with teacher's guides. No. 298-SAR: with 3 records $67.50, individually $5; No. 298-SATC: with 3 cassettes $71.50, individually $6.50, individual filmstrip with teacher's guide $10.

This study offers a perspective on the most rapidly growing nation in the world—Japan. Full-color, on-location photography, supplemented by instructional maps, authentic art and music, and authoritative narration picture Japanese people as they live and work in a highly organized and complex society. Portrays Japan as an industrial, progressive urban society; yet shows it also to be a simple agricultural country which remains deeply committed to tradition. Titles: No. 298-1: Tokyo: World's Largest City; No. 298-2: A Traditional Japanese Family; No. 298-3: Japan's Life from the Sea; No 298-4: Silk Farming at Takatoya; No. 298-5: Nagasaki and Her Shipbuilders; and No. 298-6: Okinawa: Keystone of the Pacific.

OTHER 49'ERS, THE: WHITE AND CHINESE IN THE EARLY DAYS OF CALIFORNIA. SSSS.

Traces the course of Chinese immigration to the West Coast from 1849 to 1877. Examines the causes of anti-Chinese prejudice and the growth of anti-Chinese propaganda in the 1850s, explaining why the Chinese were more vulnerable to abuse than European immigrants. Discusses the economic basis for discrimination, the intensification of hatred in the 1870s, and the culmination of anti-Chinese sentiment with the passage of the first Chinese Exclusion Act in 1877.

PEARL BUCK: THE GOOD EARTH. EDC 1972. S-C-A. col. No. 709: sound filmstrip, 15 min. With LP record $20.50; with cassettes $22.50.

A study of Pearl Buck's timeless novel, considered by many critics to be her greatest work, this program analyzes the story and gives rewarding insights into the culture, philosophy, and mystery of China.

PEOPLE OF JAPAN, THE. SCHLAT 1968. El-J. col. 49 frs with cassette.

Discusses the differences between the people of modern Japan and those of modern America, as well as the traits both groups have in common.

PEOPLE'S REPUBLIC OF CHINA, THE. SVE 1973. El-J. col. 6 filmstrips with teacher's guides. No. 299-SAR: with 3 records $67.50, individually $5; No. 299-SATC: with 3 cassettes $71.50, individually $6.50; individual filmstrip with teacher's guide $10.

This set of filmstrips on Mainland China provides a timely, in-depth exploration of the enigmatic country that has recently begun to open its doors to Westerners. Multidisciplinary in content, the set is an overview of China's geography, history, politics, economics, and culture. News photos, maps, posters, prints, paintings, and authentic Chinese music supplement the expert on-site photography. Dr. Donald E. Weatherbee, Institute of International Studies, University of South Carolina, Consultant. Titles: The Mysterious Giant; The Ancient Giant; To Feed the Giant; The Giant Looks to the Future; The Giant's Village Girl: Hsu Li-ang; and The Giant's City Boy: Sung Li.

PERCEPTION/MISPERCEPTION: CHINA/U.S.A. SCHLAT 1975. S–C–A. col. No. T358: 4 sound filmstrips, 1 silent filmstrip. Avg 87 frs, 13 min each. 1 audio cassette, teacher's guide, 30 student booklets, and set of 8 role-playing cards, $175.

A thought-provoking mini-course that focuses on the elements involved in misunderstandings between groups. In addition to introducing students to such behavioral factors as stereotyping, prejudice, and ethnocentrism, this inquiry-oriented program reveals some of the reasons why we often misperceive the values and actions of others, particularly the Chinese. American images of China and Chinese images of the United States are traced from the early nineteenth century to the present. Designed to instill both an awareness of common barriers to understanding and a willingness to overcome them, the program encourages students to reflect upon their own attitudes and images as well as the attitudes of others. The role-playing game requires students to plan a model community. Divided into two groups with conflicting philosophies—collectivism as opposed to individual freedom and private enterprise—players experience different perceptions of the goals and methods of different ideologies. Prepared by the Center for War/Peace Studies.

RELIGION AND TRADITION IN JAPAN. SCHLAT 1968. P–El–J. col. 58 frs with disc.

Shows the major religious faiths of Japan, emphasizing their origin, place in Japanese history, and effects on the daily lives of the Japanese people.

REPUBLIC OF INDONESIA. EGH 1961. El–J. 9 filmstrips. Avg 46 frs each.

Presents the land, people, and activities of Indonesia. Discusses Indonesia's crucial role in Asian and international affairs. Titles: Agriculture; Java and Sumatra; Borneo, Celebes, and Bali; The Land; Culture, Education, Transportation; Other Industries; Historic Background; The People; Important Cities.

SEEING CHINA. CORF 1968. P–El. col. 6 filmstrips. Avg 47 frs, 12 min each. No. S 115: with 3 discs $74; No. M 115-6: with 6 cassettes $68; No. C 115-6: with captions $46.

Filmstrip lets students compare the Chinese school curriculum with their own. This photo journey into Communist China highlights the education, geography, people, and events of the world's most populated nation. Students visit communal farms and villages to see both ancient and modern methods. Trips to factories, parades, and political demonstrations are seen in this controversial, changing country. Titles: Land and Resources; History; Industry and Commerce; City Life; Education; and Culture.

SEEING JAPAN. CORF 1971. P–El. col. 6 filmstrips. Avg 53 frs, 15 min each. No. S154: with 3 discs $67; No. M154: with 6 cassettes $75.

Ancient tradition and sophisticated electronics exist side-by-side in modern Japan. Explores Japan's changed political system, its industry and technology with Western and Chinese influences. Includes photographs of the traditional tea ceremony and celebration of the Buddhist Bon, with authentic music and sound effects. Titles: Land and Climate; Agriculture and Fishing; Its People; Industry and Commerce; Its History; and Its Culture.

SINGAPORE: HOW IT SERVES SOUTHEAST ASIA. EEM 1968. col. El–J. 56 frs with 12″ LP record.

Shows how the city of Singapore is located in a strategic position as a great shipping center and how the city is becoming an industrial center as well. Explains that ocean-going freighters from the west and east meet here and exchange cargo.

SOCIAL CLASSES IN JAPAN. SCHLAT 1968. P–El–J–S. col. LC FIA68-4471. 67 frs with discs.

Discusses the levels of Japanese society, their beginnings, and the ways in which Japanese society differs from our own. From "Japan, An Anthropological Study In Depth" series.

SOUTHEAST ASIA. ELKINS 1968. El–J–S. col. 13 filmstrips. Avg 50 frs each.

Young children can understand economic concepts when they are presented as simple needs in an uncomplicated society. Older students gain new insights into history and economics when they can see how an industrial revolution begins and develops. The material in each filmstrip has been organized so that reviews and maps with response activities appear frequently. This format is adapted to class activity as well as to the individual student working alone. Titles: Hong Kong 1, Shipping and Industrial Center; Hong Kong 2, East and West Work Together; Malaysia 1, Geography; Malaysia 2, Diverse People Build a New Nation; Philippine Islands 1, Geography and History; Philippine Islands 2, Man in the Tropics; Singapore, How It Serves Southeast Asia; Southeast Asia 1, Half Land—Half Water; Southeast Asia 2, Many People and Languages; Cambodia, A Center of History in S.E. Asia; Thailand 1, Temples: Centers of Culture; Thailand 2, Trades by Waterways; Thailand 3, An Ancient Economy Enters the Industrial Age.

SOUTHEAST ASIA: PAST AND PRESENT. BFA 1967. J. col. 2 sound filmstrips. Avg 51 frs. No. VS7000: with 2 cassettes $34; No. V34000: with 2 records $28.

These filmstrips are designed to show the general characteristics of Cambodia, Laos, Malaysia, Thailand, and Vietnam. Thailand is used to exemplify the climate, industry, and life-style in Southeast Asia. Daily life in typical villages is shown in a context of the background of the area, the industry, the geography, and the cultural influences. The use of rivers and waterways for cultivation, transportation, commerce, and recreation is illustrated. Titles: Living and Working in Southeast Asia, and The Cultural Background of Southeast Asia.

SOUTH VIETNAM KEY TO SOUTHEAST ASIA'S FUTURE. CAF 1964. El–J. col. 45 frs.

Discusses conditions in South Vietnam. Traces the history of the country from the partition of Vietnam in 1954 to the downfall of President Diem's regime in 1963 and the assumption of power by the military.

TAIWAN. SVE 1973. P-El-J. col. 2 filmstrips with teacher's guides. Avg 64 frs. 13 min each. No. 297-SAR: with disc $25; No. 297 SATC: with cassette $26.50.
Filmstrips describe the people, cultures, and life-styles of this small island off the mainland of China. Titles: Taiwan: An Emerging Nation. Illustrates Taiwan's exciting plan to transform a predominantly agricultural country to an industrial one. Highlights life in modern-day Taiwan. Taiwan: Agricultural and Rural Life. Examines farm life and emphasizes the changes brought about by small, individual land ownership, a recent phenomenon. Also views life among the most primitive rural dwellers, the aborigines.

TALES FROM JAPAN. CORF 1971. P-El. col. 8 filmstrips. No. M 196: with 4 discs $95; No. S 196: with cassettes $85.
The mystery and magnificence of Japanese culture is captured in this collection of children's stories that range from traditional fairy tales, legends, and fables, to more modern stories. An unrhymed haiku introduces each story. Puppets and paper sculpture represent the elements of mythology, nature, fantasy, and the supernatural that tie easily to lessons in social studies, art, and science. Titles: The Moonbeam Princess; The Tears of the Dragon; The Rolling Rice Ball; The Monkey and the Crab; The Inn of the Sparrows; The Story of the Sunset Glow; The Cranes Magic Gift; and The Man Who Made Trees Blossom.

TIKKI TIKKI TEMBO. WWSI 1970. El. col. No. SF 115: with disc $9.50; No. SF 115C: with cassette $12.75.
The reason the Chinese give their children short names is revealed with true oriental flavor in a folktale about the difficulty one child has in telling people that his brother has fallen into a well.

UMBRELLA. WWSI 1968. P. col. No. SF 105: with disc $9.50; No. SF 105 C: with cassette $12.75.
One rainy day, Momo, a little Japanese girl, found she was grown up enough to do something she had never done before. Other little children will share in the delight of Momo's adventure, which has meaning for everybody.

VILLAGE TREE, THE. VIKPI 1972. P. col. 45 frs $12.50.
The author, Taro Yashima, recalls his boyhood in Japan as typified by one summer's day spent near the huge tree that grew near the river in his native village.

Slides

ART AND ARCHITECTURE OF THE NEAR AND MIDDLE EAST. BUDEK. J-S-C. col/b&w. Avg 40 slides per set. Individually: double fr slide film (col) $10.50, (b&w) $6.50; glass mounted (col/b&w) $30; cardboard mounted (col/b&w) $22.

Titles: The Asia Minor Sites; Classical Asia Minor; Phoenician Art; The Holy Land and Its Historical Surroundings; Palmyra; Jerusalem: The Old City; The Temples of Baalbek; Gerasa: A City of the Decapolis; Petra; Persian Art; Persian Brickwork: An Architectural Marvel; Two Iranian Oasis Cities: Nein and Yazd; The Tiled Mosques and Bazaars of Kerman, Iran; The Sassanid Rock-Carvings of Taq-i-Bustan, Iran; Persepolis; Isfahan; and Iraq.

ASIAN ART. BUDEK. J-S-C. col/b&w. Avg 40 slides per set. Individually: double fr slide film (col) $10.50, (b&w) $6.50; glass mounted (col/b&w) $30; cardboard mounted (col/b&w) $22.

Titles: Ancient Art of Angkor, Cambodia; Ancient Art and Architecture of Java; Buddhist Art; Architecture of Thailand; Architecture of Pagan, Burma; Japanese Country Architecture; and Japanese Crafts Today.

A SURVEY OF JAPANESE PRINTS. ACA. S-C. No. ACA-6: 51 slides with commentary $61.

These slides were made from original prints in the collection of Judson Metzgar. The slides present the chronological development of the art from the seventeenth century Ukiyoye school through Moronubu, Harunobu, Kiyonaga, Utamaro, and Sharaku to Hokusai and Hiroshige. An additional slide shows a key color block. Mr. Metzgar's commentary includes an introduction and description of each print.

CHINESE ARTS AND CRAFTS. BUDEK. S-C-A. Over 500 slides. 40 slides per set with notes, unmounted $11.50; cardboard mounted $24; glass mounted $33.

Titles: Chinese Enamel Ware; Chinese Jade; Portrait Painting; Silk and Embroidery; Carvings in Wood, Bamboo, Ivory, Bone; Calligraphy and Writing Instruments; Chinese Porcelain; Chinese Bronze; Paintings; and Lacquer-Ware.

CHINESE PAINTING. UCSC. S-C-A. col. Book with 15 slides $25; set of 25 slides $14.50; set of 50 slides $25.50.

In these slides one will find a magnificent panorama of nearly two centuries of Chinese painting never before published and rarely seen. These most precious scrolls are jealously preserved in the imperial collection now in Formosa and in inaccessible temples.

GREAT ARCHITECTURE OF JAPAN. UCSC. El-J. Book with 8 slides $7.95; set of 50 slides $24.50.

A concise picture of the historical development of the architecture and gardens of Japan from early times right up to the Momoyama-Edo period, which ended in 1968, relating the building to the social conditions of the time.

HISTORY OF JAPANESE ART. BUDEK. S-C-A. Avg 40 slides per set. Individually: double fr slide film (col) $10.50, (b&w) $6.50; glass mounted (col/b&w) $30; cardboard mounted (col/b&w) $22.50.

Titles: Pre-Buddhist Art; Asuka and Nara Periods; Architecture of the Heian Period; Heian Period—Sculpture and Painting; Kamakura Period; Muramachi

Period; Momoyama Period; Edo Period (1615-1868)—Architecture and Sculpture; Edo Period Painting; and Modern Art.

JAPAN—A HISTORY OF ART. SAN 1965. J-S. No. 613: 240 slides $312; No. S-103: 50 slides $65.

Color slides present the history of Japan through twenty centuries as seen, remembered, and recorded by her artists. Shows the Japanese vision of life, in its richness, delicacy, and complexity of pattern, captured and clarified as never before. The original photography for the color slides was accomplished by Bradley Smith, outstanding photographer of art works.

JAPAN, A HISTORY OF ART. UCSC. S. Book with 15 slides $19.50.

The history of Japan through twenty centuries as seen, remembered, and recorded by her artists. Presents the Japanese vision of life, in its richness, delicacy, and complexity of pattern. Two hundred thirty seven works of art are reproduced, most of which have never been seen outside Japan.

JAPANESE FOLK TOYS. ACA. El. No. ACA-7: 35 col slides with commentary $38.50.

The diversity of form and materials used in various times and parts of Japan is evident in the slides which include traditional as well as contemporary toys, from the collections of Hans Conried and Charles Eames. Commentary discusses the supernatural aspect of some toys and the symbology of design and decoration.

MASKS OF JAPAN. ACA. El. No ACA-8: 30 col slides with commentary $36.

Twenty-eight of the slides show masks from the folk dance, Gigaku, Bugaku, Gyodo, Noh, and Noh-Kyogen performances. These masks illustrate various character parts which have been unchanged since remote times. Two slides, taken from sepia prints, show masked actors. Commentary gives brief history, mask description, and sizes.

MASTER PRINTS OF JAPAN—UNIYO-E HANGA. UCSC. S-C-A. Book with 15 slides $25.00; set of 25 slides $14.50; set of 50 slides $24.50.

The Japanese print is a unique art form—from the seventeenth century to the full-color works of the mid-nineteenth century. The major artists are reproduced in this book, and the history and various techniques of drawing, cutting, engraving, and printing are described.

NEAR AND MIDDLE EAST. UCSC. J-S. 7 slide sets. Avg 45 slides per set, with booklet $24.50 each.

Ancient East, Near and Middle; Ancient Iran; Ancient Near East; Gods, Men and Pharaohs; Middle East; Ancient Egypt; and Egypt.

PAINTINGS OF INDIA. UCSC. S-C. Book with 15 slides $25.00; set of 25 slides $14.50; set of 50 slides $24.50.

Covers wall paintings of the classical period of Indian art from the second to the sixteenth century: the Buddhist Caves of Ajanta which contain the greatest series of wall paintings in Asia; and the groups at Badami, Bagh, and Elura; the frescoes in the Rajaraja Temple of Tanjore.

Transparencies

ASIA (Excluding USSR). MGH. J-S-C. col. No. 410450: 6 transparencies, $40.

Approaches geography on a regional basis and considers man-land relationships. Presents a single facet of a region—population spread, transportation routes, agriculture, and industrial development.

ASIA—CLIMATE, VEGETATION, YEARLY RAINFALL. GAF. J-S. col. 10″×10″ transparencies with 3 overlays.

Presents an outline of Asia and surveys the climates and major vegetation forms. Relates the yearly rainfall to vegetation locations. From "World Geography Projects" series.

ASIAN HISTORY—CHINA. EAV. J-S. col. 4 sets with overlays.

Covers the history of China from 5000 B.C. to the present as well as physical features and population. Titles: China: An overview 200 B.C.-700 A.D.; China: An Overview 4000 B.C.-300 B.C.; China: An overview 900-1625; and China: An Overview 1650-1949.

ASIATIC CIVILIZATION. HAMMOND 1969. J-S-C. col. 9″×11″ transparencies with 4 overlays.

Twenty topics trace the growth of civilizations in Asia and other continents.

CHINA. AEVAC. J-S. No DW-11: 6 col transparencies with 19 overlays $38.50.

Presents a series of colorful views of China in six of its areas of interest: history, geography, sociology, economics, anthropology, and political science.

CHINA. IVAC. J-S. 8″×10″ transparencies with 2 overlays.

A series of five topics designed to introduce various aspects of China. Titles: Agriculture; China, Immense Country; Economic Development; Great Diversity; and Industrial Expansion.

CHINESE CIVILIZATION. GAF/WPES. J-S. col. 10″×10″ transparencies with 3 overlays.

Discusses China's family-centered society, examines ancestral worship, monarchal rule, and the four social classes; and traces the development of the Chinese civilizations.

CHINESE PHILOSOPHIES, THE. CREATV 1971. S-C-A. col. LC 72735618: 8″×10″ transparencies.

Presents and explains the great philosophies of China. From "World History & Culture Historical Development" series.

EXPLORING THE AMERICAS AND THE WORLD—ASIA. CREATV. El-J-S. Thirteen 8″×10″ transparencies with 23 overlays.

Twenty-three areas are covered in this in-depth series on Asia including the arts of China, Japan, Korea, Indonesia, East Asia, Central Asia, Nationalist China, and others.

HAWAII—HISTORICAL AND CULTURAL FEATURES. POPSCI. P-El-J. col. 10″×10″ transparencies with 2 overlays.

Depicts physical, political, and industrial features of Alaska and Hawaii from a series of four topics. From "Alaska and Hawaii" series.

HAWAIIAN ISLANDS, THE. CREATV 1971. El-J-S. col. No. H911 3 AB-01: $7.50.

The series "Exploring the Americas and the World" presents this section on Hawaii.

JAPAN. AEVAC. J-S. No. DW-17: 6 transparencies with 23 overlays $38.50.

Presents a series of colorful views of Japan in six of its areas of interest: history, geography, sociology, anthropology, political science, and economics.

JAPAN. NYT. P-El. col. 10″×10″ transparencies.

Discusses the physical, geographical, industrial, and meteorological features of Japan. Titles: Field Crops, Fishing, Fruit Crops, Growing Lessons, Lumbering, Manufacturing, Natural Resources, Pacific Basin, Population Centers, Rainfall, Relief Map of Japan, Summer Winds, Tea and Silk, Transportation, Truck Crops, and Winter Winds.

MAP READING—ASIA (Part 1). MILLIKEN 1968. El. 2 pts, transparencies with overlays.

Titles: Animal Map of Asia; Climatic Map of Asia; Map of Asia; Mineral Map of Asia; Political Divisions of Asia; Rainfall Map of Asia; Rivers, Seas, and Oceans of Asia; Surface Map of Asia; Test Map of Asia; and World Map.

MINORITY GROUPS—THE DEVELOPMENT OF A NATION. TAPUNL. El-J-S. 18 cassettes, 18 transparencies $128.25; individually $8.50.

Studies 15 ethnic groups as seen through their own eyes, discussing the groups' origins, development, participation, and contribution to the American society.

PHYSICAL GEOGRAPHY OF ASIA. AEVAC. El-J. No. AV50: 7 transparencies with 23 overlays $43.

Examines the geography of Asia; the continent which holds the greatest number of human beings within its boundaries. Titles: Contour Map; Monsoons; River Drainage; Climate Zones; Natural Vegetation; Man and the Land; and Mineral Resources.

WORLD HISTORY. EGH. J-H. col. No. 023: complete series of 45 transparencies with overlays $169.

This set graphically presents the historical changes in the world from ancient to modern times. Political maps, time lines, trade routes, and expansion and invasion charts are included. This series is useful with classes learning ancient and modern world history.

Audio Recordings and Audio Cassettes

ADVENTURES OF MARCO POLO/GENGHIS KHAN AND THE MONGOL HORDE. SCHLAT. J-S. LCs R-67-1654/1627. No. EW308: 12″ LP record $6.50.

Side A—Polo's adventures at the court of Kublai Khan, in India, and elsewhere. Side B—Genghis Khan as tribal leader, his brutal ascent to power, and his vast empire.

ASIA. LA. P-El-J. 12″ record 33⅓ rpm, 2 sides.

Contains: Asia, Giant Continent, Old and New Japan, What Is China Like. From "Spotlight Ballad" series and "Light Up the World" series.

ASIA, FOLK AND FAIRY TALES. CCMS 1966. P-El-J. No. 508: 12″ LP record, 33⅓ rpm, 2 sides $6.98.

Narrated by Christian Price, storyteller and author/illustrator of children's books. Includes: The Valiant Chattee Maker (from India), The Boy Who Drew Cats (from Japan), and The Great Stone Fire Eater (from Korea).

ASIA SOCIETY. NTR/NTREP 1961. J-S. Three 3¾ ips cassettes, $3.60 each; open reel $3.10 each.

Edwin F. Stanton, former U.S. ambassador to Thailand, chairman of the Thailand Committee of the Asian Society, and curator in chief of the National Museum of Thailand, discusses Thailand. Titles: Hands across the Sea (Part 1, 30 min; Part 2, 20 min).

A TALK WITH HO CHI MINH. XEROX/CSDI. S-C-A. No. 278: cassette, 34 min $7.50

Although Harry S. Ashmore's conversation in Hanoi with Ho Chi Minh was off-the-record, his impressions of the then president of North Vietnam and of the country, its people, and the war, are not. Mr. Ashmore went to North Vietnam to invite President Ho to attend the second Center conference on "Pacem in Terris," held in May 1967. This is the intimate, detailed report he made to the Founding Members of the Center.

A VIEW FROM INSIDE CHINA. CSDI. S-C-A. No. 516: cassette or reel-to-reel. 3¾ ips 52 min $7.50.

A lively interview conducted by John Cogley, editor of the *Center* magazine, with Barry Richman, professor of Management and International Business at UCLA and a visiting fellow at the Center. Side A deals mostly with life inside China, side B with ideological views from inside China about the world outside.

BURMESE FOLK AND TRADITIONAL MUSIC. FRSC 1956. El-J-S. No. 4436: 12″ record, 33⅓ rpm, 2 sides, $8.95.

Contains folk songs, work songs, drum-circle music, classical songs, royal music, martial music, and recent compositions. Recorded in Burma with notes by Maung Than Myint.

CHINA AND THE WORLD. LRC 1972. J-S-A. No. 316660000: 12 cassettes with maps $84.95, teacher's guide $1.95.

This cassette program begins with the Chinese version of the creation and ends with the 1970s. Special emphasis is placed on nineteenth- and twentieth-century foreign relations. The 12 lessons provide the listener with an introduction to China and its history, clarifies the reasons for China's growth, its decline, and reemergence as an important member of the world community.

CHINA: ECONOMIC DEVELOPMENT IN A HUMAN CONTEXT. CSDI. S-C-A. No. 519: cassette or reel-to-reel. 3¾ ips 59 min $7.50.

John G. Gurley of the Economics Department of Stanford University advances the thesis that economic development in Communist China must be understood as an attempt to achieve socialism by building up the entire country simultaneously, down to the poorest peasant, in order to promote the sense of equal worth of all persons in the society.

CHINA OBSESSION. CSDI. S-C-A. No. MD 528: cassette or reel-to-reel. 3¾ ips 29 min $7.50.

We will never be able to cope with the problems of Southeast Asia or to arrive at solutions with honor or wisdom until we recognize how much our involvement with that continent has been rooted in a policy of containment of China. George M. Kahin, Southeast Asian specialist, leads the discussion. The presentation includes an interesting explanation of how the Chinese Communists came to put primary emphasis on the peasants.

CHINA PROBLEM, THE. AMIDON 1969. J-S-C. 10 cassettes, 20 min each with teacher's guide and 6 transparencies $74.25.

A look at China from 1911 to early 1969 gives background for events to come in the months ahead when China "reenters the world," so to speak. Educator, lecturer, and expert on China, Dr. Siegelmann explores contemporary Chinese history.

CHINA WITHOUT POVERTY. CSDI. S-C-A. No. MD 268: cassette or reel-to-reel. 3¾ ips 53 min $7.50.

Events in China today must be understood in the context of the incredible chaos and poverty that existed when the Communists came to power. Center Fellow Harvey Wheeler interviews Franz Schurmann of the Center for Chinese Studies at the University of California about the political innovations of the Mao government, especially with regard to economic development. They are joined in the conversation by James O'Connor, professor of economics at San Jose State College.

CHINESE CHILDREN NEXT DOOR, THE. EGH. P-El. 12″ record, 33⅓ rpm, 2 sides.

Includes the story The Chinese Children Next Door read by Pearl Buck. Designed to develop an appreciation of the Chinese culture.

CHINESE FAIRY TALES. CAED. P-El. LC 73-750444. 12″ record, 33⅓ rpm $6.98; cassette $7.95.

Presents several Chinese fairy tales by Isabelle Chang including such well-known tales as Teardrop Dragon, The Tigers Teachers, The Chinese Red Riding Hood, The Faithful One, and The Sparrow and the Phoenix. Read by Siobhan McKenna.

CHINESE FOLK SONGS. NTR/NTREP 1961. El-J-S. No. 006 3-02; 30 min. Cassette $3.60; open reel $3.10.

Foreign students attending the University of Minnesota present folk music of their countries. Commentary stresses the importance of folk music as a reflection of the culture, geography, climate, and characteristics of a country and its people. From "Folk Music of the Nations" series.

CHINESE FOLK TALES, LEGENDS, PROVERBS, AND RHYMES. CMSR. P-El. No. F594: cassette $7.98. Available on record with series.

Anne Pellowski tells the well-known stories, Two of Everything from the Treasure of Li Po, the amusing Mrs. Number Three, the unusual Sick-Bed Elves, the Legend of Kitchen God, the Simple Story of Rich and Poor, and The Friend Who Failed.

CHINESE POEMS OF THE TANG AND SUNG DYNASTIES (CHINESE). FSR 1963. J-S-C. 12″ record, 33⅓ rpm $10.

Lo Kung-yuan, a teacher of the Chinese language at St. John's University, New York, reads in the Peking dialect of Northern Chinese. The poems Mr. Lo reads, with one or two exceptions, were written in the Tang dynasty (618-907) or the Sung dynasty (960-1279). Since those times the pronunciation of Chinese has altered to a degree that can only be estimated by linguists.

CONSIDERATIONS FOR THE 21ST CENTURY. CSDI. S-C-A. No. 479: cassette or reel-to-reel, 3¾ ips 29 min $7.50.

If we cannot break free from the nineteenth-century myths underlying our foreign policy, we may not survive the twentieth century to enter the twenty first. Pulitzer Prize winner Harry S. Ashmore is in good form as he summarizes a three-day conference in which Japanese leaders and American legislators considered the steps necessary for a rapprochement with China. Masumi Ezaki, former Japanese minister of defense, adds a footnote.

FOLK MUSIC OF JAPAN. FSR 1959. El-J-S-C. No. FE4429: 12″ records, 2 sides, $8.95.

The abundant folk music of Japanese religious songs, work songs, ballads, children's songs, and dancing songs are sung at festivals, wedding banquets, and other feasts. A great number of regional songs, many of whose origins have long ago been lost in antiquity.

HANUNOO MUSIC FROM THE PHILIPPINES. BEE. El-J. Two 12″ records, 33⅓ rpm $7.95.

This is a scholarly recording by Dr. Harold C. Conklin demonstrating all kinds of instruments, chants, and calls by the Mangyan tribe called Hanunoo who live in southern Mindoro, only 140 air miles from Manila.

HAWAIIAN CHANT, HULA, AND MUSIC. FRSC 1972. El-J-S. No. FW8750: $6.98.

Recorded in Hawaii by Jacob Feuerring, these 14 authentic traditional selections including prayer-offering, tributes, legends, and serenades are played on native instruments and sung by Kaulaheaonamiku Kiona.

HAWAIIAN MUSIC. UCO. El-J-S. 3¾ ips 1 track tape, 20 min.

Designed to introduce the people of Hawaii through their music. From "Understanding People through Their Music" series.

JAPAN—A SERIES. DEMCO. P-El-J. Four 12″ records, 33⅓ rpm, 8 sides.

Presents several facets of Japanese life. Titles: Discovering Downtown Tokyo; Exploring Rural Japan; Finding Friends in Tokyo; and Making a Home in Tokyo.

JAPANESE AMERICANS. EDR. J-S-C. No. 455.23: 12″ LP record, side A—10 min; side B—9 min, $11.50.

The late nineteenth-century settling of the Japanese—the Issei—first in Hawaii, then in the United States; the "Yellow Peril" and the exclusion laws; success at farming; the Alien Land Bill; the second generation—the Nisei; successes in education; World War II, the detention camps, and the 442nd; the end of discriminatory laws; acceptance in business, the professions, and community life.

JAPANESE HAIKU. UM 1961. S-C. Cassette. Approx $6.50.

Presents the world-famous Haiku of Japan and describes this art-form in English. From "Enjoyment of Poetry" series.

JAPAN: HER VOICES AND PEOPLE. KEY 1975. El-J-S. LC R62-579. No. KLP-740: 12″ LP record, 33⅓ rpm $5; cassette $7.

Recorded in Japan by Robert L. Niemann, this record points out with a broad stroke the culture of this great people. American pop, Nipponese style; major-league baseball; and Kabuki theater are heard.

JAPAN: THE FREE WORLD IN THE FAR EAST. DOUBLE. J-S-C. 3¾ ips 4 track tape, 15 min.

Traces the growth of Japan in the postwar period to a position of sixth largest in gross national product and tells of her position of responsibility and influence in building the free world in the Far East. Discusses areas of common concern and comments on China.

JAPAN THROUGH AMERICAN EYES. UCO. J-S-C. 3¾ ips 1 track tape, 30 min.

Describes the customs and habits of the Japanese people as seen by the American people.

KOREA, FOLK AND CLASSICAL MUSIC. FRSC 1959. El-J-S-C-A. No. 4424: 12″ record, 33⅓ rpm $8.95.

Presents Korean classical music "Ah Akk" played by an orchestra associated with the court and Confucian rituals, with introduction and notes by Kyung Ho Park. The performance still is, to a great extent, limited to court and religious occasions such as Confucian rituals.

MADAME BUTTERFLY—PUCCINI. CDS. S-C-A. Three 12″ LP records, 33⅓ rpm, 6 sides.

Presents Puccini's famous and well-known opera *Madame Butterfly* with Japanese setting, performed by Clara Petrella, Ferruccio Taglianini, and others.

MIKADO, THE. EDRECS 1970. J-S-C. 12″ record, 33⅓ rpm.
Features the complete musical compositions of *The Mikado*. From "Opera and Operetta Sets" series.

MUSIC OF ASIA: JAPAN/CHINA/OKINAWA. FRSC 1964. J-S. No. 8885: 12″ record, 33⅓ rpm, 2 sides $5.95.
Native instruments are used to play imperial court music and excerpts from Cantonese opera. Music included of Japan, China, and Okinawa. Side A: Shinto, Goeika, Mikagura-Uta, and Gagaku. Side B: Chikuzen Biwa, Utai, and Shigin music.

NOH PLAYS (JAPANESE). CAED. S-C. 12″ LP record $6.98; cassette $7.95.
Recorded in Tokyo, two Japanese dramas, *Kantan* and *Hagoromo*, are chanted and sung by the foremost Noh companies, accompanied by the exotic musical instruments traditional in these performances.

OUTSTANDING ASIAN AMERICANS. UMINN. El-J-S. 2 programs, 10 min each. Cassette $1.80 each; reel $2.57 each.
Two programs presenting outstanding American citizens of Asian descent. These names, some not often heard, will come as a pleasant surprise—especially their accomplishments.

RELIGIOUS MUSIC OF ASIA. FSR 1967. J-S-A. No. 4481: 12″ LP record, 2 sides $8.95.
Devotional music recorded in Eastern mosques, Indian temples, monasteries in Nepal, Taiwan, and Japan. The selections are a sample of the musical traditions of the major religions of Asia. Recorded on location in the middle of cities and in rural monasteries, they reflect, in sound, the actual conditions of life, not the controlled acoustics of a studio. Buddha's birthday is celebrated to the accompaniment of an American-style brass band in central Taiwan. Notes by Charles A. Kennedy.

SOUTH SEA ISLAND TALES MANN TUPOU. CAED. P-El. LC-73-75-1131. 12″ LP record $6.98; cassette $7.95.
Recorded by Erick Berry, this record includes The Magic Banana, The Story of Hine—Moa and Tutavekai, The Three Monsters of the Sea, and Three Authentic Legends.

SUPPOSE THEY GAVE A WAR AND NO ONE CAME? CSDI. S-C-A. No. 482: cassette or reel-to-reel. 3¾ ips 30 min, $7.50.
Japan, which has a constitutional prohibition against war, stands in a unique position to usher in the warless world. William O. Douglass, former Associate Justice of the U.S. Supreme Court, interrupted the Conference on China Policy with an impatient plea that we break with our bankrupt political policies and seek innovative paths to peace under law. He was joined by Senators Fulbright and Hatfield and their Japanese counterparts in a moving montage that demanded respect for all living things, including man.

TALES OF CHINA AND TIBET—BY ISABELLE C. CHANG. CAED. P-El. LC 72-750988. 12″ LP record $6.98; cassette $7.95.

Aesop-like fables of animals and legendary people, including The Oracle, Candy Man, The Noble Frog, and other charming stories are read by Siobhan McKenna.

THIS IS MY COUNTRY—EAST ASIAN COUNTRIES. WILSHH. P-El-J. $1\frac{7}{8}$ ips cassette.

Issue-oriented, open-ended, and designed to promote critical thinking and student involvement, this cassette presents interviews with people from India, Thailand, Japan, and Taiwan.

VIETNAM. MR 1972. El-J-S. 12″ record, $33\frac{1}{3}$ rpm $5.98.

Presents the National Vietnamese Ensemble in songs and dances of Vietnam.

VIEWPOINT: ASIAN—THE TENSIONS OF A NON-WESTERN NATION. NEA. J-S. No. 388-12002: cassette, approx 30 min. Complete set $43.45.

Taped during spontaneous, round table discussions of concerned educators from the minority group. Speakers: Mary Kashiwagi, Seattle; Ted Lou, Flint, Michigan, and Sunsiko Suyenaga, Sacramento, California. Series.

Video Cassettes

ASIA—AN INTRODUCTION. BFA 1972. C-A. 20 min col. $\frac{3}{4}$ inch.

Explores the unique characteristics of each major region, comparing and contrasting life-styles, economics, and physical geography of Asia's various regions. Includes end-of-unit review of the vast Asian continent.

ASIAN AMERICAN HERITAGE. GPITVL. S-C-A. 30 min 2 inch.

Introduces viewers to the many aspects of a rich heritage that have become blended into the American way of life—food and dress, language, poetry, art, and religion.

ASIAN EARTH. ATLAP 1954. J-S-A. 22 min col. $\frac{3}{4}$ inch.

The full cycle of daily and seasonal life of a Hindu family of the lower Ganges River and the relationship of the farmer to the landowner and the money lender give an idea of the enormity and complexity of the problems facing the Indian government.

BORN CHINESE. BBCTV/TIMELI. J-S-C. 57 min b&w. Video $230; 16mm $330; rental $40.

One person in every four on the face of the earth is Chinese, yet to Westerners all Chinese are somehow the same—distant and enigmatic. We enter into the daily life of the Lung family. Linda Lung and her husband left Red China soon after the revolution. They now live in an apartment in one of Hong Kong's huge government housing blocks with their two small children and a sister who works in a factory.

CHINA; MAO TSE-TUNG'S SYSTEM. BBCTV/TIMELI. J-S-C. 35 min col. Video $300; 16mm $125; rental $45.

A BBCTV crew was allowed to shoot many scenes of life and politics in China today. The resulting documentary portrays China as a completely monolithic society with one mind, one direction, one all-knowing leader, Mao Tse-tung. The people appear to be well-fed, well-housed, and well-clothed, and at the same time illiteracy is being wiped out.

CHINESE IN CALIFORNIA. KQED 1963. P–El. 20 min b&w 2 inch.

Describes points of interest in the San Francisco Bay area, including industries, recreation spots, bridges, and historical sites and concentrates on the Chinese Americans.

FELIX GREENE'S CHINA. TIMELI. J–S. 25 min col. Set video $1,400, 16mm $2,000, rental $200; individual video $235; individual 16mm $330; individual rental $40.

For five months in 1972 Felix Greene roamed through mainland China with his family and his camera and sound equipment. He went where no Westerners have gone since the revolution, and he filmed wherever he went. The result is a complete and professional film coverage of China. Titles: The People's Communes; Eight or Nine in the Morning; Self Reliance; The People's Army; Our Nation, Many People; Medicine in China; and Friendship First, Competition Second.

JAPANESE MOUNTAIN FAMILY. BFA 1972. P–El–J. 15 min col.

Illustrates family spirit and the details of rural life in contemporary Japan as portrayed by Yuji, son of a woodcutter, and his family living in the forested mountain country.

TOKYO THE FIFTY-FIRST VOLCANO. BBCTV/TIMELI. J–S–C–A. 30 min col. Video $280; 16mm $400; rental $40.

This film is about the quality of life that this extraordinary place has to offer. It is a city of superlatives: The world's fastest trains, the worst smog, the most bars, the biggest nightclubs, the most inadequate sewage system, the best riot police, the most violent students, and the largest newspapers; not to mention the largest population with eleven million people and hundreds of thousands pouring in every year.

Study Prints/Pictures/Posters/Graphics

CHILDREN OF AUSTRALIA AND THE PACIFIC ISLANDS. SVE. P–El. 8 col study prints with texts $8.

Shows happy, attractive children of Australia, New Zealand, Hawaii, Sumatra, Philippines, Sulu Islands (Moro), Samoa, and Sarawak (Malaysia) in settings indicative of their background.

CHINA: A CULTURAL HERITAGE. JACK. El–J. SBN 670-21809-X: 9 exhibits, 4 broadsheets, contents brochure $3.95.

Describes and illustrates the most important features of China's art, drama, literature, philosophy, craftsmanship, and technology, setting them in chronological perspective. Exhibits include a copy of the Analects of Confucius, a fifteenth-century hand-scroll painting, a Cultural Revolution propaganda poster, and instructions for making a Chinese kite.

CHINA: TEACHER'S STARTER KIT. SSSS. El. No. CW 201: $10.50. Contains paperback, reprints, visual materials, and lesson plans designed to provide introductory background material for teaching about China. Included in the boxed set are the following: China: Readings on the Middle Kingdom, by Leon Hellerman and Alan L. Stein; Confucianism and Taoism, by A. Jeff Tudisco; Quotations from Chairman Mao Tse-tung; wall map of China plus guide; Understanding U.S.-China Relations, an Intercom booklet; picture post card series depicting Chinese ballet, Red detachment of women; reprints from magazine articles and Department of State Bulletin; and teacher's guide on above materials, bibliography, helpful exercises, and resources.

JAPANESE LIFE. DPA. El-J. No. PC-J 707: series of 5 col 20″ × 15″ charts $2.50.

Charts depict the various aspects of Japanese society: work, family life, religion, education, and traditions.

UNESCO STUDY PRINTS. SSSS. El-J-S. Asia study prints 18″ × 12″ with study notes. Complete set $49.50; individually $7.95.

Eight carefully selected photographers portray each country, highlighting characteristic features through its people, places, and activities. Included are: Burma, Cambodia, India, Indonesia, Japan, Mongolia, and the Philippines.

WAR IN VIETNAM. DPA. J-S. No. DPA 12: 10 b&w photos on glossy stock, $6 series.

Includes U.S. helicopter over Saigon, American troops encountering Vietcong in the jungle, Marines carrying body of dead buddy, Vietcong prisoner being led by a rope around his neck, troops dashing to helicopters under heavy fire during search-and-destroy operation, President Johnson pinning medal on a sergeant, and Ho Chi Minh at Geneva Peace Conference (1954).

CHAPTER III

The Native Indian American

by S. Gabe Paxton, Jr.,
Bureau of Indian Affairs,
U.S. Government

"Culture" has many meanings to various people. Simplified, culture is whatever happens to a person internally and externally on any one day—thoughts, needs, fears, attractions, aversions, hopes, life style, daily experiences, biases, rituals, habits, and so on. Culture is the sum of all learned behavior in the life cycle.

There are also other factors and other cultures (some even say subcultures) which affect and condition the individual and modify the peer culture, the community or tribal culture, the assumed culture in a marginal or non-Indian world, the school culture, and so on, seemingly endlessly. This idea of culture is further complicated if the individual compares the *actual* cultural self-concept with the *ideal* cultural self-concept of the larger environment.

What has been stated so far is certainly true of all people of all races. It is no less true of a group of people called Native Indian Americans. Even considering that every individual of every race is different and unique, the Native Indian American has a special uniqueness in America by virtue of being the pre-Columbian inhabitant and possessor of the American continents. In addition, the Indian, by right of the U.S. Constitution and numerous national commitments, treaties, and policies, has a special relationship with the federal government.

It has not always been recognized that Native Indian Americans and Alaskan natives do not have a culture which is unitary or alike. In 1772 the attitude was "He who has seen one tribe of Indians has seen all." This attitude appears to have remained over the years. Even now there are some people who do not realize that Indians are quite variable, and that the Native Indian American culture is not one culture but many, often at opposite ends of a continuum of human behavior. The basic assumption of this chapter is that Native Indian Americans *are* different, not only from non-Indians but also tremendously different among their various tribal groups and subgroups. Assuming this statement to be true, there are some definite implications to be considered by the educator.

1. Contemporary Native Indian American youths find themselves stereotyped and falsely characterized as being:

a. romantic woodland children of nature;
b. vanishing Americans;
c. defeated horsemen;
d. noble savages;
e. ignorant heathens;
f. drunken, lazy recipients of unearned resources;
g. illiterate, nonintellectuals who are good only with their hands, drawing pictures, arts and crafts, music, or repetitious factory benchwork;
h. passive, nonverbal, native aborigines;
i. simple-minded red men who are unable to understand complex relationships; and
j. members of a homogeneous Indian society rather than a modified multiethnic Native American society.

Each of these stereotypes is false. They confuse Native Indian American youths when they are unable to fill these expectations, and such degrading misrepresentations must be counteracted by the discerning educator.

2. Contemporary Native Indian American youths maintain cultural, tribal, or racial identities which are uniquely different from most other Americans. Many of these ritual, ceremonial, or kinship differences may not be clearly understood by the educator, but they should be accepted as being just as valid to the Native Indian Americans as Valentine's Day, Halloween, Thanksgiving, Lent, and other such observances are to other Americans.

3. As are all other students, Indians are subjected hourly to numerous stimuli. These stimuli are either ego-enhancing or ego-assaultive. There is no middle ground. They are either growing and developing or their self-images as worthy human beings are being destroyed insidiously. If their cultural life style is degraded as being primitive and with no meaning, the educator is providing a grave disservice.

4. Contemporary Native Indian American youths, in being asked to reject their own culture, are subject to becoming as confused and as neurotic as many of their peers. Unable to fill their expected role they become maladjustive and their learning and development are inhibited.

5. Contemporary Native Indian American youths are faced with a failure expectancy whereby they are conditioned to such self-concepts as "I can't do it"; "I am not important"; or "I am not smart." This may result in an Indian adult who says, "I can't compete in contemporary life."

6. Contemporary Native Indian American youths are often faced with the idea that they must be more verbal, but not too verbal; be more self-assertive, but not too much; be Indian, but a nice acculturated Indian.

7. Contemporary Native Indian American youths are also confronted with the attitude that they are being prepared to participate in an Anglo-oriented society. However, this approach is not sound as the American society is not just

Anglo-oriented. The Swedish, Italian, Spanish, French, African, German, Irish, Oriental, and other cultures, as well as that of the Indians, also had a part in orienting, fashioning, and developing what we call the American society. It is a diverse, multiethnic, and modified modern society.

8. Contemporary Native Indian Americans who become educated often find themselves characterized as co-opted Indians, those who having been educated, are then selected, preempted, or chosen to perform the tasks of the larger society. However, they may find themselves still not being accepted by the "larger" system. One wonders if this is a pseudo co-optation rather than a true co-optation—a matter of tokenism.

HISTORICAL MILESTONES

Native Indian American people are extremely diverse and vary in life styles and languages. When the Europeans and the Native Indian Americans first came into contact, there were approximately 200 tribes whose customs, beliefs, value systems, and languages were very complex. Many writers will attempt to generalize by saying the Eastern Indian was a farmer, the Plains Indian was a buffalo hunter, the Southwest Indian was a seed-gatherer, and the Pacific Coast Indian was a fisherman. Such generalized characterizations presented in textbooks and numerous media are fallacious. For instance, while some Eastern Indians were farmers, some were also hunters and fishermen. A particular Eastern Indian may have been all three—farmer, hunter, and fisherman. In another instance, the generalization of the Southwest Indian as a seed-gatherer or dry land farmer may be true for a particular group of individuals; however, there were also skilled irrigation farmers among the Indians of the Southwest.

The foregoing has been emphasized to illustrate the danger of generalizations in describing a group of human individuals who just happen to be Native Indian Americans. Therefore, in the attempt to present historical milestones for a group of complex and highly varying Native Americans, this writer does so with the idea that a particular tribe or subgroup may have a history which is modified from the general pattern.

Prehistorical Period

Scientists continue to add to their store of knowledge as to the origin of Native Indian Americans. Controversy arises when scientists discuss both the origin and the times of migrations of the first Americans. Therefore, perhaps it is safer to say that many thousands of years ago, groups of people came to the American continents from Asia across a land bridge, where the Bering Strait is now. The theory is that during this time the sea was lower, exposing land between Asia and Alaska. By 9000 B.C. evidence indicates that various migrating groups had reached the tip of South America. When the Ice Age ended about ten thousand years ago the land bridge was flooded. Since that time the civilizations of Native Indian Americans developed to a high level, through trial and error. When the European explorers arrived, they failed to understand the complex nature of the "different" cultures which they encountered, falsely interpreting instead that the newly discovered first Americans were barbaric and primitive savages. As a matter of fact, the daily life cycle of the Native Indian Americans was extremely complex.

Early Historical Period

The early contacts with the Native Indian Americans, thus, were based on wrong assumptions and fallacious reasoning by the Europeans, including the first mistake that the Native Indian Americans were "Indians." Acting on the baseline view that these new people were "different," and subhuman beings, the early European explorers then proceeded, with conscience unimpaired, to treat the Indians on an unequal basis, to the extent of violating their property and personal rights.

The Mission Period

Since the Native Indian Americans were classified as different, the early policy of Spain, France, and England was to change and "civilize" the representatives of the new culture. Not long after the discovery of America, Pope Julius II solemnly declared that the Indians were descendants of Adam and Eve. There was also a popular belief that the Indians were descendants of the children of Babel, people in the Bible who built the Tower of Babel, tried to reach to the sky, and incurred the wrath of God. The idea was that the Indians had been scattered and cast into a "primitive existence" because of their sins. Even today, the Mormons still teach that the Indians are descendants of the Ten Lost Tribes of Israel. Indians also have been thought to be descendants of the Egyptians because they built the huge pyramids in South America, or to be descendants of the Romans or Carthaginians.

Therefore the early Catholics and Protestants sought to Christianize the Native Indian Americans. Beginning with a Jesuit mission school in Florida in 1568, the task was pursued vigorously. By 1617, King James I called upon the Anglican clergy to provide funds for educating the children of the barbarians. The College of William and Mary was established as a college for the "children of the infidels."

The goals of the Jesuits, mainly French, were to follow the order of Louis XIV to "educate the children of the Indians in the French manner." Children were removed from their families and tribes. They were taught the French language and the traditional academic subjects. Singing, agriculture, carpentry, and handicrafts were also included—the first indication that Indians were "good with their hands." The Spanish Franciscans gathered the people into villages around missions. The schools taught Spanish, but did not emphasize the academic subjects, placing greater stress on those subjects with which the natives could "use their hands." The English founded Dartmouth for the education of the youth of Indian tribes, English youths and others. These early attempts at education were to transmit the western culture and civilization, with no attempt to incorporate Indian languages, culture, or history into the curriculum.

Historically, then, from the original clashes of Indian and non-Indian cultures came a resolve by the Europeans to submerge, assimilate, or erase the little-understood and different Indian cultures. These early encounters failed in their goals and the problems of the European-Indian encounters were not solved.

However, the Native Indian American cultures were modified. Complicating the picture was the fact that the non-Indian Spanish, French, and English cultures were not unitary. They were different from each other; different in speech, religion, dress, life styles, and in sociopolitical organizations. These European cultures, in turn, met not a unitary Native Indian American culture, but many diverse cultural groups whose habits, speech, religion, dress, life styles, and sociopolitical organizations were different. So the Native Indian Americans did not change drastically. Bombarded by cross-cultural stimuli, both beneficial and adverse, the Indian tribes did modify their cultures in order to survive, but only slowly through the decades. Through it all, the composite "generalized" Native Indian American resisted and refused to become a vanishing part of the American melting pot. The term "Vanishing American" may have been wishful thinking on the part of the newly developing American nation, but it was not true. The Native Indian American refused to surrender a different and unique identity, even though it had been tragically and severely damaged. The Native Indian American was not submerged, assimilated, or erased during the early historical period.

The Treaty Period

The signing of the treaty between the United States and the Delaware tribes in 1778, soon after the birth of the United States, established treaties as the primary legal basis for federal policies in regard to the Native Indian Americans. The colonial period over, the new United States of America treated Native Indian Americans as foreign nationals. The earliest treaty which provided for Indian education was signed in 1794 in which the federal government promised to provide a tribe with teachers "in the arts of the miller and sawyer." Similar provisions, usually in exchange for Indian land, were common elements in treaties for the next 80 years. Indian education was influenced by a nationwide religious awakening which took place in the United States at that time. The Bible was the book; the primer reader and the hoe were the weapons of those who sought to teach the natives "morals" rather than physically exterminate them. Education was thought of as a weapon to destroy the Native Indian American languages and customs, thus their culture. Vocational education was stressed and remained mostly in the hands of the missionaries. Off-reservation boarding schools were established emphasizing strict military discipline, removal of the students from their homes, and work and study programs including a system in which Indian students lived and worked with white families. During this time tribal identities and tribal languages were discouraged in the schools.

The purpose of the treaty period did not differ much from the purpose behind the efforts of the missionaries. Both the government and the missionaries sought to civilize the Indian. Government leaders realized that if the Indian could be converted from hunter to farmer, the Indian would require less land and be easier to contain. By 1871, when the last treaty was signed, Indian tribes ceded almost a billion acres to the United States. In return, the government pledged education, health care, and technical and agricultural training. Beginning in 1802, Congress appropriated money for the "civilization of the aborigines." This civilization fund was appropriated annually until 1873.

The Allotment Period

After 1887 there was a deliberate attempt to convert all Indians to farming, to break up the reservations, and to eliminate federal responsibilities for the signed treaties. In 1901 the commissioner of Indian Affairs reported that rations and annuities should be abolished, then the educated Indian should be thrown on his own resources, and the settlement of the Indian question would follow. This fitted the ethics and value system of the United States citizenry at that time. Native Indian American children were cajoled, threatened, bribed, forced, and otherwise induced to go to school so that they could take upon themselves the outward semblance of civilized life.

The Dawes Severality Act of 1887, then, provided for land allotments to individual Indians as a means of breaking up the tribal structure. The actual result was to diminish the Indian tribal economic base from 140 million acres to about 50 million acres. Indian family social organization was severely disrupted. The newly established boarding schools were often abandoned army posts. They were operated in a rigid military fashion, with heavy emphasis on vocational education. The schools were designed to separate children from their reservations and families, strip them of their tribal lore and mores, force the complete abandonment of their native language, and prepare them for never again returning to their people. Although many Indian families resisted, the official policies of forced assimilation continued until 1928.

The Meriam Report and the New Deal Period

In 1928, shortly before the administration of Franklin D. Roosevelt, a report was issued by Lewis Meriam of the University of Chicago, through the Brookings Institution in Washington, D.C., which had significant impact on Indian affairs. The Meriam Report led to a creative and innovative period under the commissioner of Indian Affairs, John Collier. The Meriam Report stated that Indians were excluded from the management of their own affairs, and that they were receiving poor quality of health and education services. The report condemned the practice of taking children from their homes and placing them in boarding schools. It called for a relevant curriculum in both Bureau of Indian Affairs schools and in the public schools. According to Meriam, the public schools with their traditional curriculums, were doing no better than the Bureau schools. He stated that the most fundamental need was a change in point of view.

A series of changes and approaches were initiated. The Allotment Act was ended. The Indian Reorganization Act of 1934 laid the groundwork for more autonomous tribal governments. Programs were started in bilingual education, adult basic education, training of Indian teachers, Indian culture, and in-service teacher training. However, the advent of World War II and a changed congressional attitude brought a halt to progress. This attempt to restore recognition of Indian languages and cultures faltered.

The Termination Period

In 1944, Congress called for a return to the pre-Meriam policies. It criticized Indian day schools for adapting education to the Indian and to his way of life. The House Select Committee on Indian Affairs offered recommendations on achieving the "final solution of the Indian problem." The policy was to make Indian children better Americans rather than to equip them to be better Indians. Many Indian children were moved into public schools which had no special language or cultural programs for them. Termination policies accelerated causing a termination syndrome which only partially ended in 1958 when the secretary of the interior announced that no tribe would be terminated without its consent.

The Beginning of the Pan-Indian Period

Throughout the 1960s the termination policy resulted in unrest, confusion, disorientation, and a general feeling on the part of Indians that they were living within a framework of no federal policy. By 1965, the Bureau of Indian Affairs had shifted to a program of economic and community development. There had been a growing interest in special programs for language instruction. The goals for Indian education began to move toward maintaining respect for Indian culture and the dignity of Indian people.

Two forces helped to develop a new Pan-Indian movement, through which a person identifies himself first as an Indian and second as a person of a particular tribe. The first influence was the growing responsiveness of reservation tribal governing bodies to seek self-determination. Another influence was the impact of thousands of Indians relocated during the 1950s and 1960s in urban centers. In an alien environment, the urban Indians often found Pan-Indianism to be a stabilizing element; perhaps a permanent part of the adaptation of the Indian migrant to the urban centers.

Indian Awareness Period

The present period of "Indian Awareness" in the 1970s is a developing one based on an understanding of previous policy failures. It can be speculated that "some" and "many" Indians, both old and young, are more aware of themselves as Indians. It can be hypothesized that they are more aware of their personal and civil rights; of their dignities as human beings; of their awareness that they are proud contributors to the family of human beings; and that they can have equal status with others. They are aware that self-choice, self-determination, and self-expression without degradation or forced assimilation should be the means for improving their position within the total society. Today Native Indian Americans want their children to be educated in a school climate which has no prejudice, racial intolerance, or discrimination. They want teachers and school systems to protect their children's integrity, individuality, and cultural identity.

SPECIAL EDUCATIONAL NEEDS OF THE NATIVE INDIAN AMERICAN

Native Indian Americans are culturally different and this state is not a negative but a positive force for learning. An appreciation of these cultural differences by the educator may go a long way in undoing some of the paternalistic prejudicial, and presumptuous educational practices of the past.

While there are specific exceptions, most of the schools that teach Native Indian Americans are subject to criticism that the curriculum is irrelevant to their needs. This criticism is directed to federal, public, and mission schools, and includes textbooks, library books, and other instructional media.

Most Native Indian American parents agree that the mastery of English is important. Some schools approach this problem by utilizing programs of teaching English as a second language. However, the lack of trained teachers limits this approach. In addition, the materials often have a strong Spanish-English bias which may not be applicable for use with Native Indian Americans. Some schools with high Indian enrollments use a bilingual, bicultural approach. Limitations include the lack of trained teachers and inadequate funding and materials.

Indian languages are no longer vetoed in some schools as a matter of official policy. However, some educators resist bilingualism because they still believe in the melting pot theory, with Native Indian Americans being subjected to a one-way assimilation. Careful implementation of bilingual programs may be possible as successful programs are demonstrated and the approaches disseminated, especially in the early grades.

Special consideration must be given to the needs of teachers who work with Native Indian Americans. There is a need to sensitize them to the sociocultural differences which they encounter with Native Indian Americans. This is not only a problem to be dealt with by the teacher-training institutions but also by the administrators and supervisors who provide in-service training for the teachers. Socially disadvantaged youth are often characterized as being from low economic backgrounds, as having low social status in the community, and as having low educational achievement. Their families are characterized as having tenuous or no employment, as having limited participation in community organizations, and as having limited ready potential for upward mobility. The teacher is told that Native Indian Americans come from depressed social and economic situations, that they are further handicapped by ethnic and cultural caste systems, that they come to the "dominant society" school disadvantaged to the degree that the home culture has failed to provide them with the experiences normal to the kinds of children the schools are used to teaching. These are generalizations which may or may not be true, according to local tribal and individual differences. Therefore, the teacher should not be trapped into the failure expectancy that such teachings and attitudes provide. Indian children today are a product of a modified culture and display many traits of their native culture. But they are also the by-product of many multicultural influences.

Many Native Indian Americans in their earlier years are trained at home to believe that their traditions are proud and fine. It is then a shock to the ego for them to discover the white world expects them to forget Indian culture and traditions and immediately adopt a foreign way of life. In many Native Indian American cultures there is a deep-set historical distrust of "they" in the "we-they" relationship.

Learning Styles and Characteristics

Educators who have been fully conditioned to the concept of individual differences will recognize that "Indianness" is another "difference." Therefore, they will have no difficulty in adjusting ultimately to the fact that differences in learning style and pace are quite as variable among Native Indian Americans as they are with all other children.

Native Indian Americans often differ from others in their level of acculturation. Historically, they have learned by doing, primarily because culture and language had not been reduced to writing. The middle-class teaching approach and temptation, however, is to teach entirely by words and books. Thus, many Native Indian Americans have difficulty in learning, not because they are intellectually inferior, but because English is a second language and results in difficulty with meanings, interpretations, and relationships.

Students learn through all their senses and some learn better through one sense than through another. Therefore, learning for some comes through auditory, for others through visual perception. Others learn through the tactile (feeling) approach. Still others learn through the kinesthetic (tracing) approach.

A multisensory approach is suggested and when the Native Indian American's best mode of reception is finally observed, that approach should be used. However, the other approaches for developmental purposes should not be neglected. The learning approach which provides the greatest success should be reinforced. The audiovisual approach with slides, filmstrips, locally prepared tapes for use at listening stations, and the use of artifacts and field trips to museums can be beneficial in reinforcing learning. Moreover, small group-learning encounters are preferred with Native Indian Americans rather than a constant verbal bombardment.

The intent is to promote a learning environment which is responsive to the students. The emphasis is that the feelings and attitudes of the environment (teacher and significant peers) affect learning. It is suggested that there should be immediate feedback communication rather than a delayed reaction on the part of both student and teacher. This type of immediate feedback helps to evaluate the learning experience.

Positive learning growth promotes positive feelings toward self, toward others, and toward learning. A rich learning program, individually prescribed, and using a multiplicity of approaches and materials should provide a rewarding experience for both teacher and student.

Criteria for Selection of Materials

Native Indian American researchers, scholars, and educators are only now, in the mid-1970s, beginning to show a concerted effort to establish criteria for the selection of media materials to use with Native Indian American students. In using pictures, projected materials, field trips, charts, photographs, tapes, records, and graphic processes, some suggestive criteria to be utilized are as follows:

1. Is the material accurate? Does the material accurately depict Native Indian Americans as they are rather than a projection of generalized stereotypes?
2. Does the material contribute to a positive self-image of the Native Indian American? Does the experience represent an enhancing force as opposed to a degrading or ego-assaulting experience?
3. Does the material depict the Native Indian American as a person of worth, whose culture has a right to exist on an equal basis in a world of many cultures?
4. Does the material contribute to an understanding that Native Indian Americans had substantial roles of lasting impact on developing the American continents?

The above criteria are only suggestive and are not exhaustive but should be a starting point as the professional educator evaluates instructional media materials and applies such criteria to the selection process. There is a need for more efforts to be taken in establishing criteria. This has been done in the case of textbooks being used in schools educating Native Indian Americans. The Indian Historical Society has published *Textbooks and the American Indian*, edited by Rupert Costo, which brought substantial attention to the fact that most of the texts being used contained derogatory and misleading information. The Indian Historical Society also published the *Index to Literature on the American Indian* (1970), *The American Indian Reader* (1970), *Handbook of the American Indian Series* (1972), *Indian Voices Today*, and a magazine of Indian Americans for young people, published six times annually, entitled *The Weewish Tree*.

Such efforts as those above should lead naturally into a consideration of all other media materials. Project MEDIA, sponsored by the National Indian Education Association, is a developing program to be considered by the educational professional who may ask to be placed on their mailing list. Project MEDIA is a federal grant program under Title IV, Public Law 92-318. The project, now in the first year of a planned five-year program, has three main goals:

1. To gather together information for an automated data base (computer) of Indian bibliographic materials. The information will be taken from books, tapes, records, films, teaching materials, articles, and more that either pertain to Indian education or feature Indians.
2. To develop a standard guideline for evaluating the information in the data bank.
3. To carry out workshops in the ten Health, Education and Welfare (HEW) regions, to inform Indian librarians and educators and to show non-Indians what is written and presented to depict Native Indian Americans and to teach them how mistakes and misjudgments can be corrected.

Implications for Research

The discerning education professional will readily see that there are many questions and few ready-made answers. The whole area of identifying and utilizing adequate instructional and media materials has hardly been touched. Beginning signs, i.e., Project MEDIA of the National Indian Education Association and the Indian Culture Section of the Bureau of Indian Affairs, are evident. As scholarly research in this area develops, a more accurate portrayal of the Native Indian American is possible through the proper utilization of media materials. Native Indian American scholars, and non-Indians who are interested in Native Indian Americans, are concerned that greater accuracy in the content of curriculums be developed. Materials need to be evaluated. Accurate resource materials need to be identified. Cognitive and affective approaches need to be developed and researched.

The establishment of criteria for evaluation of instructional media materials is an area of great need. No valid bibliography of materials now exists. Perhaps the first step in research is to identify the available materials and then apply established criteria for their use. In summary, it can be said that many factors influence the learning environment of and for Native Indian Americans, including the social atmosphere of the school and the administrative policies which prevail. Outside influences, such as the school board, the community, accrediting agencies, universities, Indian parents, and activists, all affect the system. Within the school, the decor, the interpersonal relationships of staff members, and peer attitudes are significant. Moreover, the use of proper instructional media materials in creating a learning growth potential is vital. Field studies need to be carried out in a systematic manner to determine to what extent the needs of Native Indian American students are being met.

BIBLIOGRAPHY

Native Indian American Media Guideline Sources

The reader is urged to explore the future findings of Project MEDIA, National Indian Education Association, 3036 University Avenue, S.E., Suite 3, Minneapolis, Minnesota 55414. The reader is also urged to follow the development of disseminated information from the Research and Cultural Studies Development Section of the Bureau of Indian Affairs, Indian Education Resources Center, Box 1788, Albuquerque, New Mexico.

The National Indian Training Center, Professional Library, P.O. Box 66, Brigham City, Utah 84302, lists a number of audiovisual materials as shown below. The priority of service from this library is to Bureau of Indian Affairs employees, Indians, university libraries, and those interested in Indians.

Another resource to help establish guidelines and criteria in the various states is the Native American Professional Resource Directory, published in 1973, which can be obtained for $4.50 from the Southwestern Cooperative Educational Laboratory, 2017 Yale, S.E., Albuquerque, New Mexico 87106. This directory lists 1,076 individual Indians, from numerous tribes and states, who have degree backgrounds.

A most helpful media document is *A Filmography for American Indian Education* published and distributed by Zia Cine, Incorporated, P.O. Box 493, Santa Fe, New Mexico 87501. This document, containing over 300 reviews, was prepared with the support of the Research and Cultural Studies Development Section, Bureau of Indian Affairs, Santa Fe, New Mexico.

The National Indian Education Association, 3036 University Avenue, S.E., Minneapolis, Minnesota 55414, lists very pertinent visual and instructional aids in the booklet, *Contemporary Issues of the American Indian.*

The Center for In-Service Education, P.O. Box 7541, Loveland, Colorado 80537, lists a number of Native Indian American media materials which may be of assistance to teachers of Indian units.

Listening Library, Inc., 1 Park Avenue, Old Greenwich, Connecticut 06870, has filmstrips, slides, and cassettes available concerning Indians.

Because colleges and universities with Indian related programs in the various states are important resources in helping professional educators to establish criteria and guidelines for instructional materials, some of them are as follows:

Arizona State University, Tempe, Arizona, provides studies leading to a Master's degree in Indian education.

Bacone College, Bacone, Oklahoma, is a liberal arts junior college offering courses in Indian art, arts and crafts, and music.

Bemidji State College, Bemidji, Minnesota, offers a minor in Indian studies.

Brigham Young University, Provo, Utah, has an American Indian Education Department and offers a minor in Indian studies.

Central Washington State College, Ellensburg, Washington, sponsors Indian education projects.

Dakota State College, Madison, South Dakota, has an Indian Culture study.

Eastern Montana College, Billings, Montana, offers an Indian studies program.

Eastern New Mexico University, Portales, New Mexico, has courses related to Indian people, including teaching of English as a second language.

Eastern Oregon College, LaGrande, Oregon, has an Indian studies program.

Eastern Washington State College, Chency, Washington, provides Indian history and anthropology courses.

Fort Lewis College, Durango, Colorado, offers a seminar on contemporary Indian affairs, and has several training programs for Indians.

Gonzaga University, Spokane, Washington, has an Indian program.

Haskell Indian Junior College, a Bureau of Indian Affairs School at Lawrence, Kansas, is an all-Indian School and has a developing Indian studies department.

Humboldt State College, Arcata, California, has an Indian foundation.

Mary College, Bismarck, North Dakota, has an Indian studies program.

Mount Marty College, Yankton, South Dakota, has a program of "Life and Culture of the American Indian."

Navajo Community College, Many Farms, Arizona, has numerous courses related to Native Americans.

Northeastern State College, Tahlequah, Oklahoma, has Indian related training programs, including bilingual education programs.

Northern Arizona University, Flagstaff, Arizona, has relevant courses related to Indian education, including Indian history, Indian internships, and linguistics.

Northern State College, Aberdeen, South Dakota, has various Indian related programs.

Oregon College of Education, Monmouth, Oregon, emphasizes Indian studies.

Sheldon Jackson Community College, Sitka, Alaska, is involved in training education staff for Native Americans.

South Dakota State University, Brookings, South Dakota, has summer programs in cultural enrichment for Native Indian Americans

Southeastern State College, Durant, Oklahoma, holds an annual Guidance Institute for Indian School personnel with an emphasis on Indian heritage.

University of Alaska, College, Alaska, has bilingual training programs.

University of Arizona, Tucson, Arizona, has Indian related courses.

University of California, Davis, California, has a Native American Studies program.

University of California at Los Angeles has special programs for minorities, including Indians.

University of Kansas, Lawrence, Kansas, has numerous courses on Indians.

University of Minnesota, Harvard, and Pennsylvania State University, University Park, Pennsylvania, form a consortium which offers training to Native Americans to the doctoral level in education administration. Special education programs are also offered.

University of Minnesota, Minneapolis, Minnesota, has a Division of Indian Studies with a full four-year program leading to a bachelor's degree.

University of Montana, Missoula, Montana, has a division of Indian services.

University of Nevada, Reno, Nevada, has research, language, history, and culture studies.

University of New Mexico, Albuquerque, New Mexico, has a cultural center and an Indian law program.

University of Oklahoma has numerous Indian related courses and an extensive book publishing program on Indians from the University of Oklahoma Press.

University of Oregon, Eugene, Oregon, has a Native American studies program.

University of South Dakota, Vermillion, South Dakota, has an institute of Indian studies.

University of Washington, Seattle, Washington, has an Indian studies program.

Washington State University, Pullman, Washington, has a Native American studies program.

Western Washington, State College, Bellingham, Washington, has an ethnic studies program.

Wisconsin State University, Superior, Wisconsin, has a workshop for teachers of Indian children.

Other resources are mentioned as possibly having pertinent information. The state departments of education in states heavily populated by Native Indian Americans may have excellent materials and pamphlets, especially in the states of Arizona, California, New Mexico, Oklahoma, North and South Dakota, Washington, Oregon, Nevada, and Alaska. The Bureau of Indian Affairs, Department of the Interior, Washington, D.C. 20242, also has representative pamphlets, photographs, and suggested resource materials. The Indian Education Resource Center, Branch of Research, P.O. Box 1788, Albuquerque, New Mexico, may also be of assistance. *The Journal of American Indian Education*, Bureau of Educational Research and Service of the college of education, Arizona State University, Tome, Arizona 85281, is recommended as a general resource.

Introduction to Native Indian American Studies

Bahr, Howard M.; Chadwick, Bruce A.; and Day, Robert C. *Native Americans Today: Sociological Perspectives*. New York: Harper & Row, 1972.

Collier, John. *American Indian Ceremonial Dances* (*Navajo*, *Pueblo*, *Apache*, and *Zuni*). New York: Crown Publishers, Bounty Books, 1972.

Costo, Rupert, ed. *Textbooks and the American Indian*. San Francisco: Indian Historian Press, 1451 Masonic Avenue, 94417, 1970.

Council on Interracial Books for Children. *Chronicles of American Indian Protest*. New York: Fawcett Publications, 1971.

D'Amato, Janet, and D'Amato, Alex. *American Indian Craft Inspirations*. M. Evans and Company, Inc., 216 East 49 Street, New York, N.Y. 10017, 1972.

Davis, Christopher. With an introduction by Marlon Brando. *North American Indian*. London: Hamlyn House, Feltham, Middlesex, England, 1969.

Dixon, Joseph K. *The Vanishing Race*. New York: Popular Library, 1913 and 1972.

ERIC Clearinghouse on Rural Education and Small Schools, Box 3AP, New Mexico State University, Las Cruces, New Mexico 88001. Inquire for research papers and documents on Native Indian Americans.

Fuchs, Estelle, and Havighurst, Robert J. *To Live on the Earth: American Indian Education*. Garden City, New York: Doubleday, 1972.

Huenemann, Lynn. *101 Immediately Useful Ideas and Resources for Schools and Teachers of Indian Students*. Available from the author, Lee General Delivery, Tesuque, New Mexico, 1973.

Indian Education Resource Center (Branch of Research), Bureau of Indian Affairs, P.O. Box 1788, Albuquerque, New Mexico. Various research bulletins.

Indian Historical Society and Indian Historian Press, *The Indian Historian*, *The American Indian Reader*, *Handbook of the American Indian Series*, and *The Weewish Tree* (a magazine of Indian Americans for young people), 1451 Masonic Avenue, San Francisco, California 94117. The subscription price for the magazine is $6.50.

Locke, Raymond F. *The American Indian*. Mankind Series of Great Adventures of History. Los Angeles: Mankind Publishing Co., 1970.

McGrath, James. *Art and the Indian Child* (also available are *Dance and the Indian Child* and *Music and the Indian Child*). Available from the author, Institute of American Indian Arts, Santa Fe, New Mexico.

Myers, J. Jay. *Red Chiefs and White Challengers*. New York: Simon & Schuster, 1972.

National Indian Education Association, *Contemporary Issues of the American Indian*. 3036 University Avenue, S.E., Minneapolis, Minnesota 55414, 1974.

Sanders, Thomas E., and Peek, Walter W. *Literature of the American Indian*. New York: Glencoe Press (Macmillan), 1973.

Southwestern Cooperative Educational Laboratory, *Native American Professional Resource Directory*, ed. by David Honahni, 2017 Yale, S.E., Albuquerque, New Mexico 87106, 1973, $4.50.

Special Subcommittee on Indian Education of the Committee on Labor and Public Welfare, United States Senate. *Indian Education: A National Tragedy—A National Challenge*. Washington, D.C.: Government Printing Office, 1969.

State Departments of Education (Indian Division)—Arizona: Information pamphlets; Idaho: *Books About Indians and Reference Material* and *There's an Indian in Your Classroom*; Minnesota: Research and reference material; Nevada: *Know Your Nevada Indians* and *Our Desert Friends*; and Oklahoma: Pamphlets on Indians in public schools.

Taylor, Calvin. *Instructional Media and Creativity*. Proceedings of the Sixth Utah Creativity Research Conference. New York: John Wiley & Sons, 1966.

Taylor, Theodore W. *The States and Their Indian Citizens*. Washington, D.C.: Department of the Interior, Bureau of Indian Affairs, U.S. Government Printing Office, 1972. Includes a map of Indian land areas.

von Bertalanffy, Ludwig. *General System Theory*. New York: Braziller, 1968.

Waddell, Jack O., and Watson, O. Michael. *The American Indian in Urban Society*. Boston: Little, Brown and Co., 1971.

Williams, Carroll Warner, and Bird, Gloria. *A Filmography for American Indian Education.* Zia Cine, Inc., P.O. Box 493, Santa Fe, New Mexico 87501, 1973.

MEDIA AND MATERIALS—ANNOTATED

Films (16mm)

A BOY OF THE NAVAJOS. CORF 1956. El-J. 11 min b&w/col. Rental $5 (b&w), $6.50 (col); purchase $65 (b&w), $130 (col).

This is the story of a present day Navajo boy as he herds sheep in the Arizona desert, spends evenings with his family in their hogan, and takes a trip to the trading post where he sells drawings he has made of the Navajos.

A BOY OF THE SEMINOLES. CORF 1956. P-El-J. 11 min b&w/col. Rental $5 (b&w), $6.50 (col); purchase $65 (b&w), $130 (col).

By visiting Naha's people, the Seminoles, and seeing a boy and his family and their way of life, and the boy traveling into the swamp as he returns the baby alligator captured by his dog, viewers learn of life among the Indians of the Everglades.

AGE OF THE BUFFALO. UK/EBEC 1968. El-J-S. 14 min col. Rental $6 (per day), $9.60 (per week).

With paintings by Frederic Remington and other artists of the mid 1800s, the film presents life on the Western plains—how Indians followed and hunted the buffalo for food, clothing, and shelter; how white men slaughtered the buffalo herds for sport and profit. Explains how the Indians' way of life was changed when the buffalo were gone.

AMERICAN INDIAN INFLUENCE ON THE UNITED STATES, THE. DP 1972. El-J-S-A. 20 min col. Rental $30; purchase $295.

Narrated by Barry Sullivan, this film depicts how life in the United States today has been influenced by the Indian—economically, socially, philosophically, and culturally. It follows the Indian trails which have become major highways and features nine dances and ceremonies authentically portrayed by the University of California at Los Angeles.

AMERICAN INDIAN IN TRANSITION, THE. ATLAP/UC 1974. J-S-C. 22 min col. Purchase $275.

A Native Indian American mother, living on a reservation, describes her family and tribal problems by relating her past and her dreams for the future. The film engenders an understanding and appreciation of Indian problems, concepts, and values.

AMERICAN INDIANS AS SEEN BY D. H. LAWRENCE. CORF/USC-ISC 1966. S-C-A. 14 min b&w/col. Rental $6.50; purchase $81.25 (b&w), $162.50 (col).

At the Lawrence ranch near Taos, New Mexico, where the great novelist spent most of his later years, his wife, Frieda, speaks intimately about his beliefs and thoughts. Aldous Huxley presents selections from Lawrence, which reveal his deep insights into the religious and ceremonial impulses of Indian culture as shown by various ritual dances.

AMERICAN INDIANS BEFORE EUROPEAN SETTLEMENT. CORF 1959. P-El-J-S. 11 min b&w/col. Rental $4.10; purchase $71 (b&w), $142 (col).

Before the arrival of the Europeans, North America was inhabited by Indian tribes who had occupied the continent for thousands of years. Where they originally came from, how they lived, and the five basic regions of the United States—the Eastern Woodlands, Great Plains, Southwest, Far West, and Northwest Coast are portrayed in this account of Indian life.

AMERICAN INDIAN SPEAKS, THE. EBEC 1973. J-S-C. 23 min col. Purchase $290.

This documentary lets the Indian speak about his people and heritage, about the white man and the future. Visits with the Muskogee Creek, Sioux, and Nisqually yield eloquent portraits about life on today's reservations. Highlighting the action are poetic Indian speeches interpreted by Academy Award nominee Chief Dan George.

AMERICAN INDIAN, THE—AFTER THE WHITE MAN CAME. HFC 1972. El-J-S. 19 min col. Rental $30; purchase $300.

This film presents a comprehensive study of the Indian from early migration routes to the development of the main tribes of North America. It is narrated by Iron Eyes Cody, a member of the Cherokee tribe, who is an actor, author, authority on Indian history, and popular master of ceremonies at Indian councils and powwows. Discusses such topics as: Who were the ancestors of the Indian? What migration routes did these early Indians follow? What were the names and locations of the principal tribes?

AMERICAN INDIAN, THE—BEFORE THE WHITE MAN. HANDEL 1974. J-S-A. 19 min col. Rental $25; purchase $235.

Presents a comprehensive study of the Native Indian American. It traces the early Asian descendants who migrated from Siberia to Alaska, fanned out into Mexico and the Americas, and developed many civilizations such as the remarkable Aztec empire, which lasted until the Spanish conquest.

ANANSI THE SPIDER. TEXF 1969. El-J. 10 min col. Rental $15; purchase $140.

In this tale, Anansi falls into a river and is swallowed by a fish. He is rescued by his six extraordinary sons and then is carried off by a falcon. Again, his sons save him. Anansi wants to reward the son who has helped him the most with a beautiful white globe.

AND THE MEEK SHALL INHERIT THE EARTH. IU 1972. S-C. 59 min col. Rental $20.50; purchase $550.

An account of the Indians of Menominee County, Wisconsin, the only Indian-governed county in the nation which is now losing its struggle for self-sufficiency. During the 1950s the Menominees acquired $10.5 million in their treasury and the government decided that they were ready to be "terminated" as a tribe under the supervision of the Bureau of Indian Affairs. They now have to pay taxes and purchase the land they have lived on for generations. Public services are disappearing and 70 percent of the people are under the $3,000 poverty level.

ARROW TO THE SUN. TEXF 1973. El–J. 12 min col. Rental $12; purchase $165.

From the Acoma Pueblo in New Mexico comes this classic tale of a boy's search for his father: the universal search for identity, purpose, and continuity. This recent and relevant film is designed to tell a beautiful story and inspire young people.

ARTS AND CRAFTS OF THE SOUTHWEST INDIANS. OUSD 1953. S–A. 22 min col. Rental, free.

This film is presented in two parts. Part 1 deals with nomadic Navajos and the production of their beautiful turquoise and silver jewelry and handwoven rugs. Part 2 tells about the arts and crafts of the Pueblo-type tribes, such as the Zunis, and their silver work, baskets, and pottery.

BALLAD OF CROWFOOT, THE. MGH 1974. J–S–A. 10 min b&w. Rental $12.50; purchase $125.

This graphic history of the Canadian West was created by a group of Canadian Indians who wished to reflect the traditions, attitudes, and problems of their people. Throughout the film a Dylan-style ballad is run which surveys the broken treaties and speculates wryly whether there will be a better tomorrow.

BIG POWWOW AT GALLUP. HUMBLE/OUSD. S. 20 min col. Rental, free.

This film covers the highlights of the annual Inter-Tribal Indian Ceremonial: street parades, evening dance programs, afternoon Indian sports, and exhibit hall of Indian crafts and arts with working demonstrators.

BITTER WIND. BYU 1963. El–J–S–A. 30 min col. Rental $15.90; purchase $265.

A classic, timeless film about Indian alcoholism. Filmed in the Four Corners area of the American Southwest, *Bitter Wind* is a dramatic portrayal of an Indian boy whose family is destroyed by liquor.

BRYAN BEAVERS: A MOVING PORTRAIT. IU 1969. S–C–A. 30 min col. Rental $12.50; purchase $240.

Bryan Beavers is a Maidu Indian living in a log cabin which he built by himself in the wilderness of Plumas County, California. He is a man who has experienced two distinct cultures which combined give him a unique personality. As Beavers talks about his past—Indian spirits, his ancestral history, and his life—the camera follows him about his daily tasks such as taking care of his animals, making a snowshoe, and eating.

CALIFORNIA'S DAWN (MISSIONS, RANCHOS, AND AMERICANS). KLEIN/IU 1963. El-J-S-C-A. 15 min col. Rental $7.50.

This film is a survey of California history. The film shows: missions and mission life; the important contribution of Indian labor; the tallow trade; the government offering to settle territory; the burden of proof of ownership of grantees; and the Russian settlement at Fort Ross, Russian River—evidences of Russian occupation of the country north of San Francisco.

CEREMONIAL DANCES OF THE SOUTHWEST TRIBES. AMBP 1939. S-A. 10 min b&w. Rental, free.

Presents thirteen different ceremonial dances of the southwestern Indians, such as the Pony and Corn dances of the Hopi, Horsetail and Hoop dances of the Taos, Devil dance of the Apache and San Carlos, Rabbit dance of the Kiowa, Eagle dance of the Tesuque and San Juan tribes, Rainbow dance of the Santa Claras, Deer dance of the San Juan, Mud dance of the Navajo, and Buffalo dance of the Tesuque. Includes descriptive narration and sound recording of chants and drums.

CHEYENNE AUTUMN. MFI/IDEAL. El-J-S-A. 156 min col. Rental $35.

John Ford has made a beautiful and powerful motion picture that tells a profound and passionate story of mistreatment of Indians in a strong plea for tolerance. Adapted from the novel which was based on an actual incident, the film shows the valiant efforts of Cheyenne Indians to escape to their Wyoming homeland from the wretched Oklahoma reservation.

CIRCLE OF THE SUN. NFBC/MGH 1960. El-J-S-A. 30 min col. Rental $20; purchase $300.

Taking the impressive and nostalgic ritual of the Sun dance on the Blood Indian reservation in Alberta, Canada, as its framework, this film examines the life of the Indian with honesty and perception. The conflicting attractions of tradition, with its call to heroism and greatness, and assimilation into the mainstream of Canadian life, with its economic wealth, place the Indian in a dilemma that has yet to be solved satisfactorily.

CLUES TO ANCIENT INDIAN LIFE. AIMS 1962. El-J-S-A. 11 min col. Rental $15; purchase $150.

This film shows the study of primitive man. Using ancient drawings and paintings, the film delineates the art and communication and identifies the culture of primitive man. This film also suggests ways we learn about the past, the kinds of clues ancient man left behind, and the importance of preserving these artifacts for study. Designed for all ages. Produced by Dave Estes.

DAWN HORSE, THE. STAN 1972. El-J-S-A. 18 min col. Rental $24; purchase $210.

Told by Jay Silverheels, *The Dawn Horse* is photographed in the remaining wilderness of North America. Today, the cultures of many civilizations blend into one, but once the only communities of man were Indian. Each tribe, each nation, had its dignified message of truth which frequently revealed man's deeper relationship with nature. Boniface Bonnie, Navajo singer, sings of the mountains that surround his world. A group of young Indian students perform traditional songs, including a Pawnee dance, a Sioux lullaby, and a Zuni sunrise song.

DAY OF PROMISE. BYU 1967. J-S. 22 min col. Rental $13.20; purchase $220.

Follows two Indian children from elementary school through college in the Mormon Indian Placement Program (Indian children are taken into Mormon homes and become foster children during the school year, then return home during the summer). Made for use in the Church of Jesus Christ of Latter-day Saints.

DESERT PEOPLE. SF/OUSD 1970. S-C-A. 25 min col. Rental, free.

Produced by the federal government for use in Indian education, this is the story of the Papago Indians who have lived on the desert for centuries. They find uses for nearly every growing thing. Even in this extremely dry region, they manage to farm a little and raise cattle. The story was written by the Indians themselves and by the people who have lived and worked with them for years.

DISCOVERING AMERICAN INDIAN MUSIC. BFA/UK 1970. J-S-C. 26 min col. Rental $12 (per day); $19.20 (per week); purchase $325.

Songs and dances of various tribes are performed in authentic costumes, and members of the various tribes explain the social and ceremonial functions of the music. The film ends with a composition on a computer.

END OF THE TRAIL: THE AMERICAN PLAINS INDIAN. MGH 1967. J-S-C. 53 min b&w. Rental $29; purchase $325.

Uses the still-in-motion technique, utilizing a vast number of photographs, to depict the life and culture of the American Plains Indian and the concurrent American westward movement. Covers the period between 1860 and 1890, showing the inevitable clash between the white and red man as the latter became increasingly concerned about the white man's encroachment and destruction of the Indian's physical and spiritual environment.

EXILES, THE. MGH 1961. J-S-C-A. 72 min b&w. Rental $35; purchase $430.

This film is a dramatic documentary of the problems encountered by Indians living in urban areas and caught between two conflicting cultures. Directed by Kent Mackenzie.

FIRST AMERICANS, THE. NBCTV/IU 1969. J-S-A. 52 min col. Rental $9.75.

This film tells the story of early man's migration from the Siberian tundra across the Bering land bridge into North and South America and shows a record of man's journey through the tools and artifacts he left behind. Two parts.

FIRST AMERICAN, THE—THE LAST AMERICAN. FORES 1971. J-S. 15 min col. Purchase $630.

Presents recent and past history as the late Robert F. Kennedy underlines some contemporary Indian problems, which still affect Indian students on reservations today.

FORGOTTEN AMERICAN, THE. CORF 1968. J-S-A. 25 min col. Rental $10.05.

Documents the impoverished condition of the Indian—minimal food and housing, inadequate educational facilities, limited employment opportunities, and the continued exploitation by the white man. Explores the damaging loss of identity and self-respect.

GERONIMO JONES. LCA/IU 1970. El-J-S. 21 min col. Rental $10.50.

This story depicts a brief period in the life of Geronimo Jones, a Papago Indian youth, living on a reservation in Arizona. The main focus is on the gift his grandfather, a descendant of the Apache Chief Geronimo, gave to him. We see injustices and pain, and a youngster caught between two cultures.

GLIMPSE OF THE PAST. IU 1951. J-S. 10 min b&w/col. Rental $2.75 (b&w), $4 (col); purchase $50 (b&w), $100 (col).

Shows, by means of archeologists' activities, exhibits, and dioramas, evidence of how prehistoric Indians lived. Describes the structure of their homes, their food-gathering activities, and several other phases of their culture. From the "Pre-History" series.

GO MY SON. BYU 1971. S-C. 26 min col. Rental $13.20; purchase $220.

Features Indian students at Brigham Young University, where over six hundred Indian students are enrolled full time. Discusses opportunities, needs, and goals of the Indian from the Mormon point of view.

HAIDA CARVER. IFB 1964. J-S-C. 12 min col. Rental $12.50; purchase $150.

Presents a young Haida Indian carrying on a tradition of his people. The Haida Indians have lived for centuries on the Queen Charlotte Islands off the Pacific coast of Canada. Most of them are fishermen, but this young man is encouraged by his grandfather to perfect the craft he has taught him, that of carving miniature totems from argillite, a soft dark slate. Using the legends of his tribe as subjects, he persists in an art which is gradually dying out as more and more of the Haida Indians leave the islands. A National Film Board of Canada film.

HANDS OF MARIA, THE. RMIF 1968. P-El-J-S. 15 min col. Rental $12.50; purchase $150.

Shows Maria Martinez, an Indian artist of the Southwest, working without a potter's wheel, following the ancient techniques of her people to create the exquisitely beautiful black pottery for which she is renowned. The film captures Maria Martinez' great dignity and serenity. Maria is shown firing her wares in an open kiln. Fired pots, plates, and bowls are removed from ashes to show brilliant metallic black with paintings.

HOME. SBRTC 1971. J-S. 30 min col. Rental $5; purchase $300.
The ecological crisis is depicted through scenes of modern pollution presented in contrast with an Indian chief's heart-felt love for his natural environment. He reminds the viewer that whatever befalls the sons of the earth—"to harm the earth is to heap contempt on its creator."

HOPI INDIAN ARTS AND CRAFTS. CORF 1945. P-El-J-S. 11 min b&w/col. Purchase $65 (b&w), $130 (col).
This study of the Hopi Indians centers on their distinctive handicraft. Weaving, silversmithing, basket and pottery making are all shown in detail. This film records the skill and patience in these interesting native arts.

HOPI INDIAN VILLAGE LIFE. CORF/USC-ISC 1956. P-El-J-S. 11 min b&w/col. Rental $4.10; purchase $65 (b&w), $130 (col).
This portrayal of the Hopi Indians and their mode of living as it exists today makes clear the changing character of Hopi Indian life. Meeting Bob, Ralph, Mrs. Hotewa, Grandmother White Sand, and other villagers, and observing them at their daily work, reveal a blending of old and new ways.

HOPI KACHINAS. ACI/IU 1961. P-El-J. 10 min col. Rental $6.15; purchase $130.
An in-depth study of an Indian tribe's religion and beliefs which are expressed mainly through spiritual dances. Kachina dolls, little wooden images of the dancers, are made for Hopi children as representations of various supernatural spirits, other Indians, or creatures from mythology. This film will help dispel the stereotype notions children have about the Native Indian American.

HOPI WAY, THE. SHOSPI 1972. S-C. 22 min col. Rental $21; purchase $290.
Hopis have occupied land on three southwestern mesas for 1300 years. Agricultural people, organized into self-sustaining communities in Arizona, have lived in harmony with nature and themselves, shunning most efforts at assimilation into the larger society. The movement of a large coal-mining company into the Black Mesa now threatens to upset the fabric of Hopi life. The vast mine scars the landscape, fills the air with pollutants, and brings more powerful industrial and land interests into the Hopi's traditional lands.

INDIAN AMERICA. IDI 1969. El-J-S. 90 min col. Rental $25; purchase $800.
Henry Fonda narrates this well-done documentary, the purpose of which is to help the white man understand Indians of today, their values, their heritage, and their life-style. Many Indian people from all over the United States are shown as they talk about what concerns them.

INDIAN BOY IN TODAY'S WORLD. CORF/IU 1971. P-El-J. 14 min col. Rental $8.50; purchase $175.

David, a nine-year-old Makah Indian, who has lived on the reservation all his life, is moving to Seattle to join his father. David leaves behind his friends and the many activities on the reservation and faces the challenge of growing up in a non-Indian world.

INDIAN BOY OF THE SOUTHWEST. BFA 1963. P-El. 15 min b&w. Rental $10 (3 days); purchase $160.

Indian Boy of the Southwest allows the viewer to look at life on the Hopi reservation today as seen through the eyes of a young Hopi boy, Toboya; traces the history of contact with Europeans; shows a Hopi family eating and the ways they make a living; shows their customs and traditions.

INDIAN CANOES ALONG THE WASHINGTON COAST. UWASHP 1972. P-El-J-S. 18 min col. Purchase $150.

This film demonstrates how and with what tools a canoe is carved. The traditional cedar dugout canoes of Northwest Indians are still used as fishing and racing vessels, as they have been for centuries past. The highly competitive river and saltwater races, the stocking of a king salmon hatchery, dancing, and a salmon bake are shown.

INDIAN CONVERSATION. FI 1974. J-A. 13 min col. Rental $8 (per day), $12.80 (per week).

Two college graduates, Maria DeManto, raised in an urban environment, and Francis Levier, raised on a reservation in Kansas and educated at a boarding school, explore their identities as Indians, their feelings of isolation, and their hopes for the future.

INDIAN COWBOY. OUSD. J-S. 20 min col. Rental, free.

In 1934 the Indian agency bought cattle from the drought areas and loaned them to the Indians. The film shows how 8,000 Indians now have profitable herds and have paid back a calf for every animal borrowed. Other Indians are advised to participate in the cattle program in the interests of their own security rather than to lease land.

INDIAN FAMILY OF THE CALIFORNIA DESERT. EH 1964. El-J. 15 min b&w/col. Purchase $95 (b&w), $185 (col).

A Cahuilla woman employed at the Palm Springs Desert Museum narrates details of childhood memories as Indian children and tribesmen reenact scenes of early primitive life. This film illustrates Cahuilla Indians adapting to their desert and mountain environment; their craft skills in weapon making, basket weaving, and pottery making. Depicts the creativity, intelligence, and joy characteristic of their daily living activities. Indian "accent" adds measure of realism to the film.

INDIAN HERITAGE: THE TREASURE. CSMIE/BFA 1971. El-S-C. 13 min col. Purchase $110.

Two young Indian brothers want to modernize their father's fishing methods. Why carve a dugout canoe when motorboats can be bought? But then conflict arises between Indian fishing tradition and modern laws. Their father is jailed.

The boys begin to understand that new ways will not coexist with the old, and they, too, must choose.

INDIAN HOUSE, THE. OUSD/GATEPI 1950. S. 10 min b&w. Rental, free.
Illustrates the architecture of southwestern United States including the cliff dwellings of the Indians, the Spanish influence after 1540, and the contributions of Americans from the East after 1846.

INDIAN INFLUENCES IN THE UNITED STATES. UK 1964. El–J–S. 11 min b&w/col. Rental $4 (per day), $6.40 (per week); purchase $65 (b&w), $130 (col).
This film points out that the early settlers in America learned to hunt as the Indians did, to plant crops as the Indians planted them, and to follow Indian trails; and that they used Indian names for their towns and rivers. Many aspects of Indian heritage continue to the present day in art and music, foods, the locations of many cities and highways, and in language and literature.

INDIAN LAND: THE NATIVE AMERICAN ECOLOGIST. MFI 1972. J–S–A. 21 min b&w/col. Rental $17.50; purchase $250.
In candid vignettes, Indians discuss their traditional veneration for the earth—their concept of land as being free for use by anyone who respects it as the air and water are free. When the Indians signed treaties with the settlers, one explains, they were indicating their willingness to share the land. Now that contemporary Indians see the industrialization, they want to save their reservations.

INDIAN MUSICAL INSTRUMENTS. OUSD 1955. S. 13 min col. Rental, free.
This film shows the importance of music in the Indian life-pattern; demonstrates the making and playing of different kinds of drums, rattles, flutes, and whistles. Shows specimens from the University of Oklahoma Museum. Songs and dances from various tribes are also presented.

INDIANS IN THE AMERICAS. BFA 1971. El–J–S. 16 min col. Rental $12; purchase $215.
It is believed that the first Americans migrated to these continents from Asia over 20,000 years ago. The first arrivals were probably hunters; but as centuries passed, the Indians developed agriculture and advanced civilizations such as those of the Mayans and the Incas. The film examines many of the contributions of the Indian.

INDIANS OF EARLY AMERICA. EBEC/OUSD 1957. S. 22 min b&w/col. Rental $7.50; purchase $150 (b&w), $290 (col).
Re-creates the environment and typical activities of tribes from the Eastern Woodlands, the Great Plains, the Southwest, and the Northwest. The film includes the ceremonies attending the death of an Iroquois chief and the election of his successor, a Sioux buffalo hunt, pottery making in a Pueblo village, and a potlatch ceremony.

INDIANS OF THE PLAINS–LIFE IN THE PAST. OUSD/ACA 1957. S. 22 min col. Rental, free.

The film shows how the Plains Indian lived before the white man arrived, depending on the buffalo for food, clothing, and shelter. Examples are shown of quill and beadwork decorations on clothing and moccasins, preparation of pemmican, painting of household articles, and a typical encampment beside a river.

INDIANS OF THE PLAINS–PRESENT DAY LIFE. OUSD/ACA 1957. S. 11 min col. Rental, free.

The film shows how the Plains Indians of today live on reservations in the West and earn their living by farming, sheep raising, cattle raising, tanning hides, and making moccasins for tourists. The grandson of a chief makes a warbonnet of eagle feathers and beadwork. A typical school on the reservation is shown.

INDIANS OF THE PLAINS–SUN DANCE CEREMONY. OUSD/ACA 1957. S. 11 min col. Rental, free.

At the Sun dance encampment, Indians are shown erecting a tepee, a "sweat lodge," and the "medicine lodge" where the ceremonial Sun dance takes place. It is followed by the social Grass dance.

INDIANS OF THE SOUTHWEST, OUR LAND, OUR PEOPLE, U.S.A. SERIES. MFI 1972. J-S-A. 16 min col. Rental $15; purchase $200.

Among the first Indians to give up nomadic ways were the Cochise, becoming farmers and eventually developing a system of irrigation and housing that required a high degree of organization. This film focuses on the history and culture of these peoples, their descendants, the Pueblos, and the other tribes that settled in the Southwest, including the Navajos, the Hopi, and the Zuni.

INDIAN SPEAKS, THE. NFBC/UM 1967. El-S. 40 min col. Rental $25.

Indian people of Canada tell their story. They are troubled when they see the old customs, which many feel should be preserved, being lost. They wonder what will become of the young Indians in the future. Will education be the answer? they ask. A thought-provoking portrayal of the dilemma of the modern Indian torn between the serenity of the reserve and the comforts of the city.

INDIANS, THE. XEROX 1970. J-S-C. 31 min col.

The film begins as an old Indian tells about his people and about the white men who will come to his land and try to change the Indian's way of life. The old Indian tells of his forefathers, who passed on the stories of their people by word of mouth. These stories are of the Utes and the Indians of the plains: Cheyenne, Arapaho, Pawnee, Comanche, Kiowa, and Sioux.

IN SEARCH OF A CITY. IU 1961. S-C-A. 9 min b&w/col. Rental $2.55 (b&w), $3.60 (col); purchase $35 (b&w), $75 (col).

Visits Mesa Verde National Park in southwestern Colorado. Discusses the work of archeologists and how they uncover ancient Indian cities. Shows an Indian burial ground; homes of early cliff dwellers; and workers excavating, mapping, and recording their discoveries. Explains how their work provides knowledge of early Indians. From the "National Parks" series.

ISHI IN TWO WORLDS. RTOMP 1967. J-S-A. 19 min col. Purchase $250.
Based on the book by Theodora Kroeber. Recaptures faithfully and sensitively the story of the Yahi Indians of California, and of Ishi, the last Yahi who spent most of his life leading a totally aboriginal existence. Historic still photographs and footage of great visual beauty capture the presence and spirit of the Yahi. The last years of Ishi's life in San Francisco are excellently portrayed.

ISLAND OF THE BLUE DOLPHIN (An Introduction). IU 1966. P-El-J. 20 min col. Rental $10.25; purchase $260.

An excerpt from a feature film based on the book of the same title by Scott O'Dell. Portrays the life of Chalas—on an island off the California coast in 1801. Depicts the diminished tribe, after many battles with sea-otter hunters, leaving the island for a mainland mission. Karena, an Indian girl, seeing her younger brother on the shore, dives into the water and swims back to the island. The viewer is left to decide the fate of the children.

JIM THORPE—ALL AMERICAN. MFI. El-C. 107 min b&w. Rental $22.50.
The life of Jim Thorpe, who has been acclaimed by the sportswriters of America as the "greatest athlete of the twentieth century," is portrayed in a warm and poignant film biography. Burt Lancaster stars as the Oklahoma farm boy whose athletic prowess was developed at the Carlisle Indian School in Pennsylvania. He becomes a star halfback and gold-medal winner at the 1912 Olympics in Stockholm, but his life is dogged by heartbreak and pathos.

JOHNNY FROM FORT APACHE. EBEC/USC-ISC 1971. I-J. 15 min col. Rental $7.50; purchase $185.

An Apache family moves from the reservation to the city and finds readjustment difficult as they encounter a new life-style.

KEE BEGAY, NAVAJO BOY. HSTFR/OUSD 1965. S. 27 min col. Rental, free.

This film depicts the problems facing the Navajo Indians and the help they are receiving from the Franciscan missionaries in the Southwest. Photographed on an actual Navajo reservation, the film relates the story of Kee, a Navajo boy who embodies the struggles of the Indians.

LAST MENOMINEE. IU 1966. El-S. 30 min b&w. Rental $6.75; purchase $125.

A series of interviews filmed on location in Menominee County, Wisconsin, during which various Menominees describe their doubts, their hopes for the future, and their problems which they now face during the termination of their reservation status by the Bureau of Indian Affairs. The Menominee Indians have gained citizenship, but they have lost their hunting and fishing rights and lack food as a result. They are also without doctors and hospitals, and adequate education and employment are no longer available.

LEARNING ABOUT THE PAST. IU 1951. S-C-A. 10 min b&w/col. Rental $2.75 (b&w), $4 (col); purchase $50 (b&w), $100 (col).

This film shows how archeologists work to reveal the story of prehistoric times by picturing the activities at a Mounds Indian dig. The film shows the work in the field, the sorting and cataloging of artifacts, the construction of an Indian stockade, and dioramas of various Indian cultures.

LEGEND OF THE MAGIC KNIVES. EBEC/IU 1971. El-J-S. 11 min col. Rental $6.50; purchase $150.

A totem village in the Pacific Northwest provides the setting for this portrayal of an ancient Indian legend. After an old chief realizes that the carvings of an apprentice are superior to his, he throws a knife at the guardian of the carvings, but strikes himself. He is permitted to choose any form of death, however, and selects to be a river always flowing close to his native tribe. The legend is recounted by means of figures on a totem and authentic Indian masks.

LEGENDS OF THE SIOUX. UK 1968. J-S-C. 27 min col. Rental $12 (per day), $19.20 (per week).

Filmed in South Dakota, the story relates many of the legends of the Sioux Indians. The actors and narrators are members of the Sioux tribe. It shows Indians amidst the state's most beautiful scenery.

LOON'S NECKLACE. UK 1953. El-J-S. 11 min col. Rental $4 (per day), $6.50 (per week).

This film brings to life a charming Indian legend of how the loon, a water bird, received a distinguishing neckband. Authentic ceremonial masks, carved by Indians of Pacific Canada, establish the characters of the story and clearly portray the Indian's sensitivity to the moods of nature. Rich color photography, skillful narration, and unique background music increase the effectiveness of this film for the use of art appreciation, arts and crafts, as well as language classes.

MARIA OF THE PUEBLOS. CENTRO/IU 1971. P-El-J-S-A. 15 min col. Rental $8.50; purchase $220.

The purpose of the film is to cultivate an understanding and appreciation of the culture, philosophy, art, and economic condition of the North American Indians, particularly the Pueblo Indians of San Ildefonso, New Mexico. In addition, the film presents the step-by-step process of forming, polishing, decorating, and firing the unique pottery of Maria Martinez and her family.

MEET THE SIOUX INDIAN. OUSD/IFB 1956. S. 10 min col. Rental, free.

This film shows the way of life of the Sioux Indians constantly on the move, carrying their possessions on travois. Their dependence upon the buffalo for food, shelter, and clothing is shown. Tepees are erected, meat is prepared as pemmican, beadwork and quill work are demonstrated, and corn and pumpkins are prepared for winter.

MIGHTY WARRIORS. IU 1964. El-J-S. 30 min b&w. Rental $6.75; purchase $125.

This film pictures the major encounters between the white man and the Plains Indians. Dramatizes the Battle of Little Big Horn, the Sand Creek Massacre, and the Fetterman Massacre. Points out that Americans are indebted to the Indians for a great amount of agricultural, and military and political knowledge. From the "Glory Trail" series.

MISSIONS OF THE SOUTHWEST. BARR 1967. El-J. 15 min col. Rental $15; purchase $180.

This film shows the missions as they appear today and interprets them in terms of their characteristic features, role in history, and influence in the present-day Southwest. Contributes to an understanding of our Spanish cultural heritage.

NAVAJO (Part 1). KETCTV/IU 1969. S-A. 29 min b&w. Rental $6.75; purchase $125.

Presents a visit to a Navajo reservation to discover the values held by this indigenous community. Questions are put to an Indian family to find out each member's duties, responsibilities, and privileges. Compares Navajo and modern medical practices and religious rituals and beliefs. Concludes by discussing the problems of reconciling traditional Navajo ways with modern technology. From the "Search for America" series.

NAVAJO (Part 2). KETCTV/IU 1969. S-A. 29 min b&w. Rental $6.75; purchase $125.

Presents a visit to Windrock, Arizona, to interview members of the Navajo Tribes Council. Discusses the problems of working within the tribal organizational patterns and of the continuing force of tradition. Questions and answers concerning education, agriculture, religion, and the adaptations to be made in light of modern science and new social values are included. From the "Search for America" series.

NAVAJO. MFI 1969. J-S-A. 16 min col. Rental $12.50; purchase $175.

Deep in the heart of the Grand Canyon is the ancient land of the Navajos. Here the remnants of this matriarchal society still tend their sheep, barter for necessities at the trading posts scattered every twenty-five miles or so in the area, and eke out an existence that goes from searing summer heat to frigid winter cold. The Navajos live outdoors as much as they can. But changes are in the wind, and the government irrigation dams may radically alter the Navajo's way of life.

NAVAJO, A PEOPLE BETWEEN TWO WORLDS. LINE/UU 1975. El-A. 22 min col. Rental $10.50; purchase $250.

The Navajo is a herder by nature and for the last one hundred years has roamed the mountains and valleys with his flocks and herds, seeking pasture and water. We see illustrated the old life which revolves around the isolated hogan, and the simple needs met by the trading post where the Navajo trades wool for flour, coffee, and cloth. Education is by far the most important thread for the new pattern of Navajo living.

NAVAJO INDIAN LIFE. CORF/UK 1966. P-El-J-S-C-A. 11 min col. Rental $5 (per day), $8 (per week); purchase $142.

Life of the Navajo in Arizona, Utah, and New Mexico—their daily life, their occasional jobs as migrant field hands, their hopes for the future. Describes the life of Indians living in the canyon. Shows ancient ruins of early Indian cliff dwellers.

NAVAJO INDIANS. UK 1956. El-S. 11 min b&w. Rental $2 (per day), $3.20 (per week).

Portrays the Navajos in their native environment, engaged in such activities as building a home, tilling the soil, tending sheep, carding wool, and weaving colorful blankets. The viewer also observes barter at a local trading post, the performance of native dances, a marriage ceremony, and wedding feast. The story centers around Taska and Alnaba, a young Navajo couple who are betrothed.

NAVAJO INDIAN, THE. CORF/IU 1968. P-El-A. 11 min col. Rental $4 (per day), $6 (per week); purchase $140.

This film portrays Navajo daily life and shows native arts and crafts, especially silver work and weaving; and the native habitat, customs, and ceremonials of the Navajo Indians. This film is a revision of an earlier edition.

NAVAJO LIFE. KETCTV/IU 1961. P-El-J-S. 9 min b&w/col. Rental $2.55 (b&w), $3.60 (col); purchase $35 (b&w), $75 (col).

This film shows the national monument of Canyon de Chelly in Arizona and describes the life of the Navajo Indians living in the canyon. Shows the ancient ruins of early Indian cliff dwellers; tells how the Indians farm, raise sheep, cook, and build their homes; and concludes with scenes of a trading post and an Indian rodeo. From the "National Park" series.

NAVAJO NIGHT DANCES. CORF/UK 1971. P-El-J-S. 11 min col. Rental $5 (per day), $8 (per week); purchase $130.

Provides a glimpse into a seldom seen facet of Navajo life—the family goes to a Nine Day Healing Chant. They join in the feasting and see the Arrow, Feather, and Fire dance rituals.

NAVAJOS—CHILDREN OF THE GODS. UK 1968. S-C. 20 min col. Rental $8 (per day), $12.80 (per week).

Shows how every aspect of the Navajo's life-style is spiritually related, unchanged by time, undisturbed by progress. Among many spirit forms the Navajo walks daily seeking harmony with the gods.

NAVAJO SILVERSMITH. ACI 1961. P-El-J-S. 10 min col. Rental $15; purchase $160.

A case study of an Indian craftsman who has come to grips with the white man's technology while still maintaining the values of his own culture. By focusing on a single and sensitive craftsman, this film captures the Navajo of today. Here is the blending of the old with the new; the tribal with the industrial.

NAVAJOS OF THE 70'S, THE. CENTRO 1971. El-J-S. 15 min col. Purchase $220.

This film deals with customs, history, economics, current problems, and future prospects of the Navajo Indians. Specific sequences deal with the clothing, housing, transportation, water shortages, farming, schooling, medical care, coal and lumbering industries, and language problems of today's Navajos. Myths regarding the beginning of mankind, the dislocation of the tribes from their land by the U.S. Army in 1864, and the "Long Walk" back to the old homeland are included. One rare photographic sequence shows the puberty rite of a fourteen-year-old Navajo girl.

NAVAJO, THE. JOU/IU 1969. J-S-A. 15 min col. Rental $6.50; purchase $175.

In sharp contrast with opening scenes of modern urban life in which man seems to be making his own environment independent of the natural world, the Navajos are shown to be a people whose whole way of life is integrated and spiritual. The Navajos' strong sense of identification with the environment is brought out in scenes depicting the family structure, traditions, ceremonials, and art forms of a people virtually untouched by modern civilization.

NAVAJO, THE: SHEPHERDS OF THE DESERT. RMIF 1968. P-El-J-A. 9 min col. Rental $7.50; purchase $100.

The life of the Navajo shepherds and the beauty of the unique landscape in Arizona's Monument Valley is chronicled with scenes of an Indian family performing its daily tasks. The narration describes the hogan, the methods of shearing the sheep, the processing of the wool, and the economic values of this distinct type of ranching. The mother is seen as she combs the raw wool, spins the substance into yarn, and weaves a sturdy and beautiful rug.

NORTH AMERICAN INDIAN LEGENDS. BFA 1973. El-J-S. 21 min col. Rental $20 (3 days); purchase $280.

North American Indian Legends is a beautiful recounting of Indian stories from three different regions of the United States. Opportunity for contrasts and similarities are afforded the viewer.

NORTHWEST COAST INDIANS (A SEARCH FOR THE PAST). UWASHP 1972. J-S-A. 26 min col. Purchase $200.

The Ozette Indian village at Cape Alava, Washington, has been the home of seafaring hunters for five or six thousand years. Through painstaking detective work, archaeologists and their students from Washington State University have reconstructed this abandoned village site on the basis of materials excavated—a rich variety of artifacts including pieces of baskets, bone and stone tools, combs, traces of houses, and fire hearths. Also available in 3/4" U-Matic videocassette.

NORTHWESTERN AMERICAN INDIAN WAR DANCE CONTEST. UWASHP. J-S-A. 12 min col. Purchase $150.

A developing awareness of their common cultural traits among the members of many Indian tribes is giving strength to the rise of Pan-Indian culture. One such aspect of this cultural unity is the northwestern War Dance Contest, held annually in Seattle. Here, groups and individuals from the western United States come together to compete in various styles of dancing, such as the War Dance, the Feather Dance, the Fancy Dance, and the Hoop Dance.

NORTHWEST INDIAN ART. CORF 1971. J-S-C. 11 min b&w/col. Rental $10; purchase $65 (b&w), $200 (col).

The highly sophisticated art of the Northwest Indian is shown through materials collected from six different museums. Movement and dance add meaning to the remarkable double-faced mechanical masks which were an unusual part of this culture. Demonstrates low-fire pottery methods before the potters wheel, and the high-fire pottery of Pueblo.

NOT WITH AN EMPTY QUIVER. BYU 1971. J-S-C-A. 29 min col. Rental $13.20; purchase $220.

The story of a young Indian boy fighting to overcome obstacles, combined with in-depth dialogues by Indians who have either succeeded or failed. Stresses the need for preparation to meet life rather than going forth "with an empty quiver."

ONE SPECIAL DOG. BFA 1969. P-El. 17 min col. Rental $12; purchase $220.

One Special Dog tells the story of young Indian children and their oneness with the animals around them. Shows the universal qualities of family love and concern for one another. This is a warm and understanding story of Mollie White Horse, her brother Charlie, and a stray half-tame, half-wild dog.

OSCAR HOWE: THE SIOUX PAINTER. CEF/UK 1974. J-S-C-A. 27 min col. Rental $19.50; purchase $400.

Vincent Price adds narration to the personal commentary of Oscar Howe in this new motion picture about the art, philosophy, and cultural heritage of the successful artist. Mr. Howe is a full-blood Sioux Indian, born on the Crow Creek Indian Reservation in South Dakota. He has become one of America's highly respected artists, winner of fifteen grand or first awards in national art competitions.

OUR PROUD LAND. UK 1969. J-S-A. 30 min col. Rental $12 (per day), $19.20 (per week); purchase $400.

Filmed in Monument Valley, written and narrated from the Navajo point of view, this film presents a number of sequences of modern day life of the Navajo Indians. Shown are the sheep herders, rug weavers, and the medicine man. A completed sand painting ceremony is also recorded.

OUR TOTEM IS THE RAVEN. BFA 1972. El-J-S. 21 min col. Rental $25 (3 days); purchase $295.

In *Our Totem Is the Raven*, a young Indian boy is taught the significance of his heritage by his wise grandfather, a role splendidly portrayed by Chief Dan George.

PADDLE TO THE SEA. NBCTV/CSMIE 1969. P-El-J. 8 min col. Purchase $150.

A little Indian in a canoe, carved by an Indian boy in the northern forest of Canada, is launched in the spring thaw on an epic journey to the Atlantic Ocean. There are many adventures, all photographed with great patience and an eye for the beauty of living things. Based on the story by Holling C. Holling, this is a children's film and a source for creative writing, arts, and crafts.

PEOPLE OF THE BUFFALO. NFBC/EBEC 1970. El-J-S. 14 min col. Rental $6 (per day), $9.60 (per week); purchase $185.

A revised version of *Age of the Buffalo.* Through the paintings of Frederic Remington and other artists of the mid-1800s, the film shows how following and hunting the buffalo was a way of life for the nomadic Plains Indians and how the coming of the white man threatened this way of life.

PUEBLO BOY. UK/OUSD 1964. El-A. 24 min col. Rental $6 (per day), $9.60 (per week).

The Pueblo Indians are the oldest known inhabitants of the New World, and their art, drama, religion, and democratic form of government are rooted in a thousand years of American history. *Pueblo Boy* shows the family life, education, work, and play of these early American people. Understanding their traditional dances is a feature of the film. Also of particular interest is the annual Indian festival at Gallup, New Mexico, where many tribes gather to join in a colorful celebration.

PUEBLO HERITAGE. LORIL/OUSD 1950. J-S-A. 20 min col. Rental, free.

Traces the history of the Pueblo people from Mesa Verde to the present Pueblos with emphasis on Taos, Acoma, and Zuni. Concludes with scenes of the Gallup Indian ceremonials.

RIVER PEOPLE. SF/OUSD 1970. S. 25 min col. Rental, free.

Intended for use in Indian education. From legend and history, the Pima Indians of the southwestern United States reconstructed their old way of life for this picture. Explains how they were once the richest Indian farmers of the Southwest because of their irrigation system, in use for over four hundred years.

SHADOW OF THE BUFFALO. IU 1961. P-El-J-S. 9 min b&w/col. Rental $5.25 (b&w), $6.75 (col); purchase $85 (b&w), $160 (col).

Visits Yellowstone National Park to explain the story of the American buffalo. Shows the Yellowstone herd and explains the methods used by the Indians to capture the buffalo. Tells why the white man, after the Civil War, destroyed the buffalo herds. Illustrates with film footage, dioramas, and photographs. From the "National Parks" series.

SIOUX LEGENDS. NFI/UK 1973. P-El-J-S. 20 min col. Rental $20; purchase $260.

Sioux Legends is a reenactment by Sioux Indians of several of the legends which are closest to the culture and most meaningful to the Sioux. The English narration is supported by Sioux singers who relate the same legends in Indian chants.

The film is shot with authentic museum costumes and artifacts, with reverence for all things of the universe, and with respect for the religious attitudes of the Sioux. CINE Golden Eagle, 1974.

SISIBAKWAT. FRC 1961. P-El-J-S. 18 min col. Rental $6.65; purchase $190.

A documentary film portraying the activities of a Chippewa Indian family in Minnesota as they work and play in their maple camp during April, the boiling month. Includes scenes of the family, dressed in traditional deerskin clothing, as they gather materials for their wigwam and then build it. Shows how they tap the trees, collect the sap, boil it, and make sugar.

SOLDIER BLUE. MFI 1970. S-C-A. 112 min col. Rental $65.

The conventional roles of white man and Indian are reversed in this violent and controversial western, directed by Ralph Nelson. Although other westerns have been sympathetic toward Indians, none have been as explicit as *Soldier Blue* in depicting the real story. Nelson's film suggests not only that the Indians were justified in their attacks, but that their practices actually originated with the white man. *Soldier Blue* is based loosely on the Sand Creek Massacre of 1864.

SOUTHWEST INDIAN ARTS AND CRAFTS. CORF 1973. P-El-J-S-A. 14 min col. Rental $15; purchase $192.

Using techniques passed down through countless generations, the Southwest Indians fashion beautiful and useful crafts with the raw materials that are found locally. Their fine workmanship is seen in Navajo rugs, San Ildefonso and Acoma pottery, Hipi and Zuni jewelry, Kachina dolls, and Pima and Papago baskets.

SOUTHWEST INDIANS OF EARLY AMERICA. CORF 1973. P-El-J-S-A. 14 min col. Rental $15; purchase $175.

A thousand years ago the ancestors of the Hopi, Pima, and Papago Indians were prospering in the southwestern United States. They include the Hohokam, about whom little is known, and the Anasazi, whose remains of dwellings, rock paintings, and pictographs in northern Arizona and New Mexico remind us of their early history.

STICKS AND STONES WILL BUILD A HOUSE. IU 1971. P-El-J-S. 30 min col. Rental $11.50; purchase $315.

This film traces the development of Indian architecture in southwestern United States. Initially, shelter was in the form of crude pit houses. Later, builders began using masonry construction, and finally, during the great pueblo period, built sophisticated apartment-type complexes housing as many as two thousand tenants. Early attempts to explore remaining ruins are seen in film footage photographed during archeological expeditions in the 1920s.

STOP RUINING AMERICA'S PAST. IU 1968. S-A. 21 min b&w. Rental $5.50; purchase $125.

The story of the campaign to save archeological sites in Illinois from destruction by urban and industrial expansion. Stuart Struever, professor of archeology at

Northwestern University, explains the significance of the sites. One area has been surveyed with the assistance of local residents. Struever and some of his students are shown during an "emergency" midwinter dig at an Indian crematorium. One local industry has supported this work. Struever suggests that with the help of others, the area's heritage could be saved.

SUMMER OF JOHNSON HOLIDAY, THE—NAVAJO BOY. CENTRO/UK 1971. El-J-S-C. 11 min col. Rental $12.80; purchase $170.

This film documents the summer and early fall activities of Johnson Holiday, a ten-year-old Navajo boy living on a reservation in Monument Valley in northeastern Arizona. Specific sequences in the film include: Johnson helping his father build a feed storage rack for the family's sheep and goats; Mrs. Holiday caring for her baby and weaving wool rugs; Johnson playing with his younger brother and sister; Johnson gathering wood and building a fire; the grandmother preparing to fry bread over the open cooking fire; and Johnson tending the family flock and exploring his spectacular environment in Monument Valley.

TAHTONKA. NFI/NEW 1968. P-El. 30 min col. Rental $27.50; purchase $330.

A reconstruction through paintings and live action of the decimation of the buffalo and the devastating effects on the culture of the Plains Indians. Opening sequences show large herds of buffalo and an enactment by Indian dancers of the decoy hunt ceremony used to capture game in prehorse, pregun days. The many uses of the buffalo by the Indians are also indicated. As the film progresses with scenes of the coming of horses, mountain men with guns and whiskey, and railroads with sportsmen, the extermination of the buffalo is revealed as an unwritten policy to also exterminate the Indian.

TOMORROW'S YESTERDAY. BYU 1971. J-S-A. 29 min col. Rental $17.40; purchase $290.

A documentary on Indian culture emphasizing the positive things Indians are doing to make a better world. Guide for everyone interested in western America and the Indian.

TOTEMS. NOF 1962. El-S. 14 min col. Purchase $170.

Totems originated on America's Northwest Coast—northwest from Seattle through British Columbia and southeastern Alaska. Original inhabitants (Indians) there had no written language; they carved totems to communicate ideas. Stone tools were used to carve on posts supporting community houses, and on screens (partitions) in those houses. Memorial totem poles were carved; then came potlatch, family history, and legend-bearing totem poles.

TRAIL OF TEARS. IU 1970. J-S-C-A. 100 min b&w. Rental $79.

Johnny Cash, as Chief John Ross, and Jack Palance, as President Andrew Jackson, star in this dramatization of the historical events surrounding the exploitation and oppression of the Cherokee Indian Nation in the 1830s. The state of Georgia, in seeking all Cherokee land, nullifies all Cherokee laws and further decrees that Indians are neither entitled to a trial nor may testify in court. The

Cherokees appeal to President Andrew Jackson because of earlier treaties, but Jackson refuses their pleas.

TRAIL RIDE. NFBC 1964. P–El. 20 min col. Purchase $200.
Depicts the trail ride held each summer on the Blood Indian Reserve, in southern Alberta, Canada, which brings together a group of Indian boys and white boys from the city to learn the tricks of range riding from Rufus Goodstriker, to participate in a roundup, and to listen in the evenings to an Indian storyteller. This is a delightful film, narrated in part by the boys themselves. It is an unpretentious film, simply showing boys living, learning, and having fun together.

TREASURE, THE. BFA 1970. El–S. 13 min col. Rental $13 (3 days); purchase $175.
In *The Treasure*, two Indian boys are caught between their own interests in the ease of modern life and the struggles of their father to live the good life of the old ways. Only when their father is arrested, spearheading a defense of tribal fishing rights, do the boys begin to see the worth of their heritage against today's commercial considerations.

TREATIES. SBRTC 1971. S–C–A. 30 min col. Rental $5; purchase $300.
The present day problems of the Indian are described by one who should understand them best—another Indian. Allen Neskahi, Jr., and his family show how the once divided Indian tribes have learned to live and work together for the sake of their children's future.

TRIBE OF THE TURQUOISE WATERS. OUSD 1972. S–C–A. 12 min col. Rental $8.
Shows life in a small Indian village hidden in an almost inaccessible valley in a remote part of the Grand Canyon, Arizona. The settlement is reached only by pack train, and the difficult transportation of food and supplies presents a daily problem.

TWO INDIANS: RED REFLECTIONS OF LIFE. CEF 1973. J–S–C. 26 min col. Rental $19.20; purchase $360.
This film contains a first-person experimental involvement in today's events in the creative arts within their own culture by Indian young people of high school and college age. This in-depth documentary is of two Indian high school art students and their classmates. Film includes both traditional and contemporary Indian art.

WARRIORS AT PEACE. UK/OUSD 1954. El–J–S–A. 11 min col. Rental $4.40 (per day).
Depicts the life of the Apache Indians in eastern Arizona with stress on their customs and traditions. The film explains the wickiup, the typical Apache home, and the development of fine basketry as an occupational outgrowth of their former nomadic life. Today's Apache is a successful cattleman, and his Thoroughbred breeds attract buyers from the entire Southwest. The ancient pollen-blessing ceremony is also included in the film.

WASHOE (Part 1). MGH 1968. J-S-A. 56 min b&w. Rental $25; purchase $325.

Depicts Washoe Indian life today in everyday activities, including old hand games, gambling practices, and the use of pine nuts. Highlights the Pine Nut ceremony, which includes its songs and dances. Discusses survival in the white man's world. Filmed in Dresslerville, Nevada.

WATER IS SO CLEAR THAT A BLIND MAN COULD SEE. NET/IU 1970. S-C-A. 30 min col. Rental $12.50; purchase $315.

Like other Indian nations, the Taos believe that all life is sacred—including plants—and have lived for years without upsetting the delicate balance of nature. They consider animals as brothers and when they eat animal flesh they do so only out of necessity. Every part of the animal is utilized and each person consumes only what he needs, no more. In 1906 the land of these Indians was taken from them and by special permit they can use it until 1983. The lumber companies want to start cutting the forest in the Blue Lake area, sacred to the Indians. From the "Our Vanishing Wilderness" series.

WHERE HAS THE WARRIOR GONE? CENTRO 1971. El-J-S. 13 min col. Purchase $180.

This film explores the life of Ted Cly, a typical Navajo father living on a reservation in Utah. Though he works as a tourist guide, tends sheep, and farms a small plot of land, Ted Cly, like most Navajo men, leads a life devoid of purpose and meaning. The Navajo society is that of warrior and protector. There have been no Navajo warriors for nearly a hundred years. Stripped of his role as warrior and its inherent power and respect, Ted Cly and his Navajo brother are anachronisms—men living in a society that no longer has a place for them.

WHO WERE THE ONES? MFI 1973. S-C-A. 7 min col. Rental $10; purchase $100.

This is an Indian's song of protest, expressive of the bitter memories of the past, still alive today. Written, sung, and illustrated in color artwork by three young Canadian Indians, this film is a compelling view of North American history as seen from the side of the Indian. The questions asked by the title relate to the coming of the early European colonists and the need they had of shelter against the rigors of the new land.

WOODLAND INDIANS OF EARLY AMERICA. CORF. P-El. 11 min b&w/col. Rental $15; purchase $70 (b&w), $140 (col).

Authentic reconstructions and scenes in the eastern and Great Lakes regions provide settings for this study of Woodland Indian life prior to European influence. The daily life of a Chippewa family is observed as Little Bear and other members of the family hunt wild turkey, harvest their staple food of wild rice, fish in the lake, and gather at the wigwam for the evening meal.

Filmstrips

ALONG SANDY TRAILS. VIKPI 1971. P. col. LC 74-737913. 31 frs. With discs $9.50; with cassettes $12.50.

The beauty of the desert and the variety of its animal and plant life are experienced by a small Papago Indian girl on a walk with her grandmother. An abridged presentation of *Along Sandy Trails* by Ann Nolan Clark with photographs by Alfred A. Cohn. Recommended by AASL.

AMERICAN INDIAN, THE: A DISPOSSESSED PEOPLE. GA 1970. P-El-J. col. LC 71-735586. 2 filmstrips with discussion guide. No. 3D-400 406: with two 12″ LP records $41.50; No. 3D 400 414: with 2 cassettes $46.50.

An examination of the historical and present-day realities of Indian life in the United States. Reviews conditions under which most Indians live today, discusses inadequacies in the performance of the Bureau of Indian Affairs, probes a Senate subcommittee's report on the BIA's mishandling of Indian education. Confronts Indian mistrust of white Americans. Deals with Indian concept of ownership of land; recent migration to cities; and organizations developed to handle reservation and nonreservation problems. Discussed by six Indian leaders: Wendall Chino, "Ace" Sahmount, Ernie Stevens, Janet McLoud, John Belindo, and Louis Bruce.

AMERICAN INDIAN, THE (A Study in Depth). SCHLAT 1969. J-S. col. No. T 401: 6 sound filmstrips with program guide. Avg 55 frs, 11 min. With discs $120; with cassettes $138.

This set of filmstrips spans more than four hundred centuries to bring a complete study of the Native Indian American. Covered are: Paleo Indians who first migrated across the Bering Straits from Asia to the New World; the exploitation of the Indian; the denial of freedom and dignity; values and traditions of Indian culture; religious traditions and practices; the meaning of Indian art; and the struggle of the Navajo from the tragic era of Kit Carson to present efforts to improve their standard of living and still retain their rich heritage. Titles: The American Indian Before Columbus; The American Indian After Columbus; The American Indian Growing Up; Religions of the American Indian; Arts and Culture of the American Indian; and The American Indian Today.

AMERICAN INDIAN BEFORE COLUMBUS, THE. SVE 1974. P-El-J-S. col. 4 filmstrips with teacher's guides. No. 376-SAR: with 2 discs $45; No. 376-SATC: with 2 cassettes $47.75. Individual filmstrip with guide $10.

Four filmstrips present an overview of the first settlers on the American continents—the pre-Columbian Indians. Traces the development of various Indian cultures, from the very first hunters to the complex societies that met European explorers. Titles: From Hunter to Farmer; Eastern Woodland Cultures; Advanced Indian Civilizations; and Southwest Indian Cultures.

AMERICAN INDIAN CULTURES: PLAINS AND WOODLAND. EBEC 1957. P. col. 6 filmstrips. Avg 53 frs.

Authentic paintings and scripts depict habits and customs of three important Indian cultures. Also available individually. Titles: No. FS 1: The Boyhood of Lone Raven (Plains Indians); No. FS 2: The Manhood of Little Coyote (Plains Indians); No. FS 3: The Young Manhood of Quick Otter (Eastern Indians); No. FS 4: The Travels of Quick Otter (Eastern Woodland); No. FS 5: Flamingo,

Princess of the Natchew (Southern Woodland); and No. FS 6: The Journey of the Flamingo Princes (Southern Woodland).

AMERICAN INDIAN LEGENDS. EBEC 1971. P-El. col. 6 filmstrips with 6 cassettes $83.95; 6 filmstrips with 6 records $83.95; 6 uncaptioned filmstrips $49.50.

Tells fascinating legends from representative North American Indian tribes in rich and distinctive artwork. The Indians believed that the animals were once men, that the sun, moon and stars had human qualities before being changed by magic into the forms we know today. Based on authentic stories and illustrations, the tales relate man's early attempts to explain the mysteries of nature. Titles: Hot Summer Came to the Northland; The Sons of Cloud; How the Indians Learned from the Animals; How Raven Brought the Sun; Great Rabbit and the Moon Man; and The Legend of Star-Boy.

AMERICAN INDIAN MYTHS (Part 1). EDC. P-El. col. 4 filmstrips. No. 203292400: with 4 records $51.95; individually $14; No. 203392400: with 4 cassettes $57.95; individually $14.95.

As the American frontier came to an end, a few far-sighted anthropologists began collecting what remained of traditional Indian culture. The importance of their work is only beginning to be felt. These four authentic Indian myths were chosen from a wide range of Indian cultures: the Passamaquoddy of Maine, the Cherokee of the south-central Atlantic states, the Chippewa of the Great Lakes region, and the Zuni of western New Mexico. Titles: The Magic Wigwam (23 frs); The Little Ice Man (32 frs); The Fisher Who Let Out Summer (44 frs); and Little Ugly Boy (327 frs).

AMERICAN INDIAN MYTHS (Part 2). EDC 1973. P-El. col. 4 filmstrips. No. 203292700: with 4 records $51.95; individually $14; No. 203392700: with 4 cassettes $57.95; individually $14.95.

These traditional and authentic legends are drawn from two North American Indian cultures—the Micmac, an Algonquin-speaking tribe of northern Canada, and the Oto of the Great Plains region. Illustrations and a narrative bring to life the folk literature of these two groups. A rabbit's clever scheme accounts for the turkey's red eyes. A man and his wife witness an epic battle between friendly giants and an ice monster. Ugly and reviled, Little Scar Face is miraculously transformed by a god-like warrior. Glooskap destroys the winter giant and brings summer to his people.

AMERICAN INDIAN TODAY, THE. SCHLAT 1969. P-El-J. col. LC 72-736184. 59 frs with disc $38.75. 35 student handbooks and 35 NYT reprints.

A searching look at the Native Indian American in both historic and modern roles. Shows how the Indian was victimized by the push of the white man. The program also examines their languages, arts, homes, education rights, and achievements. Stresses the Navajo history from their early years to Kit Carson.

AMERICAN INDIANS AND HOW THEY REALLY LIVED. TRA 1970. P-El. col. Complete unit 5 filmstrips $35; individual filmstrips $7.

The heritage and history of Native Indian Americans are revealed in this library of filmstrips. Here is their story told within the framework of the tribe and its special characteristics, their crafts and customs.

AMERICAN INDIANS OF THE NORTHEAST. CORF 1972. P-El-J. col. 6 filmstrips. Avg 48 frs, total 268. With records $55; with cassettes $70.

Filmstrips using an historical approach depict the cultures of the Algonquin and Iroquois Indians of the northeastern United States and southern Canada. Describes how they came to their homeland, their religious ceremonies, and effects of European encroachment. The program portrays modern Indian life in an alien society.

AMERICAN INDIANS OF THE NORTH PACIFIC COAST—A Series. CORF 1972. El-J. 6 filmstrips. Avg 51 frs, 12 min each. No. S194: with 3 records $53; No. M194: with 6 cassettes $68.

Sensitive photography, a rich collection of photographs from the Oregon Historical Society, and a poetic narration provide the framework for this series which presents an illuminating view of the history, culture, and modern life of the Indians of northern United States, Canada, and Alaska. Produced for Coronet by Reel Communications. Wayne Suttles, Ph.D., Professor of Anthropology, Portland State University, Collaborator. Titles: Lands and Tribes; Myths and Ceremonies; How They Lived; How They Changed, Arts and Crafts; and Their Life Today.

AMERICAN INDIANS OF THE PLAINS. CORF 1972. El-J. col. filmstrips. Avg 48 frs, 12 min each. No. S232: with 3 records $55; No. M232: with 6 cassettes $70.

Portrays the American Plains Indians in terms of their history, tribes, culture, arts and crafts, religion, and life today. Shows these Indians as a people closely attached to their land and nationhood, coping with their own heritage within the world of the white man. Produced for Coronet by Bill Boal Productions. Titles: Who They Are; Their Religions; How They Lived; Their Life Today; and Their Arts and Crafts.

AMERICAN INDIANS OF THE SOUTHWEST. CORF 1970. P-El-J. 6 filmstrips. 260 frs. No. S150: with 3 records $47.50; No. M150: with 6 cassettes $62.50.

A history-oriented presentation of the Pueblo tribes who inhabit the Four-Corners region where Arizona, New Mexico, Utah, and Colorado come together. Depicts the differing and varying customs, languages, and life of these people, and the changing and changeless things which give Indian culture its beauty and vitality. Titles: Who They Are; Their Handicrafts; Their History; Their Religions; Their Homes; and Their Life Today.

ANCIENT AMERICAN INDIAN CIVILIZATIONS. EBEC 1966. El-J. col. No. 11090: filmstrips in series. Avg 45 frs $57.50.

Comparing the civilizations of the Mayas, Incas, and Aztecs up to the time of the Spanish conquest, the filmstrips show the social and economic structures, advances made in engineering, science, the arts, agriculture, and geography, as well as maps illustrating geographical location, principal cities, and road systems. Titles: Incas and Their Way of Life; Aztecs, Mayas, and Incas: A Comparison; Mayas and Their Way of Life; Inca Achievements in Art and Science; Aztecs and Their Way of Life; Maya Achievements in Art and Science; and Aztec Achievements in Art and Science.

CHEROKEE NATION OF OKLAHOMA, THE. SVE 1972. P-El. col. No. 250-7: filmstrip, 85 frs, with teacher's guide $10.

This filmstrip explores the near-west region of America. The history of the Cherokee Indians is described in their present-day culture and life-styles. From "Focus on America" series.

CHEROKEE TRAIL OF TEARS. COMTEC 1973. P. col. LC 73-733376. 167 frs.

A Reading Story Library selection on Cherokees who have helped shape the course of history. Shows the disappointments, broken promises, and history of the Cherokees.

FIRST AMERICANS, THE. NYT/SSSS 1972. J-S-A. col. LC 72-73339. 4 filmstrips with teacher's guide. No. WS405R: with 4 LP records $66; No. WS405C: with 4 cassettes $78.

Filmstrips depict the lives of the early nomadic hunters in various regions of the Americas; explore the development of early settlements, artistic and cultural achievements, cultural and communal advances, the decline of early civilizations, and the formation of new ones leading to development of the Native Indian American tribes. From "Current Affairs" series.

INDIAN CIVIL RIGHTS LEADERS (Part 1). PATH 1974. J-S-C. 167 frs. With discs $55; with cassettes $59.

Depicts the views of three Native Indian American organizations: the American Indian Movement (AIM), a group spreading from Minneapolis and St. Paul, founded by urban Indians living in U.S. ghettos; the militant San Francisco based, Native Americans United, publishers of the *Warpath*; and the Alcatraz Indians, a group attempting to preserve the ecological and environmental land base originally promised and currently being eroded. Well-known Indian personalities express their views of life on and off the reservation.

INDIAN CIVIL RIGHTS LEADERS (Part 2). PATH 1974. J-S-C. col. 3 sound filmstrips.

This series depicts the views of three entirely different groups of Native Indian Americans: the Taos Leaders, Pueblo Indians from New Mexico who were the first to force the government to give back part of their sacred lands; the Indian League of the Americans, who are young East Coast Indians, mainly Iroquois, attempting to highlight and to improve conditions currently facing the Native Indian American on the East Coast; and a third group.

INDIAN CULTURES OF THE AMERICAS. EBEC 1963. J-S. col. No. EBE10630: 6 filmstrips. Avg 45 frs $49.50.

An eyewitness view of vital phases in the development of Indian culture through vivid illustrations, sketches, color photographs, and paintings. A reading script provides meaningful commentary on the Indians' contributions to North and South American history. Titles: The Incas, Mayas and Aztecs; Indians of Northwest; Indians of Southeast; Indians of Plains; Indians of Southwest; and Indians and Eskimos of Northwest.

INDIAN HERITAGE. TRA 1969. P–El. col. 6 filmstrips. $42; individually $7.

Six filmstrips explore the extraordinary life and culture of the Native Indian American. Illustrations paint a glowing portrait of the Indian's world from age-old crafts and skills to the beauty of timeless legends.

INDIAN LIFE IN NORTH AMERICA. EDC 1972. El–J. col. 4 filmstrips. No. IFC502R: with 4 LP records $51.95; No. IFC502C: with 4 cassettes $57.95.

Examines two contemporary Indian groups, the Havasupai and the Pueblos, who have kept their cultural identity intact. Shows how each tribe lives and how traditional ways have been combined with modern technology to meet modern demands. Titles: Havasupai of the Grand Canyon (parts 1 and 2); Pueblo Indians of the Southwest (parts 1 and 2).

INDIANS OF AMERICA. EGH 1972. El–J. col. No. TF58: 9 captioned filmstrips, 5 cassettes, 10 charts (C105) maps of American history $93.25; No. F58: 9 captioned filmstrips with teacher's manual and 10 Teach-A-Charts (C105) maps of American history $65; individual filmstrips $6.50; individual cassettes $5.95; extra set of charts (C105) maps of American history $9.95.

The origins of the Native Indian American are explored in this set of filmstrips—how they came to the Western Hemisphere and how they lived here before the colonists arrived. Some of the topics discussed are the skills they acquired in agriculture, the homes they built, including the adobe apartment houses called pueblos, and their tribal history, traditions, and cultures. Among some of the tribes and subtribes included in the filmstrips are the Algonquin, Iroquois, Pueblo, Pima, Apache and Navajo, Hopi, Zuni, Natchez, Creek, Choctaw, Chicasaw, and the Seminoles who were a branch of the Creeks.

INDIANS OF THE NEW WORLD. SVE 1973. J–S–C. col. No. 1023: 2 sound filmstrips 82 frs, 17 min each. With 2 LP records $41; with 4 cassettes $45.

Analyzes arts, crafts, and social life of Indians in North and South America and reveals the tie between Indians and nature, a tie broken when the delicate natural balance was upset by the European.

INDIAN VIEWPOINTS. SSSS 1973. J–S–C. col. No. SFC684R: 4 filmstrips, 2 LP records with teacher's guides $75.

Using the words of four prominent Native Indian Americans of the nineteenth and twentieth centuries, this series shows the reaction of the Indians of the Northern Plains to white conquest. Visuals combine contemporary photographs of the mountains and plains with historic photographs showing Indian life, white settlement, and the advance of the American armies. Covers the lives of Sitting Bull, the great Sioux chief who defeated Custer; Chief Joseph, the Nez Perce chief who sought peace; Plenty Coups, the Crow leader who sought to protect his people by cooperating with the Americans; and Pretty Shield, the Crow medicine woman. Each filmstrip reflects the Indian attitudes toward nature, the values the tribes nurtured, and the Indian reaction to the behavior of the white man.

INDIAN VILLAGE ARCHAEOLOGY. KIRK/UWASHP 1972. P-El-J-S. col. 88 frs with tape cassette $17.80.

Although the exact age of Ozette village on the northwest tip of Washington's Olympic Peninsula cannot yet be established, radiocarbon dating indicates it may go back five thousand to six thousand years. This filmstrip documents the rediscovery of ancient Ozette by archaeologists and their students from Washington State University and examines the remarkable and varied artifacts uncovered there.

INDIAN WORDS FROM THE END OF THE TRAIL. MULMED/SSSS 1974. El-J-S. col. Filmstrip with teacher's guide. No. MM7099R: with LP record $11.95; No. MM7099C: with cassette $11.95.

The dramatic narration, drawn from the speeches and writings of prominent chiefs, stresses the Indian's reaction to the white expansion onto the Great Plains in the decades following the Civil War, showing the final efforts of the Indians to retain their land and way of life, the shock of rapid conquest, and the lack of white concern.

LEGAL OR ILLEGAL: THE DISPOSSESSION OF THE INDIANS. SSSS. J-S-C. col. 2 filmstrips with teacher's guide. No. MM7055R: with LP record $14.95; No. MM7055C: with cassette $16.95.

Examines the various justifications, both legal and illegal, that were developed by settlers to remove the Indians from their lands. Describes why a legal basis for exploitation of newly discovered areas was considered important for Europeans, how the English system of natural law was used to justify ignoring the rights of Indians, and how decisions by the U.S. Supreme Court in the 1830s legally approved the mass dispossession of the Indians. Emphasized throughout is the theme of why men feel the need for legal sanction for what they do, possibly more than moral sanction. Multi-Media Productions.

NATIVE AMERICAN PAINTING. SCHLAT 1970. P-El-J-S. col. LC 79-73767. Pt 1: 63 frs; Pt 2: 77 frs. With discs $63; with cassettes $72.

A general introduction to the origins of the Indians and their art. A discussion of the character of Indian art and the values upon which the Indian's art is based. Part 2 offers a more specific discussion of the artwork from the Southwest and the Great Plains.

NAVAJO FOLKLORE. BFA 1969. P-El. 4 sound filmstrips. No. V81000: with 4 records $56; No. VU1000: with 4 cassettes $68.

The Navajo, having no written language, educated and entertained through the art of the storyteller. These animal tales are based on such folklore. The series was written by a Navajo Indian who heard the tales as a youth on the reservation. In the Navajo culture, each animal represents special characteristics. Produced by George C. Mitchell. Titles: Mr. Coyote and Mr. Bobcat; Mr. Coyote and Mr. Cottontail; Mr. Coyote and Lady Porcupine; and Mr. Coyote and Mr. Horn-Toad.

NORTHWEST COAST INDIAN TRADITIONS TODAY (A CONTEMPORARY LOOK AT REMNANTS OF A HERITAGE). UWASHP 1973. P-El. col. LC 72-734059. 90 frs with audiotape $17.50.

Northwest Coast Indians belong to the modern world as well as to their own ancient world. Here is the story of surviving traditions among the tribes on the ocean coast of the Olympic Peninsula. Featured in this unusual filmstrip are dugout canoes hollowed from cedar logs, the netting and preparation of fish, baskets made from swamp and saltwater marsh grasses, the making of "sand bread," masked dancing, and the exchange of gifts—all set in the magnificence of the tribes' coastal land.

SOUTHEAST INDIAN FAMILIES. CORF 1970. K-P. LO 79-735466. 4 filmstrips. Avg 52 frs each. With discs $47; with cassettes $52; with captions $31.

Each part is a documentary of the life-styles and family activities of four tribes: Apache; Hopi; Navajo; and Zuni.

SUN DANCE PEOPLE, THE (THE PLAINS INDIANS: THEIR PAST AND PRESENT). RHI 1973. El-J-S. col. 2 parts 160 frs. With discussion guide. With discs $27.39; with cassettes $33.

Two sound filmstrips depict the history of a proud people: how it was and how it is. Shows life-styles of the Indians of the Plains. Written and photographed by Richard Erdoes.

TALES OF THE PLAINS INDIANS. CORF 1973. P-El. col. 6 filmstrips. No. S266: with 3 records $57; No. M266: with 6 cassettes in Strip-sette pak $72.

Tales of courage and adventure, from the Pawnee, Cheyenne, Blackfoot, and Sioux. Shows the Indians' close relationship to nature, and how the horse, buffalo, corn, sun, and stars became so important in their lives, their religion, and their culture. Colorful art and photography are enhanced by a moving poetic narration. A Bill Boal Production. Titles: The Stars That Created the Earth; The Coming of the Peace Pipe; The Gift of Ponies; The Coming of Corn; How the Medicine Came from the Sun; and The First Buffalo.

TATANKAIYOTAKE, SITTING BULL. LEPI 1974. J-S-C-A. col. LO 73-735207. 2 filmstrips, pt 1: 60 frs; pt 2: 65 frs. With audiotape.

The life and death of the famous Sioux prophet and chief. Part 1 examines the structure of the Dakota tribes, the early life and rise of Sitting Bull, and the government's attempt to buy the Black Hills. Covers the pursuit of Indian bands by the U.S. Cavalry. Part 2 deals with Indian battles with Generals Cook and Custer, Sitting Bull's eventual surrender to the army, events which led to his death, and the aftermath of Wounded Knee.

WE ARE INDIANS: AMERICAN INDIAN LITERATURE. GA 1973. J–S–C–A. col. LC 73-736632. 2 filmstrips with discussion guide. No. 3D–409 241: with two 12″ LP records $41.50; No. 3D–409 258: with 2 cassettes $46.50.

Graphic documentation and photo essays, together with current on-location photography, illustrate history as described by major tribal leaders. Depicts life before contact with white men and traces the impact of civilization on Indian life. Features excerpts from Black Elk, Tecumseh, Cochise, Standing Bear, Chief Joseph, Santanta, and Big Eagle.

WE LEARNED FROM THE INDIANS. PSC 1963. El. col. 40 frs with captions $6.

It is often forgotten that the Indian made many important contributions to American tradition through food production, arts and crafts, and help in exploration. Filmstrip explores erroneous concepts about the Native Indian American.

WILDERNESS KINGDOM—A Series. BFA 1969. El. 4 sound filmstrips. 60 frs each. No. V87000: with 4 records $56; No. VT4000: with 4 cassettes $68.

Father Nicolas Point, a pioneer French missionary, lived with the Coeur D'Alene, Blackfoot, and Flathead Indians from 1840 to 1847. This series uses the paintings and diary of Father Point to re-create the daily life of these Rocky Mountain and Plains Indians. His unique record provides a comprehensive look at the culture of these tribes, their ways, their beliefs, and their skills. Titles: The Buffalo Hunt; Indians and Traders; Life Among the Indians; and Medicine Men and Missionaries.

Slides

AMERICAN INDIAN ART. UCSC. Book with 15 free slides $35; set of 50 slides $24.50.

The major Indian nations are represented, and there is a great variety of different art forms discussed—pottery, woodworking, masks, beadwork, basketry, and silverwork, to name a few. Includes 302 illustrations; 60 plates in full color and a full bibliography.

AMERICAN INDIAN ARTS AND ARTIFACTS. SAN. No. 678: 275 slides $357.50 (complete 275-slide set accompanied by background commentaries); No. 719: 90 slides $117; No. S-71: 25 slides $32.50.

This slide-survey of Indian arts presents the achievements of the indigenous peoples of the North American continent and provides a case study in the ability of man to live with his environment while extracting considerable beauty from his natural surroundings. Represented by prehistoric and historic examples are tribes from the Eastern Woodlands, Southeastern Woodlands, Plains area, Southwest, California region, Northwest Coast, and Alaska.

AMERICAN INDIAN MYTHOLOGY. UCSC. Over 100 b&w illus with 24 col pages, book with 10 slides $7.95; set of 25 slides $12.50.

This book is a wide-ranging survey of the North American Indians, outlining their deities and heroes of mythology and the beliefs of each region.

ART OF THE NORTHWEST COAST INDIAN. ACA. No. ACA-12: 44 slides with commentary $53.

This is an introduction to the entire Northwest Coast, showing material available from collections in California, including masks, carved figures, bowls, basketry and weaving, chests, implements, helmets, rattles, and charms, which are explained in a detailed commentary with bibliography. A map slide has been included.

CLIFF DWELLINGS OF THE MESA VERDE. BUDEK. El-J-S. col. 31 slides $30.

These slides portray the array of dwellings constructed some 700 years ago by a tribe of Indians in the southwest corner of Colorado.

HAIDA, THE. ACA 1969. El-J-C-A. No. ACA-30: 40 slides with commentary $62.

Most prolific of the totem pole carvers were the Haida. Here are examples of the house posts—simple and complex—famous poles in Juneau, Ketchikan, and Hydaburg. A commentary recounts the history of Haida carving, describes types of poles and posts, and adds a bibliography. A map slide and an 1878 photo of a Haida village are included.

INDIANS OF THE SOUTHWEST. MMPI. El-J. 50 slides $19.95.

Survey of the daily life and customs of the southwestern Indians from buffalo hunting, to cooking breakfast, to courtship.

KWAKIUTL AND SOUTHERN B.C. TRIBES, THE. ACA. El-J. No. ACA-32: 25 slides with commentary and map slides $34.50.

Large carvings in wood were produced by tribes on Vancouver Island and the adjacent mainland. Apart from the Kwakiutl—the late-starting eclectic pole carvers—most carving was confined to entrance and interior house posts; examples shown are from the Bella Coola, Salish, and Nootka tribes.

MUSICAL INSTRUMENTS OF THE AMERICAN INDIAN. ALCSC. El-J. col. 12 slides.

The various musical instruments used by Indians are shown in this series of slides. They capture the true beauty and originality of Indian music making.

PRIMITIVE ART—THE AMERICAN INDIAN. EDR 1972. El-J. col. 20 slides.

This set of 2″ × 2″ slides with captions and script presents a full range of creative production by Native Indian Americans.

TLINGIT, THE. ACA 1969. El-J. No. ACA-29: 46 slides with commentary $64.

Northernmost and largest in area of the Northwest Coast tribes, the Tlingit created a great volume of totemic art. These slides, including a map, show the ancient posts, other house posts and pillars, house frontal paintings, heraldic screens, memorial and mortuary poles, and grave markers.

Transparencies

AMERICAN INDIAN. AEVAC 1972. J-S-C. col. Eighteen 18½″ X 11″ transparencies with overlays. 2 pts $108.

Indian origins and culture in the various areas of the United States. Archaeological, anthropological, sociological, and historical considerations are taken into account.

AMERICAN INDIANS. CREATV. El-J-S. No. 970.1 Ao-SR: 24 transparencies, overlays, manual, $50.

Lives and accomplishments of Massasoit, Powhatan, Pocahontas, Uncas, King Philip, Pontiac, Joseph Brant, Tecumseh, Black Hawk, Red Cloud, Geronimo, Cochise, Sacagawea, Osceola, Washakie, Santanta, Sitting Bull, Stand Watie, Crazy Horse, Quanah Parker, Wovoka, and others.

AMERICAN INDIAN, THE–PREHISTORY. TWEEDY. El-J-S. col. No. 1810-1/1810-5: 5 transparencies with 14 overlays $28.

Indian culture before Columbus and during early European settlement, including development of corn.

AMERICAN INDIAN–WESTERN INDIANS. CREATV 1971. El-J. col. LC 72-735490. No. 970.1 AB-SS: 12 transparencies with 12 visuals.

Presents colorful pictures of some outstanding personalities of the Western Indians such as Cochise, Crazy Horse, Geronimo, Sitting Bull, Red Cloud, and others.

INDIANS. IC 1972. P-El-J. LC 72-736156. 3 pts with 11 overlays.

This series compares representative male and female dress of the five geographic groupings of Indians in the United States.

INDIANS AND SETTLERS. CIVEDF 1973. P-El. col. 8″ X 10″ transparencies.

Shows how and why the Indians and settlers clashed. From "Special Indian Unit B" series.

INDIANS BEFORE THE WHITE MAN. CIVEDF 1968. P-El-J. LC 72-734477.

Shows the prehistoric arrival of Indians in North America, ways of life in various regions, government, religion, and other areas of Indian life.

INDIANS OF AMERICA. TRA. P-El. col. 10 transparencies $29.95.

Looks into Indian life and culture including Indian homes, picture writing, weapons, pottery, clothing, food, tribes of the East, and tribes of the West.

INDIANS OF NORTH AMERICA. TWEEDY. P-El-J. col. No. 1810: 65 transparencies, 108 overlays, teacher's manual $279.

This series gives an in-depth coverage in pictures of North American Indians with subdivisions. The coverage includes: prehistory, Indians of the Southwest, Indians of the Plains, Indians of the Eastern Woodlands, and Indians of the Pacific Northwest.

INDIANS OF THE PLAINS (INDIANS OF NORTH AMERICA). TWEEDY. El-J. col. No. 1810-22/1810-35: 14 transparencies with 29 overlays $76.75.

Explains the history, development, traditions, and rituals of the Plains Indians. Good comparison with companion set, Indians of the Southwest.

INDIANS OF THE SOUTHWEST (INDIANS OF NORTH AMERICA). TWEEDY. El-J. 4 transparencies with overlays.

Tribal development, daily life, routines, culture, and arts and crafts of the Southwest Indians are explored. Good comparison with companion set, Indians of the Plains. From the "Indians of N. America" series.

INDIANS OF THE UNITED STATES. IC 1972. P-El. col. LC 72-736156. With 3 overlays.

Classifies and locates major Indian groups by regions in the United States before European discovery and settlement. From the "Indian" series.

INDIAN, THE HORSE AND THE BUFFALO. VMI. P. col. 10″ × 10″ transparencies with 9 overlays. 2 pts.

This two-part series looks at the Indian as related to the buffalo and the horse. From "Historical Geography of the United States" series.

INDIAN WARS. CES 1973. P-El. col. 8″ × 10″ transparencies.

Depicts Indian wars from 1856 to 1886. From "Special Indian Unit C" series.

NORTH AMERICAN INDIAN TRIBES. BTC. El-J. 24 transparencies with cassettes, 15 min each title, $105.84; individually $4.90.

Describes the dress, history, customs, contributions, and sections of the country the different tribes come from. Includes Apache, Black Foot, Cherokee, Cheyenne, Chickasaw, Chippewa, Mohican, Seminole, and others.

Audio Recordings and Audio Cassettes

AMERICAN INDIAN AND THE JUNGIAN ORIENTATION, THE. BIGSUR. S-C. No. 7021: 1 tape. 90 min $120.

Dr. Henderson offers an historical sketch of the white man's attitudes and actions toward the Indians. Their internal spiritual orientation contrasts sharply with the predominantly external orientation of the white man. Henderson uses case history material of a white woman "possessed" by Norwegian trolls who found her identity by assuming an Indian way of life. He relates her images to the Jungian system and the mythologies of various Indian tribes. A question and answer period follows.

AMERICAN INDIAN DANCES. FRSC/SCHMAG 1958. El-J-S. LC R-59-28. No. FD 6510: 12″ record, 2 slides $6.50.

A collection of 13 traditional dances including Night Chant (Navajo), Rabbit dance (Sioux), Sun dance, Omaha dance (Sioux), Devil dance (Apache), Eagle dance (San Ildefonso), Harvest dance (Zuni), Rain dance (Zuni), Squaw dance (Navajo), War dance (Plains), Snake dance (Flathead), Powwow dance (Canada

Plains), and Dog dance (Plains). Collection of Indian music by Ronnie Lipner and Stu Lipner.

AMERICAN INDIAN: HISTORY AND LEADERSHIP. TAPUNL. El-J-S. Tapes. 3¾ ips. Series $37.10; individually $6.50.

This series presents America's first citizens, both past and present, in their proper setting. Modern-day achievements are compared with past. Lives of famous chiefs are analyzed to show how the Indian obtained greatness through his own culture. Titles: No. 3751: Historical Background; No. 3752: Powhatan—Algonquin Chief; No. 3753: Massasoit—Wampanoag Chief; No. 3754: Pontiac—Ottawa Chief; No. 3755: Black Hawk—Sac Chief; No. 3756: Cochise and Geronimo—Apache Chiefs.

AMERICAN INDIANS AND THEIR EDUCATION. HSC 1971. J-S-C. No. HSC-T111: tape 45 min.

Dr. Robert Havighurst discusses a study he made of Native Indian Americans for the U.S. Office of Education in a speech given at the College of the Redwoods in northern California.

AMERICAN INDIAN STUDIO. CAED. P-El. LC 72-750993, LC 79-752550, LC 70-752553, LC 79-752124. 12″ LP record $6.98; cassette $7.95.

This series includes four separate Indian programs edited by John Bierhost.

AMERICAN INDIAN TALES FOR CHILDREN. TA. No. F 500/1: two 12″ LP records $11.90; No. F 4500/1: cassettes $15.90.

Anne Pellowski, former storyteller for the New York Public Library, tells these charming stories. Vol. 1: The Star Maiden, Punishment of Raccoon, Snowbird and the Water Tiger, and Why the Rattlesnake Sheds Its Skin. Vol. 2: The supernatural side of Indian legends is featured in: Dance of the Wind, Coyote's Ride on a Star, Bluejay Visits the Ghosts, Iktomi's Blanket, A Zuni Tale, and The Snow Man.

AMERICAN INDIAN, THE—HARMONY AND DISCORD. MB. J-S. No. EE414: set of 6 cassettes with teacher's guide $49.50.

Indians from four tribes—Apache, Navajo, Onondaga, and Mohawk—discuss their attitudes toward government, history, treaties, reservations, value systems, mythology and religion, and culture. The informal discussion focuses on traditional and contemporary views of Indians.

AN ANTHOLOGY OF NORTH AMERICAN AND ESKIMO MUSIC. FRSC. J-S. No. FKW4541: 2 LP records with teacher's guide which includes information on each of the 49 songs and translations of the lyrics $17.50.

A collection of ceremonial, work, and story songs of Native Indian Americans. Tribes of the Plains, the Southwest, Northwest Coast, Western Sub-Arctic, Arctic, Northeast, and Southeast are represented, including the Sioux, Walapai, Hopi, Navajo, Kwakiutl-Nootka, Iroquois, Winnebago, Seminole, and Ojibwa. Compiled and edited by Michael I. Asch.

AROUND INDIAN CAMPFIRES. TA 1971. El. 10 cassettes, 10 min each, $49; individually $4.90.

Describes everyday life, customs, and traditions that were part of the Indian heritage—hunting, food-growing activities, recreation, family life, Indian homes, tools, weapons, music, legends, and celebrations.

AS LONG AS THE GRASS SHALL GROW. FRSC 1961. El-J-S-C. LC R-67-371. No. FKW2532: LP record $6.50.

Modern Indian songs reflecting the new spirit of protest among America's native peoples. Written and sung by Peter La Farge, the lyrics recount past tragedies and encourage the Indian to have new pride and determination. Included are the Senecas (As Long As the Grass Shall Grow); Coyote, My Little Brother; Alaska; Hey, Mr. President; and The Trail of Tears.

CHIEFS AND LEADERS. TA. El-J. Complete unit 8 cassettes $39.20; individually $4.90.

The dramatic personal stories of famous Indians, from those who helped the first settlers in the New World, to those who fiercely resisted the loss of their own lands: Squanto, Pocahontas, Sacagawea, Osceola, Pontiac, Sequoyah, Tecumseh, and Sitting Bull.

FAMOUS AMERICAN INDIANS. ESP. P-El-J. No. 1100: 24 lessons on 12 cassettes $72 (sold in entire set only).

Authors Ralph Taylor and Pearl Brooks researched Indian leaders who played a great role in the American past: Black Hawk, Joseph Brant, Cochise, Crazy Horse, Geronimo, Chief Joseph, Massasoit, Osceola, King Philip, Pontiac, Powhatan, Red Cloud, Shawnee Prophet, Sitting Bull, Tecumseh, Uncas, Washakie, Wovoka, Quanah Parker, Sequoya, John Ross, Little Turtle, Hiawatha, and Chief Sealth.

FIRST AMERICANS, THE. TAPUNL. P-El. Tape 7/8 ips.

Historical sketch of Indians and their cultural life before and after the white man came. From "Indian Stories" series.

HEALING SONGS OF THE AMERICAN INDIANS. FRSC/SCHMAG. El-S. LC R-A-67-26. No. FE4251: 12″ LP record $8.95.

Nineteen songs recorded on location by Dr. Frances Densmore of the Bureau of American Ethnology, Smithsonian Institution, include representative selections from the Chippewa, Sioux, Yuman, Northern Ute, Papago, Makah, and Menominee tribes. Illustrated brochure includes text and translation of the songs, along with notes by Dr. Densmore with an introduction.

HOPI KATCINA SONGS—AND SIX OTHER SONGS. FRSC. El-J-S. LC R-64-1680. No. FE4394: 12″ LP record $8.95.

Seventeen songs and dances recorded by Dr. Jesse Walter Fewkes in Arizona during 1924. Dr. Fewkes was chief of the Bureau of American Ethnology, Smithsonian Institution, and was the first to write an account of the use of a phonograph among Indians. The collection represents a pioneer effort by a man who felt that music was a key to the understanding of the Indian's culture.

INDIAN CHILDREN. NTR/NTREP 1961. P-El-J-S-A. No. 0118-30: 15 min. Cassettes $2.90; reel-to-reel $2.40.

Presents well-known songs, poems, and dances that Indian children enjoy. From "Let's Sing" series.

INDIAN CREATION MYTHS. UM. El-J-S-C-A. No. H-90: 3¾ ips, 15 min, 2 tracks. Approx $2.50.

Documentary relates the story of Navabush, the mythical Indian hero, half-man and half-god who helped create the earth and mankind. Explains that Navabush was the inspiration for Longfellow's "Hiawatha."

INDIAN MUSIC OF THE CANADIAN PLAINS. FRSC/SCHMAG 1956. El-J. LC R-A-56-30. No FE 4464: 12″ LP record, 15 min. $8.95.

Nineteen Cree, Blood, and Blackfoot songs recorded on location by Ken Peacock for the National Museum of Canada, include traditional and contemporary greeting songs, war songs, and dance songs. Illustrated brochure details background of culture and music plus notes and translations of each song.

INDIAN MUSIC OF THE PACIFIC NORTHWEST COAST. SCHMAG. El-J-S-C. LC R-67-3057. No. 4523: 12″ LP record $17.90.

Songs and dances documented for the first time in a recording made on location by Dr. Ida Halpern at the request of the British Columbian government. Descriptive notes included.

INDIAN MUSIC OF THE SOUTHWEST. SCHMAG/FRSC 1964. El-J-S. LC R-57-849. No. FW8850: 12″ LP record $6.98.

Instrumental and vocal music of Hopi, Navajo, Apache, Zuni, Taos, San Ildefonso, Santa Ana, Mohave, Papago, and Pima tribes recorded on location by Laura Boulton. A booklet containing full descriptive notes is included.

INDIAN SUMMER. UMINN 1964. P-El. Cassette $1.80; reel-to-reel $2.57.

Mrs. V. Chipper introduces a delightful song about Indian summer, accompanied by a flute. From "It's Time for Music" series.

INDIAN TRIBES. TRA. P-El. Complete unit 10 cassettes $49; individually $4.90.

The fascinating story of regional tribes in America, how they differed, how they lived in harmony with the land and its creatures, and how they reacted to the coming of the white man. Tribes: Iroquois, Cherokee, Seminole, Sioux, Shoshoni, Choctaw, Pawnee, Crow, Hopi-Pueblo, and Tlingit.

INDIAN TRIBES, NORTH AMERICA. VALIANT/ESP. No. 1300: 24 lessons on 12 cassettes, 15 min each $72 (sold in set only).

Depicts the lives of 24 different Indian tribes from Apache to Sioux. Describes the tribes, section of the country, dress, history, mode of living, and conditions of the Apache, Black Foot, Cherokee, Cheyenne, Chickasaw, Chippewa, Choctaw, Comanche, Creek, Crow, Delaware, Iroquois, Mohican, Natchez, Navajo, Osage, Pawnee, Pima, Powhatan, Pueblo, Quapaw, Seminole, Shawnee, and Sioux.

KIOWA. FRSC 1967. J-S-C. No. FE4393: 12″ record, 2 sides $8.95.

Seven selections recorded on location at Tulsa, Oklahoma, by J. Gordon Thorton. Most of the songs are traditional and their composition date is lost in years gone by. Others date from reservation days; a few were composed in recent years to honor a special event. Notes are included on both the songs and the performers.

MUSIC OF THE AMERICAN INDIANS OF THE SOUTHWEST. FRSC 1958. El-J-S. No. FE4420: $7.95.

Selections include funeral song, stick-game song, butterfly dance, gambling songs, night chant, bird-song cycle, and other traditional songs and dances of the Taos, San Ildefonso, Zuni, Hopi, Navajo, Western Apache, Yuman, Papago, Walapai, and Havasupai tribes.

MUSIC OF THE PAWNEE. FRSC 1970. El-J. No. FE4334: 12″ record $7.95.

Forty-five Pawnee Indian songs sung by Mark Evans and recorded in 1935 by Dr. Gene Weltfish. Includes hand-game songs, deer dance songs, war songs, love songs, doctor's and society songs, sacred and Awari dance songs, plus others.

MUSIC OF THE PLAINS APACHE. FRSC 1968. El-J-S. No. 4252: 12″ LP record $8.95.

Fifteen songs recorded and edited by Dr. John Beatty, professor of anthropology, Brooklyn College, include children's songs, lullabies, church songs, dance songs, hand-game songs, and Peyote songs. Notes and background of songs included.

MUSIC OF THE SIOUX AND THE NAVAJO. SCHMAG/FRSC 1959. El-J-S. LC R-59-72. No. 4401: 12″ LP record $8.95.

Fourteen ceremonial, secular, traditional, and contemporary songs demonstrate the civility of modern Indian culture. Indian singers and musicians were recorded by Willard Rhodes during tribal gatherings for the U.S. Office of Indian Affairs. Sioux: Rabbit dance, Peyote Cult song, Sun dance, and more. Navajo: Riding song, Silversmith's song, and Corn Grinding song.

OUTSTANDING AMERICAN INDIANS. UMINN. El-J-S. 30 programs, 15 min each. Cassettes $1.80 each; reels $2.57 each.

Outstanding new and legendary names are included in this series of Indians of note including Sitting Bull, Chief Pontiac, Crazy Horse, and others.

PETER LA FARGE ON THE WARPATH. SCHMAG. El-J-S. No. R2535: 12″ LP record $6.98 (cassette available C-16).

This first album of contemporary Indian protest songs includes Gather Round; Ira Hayes, Radio-active Eskimo; and others. Written and sung by Peter La Farge.

RED HAWK'S ACCOUNT OF CUSTER'S LAST BATTLE. SSSS. No. CAD 1365R: LP record $6.50; No. CAD1365C: cassette $7.50.

Paul and Dorothy Gable's account of Custer's struggle and final defeat, based on records kept by Sioux and Cheyenne warriors, is told in the Sioux tradition of emphasizing personal bravery without recalling cruelty. The voice of the fictional "Red Hawk" is portrayed by a well-known Cherokee actor, Arthur Junaluska.

RED MAN IN MICHIGAN—A Series. UM. El-J-S-C-A. 12 documentary tapes, 15 min each, 3¾ and 7½ ips, approx $2.50 each.

Titles: Michigan Indian Tribes, Indian Creation Myths, Indian Stories of Corn, Animals in Indian Story and Song, Indian Clans and Totem Animals, Indian Spirits of Woods and Waters, The White Man Comes to Michigan, Red Man and White, Indian Religion and Belief, Indian Ceremonies, Indian Arts and Crafts, and Indian Names.

SONGS AND DANCES OF THE FLATHEAD INDIANS. FRSC/CSMIE 1959. El-J-S. No FE4445: 12″ LP record $8.95.

Nineteen songs and dances recorded by Dr. Alan P. Merriam and Barbara W. Merriam in the Arlee area of the Flathead Indian Reservation, Montana, in 1950. Love songs, sweathouse songs, stick songs, war dance songs, scalp dance songs, and many others are included.

SONGS OF THE SEMINOLE INDIANS OF FLORIDA. FRSC 1970. El-J-S. No. FE4383: 12″ LP record $8.95.

Recorded in 1931-1933 by Dr. Frances Densmore on cylinders, this record includes: corn dance, Cypress Swamp hunting and buffalo dance songs, snake and bird dances, plus songs for treatment of the sick, and songs concerning removal of the Seminoles to Oklahoma. Notes included.

WAR WHOOPS AND MEDICINE SONGS. FRSC 1964. El-J-S. No. 4381: LP record 33⅓ rpm $7.95.

Thirty-three songs, collected and edited by Charles Hofman at Upper Dells on the Wisconsin River where more than 200 American Indians from different tribes assembled for the annual Stan Rock Indian Ceremonial. The neighboring Winnebago people were joined by the Chippewa, Sioux, Zuni, and Acoma. Most of the singers were between the ages of sixty and eighty; however, younger singers made a significant contribution. Illustrated brochure includes lyrics and background to songs.

WASHOE-PEYOTE SONGS. FRSC 1964. El-J-S. No. FE4384: LP record 33⅓ rpm $7.95.

(Songs of the American Indian Native Church.) Recorded at Woodfords, California, by Dr. Warren d'Azevedo, this is a collection of five song cycles of four songs each. Notes include reprint of paper in *American Anthropologist* by Dr. d'Azevedo and Dr. Alan P. Merriam.

YAKIMA NATION, THE. CSMIE. J-S. 10 cassettes (also available individually), with study guide.

An aural record of the history and cultural traditions of the confederated bands and tribes that comprise the Yakima Nation, collected during the 1970 Johnson O'Malley summer school program at Wapato, Washington. Titles: No. C40: History; No. C41: The Treaty of 1855; No. C42: Language and Celebrations; No. C43: Tribal Government; No. C44: Education; No. C45: Food, Clothing, Marriage, and Death; No. C46: Health and Medicine; No. C47: The Longhouse Religion; No. C48: The Shaker Religion; and No. C49: Customs and Legends.

Video Cassettes

ARTHUR PENN FILMS LITTLE BIG MAN. TIMELI. S-C-A. 30 min col. Video $230; 16mm $330; rental $35.

Little Big Man is told from the point of view of 120-year-old Jack Crabb, the sole white survivor of the Battle of Little Big Horn. Crabb was raised by Indians, escaped when Custer murdered his Indian wife and child, and later insisted that he was not a renegade but a white man. Penn's insistence on viewing Custer from a distance and not devoting Little Big Man solely to one-to-one bestiality is well focused.

INDIAN ARTS AND CRAFTS. KRMATV. El–J. 30 min b&w. 2 inch video tape.

Shows various exhibits of Indian arts and crafts and explains interesting facts about beadwork of the Plains Indians, Navajo sandpainting, Southwest pottery, and the new directions Indian art is taking.

INDIAN LIFE IN THE CITIES. KRMATV. El-J. 30 min b&w. 2 inch video tape.

Views students learning about Indians by meeting Indian families, by visiting Indian homes, and by visiting the public schools Indian boys and girls attend. Presents work situations and meetings of Indian organizations

INDIANS OF THE SOUTHWEST. KRMATV. El–J. 30 min b&w. 2 inch video tape.

Develops an understanding of early Indian life in the Southwest by paying a visit to a Hopi Indian reservation.

MY FRIEND. NET 1975. J-S. No. 07012: 15 min. Video $125; 16mm $180.

Virgil, a young Navajo, and Eddie, a young Caucasian, live in the sparsely settled area of Utah where they have fished, hunted, and played games together for years. As they leave their rural elementary school and begin junior high, both sense that their close relationship may change. That prophecy is fulfilled as both boys are pressured by their ethnic groups to stay away from each other.

NAVAJO: THE LAST RED INDIANS. BBCTV/TIMELI. J-S-C. 35 min col. Video $300; 16mm $425; rental $45.

The Navajos—America's largest and most enduring Indian tribe—have kept their native language. Forty thousand still speak no English. Only recently has their language been written, since their culture has been handed down verbally through the elders of the tribe—the medicine men. This film is about the fight for their way of life against the inroads of the white man's culture.

PRIDE AND THE SHAME, THE. BBCTV/TIMELI. J-S. 30 min b&w. Video $195; 16mm $275; rental $30.

Frank and even shocking, this study focuses on the Sioux Indians of the Black Hills of North Dakota. This once proud race is seen in abject poverty, haunted by chronic unemployment, plagued by drunkenness, and living in appalling conditions, described by Lyndon Johnson as enough to bring the blush of shame to our cheeks when we look at what we have done to our first citizens.

TRAIL OF TEARS. NET. El-J-S. No. 05012: 20 min. Video $150; 16mm $230.

The Indians' struggle to maintain their identity and preserve their heritage has brought about new interest in their culture. The forced removal of the Cherokees from their homelands and their anguished exodus to the West—*The Trail of Tears*—is described. Drama, poetry, and dance reveal thoughts and feelings of the Cherokee, yesterday and today, and express the pathos of an oppressed but proud people.

Study Prints/Pictures/Posters/Graphics

AMERICAN INDIAN SERIES. PORTAL. El-J. A series of large, double-weight col posters $34.50.

Titles include: Indians of the Plains; Indians of California-Nevada; Indians of the Northwest Coast; Indians of the Southeastern Woodlands; Indians of the Northwestern Woodlands; Indians of the Southwest—The Navajo; Indians of the Southwest—The Pueblo Dwellers; and Map of Indian Tribes and Their Cultures.

AMERICAN INDIANS OF THE PLAINS. DPA. J-S. Set of forty 11″×14″ pictures $22.50.

Following 1778, when the Fort Pitt treaty was signed with the Delaware tribe, more than 400 treaties were made with the Indians—and broken. Ancestral lands, secured and guaranteed to the Indians by these treaties, were taken over mile-by-mile. Although doomed in their struggle to protect themselves, the Indians fought nearly 200 pitched battles against the U.S. military. This series includes pictures of chiefs, braves, villages, soldiers, Indian wars, and so on.

A PORTFOLIO OF OUTSTANDING CONTEMPORARY AMERICAN INDIANS. SSSS. P-El-J-S. No. ECA 51: 24 b&w posters 11″×14″ $10.

Short biographies of modern Indians. Designed to serve as role models for both elementary and secondary students, the portfolio includes Vine Deloria, Jr., LaDonna Harris, N. Scott Momaday, Annie Dodge Wauneka, Hank Adams, and Louis R. Bruce.

CONTEMPORARY AMERICAN INDIAN BIOGRAPHIES. SSSS. J-S. No. INS465: 32 photos and drawings 11½″×16″, printed on both sides of durable board, teacher's guide $4.95.

Features prominent Indians of the twentieth century, with a listing of each individual's major accomplishments. Personalities include Will Rogers, Jim Thorpe, Vine Deloria, Jr., Billy Mills, Buffy Sainte-Marie, and Allie Reynolds.

HISTORICAL AMERICAN INDIAN BIOGRAPHIES. SSSS. J-S. No. INS464: 32 prints 11½″×16″, printed on both sides of durable board, teacher's guide $4.95.

Photographs and etchings summarize the major accomplishments of prominent Indians of the past. Individuals such as Cochise, Crazy Horse, Geronimo, Hiawatha, Pontiac, and Sitting Bull are included.

INDIAN AGRICULTURE. DPA. El–J. No. PC-K7: 30″×40″ col chart, teaching notes $250.

Chief climatic regions, irrigation, and crops are shown, together with a large seasonal work cycle. Production is compared to population growth.

INDIAN RESISTANCE: THE PATRIOT CHIEFS. JACK/VIKPI 1972. P-El–J. SBN 670-39517X: 12 exhibits, 6 broadsheets, contents brochure $3.95.

Tells the unhappy story of the resistance of the Indian to the conquest of his lands from the time the Pilgrims landed on Plymouth Rock to the Indian occupation of Alcatraz in 1970. Exhibits include: pages from Thomas Jefferson's Notes on the State of Virginia; a painting of the Ghost Dance of the Oglala Sioux; and the last page of a Hopi petition of 1894.

INDIANS OF CALIFORNIA: ARROW MAKING. BARR 1964. El–J. No. 970.1-P4: eight 11″×16″ col prints $15.

Prints show arrow points of obsidian, shaping of arrow points, an arrow point bound to the shaft, a view along the main shaft, a feather split and bound to the end of the shaft, the socket made at the other end of the shaft, and arrow shafts in a skin quiver.

INDIANS OF CALIFORNIA: FOOD. BARR 1964. El–J–S. No. 970.1-P6: twenty-two 11″×14″ col prints $40.75.

Prints show fishing in rivers; gathering of fish, crabs, and shellfish; hunting wild game; stalking deer; uses made of the deer; drying of meat; gathering of roots, seeds, and acorns; heating water; cooking and eating a meal; and so on.

INDIANS OF CALIFORNIA VILLAGE LIFE. BARR 1964. El–J. No. 970.1-P7: twenty 11″×14″ col prints $37.

Tells the story of a primitive people as they lived before the white man came to the Pacific Coast. Included are the building of houses, making a bed with a rabbit-skin cover, gathering basket materials and making a basket, building a tule boat, the sweathouse, a father playing a hoop game with his children, and the medicine man teaching a boy to carry on the traditions of the tribe.

INDIANS OF THE UNITED STATES & CANADA. SVE. P-El. No. PPSSP-1300: forty-eight 18″×13″ prints with texts $48.

Explores traditional and contemporary Indian life on and off the reservations. Emphasis is on Indians as a viable segment of society, possessors of a rich heritage, and contributors to American culture.

INDIAN TRIBES IN 1650. SM. El. No. 3816: 42″×29″ col poster map $1.50.

Map of the United States shows approximate locations of Indian tribes, with pictures showing typical life-styles.

OKLAHOMA LAND RUSH, THE. VIKPI/JACK 1973. El–J. No. A12: 10 documents $3.95.

Re-creates the mad rush for home sites on land originally given to the Indians but destined to become the state of Oklahoma, including a certificate from President Polk to an Indian chief, an 1885 map of the Indian Territory showing the locations of the Indian tribes, and a lithograph of Sequoyah's Cherokee alphabet.

CHAPTER IV

The Spanish-Speaking American

by Lourdes Miranda King,
L. Miranda Associates,
Curriculum Consultants

> They [the immigrants to America] come to a life of independence, but to a life of labor—and, if they cannot accommodate themselves to the character, moral, political, and physical, of this country with all the compensating balance of good and evil, the Atlantic is always open to them to return to the land of their nativity and their fathers. To one thing they must make up their minds, or they will be disappointed in every expectation of happiness as Americans. They must cast off the European skin, never to resume it.
>
> *John Quincy Adams*
> (Niles Weekly Register, Vol. 18, April 29, 1820, p. 457.)

THE U.S. EXPERIENCE

In 1818, when John Quincy Adams spoke those often-quoted words, perhaps they were realistic given the nation-building efforts of the epoch; over 150 years later, however, the concept of "Anglo-conformity"[1] is still prevalent, as witnessed during the recent debates on the bilingual education amendments to the Elementary and Secondary Education Act of 1973.

The white dominated institutions and style of life bestowed their blessings upon millions of immigrants who achieved social and economic mobility by "casting off their skins" (their ethnicity) for the American dream. Their children have persisted in the melting pot theory—which resulted in their own assimilation—as being still valid today for other immigrant groups. The proponents of such a view overlook socioeconomic factors which caused the situation before World War II immigrations to differ from the migratory movements of 1945 and after. Nor do they take into consideration the fact that even then the promise of the American dream was not fulfilled for all immigrants.

Who are most of the "forgotten," those invisible people bypassed by the American dream?[2] They are the undercounted 10.8 million persons of Hispanic origin or heritage who live in the United States.[3] Their backgrounds are varied: immigrants from Central and South America, and Spain; refugees from Castro's Cuba; migrant Americans, Puerto Ricans, and a native minority—Mexican Americans, or Chicanos—seeking to improve their economic status after centuries of neglect; as well as successful professionals from many countries. The group constitutes a heterogeneous mass of persons from the former Spanish colonies and the Spanish-speaking countries of the world. This group has alternately been given the generic label of Spanish speaking, although some speak little or no Spanish whatsoever; Spanish surnamed, when many bear names such as Pierluissi, Petrovitch, Colbert, or Creitoff; Latin Americans, or *latinos*, although the majority group settled in the United States prior to the seventeenth century; and Spanish origin or ancestry, yet many of the faces reflect their Indian and African forebears. The effort to ascribe a label to an amalgam of people reflects the stereotype which equates all persons of Hispanic heritage—seeing the people in terms of a region, or a language, instead of in terms of different countries of origin. This view has failed to take into account the diversity in ancestry—European, Indian, and African—and the manner in which these three major groups interact, dominate, or coexist in the ethnic composition of the people of a country.

For instance, the European ancestry dominates in countries such as Argentina and Chile, while in Peru, Bolivia, and Mexico, the Indian ancestry predominates. The African ancestry interacted strongly in Brazil and the Caribbean and its influence is seen not only in the ethnic composition of the population, but in the customs as well. There is a tradition of coexistence between diverse groups, springing from the Iberian experience of almost eight centuries of Moorish rule (711-1492) which saw Moors and Christians living side by side, expressing the fusion in well-loved art forms—*mudejar*, Moorish art in Christian lands, and *mozarabe*, Christian art in Moorish lands. That fusion in architecture had its expression in the Western Hemisphere in the form name *tequitqi* by Jose Moreno Villa, from the *nahuatl* word for servant, in which the Indians put their characteristic details into the European structures.

This brief description shows how by racial composition, Spanish Americans do not belong to the great groups of white or black races, but to the *mestizo*—part European, part Indian, part African—an intermediate point between the races. It further suggests one of the reasons Spanish Americans have been ignored by progress in the United States. They are of a culture in which racial barriers, in a brutal sense, are impossible, since among the members of one family skin color may vary from fair to dark. Moreover, the receiving culture has not permitted persons of different skin colors to enter the mainstream of American life.

The attempts at categorization of people of diverse countries of origin also does not take into consideration the diversity in languages. For instance, in Paraguay, almost 43 percent of the population speak an Indian language, *guarani*; in Ecuador, 7 percent speak only *quechua*. Indian dialects are spoken in Bolivia, Peru, and Guatemala. Argentina, where there are very few Indians left, still has bilingual regions such as Santiago del Estero where quechua and Spanish are spoken, and Corrientes and Misiones, provinces in which guarani and Spanish coexist. Hundreds of languages survive, among them the nahuatl spoken by half a million people in Mexico, the *aimara*, and many others spoken in more limited areas.

This view also has failed to take cognizance of differences in historical development, degrees of urbanization, experiences in government, religions, traditional rivalries between countries, and international disputes, or any of the factors which define a nation—and its people—as such.

The homology in denomination has produced a uniformity in the way the Spanish American is perceived by the white American society—an image which leads to false cultural assumptions and expectations. The image of the mysterious, unpredictable, charmingly irresponsible and indolent latino has been reinforced by Hollywood films and television commercials. Without too much effort pictures of Chiquita Banana, Frito Bandido, Speedy Gonzalez, dozers under sombreros, a myriad of screen lovers, servants, and villains float through our imagination. If it were only limited to floating through our minds, it would be bad enough. However, these stereotypes have served to justify the discrimination and exclusion of Spanish Americans from full participation in the life of the United States. After all, they are only capable of subordinate status; are not so many of them employed as unskilled workers—if at all? That must mean they are suited only for menial labor and is proof enough that they belong in that category. They deserve that status, so the notion goes, supported by the occupational data.[4] These misconceptions have had disastrous effects in terms of societal neglect and indifference, attesting to the low esteem in which Spanish Americans are held, and corroborated by official statistics.

Although statistical and demographic data now available understate the true totals, a look at the Census Bureau's Current Population Reports presents a dismal picture.[5] Spanish Americans, the second largest minority in the United States, comprise nearly 5.2 percent of the entire population. They rank at the bottom of the scale in any of the key indicators used to measure well-being. Americans of Hispanic extraction generally earn less, have less education, and have larger families than the rest of the population.

A Profile

In March 1974 American families of Spanish origin had a median income of $8,720, whereas the median for all families in the United States was $12,050. Real income, or purchasing power for persons of Spanish background was unchanged from 1969 to 1973, while it increased 4 percent for the entire population. About 22 percent of persons of Spanish origin had incomes below the low-income level; ranging from a high 34 percent for persons of Puerto Rican origin to 8 percent for those of Cuban origin.

The Spanish-background population is a young population, with the proportion of persons under five years old at 13 percent, and the proportion over age 65 being 4 percent, compared to 8 and 10 percent respectively in the total population. The proportion of population under 20 years of age is a high 51.5 percent; its median age is 20 years compared with the median of 28.5 years for the population as a whole. This is especially significant in view of their consistently low educational attainment (9 median years of schooling), the large size of the families (about 34 percent contained 5 or more persons in the family), and the high birth rate.

Although there are no official projections for the Spanish-origin population in the United States, and even available figures are unreliable (Spanish- origin identification was only in limited use for the first time in 1970), and there are no vital registration statistics for Spanish-origin persons (birth and death records asking for race, not ethnic origin), it is safe to assume that the Spanish-origin population will continue to increase. This assumption is based on Census Bureau computations which cite a rate of natural increase of 1.8 percent per year, or 5.5 percent for the period between 1970 and 1973. In this same period about one-half million immigrants were admitted to the United States from all Spanish-speaking countries.[6]

About 19 percent of all persons of Spanish background 24 years of age and older had completed less than five years of school, compared to about 4 percent for the entire United States population. Only about 36 percent of Spanish origin persons 25 years old and over had completed four years of high school or more, compared with about 61 percent of the total population. Recently, there have been some gains in educational attainment; 52.5 percent of Spanish origin per-

TABLE 1. **YEARS OF SCHOOL COMPLETED BY PERSONS OF SPANISH ORIGIN 25 YEARS OLD AND OVER IN THE UNITED STATES, MARCH 1974**

Years of School Completed and Age	*Total Popu-lation*	*Spanish Origin*				
		Total	*Mexican*	*Puerto Rican*	*Cuban*	*Other Spanish*[a]
Percent Completed Less Than 5 Years of School						
Total 25 years and over	4.4	19.4	26.5	17.6	8.9	6.0
25 to 29 years	1.2	9.1	12.6	7.5	(B)	2.8
30 to 34 years	1.3	9.6	14.6	9.0	(B)	1.6
35 to 44 years	2.2	16.3	22.3	18.0	3.8	2.8
45 to 54 years	3.4	23.1	32.0	23.0	9.3	6.1
55 to 64 years	5.3	29.8	39.9	(B)	16.1	11.0
65 years and over	11.9	47.4	63.6	(B)	(B)	(B)
Percent Completed 4 Years of High School or More						
Total 25 years and over	61.2	36.4	29.1	29.6	47.7	55.9
25 to 29 years	81.9	52.5	46.7	39.6	(B)	73.7
30 to 34 years	77.9	48.2	41.9	40.3	(B)	64.0
35 to 44 years	70.4	38.3	31.0	29.5	52.0	60.1
45 to 54 years	63.0	30.2	20.6	18.8	49.0	54.0
55 to 64 years	50.0	17.4	9.6	(B)	30.2	31.2
65 years and over	33.1	13.3	5.2	(B)	(B)	(B)

[a]Includes persons of Central or South American and other Spanish origin.
B Base less than 75,000.

Source: U.S. Bureau of the Census, Current Population Reports, p-20, No. 267, 1974.

sons in the 25 to 29 age bracket had at least completed high school, compared with 81.9 percent of the total population. In 1972, 47.6 percent of Spanish origin persons between the ages of 25 and 29 had completed four years of high school or more, a gain of about 5 percent. (See Table 1.)

Over half of employed men of Spanish origin (56 percent) work in blue-collar jobs, mostly concentrated in the lower paying occupations, such as operatives and laborers. The unemployment rate averaged 7.5 percent in 1973, accounting for 6 percent of total unemployment in the United States. This rate varies considerably between groups; higher for Puerto Ricans and for teenagers, lower among Cuban-origin persons.[7] (See Table 2.)

About two million, or 83 percent of Spanish-origin families, live in metropolitan areas; the proportion is much higher for Puerto Ricans (19 out of 20) than for Mexican Americans (3 in 4). The latter also have the greatest proportion (11 percent) working as farm laborers.

The figures cited represent the averages for all persons of Spanish origin in the

TABLE 2. **MAJOR OCCUPATION OF EMPLOYED MEN OF SPANISH ORIGIN 16 YEARS OLD AND OVER IN THE UNITED STATES, MARCH 1974**

Occupation	*Total Men 16 Years Old and Over*	*Spanish Origin*			
		Total	*Mexican*	*Puerto Rican*	*Other Spanish*[a]
Total employed/ thousands	51,678	2,236	1,344	271	621
Percent	100.0	100.0	100.0	100.0	100.0
White-collar workers:					
Professional and technical	14.1	6.7	5.2	4.5	11.0
Managers and adminis. except farm	14.1	7.3	5.7	9.7	9.8
Sales workers	6.1	3.0	2.7	4.1	3.4
Clerical workers	6.6	7.0	5.0	13.8	8.4
Blue-collar workers					
Craft and kindred workers	20.9	17.6	19.2	10.8	17.4
Operatives, including trans.	17.9	27.0	26.9	31.6	25.3
Laborers, except farm	7.3	11.5	14.2	7.8	7.1
Farm workers:					
Farmers and farm managers	3.0	0.4	0.4	0	0.3
Farm laborers and supervisors	1.8	7.4	11.4	1.1	1.5
Service workers	8.2	12.0	9.3	16.7	15.8

[a]Includes men 16 years old and over of Cuban, Central or South American, and other Spanish origin.

Source: U.S. Bureau of the Census, Current Population Reports, p-20, No. 267, 1974.

United States. A clearer picture evolves once we look at the salient features for each group. Unfortunately, space limitations only allow for a brief overview, meant more as an introduction than an analysis.

The Mexican American or Chicano

Of the 10.8 million persons of Spanish origin in the United States, persons of Mexican origin account for six and one-half million, according to the Bureau of the Census. Mexican Americans, a heterogeneous group in itself, represent about 59 percent of the total population of Spanish extraction, the largest single group of Spanish Americans. Although Chicanos,[8] as is the case with the other Spanish American groups, can be found throughout every state of the United States, their concentration is greatest in the five southwestern states of Arizona, California, Colorado, New Mexico, and Texas. Sizable numbers also live in the north central area of Illinois, Michigan, Indiana, and Ohio. Of all Spanish-origin groups, Mexican Americans are less concentrated in urban areas, which has been a contributing factor toward their cultural isolation, as well as lessened their interaction with the white society, including the deliberate segregation traditional in the Southwest. About 24 percent of Mexican American families live in rural areas, an exception to the norm of urbanization for Spanish-origin persons. Still, 76 percent of the Chicanos live in metropolitan areas; less than half live in the central cities of those areas. The implication is not that the Mexican American lives in the affluent suburbs, but in poverty sections such as the *barrios* found outside the central cities throughout the Southwest and West.

Even though the Mexican American is the oldest native minority of the Spanish-origin groups, they have one of the lowest educational levels: 26.5 percent of persons 25 years old and over had completed less than five years of school, attesting to the educational neglect of which they have been victims. The *Mexican American Education Study* conducted by the U.S. Commission on Civil Rights between 1969 and 1974, found a dropout rate of 40 percent among Chicano students—for every ten Mexican American students who enter the first grade, only six graduate from high school. It reported the failure of the schools as reflected in reading ability, grade repetition, and general overage of the student in relation to grade level. The educational outcomes were the following: the proportion of Chicano students reading six months or more below grade level was twice as large as the proportion of white students; they are more than twice as likely to be required to repeat a grade as white students, and as much as seven times more likely than white students to be overage for their grade.

The history of Mexican immigration to the United States explains why we refer to them as both a native minority and an immigrant group. The Mexican presence in the United States dates back to the early Spanish explorations of North America by men such as Juan Ponce de León, discoverer of Florida in 1512; Alvar Nuñez Cabeza de Vaca, who crossed the entire south of North America on foot; Francisco Vázquez de Coronado in 1540; Hernando de Soto; Pedro Menéndez de Aviles, colonizer of Florida (St. Augustine was founded in 1565); and many other brave men.[9] There were Spaniards and Mexicans living in what is now the Southwest three hundred years before the first American immigrants settled in the region during the mid-nineteenth century. Juan de Oñates, founder of El Paso, Texas, became the colonizer of New Mexico in 1598.[10] True to Stanley Lieberson's theory on race and ethnic relations, subordinate indigenous populations are less rapidly assimilated than migrants who come into an established society in their new environment.[11] The white settlers arrived to lands belonging to the newly established Mexican republic after gaining its independence from Spain. The white settlers did not migrate to a subordinate position in the southwestern lands, exacerbating the tensions which led first to the Republic of Texas in 1844, to the state of Texas a year later, and to the Mexican-American War in 1846. The treaty which concluded that war in 1848, the Treaty of Guadalupe Hidalgo, ceded all Mexican territory north of the Rio Grande to the United States. It also granted automatic American citizenship to all those persons living in the territory encompassed by the treaty. Gradually, the indigenous group lost political and economic control as they were stripped of their land. In 1902 Congress passed the Reclamation Act which completed the dispossession of land from Mexican Americans.

Immigration in the true sense of the word sprang from the need for cheap labor as the Southwest and West developed. In the classical migratory pattern reflecting the relationship between conditions in the country of origin, especially economic, and the corresponding better outlook of the receiving country, the first large migration from Mexico coincided with the Mexican Revolution of 1910 and the years which followed, leading to the labor shortages with the advent of World War I. It is estimated that some 678,000 Mexicans immigrated to the United States between 1911 and 1930. Some were highly educated political refugees, the majority were low-paid laborers, who settled mostly in the agricultural areas of the Southwest and California. By 1928 a confederation of Mexican labor unions was organized in Los Angeles and agricultural strikes during that period were ruthlessly brought to a halt by arrests and deportations. The second large Mexican immigration into the United States has taken place in the past thirty years, from about 1940 to the present. These recent immigrants have come to live mostly in urban areas. Their ranks are increased by the people living in Mexico and crossing to work in the United States, authorized resident aliens who come across the 1,945 mile U.S.-Mexican border—"economic refugees," as they have been termed by some.[12] Although not all of them are Mexican nationals, 1971 figures cite the proportion as about 80 percent Mexican.

The successive waves of migration, initial agricultural settlement patterns with higher concentration in rural areas, contact through the common border with Mexico, and the tendency to migrate to areas which already have a sizable population of Mexican Americans, have served to reinforce Mexican culture and accentuate the ethnic identity of Chicanos.

The Puerto Ricans

The second largest group of Spanish-origin persons in the United States are the Puerto Ricans, numbering some one and one-half million according to Census Bureau figures, and over two million as estimated by community agencies based on city population counts. They are the most impoverished minority in the United States, with over 34 percent of this population living in poverty conditions. These figures do not include the three million Puerto Ricans on the island of Puerto Rico. The Puerto Ricans primarily reside in the highly urbanized centers of the Northeast—in New York City, which accounts for about 60 percent of the total Puerto Rican population in the United States; New Jersey, Connecticut, Massachusetts, Pennsylvania, and in Michigan and Illinois. However, Puerto Ricans are dispersed throughout many other states, with substantial numbers living in urban areas in states as far north as Maine and as far west as California and Hawaii. Wherever the state, 97 percent live in metropolitan areas, and of these, 81 percent live relegated to the innards of the central cities.

As is the Chicano population, the Puerto Ricans are a young group with a median age of 18.8 years. In places such as New York City, for instance, not only is it the youngest but also the newest immigrant group, with all that this implies in terms of entering a highly skilled employment market, occupying the dilapidated housing vacated by other groups, and arriving in cities overextended in services.

Puerto Ricans are at a greater disadvantage in the society at large and when compared to all other minority groups in respect to income, employment, and education. The severity of the situation can be partially gleaned from the official statistics. As of March 1974, median income for families of Puerto Rican origin was $6,779, lower than Blacks, Chicanos, and other Spanish-origin groups, and almost half that of the $12,050 average for the entire population. Unemployment is very high at 11 percent; those who do find work are concentrated in lower paying occupations such as operatives and laborers (almost 40 percent). The situation is further compounded by the inordinately high numbers of households headed by Puerto Rican women, one-third (33 percent) of all families, three-fifths of which are living in poverty.

When we examine educational attainment, the situation is not any better. Puerto Ricans lag behind the Mexican Americans and the overall population in education, with eight median years of schooling completed. Approximately 29 percent of Puerto Ricans 25 years and over have completed four years of high school or more; only 1.5 percent have attended four years of college. In New York City, the contrast is even sharper—only 15 percent of the Puerto Rican residents have graduated from high school, as compared to 48 percent for nonwhite students. This, in a state which in 1970 enrolled 301,020 Puerto Rican children, 22.8 percent of the total school population. Drop-out rates oscillate between 70 and 85 percent. For those who remain in school, their achievement, as measured by the New York City Board of Education, hardly seems worth the effort: approximately 85 percent read below grade level.[13]

The Puerto Rican is locked into the cycle of failure—little education and low income.

The Puerto Rican migration to the United States is considered one of the greatest peacetime population movements and the first "airborne migration" in contemporary history. It reached its peak in the post-World War II years, when the average yearly migration was roughly equal to Puerto Rico's annual population increase.

Several factors have contributed to this extraordinary movement of peoples. For one thing, Puerto Ricans, as American citizens (the Jones Act of 1917 granted automatic American citizenship to Puerto Ricans), have free entry into the United States. Easy access and low air fares between Puerto Rico and the United States have also been contributing factors as have the critical economic conditions in Puerto Rico, coupled with the postwar boom in the United States. In addition, the government of Puerto Rico has not discouraged migration but has seen it, rather, as a way to solve the island's overpopulation and massive unemployment problems. Thus, Puerto Rican migration differs from other immigration movements in the United States by being an immigration of U.S. citizens—similar to the traditional migration from rural states to the urban centers, yet different in that the people included come from another culture and speak a language other than that of the dominant society. It is also characterized by a high degree of mobility, and frequent travel between the island, never far away emotionally, and the "mainland." The result is that Puerto Rican culture is constantly being reinforced by the continuous flux between the two points.[14]

The Cubans

According to Census Bureau figures, there are 689,000 Cubans in the United States, and 705,000 Central or South Americans, representing respectively 6.1 and 6.5 percent of Spanish-origin population. Together they constitute the third largest identifiable group of Spanish Americans in the United States. Their situation is markedly different from the Mexican American and the Puerto Rican in that the latter is basically composed of a group of Americans who have been granted citizenship as a result of an armed conflict in which the United States won, gaining sovereignty over the land and peoples of a cultural background at variance with the white-American, while the Cuban, Central, and South American presence in the United States responds to the traditional pattern of immigrants or political refugees from foreign countries. It is revealing of United States power relationships and application toward the people it colonizes, that, of a combination of colonized, native, and immigrant persons, it is the colonized Americans who fare worse in the U.S. metropolis, as seen in the data presented for the Chicanos and Puerto Ricans.

The island of Cuba was under U.S. hegemony after obtaining independence from Spain in 1898, until 1934, when the sugar politics and the revokement of the Platt Amendment allowed for armed intervention in Cuba. Cubans come to the United States as citizens of a sovereign nation with a degree of experience in self-government and self-determination. It is not surprising, then, to find that of all the Spanish origin groups, the Cubans have the highest level of employment, highest income, and highest educational attainment. Their median income is $11,190 (according to the Census Bureau). Only 7.5 percent of the Cuban population in the United States live in poverty conditions, a striking difference from the other groups, including Central and South American (13.5 percent). In common with other Spanish American groups, the Cuban population resides primarily in metropolitan areas, 91.4 percent of the total, but not in the central cities as the Puerto Ricans. Approximately 39 percent live outside the central cities of metropolitan areas. They are concentrated mostly in Florida—particularly in Miami and Tampa—New York, New Jersey, southern California, and Illinois.[15]

In contrast to the Chicano and Puerto Rican population, the Cuban in the United States has a median age of 35.3 years; their age distribution most closely resembles that of the total population of the United States. Their age and income reflect the Cuban conditions prior to entering the United States which consisted mostly of white-collar workers and professionals with a high level of education; their high educational attainment is corroborated by statistics for the Cuban population in the United States: median educational attainment is eleven years, over half (52.8 percent) of the population 25 years and older have completed four years of high school or more, only 8.2 percent of this same age group has completed less than five years of school, and 13.2 percent of the total population 25 years and older have completed four years of college or more.

The major influx of Cubans into the United States consisted initially of the persons who were most able to get out of Cuba during the political turmoil of the Cuban Revolution which brought Fidel Castro to power in 1959. Cubans did not come to the United States as the immigrants of former times, but as political exiles and refugees under the aegis of the United States government—459,835 Cubans have registered in the Cuban Refugee Program. For the past 12 years, the government has pumped, and is continuing to pump, millions of dollars ($525 million in the past four years alone) into the unlimited Cuban Refugee Program approved by Congress in June 1962 and administered by the Department of Health, Education, and Welfare. In 1974 alone the fiscal appropriation was $129 million. It includes, among other benefits, financial assistance to Cuban emigres; open access and entry into the United States; aid in processing port of entry requisites; broad employment and training services, including job counseling and referrals; vocational training; English language classes; special financial allocations to social service agencies who furnish aid to the newcomers; and authorization for the Cuban Student Loan Program.[16] The generosity of the U.S. government has encompassed all government agencies, including the armed forces.

It has only been in the past five years that a working-class wave of Cuban immigrants has arrived in the United States, moving not into the center cities as much as to suburban localities. It is much too early to measure statistically their situation in the United States, yet we know that they arrived drained of emotional energy after long waiting periods in Cuba, their family ties strained and traumatized.

CULTURAL NEEDS

The previous section has given a glimpse of the diversity among the major groups of Spanish Americans in the United States: their heritage, geographic distribution, numbers, composition, chronology, and patterns of immigration, and has offered some insights into the status and comparisons between conditions of each. We must not confuse diversity with dissimilarity, as a result of it.

There is one common link which binds the Spanish American. That link is the continuity fostered by at least three hundred centuries (five hundred for some) of a similar culture and language. Of any single ethnic minority the Spanish Americans have resisted "melting" by refusing to abandon their cultural and linguistic heritage. The Spanish language has persisted, in spite of the overwhelming attempts to forcibly assimilate the Spanish American linguistically. As of 1972, Spanish was spoken in the homes of about 65 percent, or six million of all Spanish origin persons.

Historically, economic, social, political, and legal pressures have been used in an attempt to eradicate the Spanish language from ethnic communities. As recently as five years ago it was against the law to use Spanish as the language of instruction in some Southwestern states and California; states brimming with Spanish names of cities, towns, streets, mountains, and rivers. In Puerto Rico, English was the language of instruction in the island's public schools until the law was repealed in 1948, and Spanish once again became the common language. The result was that generations of Puerto Ricans grew up without learning the fundamentals of either English, Spanish, or subject matter. They were taught about American heroes, holidays, and historic events, as opposed to learning about Puerto Rican events and those things which would develop national consciousness and a pride in their cultural legacy and language. Puerto Ricans were truly imbued with the purpose of education—to transmit the culture of a people to the younger generations—except the culture that was transmitted was not their own. Puerto Ricans are a part of a larger cultural world, and it is not Anglo-Saxon, but Hispanic. Much has been written on the subject of attitudes of the Spanish American minorities and of Latin America, so much of it misleading and self-serving generalizations that I hesitate to add more words which might reinforce the already legendary stereotypes perpetuated by the "authoritative" works of so many scholars. Nevertheless, I will attempt to describe in general terms only those traits which, in my experience, have created barriers to understanding and blocked communications and learning.

Style of Reasoning

In referring to patterns of logic, we should bear in mind that cultures, as peoples, possess and use reasoning in a blend of both the deductive and inductive; it is a matter of which one outweighs the other. Any one person may be at certain times particularistic in a judgment, at other times the person may be universalistic. Yet, the pattern of communication—not the content—to which the Spanish American is more responsive, is the manner of presentation which deals more with that style of reasoning which is associative, deductive, and universalistic. This pattern deals in broad ideas and theories, guided by the association of ideas, impressions, feelings, and intuitions. In contrast, the approach more often used by persons of Anglo-Saxon heritage is the inductive which deals with specifics and draws a strict differentiation between the relevant and the irrelevant, the practical results in a given particular problem, the case-particularistic. Nothing illustrates the differences in logical attitudes better than the comparison between the U.S. legal system drawn from English common law and the civil law of Roman background prevalent throughout the Spanish-speaking countries. The former has evolved from a case-by-case analysis, inductively; the latter is codified to include all aspects of human conduct, the general principle to be applied, yet allowing for moral judgments and shades of meaning.

Persons accustomed to the deductive and associative approach require that the theory underlying a case in point be thoroughly explained in broad terms, not strictly as a statement of fact, that related material be brought in, and associative and emotional matter given full play. The distinction between work friends, school friends, neighborhood friends, church friends, and other types of friendship which one sees in the United States, is not made in the Hispanic mind. Friends are all encompassing, friendships are universal. You are either friends or you are acquaintances; not friends for certain occasions or environments. And if you are friends, that tie is very strong and includes a strong sense of obligation.

Relationships

The Spanish American places a great deal of importance on the value of interpersonal relationships. Personal contact is emphasized within the associative, universal framework. For instance, if you as the teacher have requested a meeting with Spanish American parents for a teacher-parent conference, before you lead into Julio's grades and progress in school, it would improve communications to have some personal exchange, such as asking Julio's parents about the children at home, the health of a sick relative, or to offer some insight into your own personal life that would contribute toward the feeling that the parents are getting to know you, and you them. This exchange would take place within the parameters of respect and formality in relationships which characterize Hispanic culture, observing the customary courtesies, formalities, and ceremonies associated with interpersonal relations, such as posture, words of deference (clichés), shaking hands at the beginning and at the end of an encounter, embracing if there is familiarity, standing up for greetings and departures, accompanying a guest to the door, and many others. Above all, a bantering or joking attitude among strangers in a situation which prescribes formality is offensive to the Hispanic person. This is a privilege reserved for persons (friends or relatives) with whom one has a deep relationship based on affection and trust, in which case the culturally imposed walls of formality are let down.

The requisite rituals in the culture of Spanish Americans are very much related to the individual's sense of dignity based on a high sense of individualism, or inner integrity and moral values. Any action, or nonverbal clue, which violates the respect due an individual or which violates the way human beings should deal with one another, directly affects the person's dignity and is cause for turning off, terminating the relationship, or aggression in its extreme.[17]

Family Structure

The man is nominally the head of the family in the extended family which is still the ideal traditional cultural norm, although the nuclear family has made inroads in areas where the economy has become more industrialized, resulting in the emergence of an urban working class. Regardless of the size and the new changes in roles for the members of the family, family ties are very strong and extend to relatives beyond father, mother, and children.

The traditional delineation of roles is the prevalent one: the husband is dominant, and the authority figure; he is the principal source of income and material well-being. The woman is a good mother and wife. There is a double standard of behavior. These relationships have become increasingly hard to maintain after migration to the United States or with the increased economic burden on the low-income family—the norm for Spanish Americans in the United States. Women have increasingly taken jobs outside the family so that their earnings will lift the family out of poverty. This in turn has created conflicts in the family unit as a consequence of the ambivalence between the ideal and the real inherent in the adherence to a traditional cultural norm and the necessity to work. Women are still principally responsible for child rearing, irrespective of the economic situation.

Children are provided with a liberal amount of affection, and taught to obey and respect all adults, which may be interpreted as shyness or lack of aggressiveness in the American school system. Their reaction upon being scolded is culturally prescribed; the child will look down, not into the adult's face. This is considered a sign of respect on the part of children toward figures of authority.

Religion

The predominant religion of the Spanish Americans is Catholicism, but there are many Protestant sects which have grown in numbers among the Spanish Americans—Seventh Day Adventists, Baptists, Jehovah's Witnesses, Methodists, and Pentecostals are some of the most popular. Protestants are distinguished from Catholics by their more faithful habits of church attendance and greater compliance with their church rules.

The attitude toward the Catholic church is of a more relaxed, unorthodox nature, as compared with the American Catholic. Spanish Catholicism can be seen more as a function of culture than of worship. Catholic rites such as baptism or confirmation are the source of a family relationship which extends the family circle even wider, to the *compadrazgo*, or godparent. Godparents become members of the family, if they are not already so, and coparents to the children they accepted to accompany to baptism. The word *comadre* for the godmother, and *compadre* for the godfather, literally means comother or cofather. The relationship of affection and obligation which the terms imply is very real.

EDUCATIONAL NEEDS—BILINGUAL EDUCATION

Any discussion on the education of Spanish American students must take into consideration the social, cultural, and educational characteristics of the Spanish American population: they come from a poor-class home or lower income levels; they have a lower level of educational attainment than the overall population; they were born into, or now live in a different cultural environment from the majority of the students around them; in many cases they are not white by American standards but perceive themselves as nonblack; they live within a conflict of cultural and social values—those they are expected to accept and relate to in school, and those they learn at home; and, in many cases, they speak only a foreign language—Spanish.

> The failure of the San Francisco school systems to provide English language instruction to approximately 1,800 students of Chinese ancestry who do not speak English denies them a meaningful opportunity to participate in the public educational program and thus violates (section) 601 of the Civil Rights Act of 1964, which bans discrimination based "on the ground of race, color, or national origin," in "any program or activity receiving federal financial assistance," and the implementing regulations of the Department of Health, Education, and Welfare.
>
> *Lau et al.* v. *Nichols et al.*, No. 72-6520, decided January 21, 1974.

Recently, the U.S. Court of Appeals for the 10th Circuit upheld an earlier decision, *Serna* v. *Portales Municipal Schools*, which held that bilingual-bicultural education is a right of non-English-speaking children under Title VI of the Civil Rights Act of 1964. It ruled illegal the failure of the New Mexico school district of Portales to provide special instruction for Spanish-speaking pupils who comprise 34 percent of the district's elementary school population. The combination of *Lau* v. *Nichols* and that of *Serna* v. *Portales* provides a solid legal base for enforcing the principle of special obligations to non-English-speaking children nationally. The legal machinery which until five years ago was employed to deny equal educational opportunity and smother the spirits of millions of Spanish American children, has now swung full cycle and is finally agreeing to grant them their educational due.

The failure lies not in the children, but in the educational system which has refused to intervene in the cycle of exclusion which has been their fate. As stated in the Kerner Report, "the problem is the one who causes it, the prejudiced and biased 'non-disadvantaged,' the 'white' people responsible for the poverty of those 'disadvantaged.'" The system has placed children representing some 28 percent of the Spanish-origin children enrolled in the California school system in classes for the mentally retarded, when the overall incidence of mental retardation in the United States for any segment of the population never exceeds 2 percent. The system had been administering intelligence tests in English and not in the primary language used in the home—Spanish. After retesting in a Spanish IQ test, children scored 40 and more points higher than they had scored in the Stanford-Binet Intelligence Test.[18]

Students have entered school not knowing English and speaking only Spanish, yet they have been prevented from speaking and learning in their own language, and they sit in the classrooms day after day, frustrated, bored, not understanding what is going on in the class, and eventually dropping out of a school system which leads them to believe there is something wrong with them because of their language and their culture, destroying their self esteem. Even those second and third generation Spanish American students who speak English as well as their American contemporaries, and know little or no Spanish, are tracked into vocational courses and treated as unsuitable college material. In the student's own words: "And often the things teachers discussed had no meaning in my life, but I tried to pretend they did. Teachers were always talking about getting a good breakfast—orange juice, cereal, milk, bacon, and eggs. But these foods didn't mean anything to me. Our family had tortillas with beans and cheese or chorizo." Rachel, a 21-year-old college student, says, "When I was in high school, I told my counselor I wanted to go to college, but she said, 'Don't try to achieve that. It's not for you. Instead, why don't you try secretarial studies?' So I took secretarial studies, but still I wanted to go to college. I went to junior college for two years to try it. And then I went on to California State L.A. I'll graduate this year."[19]

For years, the answer to this educational impasse has been to establish English as a second language (ESL or ESOL) programs within the schools. The object of these programs is to increase the English language skills of the non-English-speaking children. Students are pulled out of their regular classrooms for a one hour class in English language daily or, more likely, weekly, when the school has a few Spanish-speaking students. Most school administrators favor this type of minimal instruction; they also believe in the melting pot myth of assimilation; some people might even call them ethnocentrics. Some authorities today feel that they are misinformed. They have not been aware of the close relationship between low achievement, feelings of alienation, and suppression of a child's cultural identity. Those students who identify with their cultural background have been found to do better in school, and conversely, if the schools and their administrators are aware of this, they have opted for the cosmetic solution by having the ESL teacher celebrate the *Cinco de Mayo* or the *Grito de Lates* (Mexican and Puerto Rican holidays), or by having a fiesta with *guacamole* and *lechon*. This "cordial" or colorful folk aspect is not teaching the culture.

Studies by E. Lambert in Canada have shown that students who learn to read first in their native language have an advantage over students who must learn first in English. It is the arbitrary imposition of an unknown language when a child enters school that starts the slow but certain road to dropping out, or being pushed out, of schools. The child who learns to read first in Spanish is learning in a writing system which is very regular, with close correspondence between sounds and letters. As has been found out, a major factor in the success of initial reading instruction is the learner's ability to recognize the relationship between sound and symbol. Learning in a language where the writing system closely parallels the phonetic system builds the basic skill of reading. This basic skill is readily transferable from one language to another; it does not have to be relearned. Children must develop their first language, as well as English. It is their medium of communication with their community and the past of their people. It is the means of expressing and reinforcing their personalities. It is, and will always be, the intimate medium of first affection and knowledge. And in the final analysis, the children do not learn—English or Spanish—but drop behind in school content areas or eventually drop out altogether. Therefore, let us not fall into the trap of calling ESL programs bilingual education.

Bilingual education does not represent a panacea for the Spanish American students, but it goes a long way toward the needed educational reforms. Its main critics among Spanish Americans take exception not to the concept of bilingual education, but to the fact that it has only reached a miniscule number of those it should be reaching. In New York City the programs which have been implemented have been successful, but they have only begun to scratch the surface. Of the 21 percent Spanish-speaking enrollees in the New York City schools, the bilingual education program serves only 3 percent or 30,000 out of 260,000 Puerto Rican students.[20]

A well-conceived bilingual bicultural education program will be successful if it also takes into account cognitive styles as the Spanish American child performs better in situations deemphasizing competitiveness and asserting cooperation; on tasks requiring visual and motor skills, employing learning materials which stress the visual, rather than the auditory, and with textbooks which reflect their reality.

The U.S. Office of Education administering Title VII of the Elementary and Secondary Education Act passed by Congress in 1968, defines bilingual, bicultural education as "the use of two languages, one of which is English, as mediums of instruction for the same pupil population in a well organized program which encompasses all of the curriculum and includes the study of the history and culture associated with the mother tongue. A complete program develops and maintains the children's self esteem and a legitimate pride in both cultures." Thus, the goal is not merely to teach English to non-English-speaking children, but to teach reading and writing in the student's first language, to teach subject matter in the student's native language, and to enhance and preserve the student's dominant culture. With such standards, it can be seen how the benefits of bilingual education are not limited to the Spanish American, French American, Asian American, Native Indian American, Russian American, and other major ethnic groups, but to all English-speaking students as well, enriching as it increases respect and understanding for cultures other than their own, seeing them as the constructive force which they represent in our society. Not to mention the students own bilingualism, ensuring that in years to come they will be able to function effectively in another language and culture.[21]

There are several categories of bilingual education as defined by Joshua Fishman:[22]

1. Transitional Bilingualism, in which Spanish is used in the early grades as a remediation attempt while the student is being prepared to shift languages. This program is couched in terms such as "increasing the achievement level," "master subject matter" and/or "adjust to school," but it makes no mention of acquiring fluency and literacy in both languages. The goal is to help the children arrive at the point where they will be able to pursue a program of studies in—guess—English.
2. Monoliterate Bilingualism is intermediate in orientation between transitional bilingualism and language maintenance. It stresses aural-oral skills in the native language.
3. Partial Bilingualism, which seeks fluency and literacy in both languages, restricting literacy in the mother tongue to subject matter related to the ethnic group and its cultural heritage. The mother tongue is not used in other curricular areas.
4. Full Bilingualism, in which students develop all skills in both languages for all subjects. This is the ideal type of program for it maintains and develops the native language and English.

A. Bruce Gaarder has described how a full bilingual program and classroom practices could be organized within an "equal time, equal treatment" or "unequal time, unequal treatment" program.[23]

Regardless of the structure selected, the value of a full bilingual-bicultural education (a good bilingual program *is* bicultural) accompanied by adequate training of teachers, community collaboration, and authentic quality and honest learning materials, is undeniable.

NOTES

1. Milton Gordon, *Assimilation in American Life; the Role of Race, Religion, and National Origins* (New York: Oxford University Press, 1964).
2. Julian Samora, *La Raza: Forgotten Americans* (Notre Dame: University of Notre Dame, 1966).
3. U.S. Commission on Civil Rights, *Counting the Forgotten: The 1970 Census Count of Persons of Spanish Speaking Background in the United States* (Washington, D.C.: U.S. Government Printing Office, 1974).
4. Ozzie G. Simmons, "The Mutual Images and Expectations of Anglo Americans and Mexican Americans," *Daedalus* 90 (1961): 286-299.
5. U.S. Bureau of the Census, *Current Population Reports*, P-20, No. 267, "Persons of Spanish Origin in the United States: March 1974" (Washington, D.C., July 1974). Although census data are used throughout the chapter, this does not imply an acceptance of their figures as definitive. Their miscounts of the Spanish origin population is estimated to be 30 to 40 percent low.
6. U.S. Bureau of the Census, *Current Population Reports*, P-20, No. 250, "Persons of Spanish Origin in the United States: March 1973" (Washington, D.C., May 1974), p. 9. Also, conversations with staff members of the Population Division, Spanish statistics staff, U.S. Bureau of the Census.
7. U.S. Department of Labor, *News*, April 3, 1974.
8. *Chicano* as used here is synonymous with Mexican American, and not with all Spanish origin persons in the United States as is frequently heard. The term is today used to identify the Mexican American who is proud of his or her heritage. It is a term long used by the upper class in Mexico to describe lower-class Mexicans. In the United States the lineage distinction was made by stressing the Spanish, as opposed to the Mexican, ancestry. People from southern Colorado and northern New Mexico call themselves *Hispanos*; Mexican Americans are those in the rest of the Southwest.
9. U.S. Commission on Civil Rights, *Mexican American Education Study*, v. 6, "Toward Quality Education for Mexican Americans" (Washington, D.C.: U.S. Government Printing Office, 1974), p. 1.
10. Dario Fernandez Flores, *The Spanish Heritage in the United States* (Madrid: Publicaciones Espanolas, 1971).
11. Stanley Lieberson, "A Societal Theory of Race and Ethnic Relations," *American Sociological Review* 26 (1961): 902-910.
12. "The Illegal Aliens," *Washington Star-News*, November 17-20, 1974, p. 1.

13. U.S. Commission on Civil Rights, *Hearing*, New York, 1972 (Washington, D.C.: U.S. Government Printing Office, 1973).
14. Jose Hernandez Alvarez, *Return Migration to Puerto Rico* (Berkeley: University of California, 1967).
15. Edward J. Linehan, "Cubas Exiles Bring New Life to Miami," *National Geographic* (July 1973): 68-94.
16. Migration and Refugee Assistance Act, Public Law 87-510, 87th Congress, H. R. 8291, June 28, 1962. The Act does not specify a termination date. In 1971, $112 million were appropriated; $139 million in 1972; $145 million in 1973; and $129 million in 1974. For fiscal year 1975, the Cuban Refugee Program has requested $78 million, the lowest amount since the beginning of the program. This observation was obtained through conversations with employees of the Cuban Refugee Program.
17. Cole Blasier, "Studies in Social Revolution: Origins in Mexico, Bolivia and Cuba," *Latin American Research Review* (Summer 1967): 28-64.
18. Anthony Lauria, "Respeto, Relajo and Interpersonal Relations in Puerto Rico," in *The Puerto Rican Community and Its Children*, comps. Francesco Cordasco and Eugene Bucchioni (Metuchen, N.J.: Scarecrow Press, 1972), pp. 36-48. Also see Hilda Hidalso, *The Puerto Ricans* (Washington, D.C.: National Rehabilitation Association, 1970).
19. Mary Ellen Leary, "Children Who Are Tested in an Alien Language—Mentally Retarded," *The New Republic*, May 30, 1970, pp. 17-18.
20. Frank Sotomayor, "Para Los Ninos—For the Children: Improving Education for Mexican Americans," U.S. Commission on Civil Rights, Clearinghouse Publication 47, October 1974, p. 8.
21. U.S. Commission on Civil Rights, *Hearing*, New York, 1972, pp. 161 and 337.
22. Joshua Fishman, "Bilingual Education in Sociolinguistic Perspective," *TESOL Quarterly*, no. 4 (1970): 215-222.
23. A. Bruce Gaarder, "Organization of the Bilingual School," *Journal of Social Issues* 39, no. 2 (1967): 111-120. Also see Muriel R. Saville and Rudolph C. Troike, *A Handbook of Bilingual Education*, rev. ed. (Washington, D.C.: Teachers of English to Speakers of Other Languages, 1971).

MEDIA AND MATERIALS—ANNOTATED

Films (16mm)

AMERICAN TROPICAL. IU/NET 1972. S-A. 30 min col. Rental $11.50; purchase $315.

The story of the struggle surrounding the mural, "American Tropical"—showing a man crucified upon a double cross under the eagle of U.S. currency—painted by Mexican political artist David Alfaro Siqueiros in 1932 in Los Angeles. After two years the entire mural was covered with whitewash. Siqueiros was painting the plight of the Mexican American at a time when over two million Mexican

American citizens were being deported to Mexico on buses chartered by the Los Angeles Welfare Department. The mural has recently been restored and preserved, and the film shows the delicate process involved.

AND NOW MIGUEL. USIA 1953. El-J. 60 min b&w. Rental $11.50.
The story of a boy of Spanish ancestry living in the Southwest whose family raise sheep. Miguel has a great desire to be accepted on an equal footing with his father and older brothers.

BIRTH OF A UNION. IU 1966. S-C-A. 30 min b&w. Rental $9.50; purchase $165.
The story of how the National Farm Workers Association, a new labor union, came into existence. This film documents the unique problems of picketing nearly four thousand acres of vineyards, the mundane problems of keeping the small band of union workers fed and clothed, repairing the automobiles and other equipment needed, and recruiting more members. Interviews are presented with people behind the union movement as well as the representatives of the growers, the local police, and several of the local clergy.

BOLIVAR: SOUTH AMERICAN LIBERATOR. CORF 1962. El-J-S. 11 min col. Purchase $130.
Biography of Simon Bolivar, liberator of five South American countries. His birth into a wealthy, land-owning family of Caracas, the factors which led him to abandon fortune and position to pursue his dream of a united South American continent, and the historic meeting with San Martin are pictured.

BRENTANO FOUNDATION BILINGUAL FILM SERIES, THE. CAROUF 1971-1972. El-J. col. Purchase, see below.
This is a series of films on various subjects. Titles: First Day, New Friends/Primer Dia, Neuvos Amigos. Classroom. Introductions to national origins. 6½ min, $75; Counting and Colors/El Contar y Colores. Classroom. Sentence structure using numbers and color. 9 min, $100; Pepe Teaches Us/Pepe Nos Ensena. Review of first two films, and introduction of words for parts of body. 7 min, $75; A Day in the Park. Field trip. Children meet mounted policemen and ride horses, play football, have a picnic, and learn to pick up picnic debris.

CHICANO. MGH/UTEP 1970. J-S-A. 30 min col. Rental $25; purchase $375.
Among most Western Indian tribes it was customary for a young boy to undergo a strong and symbolic spiritual experience before he was accepted as a man and warrior. Once attained, the young man's guardian spirit became a strong and personal force upon which much of his future success as a warrior and hunter depended.

CHICANO FROM THE SOUTHWEST. EBEC/UCO/UWY 1970. P-El-J. 15 min col. Rental $9 (3 days); purchase $185.
Traces the life of a ten-year-old Mexican American boy's family of migratory workers, their move to Los Angeles for financial security, and problems he faces as the family is torn between family customs and fast-paced city life.

CHILE. MGH 1961. El-J-A. 15 min col. Rental $15; purchase $235.

Through the eyes of several eighth-grade children in a Santiago school, the viewer is taken through various regions of Chile: the northern arid desert, the great copper mine of Chuquicamata, the rich and fertile farming central region, the great forest region of the cold and rainy south. Major cities are shown, something of the people, and basic industries are discussed.

COLOMBIA AND VENEZUELA. EBEC 1961. El-S-C-A. 19 min b&w/col. Purchase $130 (b&w), $255 (col).

Uses map animation and live photography to give an overview of surface features, climate, natural resources, and major industries of Colombia and Venezuela. Pictures contrasted ways of living of a Colombian coffee grower, a lake Maracaibo oil worker, and a Venezuelan professor.

COMO SE HACE UNA PINATA. ATLAP/UTEP 1969. P. 11 min col. Rental $6.50.

Children viewing this film will not only share the experience of making the pinata with the skillful little girls of the film, but will be eager to try their hand at this popular Mexican art. Designed for both Spanish-speaking children and for the teaching of Spanish as a second language; an attached list of words is used throughout the narration with their meaning in English. This film can also be used with or without sound in art classes.

CORTEZ AND THE LEGEND. MGH/UTEP 1968. J-S-A. 25 min col. Rental $40; purchase $610.

Outstanding coverage of the civilization of the Aztecs and their conquest by Cortez. Considers the forces enabling Spain to build a great colonial empire, how European culture affected early American civilization, the epic clash between Cortez and Montezuma, the cultural heritage of modern Mexico, and the significant features of topography and climate of Mexico.

"DECISION AT DELANO." QED/UC 1967. J-S-A. 26 min col. Rental $23; purchase $295.

A multiple award-winning documentary about the Mexican American farm workers' nonviolent struggle for a voice in our society. Includes interviews with Cesar Chavez and Robert F. Kennedy. An outgrowth of the 1965 strike at Delano, a grape-growing community in California.

DISCOVERING THE MUSIC OF LATIN AMERICA. BFA 1969. El-J-S-A. 20 min col. Rental $15; purchase $260.

Demonstrates that the music of Latin America is a blend of many cultures, of which the Indian and the Spanish are most dominant. Surveys instruments and dances of the Indians. Includes examples of pre-Columbian instruments. Shows how Spanish conquistadores introduced the stringed instrument into the New World. Presents some modern derivatives such as the popular dance rhythms of the tango and rhumba. Concludes with costumed dances from a Bolivian fiesta.

ECUADOR. MGH 1963. El-J-S-A. 16 min col. Rental $15; purchase $215.

Excellent overview of Ecuador, its population, religion, transportation; some of its largest cities, products, exports, and Indian marketplaces. The Galapagos Islands, their volcanic origin, and animal and plant life on them are briefly discussed.

EDUCATION AND THE MEXICAN AMERICAN. UCEMC 1969. S-C-A. 57 min col. Rental $21; purchase $340.

This film points out the efforts of the Mexican American minority to obtain more meaningful education for its children through a massive protest in reaction to society's slowness to provide better education.

EL MUNDO DE UN PRIMITIVO: VELASQUEZ. UTEP. El-J-S. 20 min col. Purchase $180.

An excellent film about the works of the renowned Honduran primitive painter J. A. Velasquez. Highly recommended for young audiences who can gain awareness of the capacity of a creative Latin with no professional training. Spanish narration by Marla E. Walsh; English narration by Shirley Temple Black.

EL POLICIA (THE POLICEMAN). EBEC/UTEP 1966. El-J-S. 16 min col. Purchase $200.

Illustrates with good photography and narration the workings of the police in a metropolitan area, and shows them as protectors of the people.

EL SONIDO Y COMO SE VIAJA. EBEC/UTEP 1963. El. 11 min col. Rental $70; purchase $175.

The definition and causes of sound are well presented in this film with a fairly good translation of Spanish. Demonstrates the difference between one sound and another. There is an English booklet to accompany the film.

EL TEATRO CAMPESINO. NET/IU 1971. S-C-A. 61 min b&w. Rental $13.50; purchase $265.

A history of El Teatro Campesino (the Theater of the Farm workers) from its beginning in the fields boosting the morale of striking Mexican American farm workers and winning over nonstrikers to its present role as the theater committed to social change on a broad front. In promoting the solidarity of Chicanos, the theater presents plays and music stressing the relationship between economic advancement and politics. The group, directed by Louis Valdea, performs musical numbers, a satirical skit, a puppet show, and an excerpt from a full-length play.

FELIPA: NORTH OF THE BORDER. LCA/IU 1971. El-J. 17 min col. Rental $8.60.

Shows a young Mexican American girl helping her uncle to learn English so that he can pass the driver's test and thus maintain his dignity as a working member of society.

FORGOTTEN VILLAGE. CCMS 1941. J-S-C. 60 min b&w. Rental $35.

Among the high mountains of Mexico, the ancient life goes on with little change in a thousand years. Now, from the cities of the valley, new thinking and new techniques reach out to remote villages. The old and new meet and sometimes clash, but a gradual change is taking place among the villagers.

HARLEM CRUSADER. EBEC 1966. J-S-A. 29 min b&w. Purchase $200.

Documentary close-up study of activities of a social worker in Spanish Harlem over a five-year period. Skillfully woven, impressionistic views portray a slum-dweller's dilemma. Highly personalized, the film depicts problems to be found within a single-block radius of the "inner city" of mid-Manhattan where three thousand people, mostly Puerto Ricans, dwell. Excellent photography; valuable film for urban problems discussion groups.

HEALER, THE. MARYKN 1972. J-S-A. 24 min col. Rental, free; purchase $250.

This is the story of a man who came to be a god to the Aymara Indians of Peru, but instead found God in a way he did not plan to. It is a true account of this missionary's friendship with Marcellino, a priest of the Aymara religion—a witch doctor. It is a film rich in the religious customs and beliefs of the Aymara Indians. Captured in verity filming is the spirit of a people set against the life-and-death struggle they face each day.

HENRY, BOY OF THE BARRIO. ATLAP/UC 1968. S-A. 30 min b&w. Rental $30; purchase $225.

Presents a two-year documentary study of a Mexican American boy's search for identity in a ghetto neighborhood of a major southwestern city. Growing up with his Indian mother, his Mexican heritage, and the white society creates problems for him. Viewer becomes aware of Henry's thoughts and feelings as he reacts to the death of his father, alcoholism of his mother, frustrations of school, and his stealing.

HUELGA. MGH 1966. J-S-A. 50 min col. Rental $30; purchase $690.

In September 1965 a small loosely knit group of Mexican and Filipino American grape pickers began a walkout from their jobs demanding union recognition, the right to collective bargaining, and a minimum wage. Thus began the now famous Delano Grape Strike. *Huelga!* (Spanish for "strike") is a unique and moving historical documentary about the struggle to raise the standards of living of all farm workers.

I AM JOAQUIN. ETCO/UTEP 1971. S-A. 30 min col. Rental $7.50; purchase $300.

The film is a contemporary epic poem set to graphic prints of the years of struggle Mexican Indians have gone through, their heroes, and their history, up to their life in America today.

ILLEGALS, THE. UTEP. J-S. 20 min col. Rental $12; purchase $300.

Narrated by Lalo Delango, then director of the Colorado Migrant Council, this film shows ways that illegals (wetbacks, mojados, and so on) cross the Mexican-American border in search for work in the United States. Discloses the tragic suffering caused by brown slavery in the United States. In a series of interviews government officials, laborers, businessmen, and social workers put forth the political, economic, and social conditions that help perpetuate the immoral exploitation of Mexican and Chicano people.

JOSE MARTINEZ—AMERICAN. PCBNM 1964. J-S-A. 29 min col. Rental $5.

Views of life of the major Spanish American minority groups—Puerto Ricans, Mexicans, and the Spanish descendants of New Mexico. Surveys the progress made by such groups, emphasizing their cultural heritage and their growing middle class.

JULIO POSADO DEL VALLE. PAN/UTEP. El-S-A. 17 min col.

A visit to this artist's studio in San Juan, Puerto Rico. One facet of today's Puerto Rican culture is conveyed through an interesting narration, good photography, and fine background music.

LATIN AMERICAN COOKING. BAILEY 1969. J-S-A. 22 min col. Purchase $275.

Introduces Latin American cooking using modern cooking equipment; discusses Indian and Spanish heritage in Latin American cooking; shows preparation of tortillas, tamales, enchiladas, Argentine beef roll stuffed with vegetables and egg, anticuchos, mole poblano, and other dishes popular in Latin American countries.

LAWLESS, THE. BRAN. J-S. 83 min b&w. Rental $22.50.

A stirring indictment of racial discrimination, showing how an American boy from an unwanted minority group (Mexican field workers) is charged with a crime he did not commit and saved from a lynch-hungry mob by a newspaperman who stirs responsible citizens to action.

MAKING A PINATA. ATLAP 1969. El-J. 11 min col. Rental $15; purchase $150.

Young children demonstrate how a pinata is made of papier-maché formed around a balloon and decorated with tissue paper ruffles. Includes suggestions for special pinatas for Valentine's Day, Easter, Halloween, and Christmas. Shows students how much fun it can be to create a colorful means of celebrating special occasions.

MANUEL FROM PUERTO RICO. EBEC 1968. P-El. 14 min b&w/col. Purchase $95 (b&w), $185 (col).

Here are the problems of a Puerto Rican youngster engaged in two cultures—one inherited from his family and the new one he copes with in his neighborhood and school. The pressures are acute—his desire and need to "belong," his struggles with a different language, his homesickness, plus his parents' attempts to cling to their own customs and traditions.

MEXICAN-AMERICAN BORDER SONGS. NET/IU. El-J-S. 29 min b&w. Rental $6.75; purchase $165.

Presents border songs and their background on location around Rio Grande City and Brownsville, Texas, and Matamoros, Mexico. Visits homes and saloons to record Mexican folk songs. Guest participant is Dr. Americo Paredes, an authority on folk guitar styles in songs of the Rio Grande border.

MEXICAN-AMERICAN, ITS CULTURE, ITS HERITAGE. CGW 1970. El-J-S-C-A. 18 min col. Rental $23.50; purchase $235.

Ricardo Montalban, narrator, brings the story of his own Mexico to this film. In order to trace the contributions of the Spanish, Mexican, and Indian people to the growth of Mexico and the United States, a single melody, "La Adelite," is followed from its Aztec origin, through the Spanish, French, and revolutionary period, to the settlement of the American West. The film points out the contributions made by those people to our language, music, industry, and entertainment.

MEXICAN-AMERICANS: AN HISTORIC PROFILE. ADL/MPEMC 1971. S-A. 28 min b&w. Rental $10; purchase $125.

Maclovia Barraza traces the history of the Mexican American from the time of the Spanish Conquistadores to the present. Illustrates the influence that Mexicans have had on American history in both heritage and culture. Archive drawings, still photographs, and documentary film footage illustrate the lecture.

MEXICAN AMERICAN SPEAKS, THE (HERITAGE IN BRONZE). EBEC 1973. J-S-C. 20 min col. Rental $9.10; purchase $255.

Although the Spanish-speaking communities of the United States differ in origin, they share a common heritage and present aims. Focusing on the largest group—Mexican Americans—the film traces the conquest of the Indians by Spanish conquistadores and the spread of Spanish dominion in the New World. The rule of Spain disappeared, but the heritage of language, mixed blood, and culture remained.

MEXICAN AMERICAN—VIVA LA RAZA. CBS/MGH 1972. J-S-A. 47 min col. Rental $27; purchase $355.

Until recently Mexican Americans (Chicanos) were practically invisible, though numbering over five million throughout the southwestern United States. In the film, grievances of the Mexican American community in Los Angeles are discussed by political and religious leaders, the police, and Chicano leaders—both moderate and militant (a violent confrontation between the Brown Berets and the police is included). Also, the success of Cesar Chavez and Rudolfo Gonzales in organizing Chicano workers is seen as a major force in the struggle for economic and social advancement.

MEXICAN BOY: THE STORY OF PABLO. EBEC 1962. P. 22 min b&w/col. Rental $8 (per day), $12.80 (per week); purchase $165 (b&w), $325 (col).

A little Mexican boy tells in his own words how he worked to make a wish come true—then found he had to choose between having his wish and seeing his family happy. Pablo's story is told in the colorful surroundings of the mountain village in which he lives.

MEXICAN CERAMICS. BFA/UK 1967. J-S-A. 18 min col. Rental $8 (per day), $12.80 (per week); purchase $200.

Famous potters in Coyotepec, Metepec, Tonala, and Puebla are shown making and firing ceramics by techniques and methods indigenous to those regions. Shown in the film are the black pottery of the Oaxaco area, the "tree of life" ceramics of Timiteo, a master in Metepec, decorated animals and birds of Tonala, and the high-fire Talavera pottery of Puebla.

MEXICAN DANCERS. AIMS 1971. El–S–A. 18 min col. Rental $25; purchase $250.

A colorful fast-moving dance introduces a background of Mexican American communities and parts of Mexico from which the parents and relatives of these highly skilled youthful dancers have come. As high school students they have given over fifty concerts. Traditional Mexican dances, authentically costumed and set to beautiful music, dating from the early Aztec period to traditional dances found today in the coastal region of Veracruz are shown.

MEXICAN HANDCRAFT AND FOLK ART. CORF/UK 1969. El-J-S. b&w/col. Rental $5; purchase $68 (b&w), $136 (col).

This film, a second edition of *Hand Industries of Mexico*, shows that there are many craftsmen and artists in Mexico who create a great variety of goods. Natives creating jewelry and pottery, forming original designs, and copying classic statuary and ancient Indian pottery are shown. The mixed history of Mexico is represented in simple crafts and in magnificent works of art.

MEXICANS-AMERICANS; HERITAGE AND DESTINY. HFC/UU/UK 1970. P–El–J. 28 min col. Purchase $350.

Story of Roberto who feels culturally deprived and unsure of his identity as a Chicano. Narrator Ricardo Montalban cuts into Roberto's mood to lead him through his cultural past and present. Covers ancient and modern Mexican history and presents Mexican Americans who have achieved outstanding success in their work. Uses Spanish words, Mexican architecture, and music and art to illustrate their role in the American culture.

MEXICANS-AMERICANS: INVISIBLE MINORITY. NET/IU/UC 1969. S–C–A. 38 min b&w/col. Rental $11.25 (b&w), $15.25 (col); purchase $200 (b&w), $390 (col).

Documents the economic poverty of the majority of five million Mexican Americans, most of whom are in the Southwest; shows how Chicano children fall behind in school; and argues that understanding the Mexican American struggle requires sympathy for minority aspirations, which include retaining their cultural identity.

MEXICO (Part 1). MGH 1964. El–J–S–C. 17 min col. Rental $15, purchase $225.

Contrasts basic differences between regions; appraises climate, geography, topography, economy, and mode of life; and considers Spanish and Indian influences. Includes views of Monterrey, the "Pittsburgh of Mexico," and chief tourist cities, Taxco and Acapulco. Depicts economic and social changes taking place within Mexico; considers ties between Mexico and the United States.

MEXICO (Part 2) **CENTRAL AND GULF COAST REGIONS.** MGH 1964. El-J-S-C. 18 min col. Rental $15; purchase $285.

Depicts urban and rural ways of living in the central plateau with special reference to the Valley of Mexico, in which Mexico City is located. Considers *ejidos* landholding system of rural areas, movement to cities for factory work, and the historical and cultural background of Mexico. Shows cathedrals, plazas, floating gardens, and fiesta celebrations in Mexico City.

MEXICO IN THE 70'S HERITAGE AND PROGRESS. BFA 1971. El-J-S. 12 min col. Rental $8.50; purchase $155.

The blending of the old and the new in Mexico today is seen through the eyes of three Mexicans—a farmer, a butcher, and an architect. The farmer's new village, the new concrete marketplace where the butcher works, and the architect's spectacular National Museum of Anthropology symbolize the Mexicans' unique ability to blend centuries of tradition with modern technology.

MEXICO'S HERITAGE. HOE 1959. El-J-S-A. 17 min col. Purchase $200.

Depicts present-day Mexican heritage as a blend of Indian and European cultures forming a distinctive civilization. Ancient peoples conquered by the Spaniards, their art, architecture, crafts, and customs are presented. Authentic musical background at the beginning and at the end of the film may sound a bit strange at first.

MEXICO'S HISTORY. CORF/UTEP 1969. J-S-A. 16 min col. Purchase $212.

Presents basic background materials tracing the history of Mexico from pre-European times to the present. Utilizes a rich variety of original historical materials to depict the development of Mexico within the framework of four great events: the Spanish conquest of the Indians in 1519; the revolt against Spain in 1810; the Juarez revolt of 1857; and the social revolution of 1910.

MEXICO: THE FROZEN REVOLUTION (Part 1). UK 1967. C-A. 35 min col. Rental $19; purchase $900.

A graphic delineation of the political reality of Mexican history, including rare documentary footage of the uprisings of 1910-1914, and of Madero, Zapata, Vila, Huerta, and Caranza. The dominant persons, ideologies, and social forces that shaped modern Mexico are detailed.

MEXICO: THE FROZEN REVOLUTION (Part 2). UK 1971. C-A. 27 min col. Rental $17; purchase $900.

Concentrates on the 1970 presidential campaign of Luis Echeverria Alvarez, the inherited rhetoric of the PRI (Institutional Revolutionary Party), contrasted with the repressive reality of the Indian peons, Mexican farm laborers, aging veterans of Zapata's legions, and the summer of the 1968 student riots in Mexico City.

MEXICO: THE LAND AND THE PEOPLE. EBEC 1961. El-J-S. 20 min b&w/col. Purchase $150 (b/w), $290 (col).

Portrays changes taking place in Mexico, including growth of a middle-class society as a result of education and industrial progress. Pictures Mexico City, Acapulco, and Taxco. The rich Spanish heritage, products, urbanization, agriculture, roads, and tourism are discussed. *Mestizo* is defined. Indian villages and open-air markets, within a few minutes' drive of great cities, are shown.

MISSIONS OF THE SOUTHWEST. BARR 1967. El–J. 15 min col. Purchase $250.

Explores the history, purposes, and activities of missions of colonial Spain. Examines their role in the development of the old Southwest. Discusses the work of Fathers Kino and Serra in extending Spanish influence into Alta California. Points to the similarity between structural design of mission buildings in Mexico, California, and Arizona; pictures restored mission sites; and shows how missions continue to serve the communities that have grown around them.

NEW FOCUS ON OPPORTUNITY. UTEP. S–C–A. 30 min col. Rental $12.50.

Dealing with new government programs that attempt to aid the Chicano, this film depicts in a sympathetic way the problems and dreams of the Chicano of the Southwest.

"NO MORE MANANAS." PAULP 1971. J–S–A. 28 min b&w. Rental $12.95; purchase $160.

The plight of the Mexican American is sympathetically explored in this hard-hitting suspense story. Juan, who could speak only Spanish, attended a school where only English was spoken. He came to think of himself as stupid and dropped out. The film follows his trials, errors, and recovery.

NORTH FROM MEXICO. GPI/UTEP 1971. El–J–S. 20 min col. Rental $12.50; purchase $250.

This film, based on *North From Mexico: The Spanish-Speaking People of the United States* by Carey McWilliams, creates a visual and thoughtful portrait of the New Mexican American and the Southwest. It makes a bold and colorful statement about past contributions, present concerns, and future expectations. Highlighting the rich and significant contributions of the Chicano to the American heritage, the film follows the route of Coronado along the Rio Grande and into New Mexico.

NORTH OF THE BORDER. FRITH 1971. P–El–J–S. 19 min col. Purchase $235.

Presents the historical background and modern living conditions of the Mexican American in such a manner as to bear directly on the problems of this important and populous minority group and its influence on our culture, particularly in the southwestern United States. Mexican contributions to the life and culture of the United States, the missions, the architecture, the effect of the language, the distinctive food, and the *vaquero* (cowboy) with his outfit and speech are shown.

NUEVE ARTISTAS DE PUERTO RICO. UTEP. A. 20 min col. Rental $12.50; purchase $180.

A visit to the studios of nine contemporary artists in Puerto Rico. Commentary somewhat repetitive and film techniques not outstanding, but it offers a positive view of Puerto Rican culture today. Could be shown at PTA meetings in bilingual schools. Narration in Spanish and English by Jose Ferrar.

ORGANIZATION OF AMERICAN STATES. UTEP. S-C. 15 min col. Rental $12.50.

A fine film which makes the most of motion picture techniques in presenting a retrospective of Venezuelan kinetic artist J. P. Soto. Good English narration with Spanish narration available.

OUR LATIN AMERICAN NEIGHBORS. MGH 1962. J-S-A. col. Rental $15; purchase approx $260 each.

This series offers a country-by-country film study of the principal geographical, economic, and cultural aspects of South America. Family stories in each film provide continuity. Countries: Argentina, 16 min; Brazil, 20 min; Chile, 15 min; Colombia, 18 min; Ecuador, 16 min; Peru, 17 min; South America, 17 min; Venezuela, 16 min.

PANCHO. WWSI/IU 1960. P. 6 min col. Rental $6.25.

This is a story of a Mexican boy, Pancho, who captures a wild bull and thus wins a reward of a purse filled with gold, a silver saddle, and the biggest hat in "all" Mexico. Based on a book written and illustrated by Berta Hader and Elmer Hader.

PUERTO RICO—CLIMATE FOR REVOLUTION. AMDOC 1972. S-C-A. 90 min col.

Explores the life-styles of the Puerto Rican people, focusing on Puerto Rican independence rallies and protest music, the impact of tourists on the economy, and the effects of American enterprises on the island. It follows Puerto Rican emigrants to the United States and their activities as laborers. Features United Nations deliberations.

PUERTO RICO: ISLAND IN THE SUN. IU 1961. P-El-S. 18 min col. Rental $9.25.

Traces the history of Puerto Rico and surveys its geography, climate, natural resources, economy, and peoples. Highlights the island's history, including its discovery by Columbus in 1493; acquisition by the United States in 1917; and the creation of the commonwealth association with the United States in 1952.

PUERTO RICO, ITS PAST, PRESENT AND PROMISE. EBEC 1965. El-J. 20 min b&w/col. Purchase $130 (b&w), $255 (col).

Studies a bold experiment, "Operation Bootstrap," in Puerto Rico. For a despairing and impoverished Caribbean peasantry, a unique partnership between the United States and Puerto Rico has created a model democracy; turned underdeveloped and exploited sugarcane resources into a thriving industry; replaced slums with modern dwellings, and industrialized and stabilized a starving economy.

PUERTO RICO, "OPERATION BOOTSTRAP." UEVA/IU 1964. J-S-C. 17 min col. Rental $9.75.

Pictures the contemporary commonwealth and contrasts scenes of old Spanish forts with modern buildings in the heart of San Juan. Gives a brief overview of historical developments and highlights the transformation of the country's previously low standard of living to the prevailing standard of 1960. Explains the nation's close ties with the United States.

PUERTO RICO: SHOWCASE OF AMERICA. MGH/IU 1962. P-El-S. 18 min col. Rental $9.25.

Dramatizes the accomplishments in industry, agriculture, health, and welfare in Puerto Rico during the past twenty years. Pedro Lopez guides Judy Nelson, a young schoolgirl from the United States, through the country.

PUERTO RICO: SU PASADO, SU PRESENTE Y SU PROMESA. EBEC/UTEP 1965. J-S. 20 min b&w/col. Purchase $119 (b&w), $232 (col).

Good documentary with fine views of Puerto Rico. The partnership of Puerto Rico and the United States is emphasized. This film can be used as a source of discussion by the history teacher.

PUERTO RICO: THE CARIBBEAN AMERICANS. ABCTV/MP 1970. J-S-A. 22 min col. Purchase $350.

Presents the main historical facts about the island and the interesting monuments of its history. Introduces the age-old industry of harvesting the sugarcane, during which there are five months of hard work and seven months of what is called "dead time." Shows one of the newest factories on Culebra, which produces rats for biological research.

PUERTO RICO: THE PEACEFUL REVOLUTION. MGH/IU 1962. S-C-A. 25 min b&w. Rental $8.75; purchase $150.

Surveys steps taken by the U.S. and Puerto Rican governments during Operation Bootstrap to build factories, improve farms, provide housing, and eliminate illiteracy. Walter Cronkite interviews Governor Luis Munoz Marin.

QUE PUERTO RICO. ACI 1963. J-S-C. 16 min col. Rental $12.50; purchase $220.

A photographic study of the people of Puerto Rico at work, at worship, and at play, shown without narration but with full musical score. Cane cutters, women washing clothes, fishermen, and old men resting and chatting are typical of the countryside. A religious procession winds over the hills to the church. In the city, people visit cafés, stroll along the sidewalks, listen to street musicians, and take part in a holiday fiesta. Fine photography distinguishes this sympathetic portrait of a beautiful island and its people.

SANTA FE AND THE TRAIL. EBEC 1963. P-El. 20 min b&w/col. Purchase $130 (b&w), $225 (col).

Map shows trails in the United States in 1830, especially the Sante Fe Trail, used to build a profitable trade with Spanish settlements in the Southwest. Santa Fe was then a thriving settlement belonging to Mexico and the people lived under frontier conditions, working chiefly as farmers and traders.

SOUTH AMERICA. MGH 1962. J-C-A. 17 min col. Rental $12.50; purchase $240.

Excellent introduction to the continent: brief history, basic foundations of government, current economic situation, colonial past, variety of terrain and of climate, mineral resources and agricultural products, geographical features and their effects on man, and the need of transportation and of U.S. friendship. Problems are presented. Excellent discussion film.

SPAIN AND PORTUGAL: LANDS AND PEOPLE. CENTRO/CORF 1965. El-J. 16 min col. Purchase $210.

Second edition of *Spain: The Land and the People*. Surveys the endeavors of the Spanish and Portuguese peoples and their legacy of a common history and geography. Products of wine, cork, wool, meat, grain, citrus fruits and olives, and industries of fishing, mining, and manufacturing illustrate human use of the resources on the Iberian peninsula.

SPAIN AND PORTUGAL: ON THE THRESHOLD OF SUCCESS. CENTRO/MGH 1966. El-J-S-A. 19 min col. Purchase $210.

Analyzes many problems confronting the people of Spain and Portugal in their endeavor to upgrade levels of living contributive to, and resulting from, the current industrial revolution in their own and other European countries. Surveys landforms and cities and reviews historical backgrounds.

SPAIN IN THE NEW WORLD: COLONIAL LIFE IN MEXICO. EBEC 1961. El-J-S-A. 13 min b&w/col. Purchase $95 (b&w), $185 (col).

Describes colonial Mexico when it was a part of the Spanish crown. Includes views of a Spanish nobleman who was master of a great hacienda, of a priest who was a missionary to the Indians, of Indians who labored in silver mines and on the haciendas, and of soldiers, plantation overseers, and artisans of the period. Points out that many traditions which date back to Spain are still a vital part of Mexico today.

SPANISH CHILDREN. EBEC/IU 1964. El-J-S. 16 min b&w/col. Rental $8.50; purchase $115 (b&w), $220 (col).

Depicts December harvest-time activities in village of Alora, high in the mountains of Andalusia, southern Spain. Shows life-style, spirit, and traditions followed by villagers. Views of children at home, at school, in village plaza, in fields, in olive and citrus groves, learning flamenco dances, and hiking with Boy Scout troop.

SPANISH COLONIAL FAMILY OF THE SOUTHWEST. CORF/IU 1959. El-J-S. 20 min col. Rental $5.40; purchase $162.

Deals with work, play, etc., on an early nineteenth-century Spanish hacienda. Shows the relationship between the missions and ranches. Gives a very good picture of the buildings, furnishings, clothing, customs, and work on a Spanish ranch. Spanish words used and explained very well.

SPANISH COMMUNITY LIFE. BAILEY/IU 1961. El-J-S. 15 min col. Rental $7.40.

Shows life and customs of a typical Spanish pueblo near Madrid. Farmers live in the town and go out to work each day in the fields which surround the village. Birthdays, religious holidays, a procession for the saint of the town, football teams, and a bull festival are shown. Sophisticated life of Madrid shown in contrast to unsophisticated life of farm family. Authentic picture of life of the small town Spaniard.

SPANISH CONQUEST IN THE NEW WORLD. IU 1947. P-El-J-S. 16 min col. Rental $9.25.

Excerpted from *Captain from Castile*, this film presents incidents in the conquest of Mexico by Cortez from the organization of his expedition in Cuba to his advance on Mexico City. Reveals the Spanish motives and methods of conquest, and the personality and character of Cortez.

SPANISH EXPLORERS, THE. EBEC 1965. El-S-A. 14 min b&w/col. Purchase $95 (b&w), $185 (col).

Presents excellent basic background materials depicting Spain's rise to world prominence and role in discovering and shaping the New World. Examines Marco Polo's influence on Spain's entry into the Age of Exploration; discusses attempts of Christopher Columbus to find an all-water route to India; and explains significance of discoveries by Vespucci, Magellan, Balboa, Cortez, Coronado, Ponce de Leon, de Soto, and Pizarro. Utilizes map animation.

SPANISH INFLUENCES IN THE UNITED STATES. CORF/UK 1972. El-S-A. 12 min b&w/col. Rental $8.80 (col); purchase $91 (b&w), $182 (col).

Points out how the Spanish heritage influences our lives through architecture, clothing, furniture, language, customs, and religion by comparing Spanish culture with phases of American culture. Donald E. Worcester, Ph.D., Texas Christian University, Consultant.

TINA, A GIRL OF MEXICO. UK 1967. El-J-S. 16 min col. Rental $9.

Shows the daily activities of several middle-class families who share a court in Taxco. We see Tina and members of her family engaged in cooking and housekeeping activities, doing errands, shopping at the market, attending a fiesta, going to the cathedral, and so on.

UNITED STATES EXPANSION: CALIFORNIA. CORF/IU 1969. El-J-S-C. 15 min col. Rental $8.30; purchase $196.

Presents basic background materials on the development of California from its discovery by the Spanish explorers to its admission into the United States. Utilizes selected graphic materials and historical quotations. Examines the role of conquistadores, the development of Mexico, and the invasion by the Americans.

VENEZUELA. MGH 1961. El-J-S-A. 16 min col. Rental $15; purchase $210.

Size and location, physical features, history, economy (including agricultural products, mineral resources, great oil wealth of Lake Maracaibo, iron ore treasure at Cerro Bolivar), communications, contrast of great wealth and great poverty, and cosmopolitan life in Caracas contrasted with the rugged life of a farmer barely existing on barren hillside land are shown. Maps. Guitar music background.

VICUS. UTEP. S-C. 20 min. col. Purchase $165.

Narration in Spanish and English by Delores del Rio. Some words of the narrator are lost in the Spanish version, but the photography is excellent and the musical background is beautiful in this informative film about the art of the Vicus, a pre-Columbian culture in Peru.

VOICE OF LA RAZA. GREAVES 1970. P-El-J-S-C-A. 54 min col. Rental $120; purchase $380.

A candid report on job discrimination from *los barrios* of Spanish-speaking America. The camera follows actor Anthony Quinn as he travels about the country exploring this and other problems encountered by Latin and Chicano communities from New York to Los Angeles. The resulting dialogue encompassing the most urgent social and cultural issues of the day is the voice of *La Raza*, full of anger and self-searching pride. Filmed in candid camera technique, the film has won four festival awards. Produced for the Equal Opportunity Commission.

WHO NEEDS YOU? AIMS 1971. P-El-J. 11 min col. Rental $15.

Concept: the group member and the individual. In this film, Rudy, who is from a Mexican American background, sees how to view his difference as an asset. As they identify with Rudy, viewers will have an opportunity to realize that each one of us is unique, and to consider how to use one's individuality to evoke discussion.

YO SOY CHICANO. IU/UTEP 1972. J-S-C. 59 min col. Rental $20; purchase $550.

The Chicano experience—from its roots in pre-Columbian history to the present—is dramatically portrayed by actors who re-create key events and portray individuals in Mexican history and through interviewing Chicano leaders. Mexican Americans, who comprise five percent of all Vietnam casualties, have been subject to racism and exploitation throughout their history.

Filmstrips

AGRICULTURAL REVOLUTION IN MEXICO. EBEC 1965. El-J. LO F1A67-3261: 59 frs with cassettes $10.

Depicts Mexico as a totally agricultural country struggling to become industrialized; shows the continuing revolution in agriculture; discusses subsistence farming, division of large haciendas, introduction of modern machinery and scientific technology, and government subsidizing efforts to develop a sound economy for the people of Mexico.

AMIGOS LATINOS (English). DIS/FP 1964. J-S-C-A. col. No. 10027: filmstrip with script, 74 frs $7.

This filmstrip shows the cultural background of the Spanish Americans and their present situation in the United States including Puerto Ricans, Cubans, and Mexicans.

ARTISTIC REVOLUTION IN MEXICO. EBEC 1965. El-J. col. LO F1A67-3263. No. 7514-FSI: Filmstrip with captions, 49 frs $10.

Utilizes reproductions of murals by leading Mexican artists Diego Rivera, David Siqueiros, and Jose Orozco to depict the art and history of Mexico and the way of life of its people. Shows the continuing revolution in art and discusses influences of the church, the landscape, and Spanish and Mexican civilizations upon art in Mexico.

ARTS AND CRAFTS OF MEXICO. EBEC 1965. El-J. col. LO F1A67-3265: 49 frs with captions $10.

Discusses how the social and economic revolutions in Mexico have affected Mexican arts and crafts. Considers pottery making, production of lacquer bowls, weaving by looms, cotton hand-dyeing, stone carving, the crafts of the silversmith, and so on. Examines the influence of Indian culture in handicrafts.

AWAKENING, THE. SSSS 1969. J-S-C. col. No. MM8714: 8 filmstrips, 4 LP records, teacher's guide $80; No. MM8724B: filmstrips, English and Spanish records, guide $108.

Reviews the beginnings of massive immigration to the United States, the revitalization of folk culture, Mexican American economic contributions, and the problems of discrimination and adapting to a new language. Traces the Mexican American political and social awakening, the "Zoot-Suit" riots, the story of Reies Tijerina, early unionization and strikes, and the farm labor movement under Cesar Chavez.

BILINGUAL ADVENTURE SERIES. BES. El. col. No. AV185: individual filmstrip $8.95; AV186: individual cassette $8.95. No. AV185-186: special set. 11 filmstrips, 11 bilingual cassettes, teacher's guide $187.

Adventure stories designed to enrich vocabulary and concepts in Spanish. Recommended for use in elementary grades or Spanish classes. Titles: Las Experiencias de una Foca; Su Majestad el Leon; Papa Raton y sus Siete Ratoncitos; El Dragon de Wavel; Toomai el de los Elefantes; El Pececillo de Oro; El Anillo Magico; La Urraca Habladora; Aventura de Dos Pajaros Carpinteros; La Tela de Arana; and Aventura del Rey Pabon.

BILINGUAL ANIMAL TALE SERIES. BES. P. No. AV090: individual filmstrip $7.95; No. AV091: individual cassette $7.95. No. AV090-91: special set. 7 filmstrips, 7 cassettes $91.

Short stories of animal adventures. Titles: La Luciernaga y La Mariposa; La Casa de Los Animales; Mi Gallo; Mi Perro; El Jilguero Mudo; El Gallo Prepotente; and El Mono Fastidioso.

BILINGUAL CHARACTER SERIES. BES. El. No. AV100: individual filmstrip $8.95; No. AV101: individual cassette $8.95. No. AV100-01: special set. 8 filmstrips, 8 cassettes $136.

Picturesque Spanish stories showing strong personalities in dramatic conflicts. Titles: Calandrino y la Piedra Maravillosa; Sindo el Tonto; Quico y el Letrero; Juan Pedro y Juan Pablo; Ton, Tonico y la Tormenta; Calasin y Colason; Aquiles y su Madrina; and La Farsa de Maese Julio.

BILINGUAL LEGEND SERIES. BES. El. col. No. AV270: individual filmstrip $7.95; No. AV271: individual cassette $7.95. No. AV270-71: special set. 5 filmstrips, 5 bilingual cassettes, teacher's guides $75.

Illustrates well-known legends designed to enrich vocabulary and expand concepts. Recommended for elementary and Spanish-language students. Titles: Blancanieves y los Siete Enanitos; El Aprendiz del Brujo; El Patito Feo; La Alfombra Magica; and El Reloj Parlante.

BILINGUAL LITERATURE SERIES. BES. El. col. No. AV255: individual filmstrip $8.95; No. AV256: individual cassette $8.95. No. AV255-56: 5 filmstrips, 5 bilingual cassettes, teacher's guides $88.

Acquaints elementary level students with famous literature that has delighted children for generations. This series includes three stories.

BILINGUAL PRIMARY SERIES 1. BES. K-3. col. No. AV070: individual filmstrip $8.95; No. AV071: individual cassette $8.95. No. AV070-71: special set. 7 filmstrips, 7 bilingual cassettes, teacher's guides $119.

Longer stories for kindergarten through third grade pupils. Illustrated to capture interest. Titles: El Doctor Sabelotodo; El Oro de Tiempreza; El Colmo de la Felicidad; Los Animales Enfermos de Peste; La Artesa Magica; El Marido Grunon; and La Tinaja.

BILINGUAL STORIES (A Series—Spanish and English). CORF 1974. P-El. col. 6 filmstrips with 6 cassettes each. Avg. $75 a set.

Designed to enrich Spanish classes. Communication aids with bilingual children. Colores en Cuentos (stories about colors); Figuras en Cuentos (stories about shapes); Las Fabulas de Esopo (Aesop's fables); Leyendas Norteamericanas (American folklore); Leyendas de America Latina (Latin American folktales); Familias Norteamericanas (American families); Familias Sudamericanas (South American families); Conociendo Mexico (seeing Mexico); La Conducta en la Escuela (getting along in school); Ser Como Eres (Being You); Los Trabajadores (workers series).

CARIBBEAN, THE: PUERTO RICO. EDC 1966. El-J-S. col. No. 213172400: set of 4 captioned filmstrips $31.95; individually $8.50.

This survey of Puerto Rico introduces students to the land and people. An exploration of historic Puerto Rico, including forts, churches, and monuments. Relates the story of Puerto Rico's long period under Spanish rule. Shows that the island's geography, which ranges from near desert areas to lush rain forests, provides a variety of crops and habitats. Puerto Rico's cultural and commercial resources, no less diverse than the island's geography, reflect its Spanish heritage as well as the progressive outlook of its people. Titles: Historic Puerto Rico; Geography of Puerto Rico; Puerto Rico's People; and Puerto Rican Agriculture and Industry.

CENTRAL AMERICA: A REGIONAL STUDY. TERF/SSSS 1972. J-S-C. col. 4 filmstrips with teacher's guide. No. NYT340R: with 2 LP records $46; No. NYT341C: with 2 cassettes $48.

This social, economic, and geographic survey of Central America ranges from the pre-Columbian culture of the Mayans to a modern appraisal of the Panama Canal. Each country or group of countries is explored in terms of history, geography, political structure, social concerns, industrial development, trade, and common market cooperation. Produced by the *New York Times*. Titles: The Mayans of Central America and Mexico; The Panama Canal; Guatemala, Honduras, British Honduras; and El Salvador, Nicaragua, Costa Rica.

CHIQUITIN AND THE DEVIL: A PUERTO RICAN FOLKTALE. GA 1973. P-El. col. LC 73-733916. filmstrip with discussion guide. No. 3 D-301 885: with 12" LP record $21; No. 3 D-301 893: with cassette $23.50.

A hungry "devil" has followed Chiquitin's father home and now eats everything in sight. How to get rid of him? Chiquitin's task becomes a folk parable on the dangers of greed, and a textured portrait of life among the rural poor of Puerto Rico.

CONFLICT OF CULTURES. CCMS/SSSS. J-S-C. col. 6 filmstrips with teacher's guide. No. MM8713: with 3 LP records $60; No. MM87238: with English and Spanish records $81.

Describes the invasion of the trappers and Texas pioneers, the formation of the Texas Republic, and its effects on the Mexican population. Examines the Mexican-American War, the Treaty of Guadalupe Hidalgo, the California gold rush, and reviews the political and cultural changes brought on by the Mexican Revolution of 1910.

CUBA AND THE REFUGEES. SVE 1973. col. No. 255-SATC: set 2 filmstrips, 1 cassette, 2 teacher's guides $26.50; No. 255-SAR: set 2 filmstrips, 1 record, 2 teacher's guides $25; individual filmstrips with guide $10; individual records $5; individual cassettes $6.50.

On-location photographs and narration provide an overview of Cuba's history, economy, politics, education, and culture. Explores the peculiar problems of readjustment that Cubans face when they leave their homeland, bound for Miami. Discusses the handicaps they must overcome as they build a new life for themselves in an unfamiliar society. Two parts: The Island Country (79 frs); Miami's Cuban Community (80 frs).

CUBA TODAY. EBEC 1972. El-J. col. LO 72-736761. 94 frs, with audio tape. Filmstrip $10; record or cassette $7.

Describes Fidel Castro's rise to power, the role of the United States in Cuba's economic and political history, and a comparison of life in Cuba before and after Castro. Examines Castro's reform programs and illustrates the country's dependence on the sugarcane industry.

FABULAS BILINGUES. BES. P-El. col. No. AV030-3: 3 sets $88.50; No. AV030: 1 set $29.50.

A series of fables in Spanish and English by Dorothy Sword Bishop with an introduction by Carlos Saavedra, bilingual director, Albuquerque, New Mexico Schools. Effective for bilingual students as well as those learning Spanish or English as a second language. Titles: Tina la Tortuga. A perennial favorite, the story of the hare and the tortoise. Does a beautiful job of making haste slowly. Leonardo el Leon y Ramon el Raton. Wait till you see young students react to the idea that the king of the jungle also needs a friend! and Chiquita y Pepita. The story of the city mouse and the country mouse, where one excursion into the big town sends the country cousin running back home—absolutely content with what she has!

FAMILIES OF MEXICO AND CENTRAL AMERICA. SVE 1972. El-J. col. 4 filmstrips with teacher's guide. Avg 50 frs, 8 min each. No. F252-SAR: with 2 records $38.70; No. F252-SATC: with 2 cassettes $42.50.

Filmstrip shows structure of the family and explores the life-styles against their national and economic backgrounds. Titles: No. F252-1: A Banana-Growing Family of Honduras; No. F252-2: A Village Family of Guatemala; No. F252-3: A Modern City Family of Mexico; and No. F252-4: A Sisal-Weaving Family of Yucatan.

GILBERTO AND THE WIND. WWSI 1968. P-El. col. No. 104-7: LP disc $9.20; No. 104C: with tape $12.75; booklet $7.25.

A little Mexican boy, Gilberto, has an interesting friend who is completely unpredictable. His name is Wind. The artist's magic pen catches Wind's many moods. The whole Gilberto—hands, stance, and expressive face—reflects his changing response to his changeable playmate.

GOLDEN AGE OF SPAIN, THE. UTEP/TIMELI 1953. J-S-A. col. 60 frs.

Describes the political development of the Spanish states, Spain's exploration in the New World, and the artistic and literary achievements during the sixteenth century. Shows scenes of architecture, of Moorish and Roman structures of earlier periods, and art treasures from the Prado. Good for use in Spanish classes for a history background.

LA RAZA. MMPI. J-S-C. col. No. MM8710: complete program 24 filmstrips, 12 LP records, teacher's guide $235; No. MM8720: bilingual program, set of filmstrips with English and Spanish records $324.50.

A twelve-lesson sound filmstrip series spanning the cultures and societies of ancient Mexico through contemporary communities, movements, and individuals. Produced with the cooperation of the Southwest Council of La Raza. Dr. Julian Samora of the University of Notre Dame, Consultant.

LIVING IN MEXICO TODAY. SVE 1967. El–J. col. 4 filmstrips with 4 teacher's guides. Avg 36 frs, 14 min. No. 273 SR: with 2 records $37; No. 273 STC: with 2 cassettes $39.50.

Full-color on-location photography, supplementary maps, and narration provide a comprehensive, engrossing study of Mexico. Multidisciplinary approach to social studies interweaves geography and history. Reece A. Jones, Professor of Geography, Western Illinois University, Consultant. Titles: Northern Mexico and the Central Highlands; The Historical Triangle—Mexico City, Cuernavaca, and Puebla; Taxco, A Spanish Colonial City; Southern Mexico, the Lowlands, and the Yucatan Peninsula.

LOS PUERTORRIQUENOS. SCHLAT 1972. S–C. col. No. T327: 2 sound filmstrips with program guide. Avg 110 frs, 15 min each. With discs $44; with cassettes $50.

First-person accounts of life in America by Puerto Ricans from all walks of life. Illustrates problems and possible solutions in areas of health, education, business, politics, law and order, and creative expression. Community answers to drug addiction, infant mortality, lead poisoning, control of local health facilities, mental illness, and venereal disease. Puerto Rican Research and Resources Center, Inc., Consultants.

MEXICAN AMERICANS (Part 2: MINORITIES HAVE MADE AMERICA GREAT). SCHLAT 1968. J–S–A. col. No. T317: filmstrip with program guide, 68 frs, 17 min. With discs $30; with cassettes $35.

The early history of Spain and Mexico, ending with the courageous struggle by the Mexican American grape pickers who participated in "*La Huelga.*"

MEXICAN EPIC, THE. EFS 1968. S–C. col. 2 pts. $48; $80.

Students of Mexican ancestry will be brought in close contact with the roots and origins of their cultural heritage as it is unfolded in this exciting and stimulating filmstrip series. Magnificent paintings, murals, edifices, and the natural beauty of Mexico all combine to sing the glories of Mexico's brilliant past. Titles: Before the Conquest. Beginnings, classic Mexicans, Toltec, classic Maya, and Aztecs. From Conquest to Nation. Conquest, colonial heritage, and Mexico since independence.

MEXICAN HERITAGE, THE. SSSS/BFA. J–S–C. col. 6 filmstrips with teacher's guide. No. MM8711: with 3 LP records $60; No. MM8721B: with English and Spanish records $81.

Describes the development of civilization in pre-Hispanic Middle America, including the establishment and advancement of the Aztec empire and daily life in pre-Hispanic Mexico. Examines the Spanish conquest of Mexico, and the combination of Spanish and Indian influences in the development of Mexican folk culture.

MEXICO IN THE TWENTIETH CENTURY. BFA. 1974. J–S. 6 sound filmstrips. Avg 49 frs. No. VE2000: with 6 records $78; No. VSV000: with 6 cassettes $90.

This series offers a number of opportunities to study significant similarities and differences between the student's own culture and environment and that of contemporary Mexico. A varied geography and a long history of interaction between Indian and Spanish cultures contribute to the diversity of life-styles in modern Mexico. As work, play, culture, and transportation are explored in the filmstrips, the student becomes aware of the unique assets and problems of Mexico's social and physical environment. Titles: Mexico's Physical Heritage; Mexico's History; Mexicans at Work; Mexicans at Play; Mexican Art, Architecture, and Education; and Mexicans on the Move.

MEXICO IN TRANSITION. EBEC 1965. P-El-J. col. No. 10880: series of 8 filmstrips. Avg 50 frs each. With captions $65.90. Also available in non-captioned version with Spanish script.

This filmstrip presentation of a totally agricultural country struggling to become industrialized shows the continuing revolutions in agriculture, industry, education, and art. Captionless frames for extended study and carefully phrased questions inserted throughout each filmstrip help students discover for themselves the problems and progress of the Mexican people. The skillful use of reproductions of murals by leading Mexican artists provides a study of the art and history of the country and of the life-style of the Mexican people. Titles: The Land of Mexico; The People of Mexico; Mexico in Revolution; The Agricultural Revolution in Mexico; The Industrial Revolution in Mexico; The Artistic Revolution in Mexico; Three Farmers of Mexico; and Arts and Crafts of Mexico.

MEXICO: ITS LAND AND PEOPLE (Parts 1-4). RHI 1973. El-J-S. col. 4 sound filmstrips. Avg 239 frs. $54.96.

Every facet of Mexican life is covered, with emphasis on the effects of change and development on the Mexican culture.

MEXICO: OUR DYNAMIC NEIGHBOR. NYT/SSSS. J-S. col. 6 filmstrips, 3 posters, teacher's guide. Avg 66 frs. No. NYT330R: with 4 LP records $87; No. NYT331C: with 4 cassettes $91.

This colorful, in-depth, multimedia appraisal of Mexico ranges from Aztec times to the present. The student is introduced to history, culture, people, geography, and economy through the dramatic impact of narrative content that is skillfully coordinated to the visual force of original art, photographs, dioramas, and paintings from the National Museum of History at Chapultepec Castle in Mexico City. Titles: Conquest of Revolution; Geographic Contrasts; Life-Styles; Economic Success Story; Artistic Heritage; and Mexico City: Vital Metropolis.

MIAMI'S CUBAN COMMUNITY. SVE 1973. El-J-S. col. LC 73-734540. 80 frs, 18 min with disc or cassette.

This filmstrip looks into the lives of some of the Cuban refugees who fled their native country to move to Miami shortly after the Cuban revolution in 1959. It tells about their exodus from Cuba, their early days in Miami, and emphasizes their current experiences in their new home.

OUR MEXICAN NEIGHBORS. CORF 1970. P-El. col. No. 831: complete set of 21 super 8mm films in Technicolor cartridges with study guides $462; individual cartridge (Kodak on request) $22.

This series of films shows the diversity of Mexican life using the comparisons and contrasts found in the subject matter to illustrate how the Mexican people are influenced by their environment. The dynamics of social development and change are highlighted as life-patterns are examined in a wide range of occupations and places. The various climate areas seen in these films include jungles, coastal plains desert, highlands, and mountains. Archeology, history, and ancient ways of life are included. It is emphasized, however, that Mexico, like many other nations, is a country in transition, moving from an agrarian economy to a mixed economy, with a large industrial sector characterized by the growth of Mexican cities.

PANCHO. IU/WWSI 1960. P-El. col. 47 frs. No. SF145: with disc $9.20; No. SF145C: with cassette $12.75.

In this Mexican story of a boy against bull, children thrill to the wild excitement, exotic setting, and triumphant conclusion so wonderfully woven together by the authors. Good illustrations feelingly convey much of the folk life and customs of this colorful land.

PEOPLE OF MEXICO, THE. EBEC 1965. El-J. col. LO F1A67-3259. 52 frs. $10.

Describes the people of Mexico and the role they play in the continuing revolution in agriculture, industry, education, and art. Examines effect of Spanish invasion upon the Indian population and discusses blending of Indian and Spanish cultures and the evolution of the *mestizo*.

PLAINS OF YUCATAN, THE. RMIF 1969. J-S. col. LC 71-737241. 50 frs.

Through the detailed examination of the ruins at Uxmal, this filmstrip shows the classic period of the Mayan culture, its architecture, sculpture, and ceremonial rites.

PORTRAIT OF A MINORITY, SPANISH-SPEAKING AMERICAN. SCOTT/SSSS 1972. J-S-C. col. 2 filmstrips with teacher's guide. No. SED562R: with 2 LP records $35; No. SED562C: with 2 cassettes $37.

Traces the history of the Spanish subculture and its growing influence on contemporary America, and looks at the differences, problems, and goals of Spanish-speaking Americans.

PUERTO RICAN (Parts 1 and 2). SCHLAT 1973. J-S. col. LC 73-732512. No. T317: 2 filmstrips, program guide. Avg 90 frs, 17 min each. With discs $30; with cassettes $35.

First-person accounts of the current condition of the Puerto Rican community; language barriers, differences of customs, lack of education, job discrimination, and life in New York, Cleveland, Chicago, and other areas. This filmstrip portrays the social, psychological, and economic cycle that traps the newest immigrants, the Puerto Ricans, and traces the struggles, contributions, and triumphs in their quest for the American Dream. Honors Award, American Film Festival. From "Minorities Have Made America Great" series.

PUERTO RICAN SERIES. BES. J-S. No. AV470-5-4: 4 filmstrips, 4 cassettes $75; No. AV471-6-4: with records $67.50; No. AV470: Pt 1. set of 2 filmstrips, 2 cassettes, teacher's guide $36.50; No. AV471: with records $32.50; No. AV475: Pt 2. set of 2 filmstrips, 2 cassettes, teacher's guide $40.50; No. AV476: with records $36.50.

A two-part bilingual program succinctly presenting the history and culture of Puerto Rico, as well as present-day problems and accomplishments of the island culture. Part 1. Puerto Rico: History and Culture. A survey of Puerto Rican history from the fifteenth century to the present, including examples of its rich cultural and artistic traditions. Part 2. Modern Puerto Rico. The recent dynamic growth of Puerto Rico has made a huge impact on the life-style of the Puerto Rican people.

PUERTO RICO AND THE PUERTO RICANS. UMM 1968. El-J-S. col. LC 78-734754. 2 pts. Avg 55 frs. With discs $28.50; with cassettes $32.50.

Depicts the everyday life and culture of the Puerto Ricans and how these elements influence their lives when they immigrate to the States. Authentic Puerto Rican music, a native narrator, and colorful photographs hold listener's attention. Includes who they are, where they came from and why, and the contributions they are making to their newly adopted cities in the United States. In English and Spanish.

PUERTO RICO: AWAKENING COMMONWEALTH. SVE 1973. El-J. col. 4 filmstrips with 4 teacher's guides. No. 254-SAR: with 2 records $45; No. 254-SATC: with 2 cassettes $47.75.

On-site photography combines with provocative narration to present an overview of modern Puerto Rico, with its extremely arable land and favorable climate and contrasts the affluence and the poverty that exist because of, and despite, these conditions. Thomas Matthews, Ph.D., Institute of Caribbean Studies, University of Puerto Rico, Consultant. Titles: Agribusiness in Puerto Rico; Sugarcane: Sweet Taste of Success; San Juan: A Citizen's-Eye View; and Spanish Harlem: Mainland Puerto Rico.

PUERTO RICO: HISTORY & CULTURE. UMM 1969. P-El-J. col. LC 74-734753: 2 pts, 58 frs each. With records $36.50; with cassettes $40.50.

Traces Puerto Rican government from the time of Columbus' discovery in 1492 to its freedom from Spanish rule in 1898, when the country became a U.S. territory. The second part points out the influence religious tradition has had on the people and their way of life. In English and Spanish.

SANTILLANA BILINGUAL AUDIO-VISUAL PROGRAM. BES. K-El-P. No. AV705: 3 filmstrips, 3 cassettes $89.50; Nos. AV706, AV707, AV708, and AV709: 4 filmstrips, 4 cassettes each $119.50; No. AV710: complete set of 19 filmstrips, 19 cassettes $565.

Progressive, bilingual program designed to meet the specific needs of Spanish-speaking children in the United States by providing a firm foundation of basic language skills that inspire K-El level students to future study. Level 1 titles: No. AV705: Mira y Lee; No. AV706: Lee y Trabaja; and No. AV707: Trabaja y Aprende. Level 2 titles: No. AV708: La Ciudad; No. AV709: Otros Amigos, Otras Culturas.

SEEING MEXICO. CORF 1968. El-J-S. col. 6 filmstrips. Avg 50 frs, 10 min. No. S133: with 3 records $45; No. M113: with 6 cassettes $60; No. C113: captioned $37.50.

This series shows modern and historic Mexico—its cities, rural areas, agriculture, and some of the major industries which are helping her become a modern, industrial nation. Striking photographs show the varied landforms of the Sierra Madres, plateau and coastal plains, and the colorful Indian and Spanish traditions which remain an important part of Mexican life. Norman Carls, Ph.D., Chairman, Department of Geography, Shippensburg State College, Pennsylvania, Collaborator. Titles: Land and Climate; Agriculture; Industry and Commerce; Its People; Its History; and Its Culture.

SPANISH-AMERICANS OF NEW MEXICO, THE. SVE 1971. El-J-S. Filmstrip with guide 84 frs. No. P250-9R: with record $12.50; No. P250-9T: with cassette $14.50.

Conflict continues to erupt between the descendants of land-grant Spanish settlers and the U.S. government over the land the descendants live on. This filmstrip examines the causes for conflict and shows modern society's threat to the traditional way of life of these people.

SPANISH HARLEM "MAINLAND PUERTO RICO." SVE 1973. P-El. col. 64 frs. With discs $45; with cassettes $47.75.

Explores the living conditions of Puerto Ricans who immigrate to New York's "Spanish Harlem" in search of a better life. Gives authentic details of their experiences, their frustrations, language difficulties, and aspirations in a new land.

TESERO DE CUENTOS DE HADAS. SPA 1973. K-P. col. Complete set of 4 filmstrips, 4 LP records, teacher's guide, reading script in primer type, Spanish and English versions $69.95; with cassettes $79.95; individual filmstrips with record $16.50; individual filmstrips with cassette $18.50; individual teacher's guides $1; individual reading scripts $1.50.

The four well-known fairy tales in this collection were chosen for their universal appeal and because they provide the bilingual child with an introduction to the world of literature. Each story is a dramatized version of the original and is illustrated by a young American artist. Titles: The Frog Prince; Rumpelstiltskin; The Emperor's New Clothes; and Little Red Riding Hood.

THREE FARMERS IN MEXICO. EBEC 1965. El-S. col. LC F1A67-3264. 66 frs with captions $10.

Describes agricultural aspects of Mexico from the point of view of three farmers, showing traditional methods and new innovations in the field. Farmers represent a warm lowland area, a desert valley region, and a cooperative farming village.

Slides

ART OF LATIN AMERICA SINCE INDEPENDENCE. SAN. S-C-A. col. No. 634: 196 slides $254.80.

The slides in this edition present a historical survey of the cultural development of Latin America from 1800 to the present. Slides document the exhibition, Art of Latin America Since Independence, at the Yale University Art Gallery, directed by Stanton L. Catlin.

COSTA RICA. BUDEK. El-J-S. col. 37 slides $22.

Presents a regional analysis of Costa Rica covering population, agriculture, industry, communications, and trades.

EL GRECO. POPSCI. S-C-A. col. 12 slides.

Presents twelve of El Greco's works including "Adoration of the Name of Jesus," "The Agony in the Orchard," "Ascension of the Virgin," and others.

HISTORY OF LATIN AMERICAN ART & ARCHITECTURE. UCSC. El-J-S. Book with 8 slides $8.95 (pb $5.95); set of 25 slides $11.50.

Richly illustrated survey of 3,000 years; from the monoliths of the Olmecs to the fabled cities of the Aztecs and Incas, to today's soaring, modern capitals.

HISTORY OF SPANISH ARCHITECTURE. BUDEK. Individually: double-frame slide film (b&w) $6.50, (col) $10.50; cardboard mounted (b&w/col) $22; glass mounted (b&w/col) $30.

Titles: The Roman and Visigothic Era; Pre-Romanesque (Asurini, Early Muslim, and Mozarabic Architecture); Romanesque Architecture; Romanesque and Medieval Fortifications; Later Muslim Architecture and Its Effect in the North; Gothic Architecture (first half); Gothic Architecture (second half); The Early Renaissance; The High Renaissance; and The Baroque, Neoclassicism, and the Nineteenth Century.

MEXICO. BUDEK. El-J. col. 40 slides $30.

Shows the differences in landforms, climate, vegetation, economy, and cultural activity in Mexico.

MEXICO—A HISTORY IN ART. SAN. J-S. col. Nos. 665, 666, and 667: 30 slides each, $39 each; No. 672: 266 slides, $345.80.

Illustrations have been reproduced in high quality slides. This 266 slide survey provides a visual chronology of the development of Mexico. The history of ancient and modern Mexico is shown in the sculpture and painting of its great artists from prehistoric to modern times; how life was lived in the first villages; the splendor of the classic city-states; the tumultuous rise of the Aztec empire and its fall to the conquistadores. Titles: Ancient Mexico; Colonial Mexico; and Modern Mexico.

MEXICO'S MODERN CAPITAL CITY. BHAWK. El-J-S. col. 26 slides.

Presents a panorama of Mexico City with its skyscrapers and neon lights, the new city hall, Chapultepec Castle, Columbus Circle, and Alameda Park.

THE NATIONAL MUSEUM OF ANTHROPOLOGY, MEXICO. UCSC. S-C-A. col. Book with 6 free slides $10.00; set of 50 slides $24.50; set of 100 slides $47.00; set of 150 slides $67.50.

The ancient roots of Mexican civilization as seen in the arts and artifacts in the National Museum of Anthropology range from primitive civilizations to the most polished examples of sixteenth-century Aztec culture.

PRE-COLUMBIAN ART IN LATIN AMERICA. ACA 1969. S-C-A. No. ACA-28: 63 slides with commentary $75.50.

Including the arts from cultures in Mexico, Central America, Colombia, Ecuador, and Peru in all periods of development, this series serves as an outline of the subject. A definitive commentary, two map slides, and a chronology chart slide are included.

PUERTO RICO. UCSC. El-J-S. col. 32 slides.

This beautiful set of 2″ × 2″ slides takes the viewer on a trip through the island of Puerto Rico showing highlights of Puerto Rico's growth and history.

SOUTH AMERICA. UCSC. El-J-S. col. 32 slides.

Depicts Peru, Brazil, Chile, Bolivia, Colombia, Argentina, and Uruguay—countries accented with Spanish heritage.

SPANISH COLONIAL LIFE. SAN. El-J-S. col. 25 slides.

Presents examples of significant Spanish art and architecture from the mission fields established in Florida, New Mexico, Texas, Arizona, and California which reveal the Spanish influence upon American life and culture.

SPANISH PAINTING IN THE METROPOLITAN MUSEUM. ALCSC. S-C. col. 20 slides $27.

This series shows the many fine paintings of Spanish artists whose works are located in New York's Metropolitan Museum.

3000 YEARS OF ART IN MEXICO. UCSC. J-S-C. Book with 8 free slides $9.50; set of 50 slides $24.50.

A comprehensive, scientifically ordered panorama of the ancient cultures of Mesoamerica, from prehistory to the Spanish conquest and the still continuing heritage, the plan follows that of the museum itself, denoting the relationship between the building and its collection in the National Museum of Anthropology in Mexico City.

Transparencies

AGE OF EXPLORATION AND DISCOVERY—THE SPANISH. WPES. J-S. col. 10″ × 10″ transparencies with 2 overlays.

Describes the Spanish discoveries in the New World and discusses the explorations of Columbus, Ojeda, Balboa, Ponce De Leon, Cortes, Pizzaro, De Vega, De Soto, and Coronado.

EXPLORATION AND COLONIZATION. MILLIKEN 1968. P-El-J. 2 pts.

A two-part series of European exploration and colonization in the world. The following are those of interest to students of Spanish exploration: Explorers

Who Sailed for Spain; Spanish and Portuguese Claims; and Spanish Influence in the New World.

MEXICAN AMERICAN. CREATV 1971. El-J. No. 301.45A-SS: 12 transparencies, overlays, manual, $26.40.

Famous people of Mexican descent who helped make Texas a state, such as: Panchita Alanez, Santos Benavides, Jesus Cuellar, Jose Maria J. Carbajal, Jose De Escondon, Manuel Joaquin Gonzales, Jose Antonio Navarro, Juan Seguin, Juan Martin Veramendi, Antonio Zapata, Ignacio Zaragoza, and Lorenzo De Zavalo.

MEXICO. AEVAC. J-S-C. No. DW-18: 6 transparencies with 22 overlays $38.50.

Deals with facts, figures, and statistics on Mexico through history, geography, sociology, anthropology, political science, and economics.

PUERTO RICO AND THE VIRGIN ISLANDS. CREATV 1973. El-J-S. col. No. J911.3AB-01: transparency $7.35.

Highlights the features of two island commonwealths. From "Exploring the Americas and the World—in the United States" series.

PUERTO RICAN EXPEDITION. POPSCI. El-J-S. col. 10″ × 10″ transparency with overlay.

Pictures the expansion of the United States between 1803 and 1845 with emphasis on the Puerto Rican island.

SPANISH-AMERICAN WAR 1898-99. CREATV 1974. J-S. col. No. 973 TPB 06: 9″ × 11″ transparencies with cassette and work sheets $7.50.

Traces the sequences and high points of this American war. From "American History" series—The U.S.A. in Transformation 1865-1917.

SPANISH VOCABULARY (COGNITIVE SYSTEM). 3M/MMAMC 1967. J-S-A. Series transparencies.

This series deals with words and is intended to focus on vocabulary-building in the cognitive domain.

SPANISH—WORD AND NUMBER GAMES. 3M/MMAMC 1965. S-A. 19 transparencies with overlays.

This series is an interesting and enjoyable way to evaluate Spanish and non-Spanish-speaking learners in the classroom.

Audio Recordings and Audio Cassettes

CACTUS CURTAIN, THE. XEROX. J-S-C. No. CSD1257: 30 min cassette $14.95.

Ernesto Galarza became a leader of the Mexican American community at the age of eight simply because he knew two dozen English words. Since that time he has worked ceaselessly for the betterment of his people, emerging as one of their most eloquent spokesman. In this moving and frequently anecdotal account of the Mexican American's slow progress toward equality, Galarza demolishes some of the myths surrounding their struggle and proposes ways of making it more effective. A program from the Center for the Study of Democratic Institutions.

CUBA: THE KEY WORD IS HOPE. CSDI. J-S-C. No. 506: 26 min cassette $7.50.

Professors Richard Lichtman and Franz Schurmann of the University of California at Berkeley report on their trip to Cuba. Both stress the sense of community and feeling of cooperation in building a future for the whole people. Comparisons are drawn to life in the United States as both speakers describe why they were personally so deeply moved by their Cuban experience.

EL TESTAMENTO. CMUSIC. J-S. 12″ LP record 33⅓ rpm, 2 sides $5.95.

Love songs and comical songs showing Spanish or Indian influence were collected and rendered with genuine feeling by Alex J. Chavez. Titles: El Testamento; Julia Mia; La Vieja y sus Animalitos; El Caballo; Don Simon; El Burrito; El Carrito de la Parranda; El Bueyecito Canelo; Morena; La Indita; El Pavo Real; Tecolotito—1; Tecolotito—2; El Asturiano.

ENGLISH FOR SPANISH-SPEAKING PERSONS. MB. J-S-A. No. HCOC-3031: set of 2 cassettes only, with manual and dictionary, $12.95.

Modern techniques are used in this boxed set designed to help Spanish-speaking persons learn English more readily. The illustrated manual contains more than one hundred lessons in such areas as using the telephone, a train trip, at the drugstore, buying flowers, plus lessons in vocabulary and grammar.

FOLK SONGS AND DANCES. WIBLE. P-El-J. 33⅓ LP record $5.95.

Features instrumental and vocal pieces recorded by Dr. William Marlens.

FOLK SONGS OF MEXICO. FRSC 1959. El-J-S. No. FW8727: 12″ LP record $6.98.

Eighteen lovely songs from the various regions of Mexico, each telling a story—some sad, some joyful, some of love.

"LA MULA NO NACIO ARISCO." XEROX. J-S-C. No. CSD 1255: 49 min cassette $14.95.

There is an old Mexican saying: "The mule wasn't born stubborn—his life made him that way." Likewise, the much-criticized apathy and skepticism of the Mexican American can be attributed to a life of deprivation which exceeds even that suffered by the black community. A group of scholars and government officials examines the factors which have contributed to the Mexican American's exclusion from the benefits of our society.

LET'S LEARN SPANISH SONGS. EAV. J-S. Each tape $80.

These tapes follow the hear, repeat, and learn method. Each song is sung through completely, then repeated phrase by phrase for student repetition; the accompaniment only is then played, with the singer keying in the students by singing the first word or two of each line. Titles: No. 92T 701: Aquelarre, Los cordones; Tres hojitas, Madre; Canto de pescadores; Serranilla; Soy tolimense;

Las mananitas. No. 92T 704: Christmas carols; La Virgen lava panales; Esta noche los pastores; Hacia Belen va un borrico; El buen rabadan; Ya viene la vieja; Alegria.

LET'S VISIT MEXICO. EAV. S-C-A. Automatic and manual projection cassette only. No. 93TF 866: set of tape with sound filmstrip $17; No. 98TF 859: set of cassettes with sound filmstrip $18.
The scenic beauties of Mexico, its modern industrial developments, and the university are shown along with the more primitive parts of the country to give a comprehensive picture of Mexican life. The correlated narration in Spanish describes and discusses the contrasts in the country. Teacher's notes and full text of the narration in Spanish as well as an English translation are included.

LET'S VISIT SPAIN. EAV. S-C-A. Automatic and manual projection cassette only. No. 92TF 516: set of tape with filmstrip $17; No. 98KF 857: set of cassettes with filmstrip $18.
The contrasts of contemporary Spain are photographically depicted: cosmopolitan Madrid, primitive fishermen and farmer, a bullfight, festivals from Andalusia, Castile, Catalonia, Galicia, Aragon, and Extremadura. The correlated narration in Spanish offers commentary on each frame by native speakers.

MEXICAN FOLK DANCES. BOWMAR. P-El. 12″ LP record, 2 sides.
Presents eight popular Mexican folk dances: La Raspa; Chiapenecas; La Baniba; La Jesuscita; Chichauhua; La Cucaracha; La Burrita; and Jarabe.

MEXICANOS OF THE SOUTHWEST, THE. UK. S-C-A. No. T9298: record 40 min.
Conference on the Role of Higher Education for Compensatory Education, June 17-19, 1965, general session 3. Dr. Sanchez speaks on the Mexicanos of the Southwest and emphasizes the need to educate educators.

MEXICANS BRING US RHYTHMS. NTREP 1961. P-El. No. 0155-18: 15 min cassette $2.90; open reel $2.40.
Musically explores the concept of brotherhood by considering the contributions of composers of different nations. From "Music Unites Us in One World" series.

MEXICAN SING ALONG (VOCAL SPANISH). CMUSIC. P-El. 12″ LP record 33⅓ rpm, 2 sides.
Presents Mexican folk songs played by an instrumental group as an accompaniment for class singing.

MEXICANS IN THE UNITED STATES—EDUCATION. UK. S-C-A. No. T-1609: 2 reels 7 min.
Mexican American education in the United States. Recorded at Monterey, California, March 1, 1969. U.S. National Defense Educational Act.

MEXICO, ITS SOUNDS AND PEOPLE. CMSR. 12″ LP record $10.
Features Carlos Gestel, who narrates a tour of Mexico, and includes typical sounds such as church bells, carols, children playing, street noises, and bullfights.

MODERN METHOD ENGLISH COURSE FOR SPANISH-SPEAKING PEOPLE. MB. J-S-A. No. HCX-386: set of four 12″ records 33⅓ rpm, with illustrated instruction manual and pocket dictionary $11.95.

A unique system combining correct pronunciation of English words with illustrations of objects and actions in a manual. Includes one hundred lessons with complete translation in manual plus a Spanish-English pocket dictionary. Students begin holding simple conversations in English almost immediately.

NEW WORLD, NEW LINES SERIES. NTREP. J-S-A. No. 0164: 30 tapes, 3¾ ips, 15 min each. Cassette $2.90 each; open reel $2.40 each.

Features our Pan-American neighbors, past and present, and provides an understanding of their history.

PUERTO RICAN PEOPLE. EDRECS. P-El. 12″ LP record 33⅓ rpm, 2 sides.

The story of the Puerto Rican people and their history as related to America. From "They Came to America" series.

PUERTO RICANS. EDR. No. 455.19: 12″ LP record. Side A, 8 min; side B, 5 min; $11.50.

From Spanish subjects to American citizens; Indian and African slaves—a blending of races; Spanish misrule; the Spanish-American War; an American colony; American citizenship—1917; self-rule—1947, the first Puerto Rican governor, Luis Munoz Marin; Operation Bootstrap—raising living standards; the Commonwealth of Puerto Rico—1952; and migration to the mainland.

PUERTO RICO—SELECCIONES POETICAS. SMC. El-J. 12″ LP record 33⅓ rpm, 2 sides.

A Spanish-language record in which Rafael Bartolomei, Puerto Rican poet and elocutionist, reads 15 collections of Puerto Rican poetry against a musical background.

SONGS IN SPANISH FOR CHILDREN. LEART. P-El. 12″ LP record $15.

Performed by Maritita, Jesus de Jerez, and Juan Rojas with children's chorus and orchestra. Titles: El Barco Chiquitito; Cantos de Animalito; Los Pichones; Los Quehaceres de la Semana; Arrurru; A la Vibora de la Mar; Los Meses del Ano; Diez Ninitos; Desde Musico He Venido; Mi Granja; El Zapatero; El Mandado; Nina Despierta; and La Rana.

SOUTH AMERICA. UMAVC. J-S. tape. 2 tracks 15 min.

This tape includes music of South America, such as La Chacavera, folk dances from Argentina, and work and folk songs from other South American cultures.

SPANISH LIFE AND HUMOR. EAV. El-J. Six 12″ LP records, 12 sides.

This series is in Spanish and presents the life-styles in various Spanish-speaking countries of the world. Includes selections from the works of significant writers of the past and present. Contains oral exercises to test listening comprehension.

SPANISH SONGS. SCHMAG. J-S-C. 12″ LP records $6.98 each.

In record annotations the term "classic" refers to traditional Castilian Spanish, the official and literary language of Spain. "Latin American" refers to the

Spanish spoken in Central and South American Countries. Titles include: Cantos de las Posadas—Christmas folk songs from Spain and Mexico sung in Spanish—Fum Fum Fum—Natividad, and more (No. R7745); Children's Songs from Spain—folk songs from three Spanish provinces, some sung in classic and some in Latin American Spanish—Lavante Jose, Mi Burro, and many more (R7746); Christmas Songs of Spain—secular and religious songs recorded in Spain, with bilingual text (R6836); Folk Songs of Mexico—eighteen popular folk songs recorded in Oaxaca, Mexico, with bilingual text (R8727); and Vamos a Cantar (Let Us Sing)—collection of popular children's songs sung in Latin American Spanish—includes songs from Spain, Mexico, Ireland, Germany, and the United States, with bilingual text (R7747).

SPANISH STORIES AND POEMS. SCHMAG. J-S-C. 12″ LP records $6.98 each.

Selections include: Don Quixote—fifteen excerpts from Cervantes' novel read in classic Spanish by Jorge Juan Rodriguez (R9930); Ninos. . .Dejad Que os Cuente un Cuento—Rumpelstiltskin, Cinderella, and four other fairy tales—narrated in classic Spanish by Jorge Juan Rodriguez (R7833); Oral Anthology—Spanish-American Poetry of the 20th Century—poetry of Mistral, Reyes, Vocos-Lescand, and others—read in Latin American Spanish by Octavio Corvelan, with bilingual text (R9926); Paso A Paso (Step by Step)—richly varied selection of nursery rhymes (R7824); and Spanish Short Stories (R9931).

SPANISH TODAY. EAV. El-J. No. 99K Series 257-267: cassettes. 10 to 15 min each with teacher's notes $8 each.

An excellent cassette series made by native speakers to aid in teaching intermediate and advanced Spanish. Each unit deals with a different phase of contemporary Spanish life or culture. Each cassette provides comprehensive exercises with follow-up questions, repetition, and pattern drills.

TACOS AND HAMBURGERS. KEY. El-J. 75 min cassette 3¾ ips $10.

Recorded live at a graduate credit workshop for teachers. Leonard Olguin shows the educator how to teach, and then how to teach the boy and girl from the Spanish-speaking family. Along the way, he pinpoints the pitfalls that generate cultural clashes and shows how to avoid such confrontations.

TRADITIONAL SONGS OF MEXICO. FRSC 1966. El-J-S. No. FW8769: 12″ record $6.98.

From different parts of Mexico old songs nearly forgotten, and simple and easy songs with guitar illustrate the folklore of Mexico.

WHAT IS PUERTO RICO? CAED. J-S. LC 73-75 1129. 12″ LP record $6.98; cassette $7.95.

An introduction to Puerto Ricans on the island of Puerto Rico and in the big cities of the United States. Of value to both Spanish American children and those who wish to better understand the Puerto Ricans.

WHO IS THE ENEMY? XEROX. J-S-C. No. CSD 1256: 40 min cassette $14.95.

Who—or what—is to blame for the fact that Mexican Americans have lagged behind other minorities in improving their condition? Is it the educators who keep them in ignorance? Or is it the slum landlords who keep them in poverty? Or is it simply the Spanish language? On this cassette a panel of outstanding Mexican Americans consider these and other explanations. A program from the Center for the Study of Democratic Institutions.

Video Cassettes

AVENIDA DE INGLES. KPBSTV/GPITVL. P. Thirty 15 min lessons b&w $52.50 each.

Designed for Spanish-speaking children who upon entering school find themselves faced with a number of problems—a language barrier, cultural differences, and adjustment to a new and foreign routine. The series represents a presentation of what is known about linguistics and the role of motivation in language learning.

CARRASCOLENDAS. KLRNTV/GPITVL. P. 30 min b&w $65. With printed materials.

The aim of the *Carrascolendas* telecourse is to facilitate the bilingual education of Mexican American children. The Spanish word *Carrascolendas* translates as local festivals. The *Carrascolendas* series features elementary school children and unusual residents of the imaginary *Carrascolendas* community.

CHICANOS IN TRANSITION. UTEP. El-J-S. 18 min b&w. Video tape.

Narrated by Philip D. Ortego and filmed in El Paso, Texas, this tape shows prominent Chicano politicians and artists. Part of a proposed series.

HISPANIC CULTURAL ARTS. GPITVL. P-El. 30 min 2 inch video tape.

Discusses and explains language, music, dance, architecture, and art with visual techniques to help make children aware of the influence these cultural elements have had in the Southwest. Visits historical and modern homes to show Spanish influence.

HISPANIC HERITAGE. GPITVL. P-El. 30 min 2 inch video tape.

Views students and visits small towns to trace important aspects of the Spanish-speaking heritage and to emphasize many of the contributions that have blended into the American way of life.

HISPANIC LIFE IN A CITY. GPITVL. P-El. 30 min 2 inch video tape.

Focuses on the fifty thousand Spanish-speaking Americans now living and working in the Denver area and how they feel about their lives. Shows these people in their work world and in community activities.

NOTICIAS A FONDO. GPITVL. El-J-S. 2 series of sixteen 20 min lessons $57.50 each.

The Spanish-language version of Places in the News, the popular weekly current-events series distributed by GPN. The primary purpose of this series is to provide a source of news for intermediate level Spanish-speaking students attending bilingual schools or classes.

PUERTO RICO, USA. PEI. J-S-A. 11 min col 3/4 inch video cassette.
Explains the unique position of Puerto Rico as the United States' only commonwealth and shows the beauty, topographical variety, and historic locations on the island.

Study Prints/Pictures/Posters/Graphics

CHICANO POSTERS. UPMPD. J-S. Set of 5 col posters $2.
Colorful posters depict the Spanish-speaking American's new sense of self-identity. Includes the Servant Congregation poster in Spanish.

MEXICO. UTEP 1962. El-J. No. 917.2-P2: thirty-five 11″ × 14″ b&w study prints.
Prints include: thatching the roof, an arrow-weed house, mesquite beans, an outdoor oven, picking cotton, yoke of oxen in a corn field, cutting corn with a curved machine, grinding corn, tortilla making, carrying clay pottery, burro under a load of hay, a riverboat, Mexico City, the great cathedral of Mexico City, the floating gardens of Xochimilco, Central Mexico, Mount Popocatepetl, and others.

MEXICO AT WORK AND PLAY. UTEP. El-J. No. 917-P1: 20 col study prints.
Contents: corn harvest, making tortillas, water carrier, going to market, in the market, gathering maguey, weaving, a serape vendor, washing clothes, Sunday, the potter, decorating gourds, making masks, glass blowers, making candles, making toys, musicians, Xochimilco, All Souls Day, and a girl from Tehuantepec. Latin American village.

MEXICO, CENTRAL AMERICA & THE WEST INDIES TODAY. SVE. J-S. No. PSSP: 48 prints in 6 sets $54.
Provides insight into modern living and the problems that come with progress. Included are Mexican cities, the countryside, and arts and crafts. Costa Rica, Nicaragua, Panama, and the West Indies are also shown.

MEXICO, CRAFTS AND INDUSTRIES. UTEP 1968. El-J. No. 917.2-P5: eight 13″ × 18″ col study prints.
Contents: pottery painters at work, a silversmith at work, building with adobe bricks, drying sisal, printing textiles, a fisherman at work, refining petroleum, and the port of Vera Cruz. From "Mexico, Central America, and the West Indies" series.

PORTFOLIO OF OUTSTANDING AMERICANS OF MEXICAN DESCENT. SSSS. El-J-S. No. ECA 10: thirty-seven col 11″ × 14″ portraits $10.
Includes biographical sketches in both English and Spanish of important and famous Mexican Americans. Among individuals portrayed are Cesar Chavez, Ernesto Galarza, Congressman Henry Gonzalez, Congressional Medal of Honor winner Rodolfo P. Hernandez, Julian Nava, Congressman Edward Roybal, Ambassador Raymond L. Telles, and Judge Carlos M. Teran.

PROMINENTES CHICANOS Y CHICANAS. SSSS 1974. El-J-S. No. ECA 20: twenty-four 11″ × 14″ b&w posters $10.

Each sheet contains a line-drawing portrait, biographical highlights, and a discussion in both Spanish and English of the career of a prominent Mexican American. The set includes Vikki Carr, James Plunkett, Rueben Salazar, Reies Lopez Tijerina, Romana A. Banuelos, and Roberto A. Mondragon.

SOUTH AMERICA TODAY. SVE. El-J. No. PSSP-900: 48 col study prints in 6 sets $54.

Covers important aspects of the life and culture of South America's Spanish-influenced nations: Ecuador, Colombia, Peru, Bolivia, Brazil, Argentina, Paraguay, Uruguay, and Chile.

SPANISH-AMERICAN WAR PERIOD, THE. DPA. J-S. No. DPA 120 (7): 10 b&w photos on glossy stock $6.50.

Includes President McKinley and his cabinet, recruiting posters of 1898, the battleship *Maine* arriving in Havana, Sixteenth Infantry at San Juan Hill, Roosevelt and the Rough Riders, Admiral Dewey with President McKinley, and American troops in the trenches.

SPANISH INQUISITION, THE. JACK. El-J. SBN 670-66112-0: 8 exhibits, 6 broadsheets, contents brochure $3.95.

Assesses the real nature of the long-feared organization and its role in Spanish life. Exhibits include a pact with the devil, said to have been written in a nun's own blood; contemporary engravings of an *auto da fe*; and a ballot sheet on English sailors who suffered at the Inquisition's hands.

UNA PERSPECTIVA DE MEXICO. SSSS. El-J-S. No. ECA: twenty-four 14″ × 11″ b&w/col photos with teacher's guide $100.

Study prints contrast the past and present of Mexico as well as its rural and urban societies. Captions are in English and Spanish.

CHAPTER V

Other Ethnic Minorities on the American Scene

by Harry A. Johnson,
Professor of Education,
Virginia State College

As stated at the outset the purpose of this book obviously is to focus on four major American minorities. However this final chapter recognizes the great contributions of other American minorities. Although diverse, there is a strain of common experiences which these minorities have experienced at some time or place in their history. They include American Jews, migrant Americans, Eskimos, European immigrants, and others. Each of these groups has lent to the American culture much of its rich culture and tradition. They, too, may claim inadequate and inaccurate representation in our history and the instructional materials produced to teach about them.

America was a land of immigrants. They came early from Europe representing different national origins, creeds, and shades of skin color. Their struggle for economic and political power, status, and upward mobility is a ringing tribute to American democracy. Religious freedom and the flight from persecution lend a special place to these pioneers. From the revolutionary period to the present day, over 50 million immigrants have come to America. To them, survival often meant a loss of identity. Therefore in seeking their own cultural identification, the Irish sought out the Irish, the Germans the Germans, the Poles the Poles, the Italians the Italians, each forming a self-enclosed ghetto where old world traditions and languages could be maintained. Immigrants who came to this country in its infancy looked upon the schools with great awe and respect. The schools in turn, providing for children from diverse cultures, nations, and religious backgrounds, sought to find a strong theme of nationalism and dwelt upon unity, thus suppressing the diversities. Since there existed a tendency to accept the values of the more privileged and prestigious groups, minorities developed conflicts within their own cultures, often feeling an unworthiness in their native cultures.

Times have changed and America is coming of age. Children and youths are encouraged to be proud of their parents' culture and recognize the unique contributions of these cultures to the development of our country.

Although Jews represent only 3 percent of the total population of the United States, they play an important role in literature, art, science, medicine, philosophy, law, government, television, motion pictures, music, and theatre. This ethnoreligious minority has produced a cultural impact that is out of proportion to its numbers. This country is primarily based on a Judaic-Christian heritage and knowledge of the Judaic culture as it exists in the American Jewish community is essential for a better understanding of the total American cultural scene.

Long years of ethnic bias in instructional materials has been standard fare in American schools. These standard materials should reflect our pluralistic society, but have tended to reflect a long embedded bias found in our broader society. The recognition and acceptance of cultural pluralism in our democratic society is a professional responsibility for our curriculum planners, administrators, and classroom teachers.

The degree to which these ethnic groups have encountered problems and progress has differed. Their visibility as minorities, their degree of progress, and their encounter with prejudice have substantially differed.

No effort is made here to comment separately on each of these other minorities, but this chapter, pursued in less depth than the others, attempts to provide annotated materials focusing on people, their differences and likenesses, the recognition of their cultures, and the contributions to the growth and development of this great land.

The selection process used in the first four chapters was not so rigidly followed here. For a number of reasons this was necessary. There is a dearth of materials on some of these other minorities; some are not considered minorities in the strictest sense and some are not categorized as underprivileged or disadvantaged. Additional materials which criss-cross several ethnic groups were placed in this section because they did not properly fit in any of the first four chapters.

Users of this guide are encouraged to include these materials in curriculum planning that deals with ethnic and racial groups. Their cultures should be recognized, accepted, and appreciated as are other groups. Perhaps in a special book, at a future time, these other minorities may be dealt with in depth as they so richly deserve.

MEDIA AND MATERIALS—ANNOTATED

Films (16mm)

ALAHU AKBAR: FAITH OF FOUR HUNDRED MILLION. ACI 1970. J-S-C-A. 10 min col. Rental $15; purchase $120.

A portrait of the Islamic faith, youngest of the world's major religions and the most rapidly growing in the nations of Africa and Asia. This religion, practiced by 400 million Moslems, follows the teachings of the prophet Muhammad. A compelling film that will deepen the understanding of an important culture.

AMERICANS, THE: A NATION OF IMMIGRANTS. FI 1970. J-S-C-A. 62 min b&w. Rental $40; purchase $562.50 (set).

Based on John F. Kennedy's book *A Nation of Immigrants*, this five-film series traces the coming to America of more than fifty million Africans, Asians, and Europeans from the early 1600s to the present. Survival dictated not a great melting pot but sticking with your own—Irish with Irish, Pole with Pole, Italian with Italian, Chinese with Chinese. Titles: Ellis Island; Immigrants in Chains; Immigration in the 19th Century; Immigrants in the Cities; and Immigration in the 20th Century.

A STORM OF STRANGERS. NCFP 1970. J-S-A. 27 min b&w. Purchase $195.

An award-winning film about Jewish immigration to New York's Lower East Side around 1910, told through authentic photographs of the period. The narrator, Herschel Bernardi, speaks to an elderly Jew still living on Delancy Street who remembers his arrival in New York, his family, and neighbors. The story ends as the old man looks with a sympathetic eye on the new immigrants in his neighborhood—the Blacks and the Puerto Ricans. Awards in festivals include: San Francisco Film Festival—First Prize; Melbourne, Australia Film Festival—First Prize, 1971; Landers Award of Merit, 1970. CINE Golden Eagle.

AUTUMN COMES TO THE CITY. CORF 1970. S-C-A. 11 min b&w. Rental $70; purchase $146.

This film deals with seasonal colors, sounds, and activities in the city. It is dramatically presented without narration and in a racially integrated manner. It shows changing weather, clothing, food, animals, children's fun at Halloween, and a family Thanksgiving. Children of different backgrounds are shown sharing common experiences.

BAR MITZVAH. MGH. J-S. 13 min b&w. Rental $12; purchase $175.

A careful portrayal of the ceremonies in which a Jewish youth confirms his faith. An honored estate, Bar Mitzvah (the coming of age) follows several years of study of Hebrew language, scriptures, and customs. Through the film we realize the seriousness with which Jewish boys prepare for the full obligations and privileges of their faith.

BEHIND THE NAMES. ABCTV/MLA 1963. El-S-A. 24 min b&w. Purchase $250.

Examines background of California place names—how names stem from dialects of the Indians, the Spanish language, the salty flavor of frontier America, the physical features of the land itself, the honoring of distinguished citizens, the commemoration of an event, or the expression of an idea. Describes naming of many sites in the San Francisco Bay area.

CAN WE IMMUNIZE AGAINST PREJUDICE? B'NAI B'RITH 1954. S-C. 7 min b&w. Rental $7.50; purchase $70.

Three sets of parents use different methods to prevent prejudice in their children. When racial and religious bias develops, nevertheless, the film asks where the parents have failed. The film provides an "open end" or "stop the projector" technique, at which point audience discussions can take place. Narrated by Eddie Albert.

CHILDREN OF THE KIBBUTZ. ACI 1973. P-El-J-S-C-A. 17 min col. Purchase $230.

Daily life in a cooperative agricultural community in Israel today, as seen through the eyes of the children growing up there. The narrator speaks as the mother of several of the children, who are seen studying, eating, and playing together. An interesting look at communal living in a kibbutz. CINE Golden Eagle, 1973.

CHOSEN PEOPLE, THE. NBCTV/ADL. S-C-A. 27 min b&w. Rental $10; purchase $110.

An effective dramatization of the problems of anti-Semitism in America, originally presented on NBC-TV by the National Council of Catholic Men as part of the "Prejudice, U.S.A." series. In this revealing story, Anne and her friends learn that the community club they have selected for their senior prom does not admit Jews—making it impossible for some of their classmates to attend. In seeking a reason for the club's "gentlemen's agreement," the teenagers discover irrational prejudice in their own community. Discussion guide.

COLOR! COLOR! COLOR! AIMS 1973. El-J-S. 16 min col. Rental $20; purchase $215.

This film shows many natural groupings in an impressive array and a comparative spectrum of colors: of flowers, fruits, vegetables, animals, rocks and minerals, shells, butterflies, the sky, the sea, and the earth. Finally, tenderly and beautifully, man, with groupings from the three major races, is shown: the white, the black and the yellow! An open-endedness to the film will give each viewer a most thoughtful, provocative, and individual point of view. There is a dynamic and dramatic warmth throughout the film. The impact is immeasurable.

CRUNCH ON SPRUCE STREET. PAULP 1971. S-C-A. 29 min b&w/col. Rental $12.95 (b&w), $18.95 (col); purchase $160 (b&w), $325 (col).

A sensitive portrayal of the plight of the American hardhat, for whom the future is becoming the present too quickly. A blue-collar worker is appalled when his son rejects his values and drops out of ROTC. To make matters worse, a black family wants to move into his neighborhood. Unable to comprehend his son's decision, he continues to love him and struggles to accept it. But accepting the black family is something else again.

DIFFERENCES. ACI 1974. J-S-A. 25 min col. Rental $25; purchase $315.

An American Chippewa Indian, two Blacks, a Mexican American, and a long-bearded white man relate their experiences and difficulties in learning to live within the unwritten rules of white, middle-class America. Although of different ethnic backgrounds, a certain commonality is seen as they speak.

DROP OUT NOW-PAY LATER! HFC 1973. El-J-S. 24 min col. Rental $30; purchase $300.

This film focuses on minority students, especially with Spanish-speaking backgrounds. It emphasizes the many professions and trades open to trained and educated graduates and attempts to encourage students to attend college by informing them of scholarships and student loans available for futhering their studies.

ESKIMO ARTIST KENOJUAK. MGH 1964. S-C-A. 20 min col. Rental $15; purchase $295.

Here is a strange world where, in the deepening Arctic twilight, the snow, the sky, and the very air seem to throng with shadows. The thoughts of the Eskimo graphic artist Kenojuak, are spoken: "Many are the thoughts that rush over me, like the wings of birds out of darkness." Her pictures appear, like winged birds, wavering shadows on the snow. Kenojuak, wife and mother, does her work when she is free of the duties of trail and camp. The sources of her inspiration are sensed poetically, never directly demonstrated. At the cooperative Art Center of Cape Dorset the stonecutter Lyola and the printers are making rice paper prints from Kenojuak's design.

ESKIMOS: A CHANGING CULTURE. BFA 1974. El-J-S. 17 min col. Rental $15; purchase $235.

To what extent are changes in family patterns, values, and other elements of culture related to changes in technology? Using the Eskimos of Nunivak Island in the Bering Sea, this film examines such changes as they have occurred in the lifetime of the present generation.

FRIENDLY GAME. MM 1968. El-J-S-A. 10 min b&w. Rental $15; purchase $135.

This interpretation of racist and capitalistic psychology concerns a chess game between two men. Whitey, a young, white, manicured, Ivy League gentleman, considering it the purpose of a chess club (the film's setting) "to help novices along," invites Blackie, a black man, worldly wise from his experiences with the white man's knavery, to play his friendly game.

GHETTO PILLOW, THE. MGH 1960. El-J-S-A. 21 min col. Rental $12.50; purchase $175.

This film presents an old Jewish ghetto in Europe—the births, the weddings, the synagogue, the courtships, the holidays, the daily life—as seen through the watercolors of the well-known artist, Samuel Rothbart.

GHETTO TRAP, THE. INSIGHT 1968. J-S-A. 27 min b&w/col. Rental $12.95 (b&w), $18.95 (col); purchase $160 (b&w), $325 (col).

Using a Polish ghetto family to dramatize the dehumanizing effects of poverty, the necessity of breaking the vicious cycle by hard work and education is shown.

GUIDANCE . . . DOES COLOR REALLY MAKE A DIFFERENCE? AIMS 1969. P-El-J-S. 11 min col. Rental $15; purchase $150.

Using a most unique approach, this film presents several sequences wherein ethnic origins are unidentified, but different colors are presented in varying hostile actions. The viewer is led to believe that these actions have no bearing or relationship to ethnic origin. Conclusions are left completely to the audience, in what could prove a highly stimulating discussion.

GUILTY ONE, THE. AF. J-S-A. 30 min b&w. Rental $5.

A kinescope of an original telecast from the NBC series "Frontiers of Faith." Using a role-playing technique, the film first examines the question, "Who actually is responsible for hatred, discrimination, injustice, and so on?" The film concludes with three individuals commenting on these questions as related to their churches in fashionable Chicago suburbs and in black sections of the city. Use as a discussion starter with senior highs through adults on the topic of personal and civic responsibility. A church group in Washington said: "It fitted our program need on Christian responsibility and issues today very well."

HAGGADAH OF SARAJEVO. MGH 1969. S-C. 16 min col. Rental $22; purchase $230.

Presents the most precious Jewish illuminated manuscript extant from the fourteenth century. A veritable treasury of miniature paintings, the *Haggadah of Sarajevo* is a collection of tales, poems, prayers, and ceremonial rites. The manuscript is especially significant for the historic light it sheds on the ornamentation of Hebrew manuscripts and the medieval craft of bookmaking in general.

HASIDIM, THE. VEDO 1972. J-S-C-A. 29 min col. Rental $25; purchase $345.

The Hasidim (Lubavitch-Chabad) are an extremely pious and orthodox Jewish group whose origins in Russia date back to the middle 1700s. In 1940 the previous Lubavitcher Rebbe, their revered leader, fled Europe and settled in the United States, bringing the movement with him. In *The Hasidim*, a young Hasidic rabbi is host and narrator as the camera explores the history, traditions, and practices of the Lubavitch Hasidic community of New York. Some of the internal dynamics which enable this extremely vibrant group to flourish and to strongly influence the mainstream of Jewish life are revealed in vivid film sequences shot in the synagogue, home, school, and elsewhere.

HOLIDAYS YOUR NEIGHBORS CELEBRATE. CORF 1970. P. 11 min b&w/col. Purchase $70 (b&w), $140 (col).

Americans have come from all parts of the world, bringing their holidays with them. Celebrations of Chinese and Jewish New Year, St. Patrick's Day, Dr. Martin Luther King's birthday, Greek Easter Sunday, Mexican and Puerto Rican Christmas festivities, and Hanukkah reflect the excitement and pageantry of these special holidays.

HUDDLED MASSES, THE (Part 1). TIMELI/UK 1972. J-S-C-A. 26 min col. Rental $12 (per day), $19.20 (per week); purchase $330.

New York has served as the entrance to America for thousands of immigrants. The first stop was Ellis Island. Then most immigrants went into the city and tried to make a new life. They were faced with many hardships and new experiences: corruption, political machines, vaudeville, crowded housing, and sweatshop labor.

HUDDLED MASSES, THE (Part 2). TIMELI/UK 1972. J-S-C-A. 26 min col. Rental $12 (per day), $19.20 (per week); purchase $330.

Industry, labor unions and strikes, working conditions and reforms, Theodore Roosevelt and the robber barons, schools and the process of Americanization, and sports and success were all influential factors in the transition from that of being an alien to being an American. An example of America as a melting pot is given in the form of a Columbus Day parade in which Chinese, Puerto Rican and black children are participating.

IMMIGRATION. MGH 1968. El-J-S. 25 min col. Rental $26; purchase $295.

"Give me your tired, your poor, your huddled masses yearning to breathe free." This imperative emblazoned on our Statue of Liberty has meant much to Americans, both those born within our borders and those naturalized from foreign lands. *Immigration* traces the influx into this country from the beginnings of the westward movement for a manifest destiny. It shows the contributions made by these new citizens as well as the resistance of some of the country's original population to their presence.

ISRAEL: MAKING A LAND PRODUCTIVE. MGH 1967. S-C-A. 17 min col. Rental $12.50; purchase $210.

Illustrates the developments which are taking place in modern Israel. The exploitation of its mineral wealth and farm lands and the establishment of a sound, independent economy. The film will help students understand how the people of Israel have overcome the problems imposed by a dry environment to produce green fields and productive orchards. It also demonstrates from the political point of view the need for solving the conflict between the Jews and the Arabs in order to bring about further economic and social development in Israel and the neighboring countries.

KALVAK. GPN 1971. P-El-J. 18 min col. Rental $15; purchase $160.

Kalvak explores the Eskimo expression in paint and in printing. Both modes capture the excitement and color of Eskimo life. The artists work only with elements in their own environment—the animals of the hunt, their life-style, and their rituals. Kalvak is an Eskimo woman whose artistic talent was first discovered in her sewing patterns and then translated through the use of pen and paint into beautifully sensitive compositions, innately Eskimo.

LAND OF IMMIGRANTS. CF 1966. El-J-S. 15 min col. Rental $18; purchase $205.

We are a land made up of people of different national origins, creeds, and colors who have immigrated at different times and for varying reasons. Designed to show how the character, quality, and fabric of our land has been molded by the mixture of many cultures.

MAJORITY MINORITY. CEF 1973. S-A. 23 min col. Rental $20; purchase $300.

Leonard Davis is a White Anglo-Saxon Protestant, he is a paid worker, and he ranks within the median-age and median-income groups. This documentary scrutinizes him as a representative of the nation's minority group and points out groups from which he is excluded.

MINORITIES: FROM AFRICA, ASIA AND THE AMERICAS. CORF 1972. J-S-C. 16 min col. Rental $6.50; purchase $218.

This film presents backgrounds of various nonwhite minorities and their cultural contributions to American society and points out that Blacks, Mexican Americans, Puerto Ricans, Native Indian Americans, Japanese, and Chinese have made great contributions to the American culture, although each retains its own culture.

MINORITIES: FROM EUROPE. CORF 1972. J-S-C. 14 min col. Rental $5.50 (per day); $8.80 (per week); purchase $204.

The processes by which European minorities gained economic and political power, status, and their present-day position. Film points out the European heritage of descendants in the United States.

MINORITIES: IN THE NAME OF RELIGION. CORF 1972. J-S-C. 16 min col. Rental $6.50; purchase $224.

This film, in a series on American minorities, presents historical insights into the circumstances of religious persecution in America, the gradual lessening of discrimination, and problems existing today. Received the Chris Award. Arthur Mann, Ph.D., University of Chicago, Consultant.

MINORITIES: PATTERNS OF CHANGE. CORF 1972. J-S-C. 14 min col. Rental $5.50; purchase $188.

Film explores minority conditions today and in the past and the patterns of change taking place now affecting the future of minority groups in America. Two views are presented—one, that minority groups are following patterns of change similar to such groups in the past, and the other, that today the struggle of minority groups has become harder. Arthur Mann, Ph.D., University of Chicago, Consultant.

MINORITIES: WHAT'S A MINORITY? CORF 1972. J-S-C. 14 min col. Rental $5.50; purchase $188.

Filmed interviews with people of various racial, religious, and ethnic groups give perspective to the problems of prejudice and living together. Members of various groups discuss frankly their reactions to prejudice, presenting problems that each group encounters.

MINORITY PIONEERS: A WESTERN ANTHEM. UEVA 1973. El-J-S. 19 min col. Purchase $235.

The first educational film which tells the real story of the minority pioneers, what they experienced, and what they contributed to the history of the West. A revelation to all students, *Minority Pioneers* clears away the misconceptions presented by motion picture and television dramas. It defines what it was to find their place in the sun. The music is exceptional, carefully researched for its historical and folk authenticity, further justifying this film as an anthem to the spirit and determination of the minority pioneers.

NOAH. ACI 1974. J-S-C-A. 17 min col. Rental $30; purchase $230.

Noah is an elderly Eskimo who lives at Frobisher Bay, on Baffin Island. A master carver, he is seen carving a stone figure as he talks of the changes in the life-style of his people. Scenes around the settlement and out on the snow-covered, windswept landscape point up the contrasts. He remembers when they lived an isolated, self-sufficient life, hunting seals and caribou, and trading furs for necessities they could not procure in their own barren land. Now there are snowmobiles, schools, modern houses, and airplanes to carry out their products.

NOBODY GOES THERE: ELLIS ISLAND. ACI 1969. P-El-J-S. 9 min b&w. Purchase $85.

A pictorial essay of Ellis Island, the U.S. immigration station that was the gateway to the New World for thirty million European immigrants. The film combines still and live-action photography to create a haunting memorial to the island in New York Bay which served as a major focus in the making of the modern world.

NOBODY TOOK THE TIME. AIMS 1973. C-A. 26 min b&w. Rental $30; purchase $175.

Narrated by Edmond O'Brien and produced by the famous Dubnoff School for Educational Therapy, this film is directed toward the ghetto child handicapped with learning disabilities (the one most often labeled MR). Teachers demonstrate that basic trust in themselves and others is the first need of these children. This is accomplished through love, care, and understanding—treating each child as a unique individual. A variety of highly structured classroom and playground techniques help these children learn there is order to everything, and develop language and an awareness of their surroundings. Parent involvement is encouraged.

NO MAN IS AN ISLAND. DANA 1974. S-C. 11 min col. Rental $20; purchase $160.

The John Donne poem is interpreted through film and music to emphasize the positive behavioral objectives behind the words of the poem: "No Man Is an Island, Entire of Itself." It further illustrates the various ways through which we relate to the line of the poem: "Because I Am Involved in Mankind." John Donne's words, used as the lyrics, are set to music and sung by Andrea, who also composed and arranged the musical score. *No Man Is an Island* leaves one with the realization that John Donne's words, written over 300 years ago, and used by Hemingway, "ask not for whom the bell tolls, it tolls for thee"—affects each and every one of us.

OLD ORDER AMISH, THE. VEDO 1959. J-S-A. 32 min col. Rental $20; purchase $295.

A documentary film on the distinctive Amish who have turned their backs on the world and progress to follow the scriptural virtues of humility and hard work. Honored at international film festivals in New York, Venice, and Edinburgh.

OUR IMMIGRANT HERITAGE. MGH 1974. S-C-A. 32 min col. Rental $20; purchase $440.

From the revolutionary period to the present day, thirty-five million immigrants made possible the rapid settlement of the continent and the building of the nation. This highly informative film tells the story of the diverse people who became Americans—from John Smith and his crew of English adventurers of 1607, to the Russian Jews of the early twentieth century.

PEOPLE ARE DIFFERENT AND ALIKE. CORF/IU 1967. P-El. 11 min b&w/col. Rental $5.25 (b&w), $6.75 (col); purchase $150.

This film shows that differences among people are easily seen by how they look, where they live, and what they own. But it also emphasizes the likenesses of people—they all need friendship and love, food, and a place to live.

PREJUDICE: CAUSES, CONSEQUENCES, CURES. FI 1974. S-A. 24 min col. Rental $12 (per day), $19.20 (per week).

News films, historical photographs, and interviews with psychologists are used to survey aspects of prejudice. The social distance theory of prejudice is explained. Stereotyping socialization as a cause of prejudice and an analysis of the way children's books reinforce sexual stereotypes are discussed. Consequences explored include the development of parallel institutions and legal and economic prejudices against women. Various cures are described including legal measures, interdependency, and organized resistance.

TO FEED THE HUNGRY. MGH 1971. S-A. 45 min col. Rental $30; purchase $660.

An uncompromising view of the phenomenon of hunger in America detailing both its causes and results. Shot in Chicago, the film is a series of interviews with people—black, white, young, and old. Black community leaders and politicians point up the pressing need to find alternate ways to combat hunger.

VICTIMS, THE. ADL 1966. S-A. 50 min b&w. Purchase $150.

Dr. Benjamin Spock, author, teacher, and pediatrician, diagnoses the causes of prejudice in children. He finds it a crippling disease for carrier as well as recipient. A dramatically moving film showing young people—at play, in school, and in fraternity houses—as the victims. Poignant interviews with parents. Narrated by Pat Hingle.

WE CAME TO AMERICA. SHAW/IU 1964. P-El-J. 16 min col. Rental $7.70.

Tells about the special contributions brought to America by different national groups and how America has been influenced by three cultures. May be applicable to intergroup education.

WHAT COLOR ARE YOU? EBEC/IU 1967. El. 15 min col. Rental $9; purchase $220.

Tells about the three races of man and how skin color is an advantage to those living in different regions of the world. May be suitable for a general introduction to intergroup studies.

WHERE IS PREJUDICE? NET/IU 1967. S-A. 28 min b&w. Rental $15.25; purchase $265.

Pictures twelve college students of different races and faiths participating in a workshop to test their common denial that they are prejudiced. Shows that prejudice exists in those who believe themselves to be unprejudiced. The workshop is under the guidance of Dr. Max Birnbaum, director of Human Relations Laboratory at Boston University. In two parts.

WHO ARE THE AMERICAN JEWS? B'NAI B'RITH 1968. S-C-A. 30 min b&w. Rental $10; purchase $200.

A portrait of the Jews as a 5000-year-old religious-ethnic-cultural-historic entity. The program, narrated by Dore Schary, playwright and producer, emphasizes the development of the American Jewish community during the last three centuries; its participation in community affairs, its concern for philanthropy, and its relationship to the State of Israel.

Filmstrips

ACCENT ON ETHNIC AMERICA. SSSS. El-J-S. No. MM7086R&C: $12.95 with discs; $14.95 with cassette each set. $65.00 and $75.00 for complete set.

Different ethnic groups have had widely different experiences and problems. This series examines the unique situations of six immigrant groups, both historically and as they exist today. Each unit examines the common stereotypes of one ethnic group, the culture the group brought to the United States, and how that culture affects the lives of their descendants. Multi-Media Productions. Titles: The Chinese Americans; The Puerto Rican; The Polish Americans; The American Jew; The Mexican American; and The Italian American.

AMERICAN FAMILIES. CORF 1971. P-El-J. col. 6 filmstrips. No. S208: with 3 records $55; No. M208: with 6 cassettes $70.

Pictures the daily activities and family life of six urban American families—Black, white, Jewish, Puerto Rican, Chinese, and Italian. Shows them at work and worship, their customs, and points out their different life-styles.

AMERICA'S CHILDREN. SCOTT. J-S-C. 5 filmstrips. No. JH3700: with 5 records $57; No. JH3700FC: with 5 cassettes $62.

Depicts the life and dreams of five ethnic groups: the Native Indian American, Puerto Rican, Mexican, Oriental, and Black through the eyes of their most sensitive observers—their children. The series provides the student with an emphatic understanding of some of the minorities that help make America the greatest homogeneous nation in the world. Titles: I Am a Puerto Rican; Our First Americans; Ching Dao (Island of Gold); Los De La Roya (Those from the Nation); and To the Mountaintop.

AMERICA'S OLD WORLD BACKGROUND. MGH 1954. J. col. Avg 45 frs. No. 145000: 6 filmstrips $46; individually $8.50.

This series helps students understand present-day law as the outgrowth of age-old customs. Beginning with the Dark Ages, the filmstrips follow man's social progress and increased humanity, culminating with the contributions made by the knights and barons of old England. Titles: The Dark Ages; The Crusades; Europe Awakens; Gifts from Ancient Times; Life in a Medieval Castle; and Our Heritage from Old England.

AMERICA, THE MELTING POT: MYTH OR REALITY? SSSS. J-S-C. col. filmstrip 66 frs. With record $17.50; with cassette $19.50.

Why haven't Blacks, Puerto Ricans, and Mexican Americans become assimilated into America's national life? Is the melting pot concept valid at all, or are U.S. citizens divided into different classes?

A NATION OF IMMIGRANTS. GA 1967. J-S-C. col. LC F1A-67-2558. filmstrip with discussion guide. No. 3 D-414 100: with 12″ LP record $22; No. 3 D-414 126: with cassette $24.50.

Traces immigration from Puritans to present; probes laws, policies, and conditions; includes a contemporary case history. Produced in cooperation with the Associated Press.

ARABS AND JEWS: THE CRISIS. SCHLAT 1972. S-A. col. No. T412: 6 sound filmstrips with program guide. Avg 75 frs, 15 min each. With discs $120; with cassettes $138.

A penetrating account of the volatile Middle Eastern situation which probes the issues and background contributing to underlying hatreds and periodic atrocities. Background: Biblical times, Diaspora, Arab conquest of Palestine, Jewish persecution, political Zionism, Arab nationalism, Hussein-McMahon correspondence, Balfour Declaration, Mandate Agreement, and the 1948, 1956, 1967 conflicts. Two points of view: Physical, cultural, historical, and political ties of each side to Palestine; Jewish and Arab refugee questions.

CALIFORNIA CONFLICT: MIGRANT FARM WORKERS. SVE 1972. El-J-S. col. No. 250-29: 94 frs filmstrip and teacher's guide $10; with discs $5; with cassettes $6.50.

This incisive filmstrip shows dependence of the agriculturally rich central valley of California on the migrant farm worker; highlights the life-styles and living conditions of these migrant families; and explains how recent unionization will help them achieve a better standard of living.

CHILDREN OF COURAGE. SPA 1971. P-El. col. 5 filmstrips (a series). No. SA 2008: with LP recordings $100; No. SAC 2008: with cassettes $110.

Each of these five original stories, designed to entertain and awaken pride of origin and respect for differences in ethnic make-up, has as its hero or heroine a child of special ethnic background—a Japanese American boy, a girl from Puerto Rico, a black boy, a Native Indian American, and a Mexican American boy. Titles: Donny's Star; Raquel and Perdido; Pancho's Puppets; Whistling Boy; and Teru and the Blue Heron.

CULTURALLY DIFFERENT LEARNER, THE. NEA 1970. C–A. col. No. 388-11924: 2 filmstrips, tape, booklet $15.

These filmstrips reveal the learning styles of culturally different children and are designed to improve the instruction of these children. Part 1: Learning Styles; Part 2: Using Media.

ESKIMOS OF ST. LAWRENCE ISLAND. SCOTT/HANDY 1967. El–J. col. 3 filmstrips. No. DSR2930: with 3 records; No. DSC2930: with 3 cassettes $38.

Authentic photography shows the life-style of the Eskimos—how they work, play, and hunt for food. Titles: Life in an Eskimo Village; Fun and Festivals of the Eskimo; and Hunting with the Eskimo.

ETHNIC STUDIES: THE PEOPLES OF AMERICA. EDR 1973. P–El. col. No. 514: 4 sound filmstrips, 10 min each, 4 cassettes $66.

Presents historical background and culture of American ethnic groups. Part 1: An American Town. Part 2: The First Settlers. Part 3: America Grows Up. Part 4: The Melting Pot.

EXPLODING THE MYTHS OF PREJUDICE. MB. El–J–S. col. 94 frs. With records $38.50; with cassettes $45.

This set of filmstrips brings to light a variety of myths and misconceptions which underlie racial prejudice.

FOLK SONGS OF ISRAEL. BOWMAR 1969. col. 2 filmstrips. Avg 51 frs each. No. 462: with records; No. 808: with cassettes.

Reviews the history and development of the modern State of Israel and presents the remarkable accomplishments of the new nation in communal living (*kibbutzim*), agriculture, industry, music, and the arts. Titles: Hava Nagila; Ach Ya Chabibi; Artza Alinu; Hatikvah; Zamar Noded; O Hanukah; Havenu Shalom Aleichem; Kol Dodi; Zum Gali Gali; Rad Hlayla; Rock of Ages; and B'er.

FOLK SONGS OF THE ARAB WORLD. BOWMAR 1969. P–El. col. 2 filmstrips. Avg 48 frs each. No. 463: with discs; No. 807: with cassettes.

Includes: The Arab world—Morocco, Algeria, Tunisia, Libya, United Arab Republic, Sudan, Saudi Arabia, Yemen, Jordan, Syria, Iraq, Kuwait, Qatar, and Lebanon. O Come Now, I'm Thirsty, Tafta Hindi, In Lebanon, and The Apple Tree. Also includes: Come, Little Children Come with Me (Olive Chant); The Freshness of the Breeze (My Home So Far Away); Maidens Living by the Sea; In Alexandria; Will You Come To My Birthday Party? and Ala Da 'lona.

FOLKTALES OF ETHNIC AMERICA. NYT 1973. P–El. col. 6 sound filmstrips with teacher's guide. No. 410470: with 3 records $72; No. 410471: with 3 cassettes $75.

In each of these folktales, youngsters receive a graphic portrait of the daily life in the country of their origin. The population of the United States is made up of many ethnic groups, and our literary heritage is a unique blend of many countries. These are dramatizations of folktales from Japan, Kenya, Mexico, Puerto Rico, East India, and Alaska, which have become part of America's ethnic literature.

FORERUNNERS OF EQUALITY. TERF/SSSS 1972. El-J-S. col. 8 filmstrips with teacher's guide. No. NYT290R: with 4 LP records $94; No. NYT290C: with 4 cassettes $98.

Filmstrips describe how men of widely diversified backgrounds and interests contributed to the American ideal of brotherhood. Utilizing colorful illustrations, leaders are shown who established New World colonies based on equality of man: Lord Baltimore, Peter Minuit, Roger Williams, and William Penn. The second part of the program examines individuals who fought for their own or others' rights to an equal place in life: Dr. Goldberger, Paul Cuffee, Osceola, and Thaddeus Kosciusko.

IMMIGRATION. MGH 1975. J-S-A. col. 98 frs 11 min. Complete set 2 sound filmstrips, guide, and catalog cards. No. 106471-0: with 2 records $40; No. 102706-8: with 2 cassettes $40. Individually: filmstrip $13; record $8; cassette $8.

Filmstrips vividly present the subject of immigration in its historical perspective. The filmstrips are based on the fact that we are *all*, except for the American Indian immigrants, the descendants of immigrants, and that, from this fact, some of our greatest strengths and greatest problems have arisen.

IMMIGRATION: THE DREAM AND THE REALITY. SCHLAT 1971. J-S-C-A. col. No. T313: 6 sound filmstrips with program guide. Avg 62 frs 10 min each. With discs $120; with cassettes $138.

Tells the story of immigrants to America and their confrontation with the harsh and disillusioning realities of life in America around the turn of the nineteenth century. The first filmstrip details some of the reasons why immigrants left their homes and illustrates their hopes for earning a better way of life in America. The second filmstrip opens with a more general view of what the typical immigrant expected to find in the United States. Covered are the Irish, Italian, German, and Japanese immigrants.

ITALIANS IN AMERICA. SSSS. J-S-C. col. 2 filmstrips with teacher's guide. No. ADL42R: with LP record $35; No. ADL42C: with cassette $40.

An historical overview of Americans of Italian ancestry, relating the reasons for immigration to the United States and their contributions to their new country. The program examines life in southern Italy; fleeing from poverty; establishing a new way of life, despite the impact of bigotry and prejudice; mapping the wilderness, the colonial period, opening the West, gallantry in two world wars, and Italian Americans today. Anti-Defamation League.

JEWISH IMMIGRANTS TO AMERICA. SSSS. J-S-C. col. 2 filmstrips with teacher's guide. No. SUN207R: with 2 LP records $45; No. SUN207C: with 2 cassettes $45.

This review of Jewish immigration serves as a case study of migration to America over three centuries. Covers the reasons for migration, the first Jewish immigrants in the mid-1600s, the growing persecution of Jews in Europe, the struggle in the nineteenth century to build a new life in urban America, and the contributions these immigrants and their children have made to American society.

Visuals are drawn from historic photographs vividly depicting hardships and life-styles at the end of the nineteenth century.

LIVING IN ISRAEL—NORTH TO SOUTH. EGH 1973. S. col. 8 filmstrips. No. DF231: with 4 records $71.25; No. TF231: with 4 cassettes $72. Individually: filmstrip $6.50; record $5.75; cassette $5.95.

Israel is a country of diversity, both in its geography and in its people. A kibbutz family, a family from the Mediterranean port city of Haifa, and Bedouin tribes in Israel's Negev desert are seen. The workings of a kibbutz community are described, and details are given on geography and resources of various areas. Titles: Kibbutz Families in Israel's Negev; Farming in Israel—A Desert Kibbutz; City Family in Haifa; Haifa and Acre; Jerusalem; The Jordan River and the National Water Carrier; The Negev; and Bedouin of Israel.

MAKING OF MODERN ISRAEL, THE. SVE 1975. J-S-C. 4 filmstrips with 4 teacher's guides. Avg 90 frs, 20 min each. No. 253-SAR: with 2 records $45; No. 253-SATC: with 2 cassettes $47.75.

This timely new series documents the remarkable history of Israel, a small country with limited resources, but very important in terms of world politics. Israel's unique position is crucial to the political and economic stability of the Middle East. On-site photography and authoritative narration explore the social, economic, and cultural habits of the Israeli people who settled in the land of Israel, cut farms out of the desert, and made new cities in an ancient land. Titles: Birth of a State; Building a New Nation: Israel Since 1948; A New People: The Settlers of Israel; and Jerusalem the Golden.

MIGRANT WORKER. GA 1972. S-C-A. col. 2 filmstrips. No. 413 524: with two 12″ LP records $48.50; No. 413 532: with 2 cassettes $48.50. 3 student manuals, discussion guide (LC 72-734939).

The migrant worker, depicted in interviews and photos taken on location in Florida, examines life-styles, working conditions, wages, housing, education, nutrition, racial attitudes, relations with townspeople, employers, and unions.

MINORITIES—USA. CORF 1975. P-El-J-S. col. 8 filmstrips with teacher's handbook. Avg 68 frs, 11 min each. No. S703: with 8 records $96; No. M703: with 8 cassettes $108; individual teacher's handbooks $4.50.

This filmstrip series points out the conflict between the American creed and how minorities are treated in America. Using candid case studies, documentary interviews, poetry, and photography to develop the key concepts of prejudice, discrimination, and scapegoating, this investigative open-ended approach probes the effects on the people involved. Titles: The American Dilemma; Who Am I? (Native Americans); A Piece of the Pie (black Americans); La Causa (Mexican Americans); Executive Order 9066 (Asian Americans); Two Different Worlds (Puerto Ricans); To Breathe Free (religious minorities); and Bringing About Change.

MINORITIES AND MAJORITIES. EGH 1972. P-El. LO 75-739937. 6 filmstrips. With 3 records $53.50; with 3 cassettes $54. Individually: filmstrip $6.50; record $5.75; cassette $5.95.

Dealing with child-to-child prejudice, this series is designed to teach children why there is no valid basis for bigotry and why it functionally fails. Ethnic, national, religious, and color distinctions are not discussed as issues. Titles: Me, You and Us; Being Alike and Being Different; Him, Her and Them; Faster, Bigger and Smarter; Them and Us; and I Hate You!

MINORITIES HAVE MADE AMERICA GREAT. SCHLAT 1966. P-El-J-S. col. 6 filmstrips with teacher's guide. No. WS317R: with 6 LP records $90.50; No. WS317C: with 6 cassettes $110.

Offers an appreciation of America's greatest heritage—her people. Illustrated with photographs, paintings, drawings, and prints, each sound filmstrip traces the history of a particular ethnic group in America. The series reveals many problems faced by each minority and recounts its group and individual contributions to American life. Titles: Negroes: Slavery; Negroes: Since Reconstruction; Italians; Germans; Irish; American Indians (I and II); Puerto Ricans (I and II); Orientals; and Mexican Americans.

OTHER AMERICAN MINORITIES, THE (Part 1). NYT 1973. P-El-J. col. 4 sound filmstrips with teacher's guide. No. 410460: with 2 records $52; No. 410461: with 2 cassettes $54.

This is an examination of the minority groups in America who until recently have been all but ignored by mainstream America. The Mexican American has been called America's best kept secret; the Native Indian American has been the victim of broken treaties, unemployment, and segregation; the Puerto Rican confronts a language conflict that heightens the incidence of social and economic discrimination; the Oriental, a misunderstood people. The special problems and aspirations of four minority groups in America are discussed in depth. Titles: The American Indian; The Mexican American; The Puerto Rican/The Cuban; and The Oriental American.

OTHER AMERICAN MINORITIES, THE (Part 2). NYT 1973. P-El-J. col. 4 sound filmstrips with teacher's guide. No. 410820: with 4 records $66; No. 410821: with 4 cassettes $70.

Here is an examination of the contributions of the Irish, German, Italian, and Jewish minority groups that have added so much flavor and character to American life. Gives a picture of the heritage of four groups and a deep appreciation of people who have made our country great. The historical background is explored as well as the impact on education, art, agriculture, music, food, and many other aspects of our life.

OUT OF THE MAINSTREAM. SCHLAT 1970. J-S-C. col. No. T318: 6 sound filmstrips with program guide. Avg 120 frs, 15 min each. With discs $120; with cassettes $138.

Individuals from America's poverty stricken population reveal the agony and hardship of being poor in the world's most prosperous nation. Titles: What More Can You Take Away?; Mostly Poor; You All Got to Live; A Good Citizen; Basta; and The Migrant Stream.

SEEDS OF HATE: EXAMINATION OF PREJUDICE. SCHLAT 1972. J-S-C. col. No. D326: 2 sound filmstrips with program guide. Avg 90 frs, 12 min each. With discs $40; with cassettes $46.

This filmstrip shows the overwhelming potential for harm prejudice carries and the psychological groundwork for studying prejudicial decision making. Includes interviews with people who have experienced prejudice. Designed to show young people what can happen if they do not examine their own feelings and actions toward others.

SOUTHERN APPALACHIA: AN AREA LEFT BEHIND. SVE 1972. P-El-J. col. Filmstrip with teacher's guide $10; No. P250-13R: with records $12.50; No. P250-13T: with cassettes $14.50.

Filmstrip graphically examines the poverty and other problems besetting southern Appalachia and explains their relationship to the geography of the mountainous area. Emphasizes mining activities and provides a detailed study of a farmer.

STORY OF AMERICA'S PEOPLE, THE. EGH 1972. P-El-J. col. 10 captioned filmstrips, 5 cassettes $90; individual filmstrips $6.50.

A filmstrip documentary illustrating the arrival, growth, and achievement pattern of the leading ethnic groups: the story of the Hungarian, the Italian, the Afro-American, the Spanish speaking American, Scandinavian Americans, Jewish Americans, and others.

TALL TALES IN AMERICAN FOLKLORE. CORF 1971. P-El-J. col. 6 filmstrips. Avg 45 frs, 11 min each. No. S248: with 3 records $58; No. M248: with 6 cassettes $73.

The deeds of regional characters are retold in colorful illustration, verse, music, and sound effects. History, as well as imaginative adventures, are skillfully recreated in these stories of the seaman who made the cliffs of Dover white, the Tennessee woodsman who went to Congress, the man who gave away apple seeds, the West Virginia lumberjack who invented clothespins and peanut brittle, the Nebraska farmer who saved the crops from grasshoppers, and the fireman who used the Hudson River as a hose.

UNDERSTANDING PREJUDICE. SSSS 1973. J-S-C-A. 3 filmstrips with teacher's guide. Avg 76 frs each. With discs $40; cassettes available $45.

Designed to give a fuller understanding of the nature of prejudice, the program examines how prejudice is formed, how it may be altered, how stereotyping affects the individual's perspective, and how it differs from generalizing. Part 1: Stereotyping and Generalizing; Part 2: Master Race Myth; Part 3: Scapegoating.

WHAT IS PREJUDICE? SCHLAT 1969. col. J-S-C. 160 frs. With discs $38.50; with cassettes $45.

Drawing on the celebrated works of such experts as Ashley Montagu, Gordon Allport, and Oscar Handlin, the series deals with prejudice and how it can be erased.

Slides

ALASKAN ESKIMO ARTS. ACA. El-J. No. ACA-20: 25 slides with commentary $30.

The Alaskan Eskimos were seminomads. Their artistic genius found expression mainly in the creation of wooden masks, small ivory carvings, and engravings. Included in this series are slides showing ivory implements, stone tools, engraved ivory, wooden containers, and masks of wood. The commentary has a bibliography.

ESKIMO ART. UCSC. El-J. Book with 4 free slides $4.95; set of 20 slides $9.50.

The author traces Eskimo art from prehistoric times to the present day. The volume is about evenly divided between text and illustrations. Included are one hundred photographs of examples of Eskimo art about half of which are in full color.

LIFE THAT DISAPPEARED, THE. SCHMAG. S-C-A. No. 8892: 80 slides with tape cassette, 16 min, glossary of Yiddish terms and teaching guide $50.

The Jewish experience in Eastern Europe 1935-1939, by Roman Vishniac. An International Fund for Concerned Photography program, published in cooperation with the Jewish Museum.

Audio Recordings and Audio Cassettes

ARAB WORLD, THE. CMUSIC. P-El-J. No. CN118: 12″ LP record with booklet $6.98.

The people and music of eleven Middle Eastern countries—Iran, Iraq, Israel, Jordan, Saudi Arabia, United Arab Republic, Lebanon, and so on. The instruments are pictured in the booklet.

ARCHITECTURE OF PLURALISM, THE (ASIAN, BLACK, CHICANO, FIRST AMERICANS). NEA 1972. El-J-S. No. 388.12002: 40 min cassette $46.

Representatives of four NEA caucuses exchange views on the present outlook in American schools and needed changes. Speakers are Bambi Cardenas, Lloyde Elm, Paul Tanaka, and Lavni Wynn. A human relations booklet is included.

CHILDREN OF COURAGE. MB. El-J. No. T SAC 6069/73: 5 cassettes $29.75.

Pride of origin and respect for differences in ethnic make-up are encouraged in these creatively conceived American ethnic tales. Each story has as its hero or heroine a child of a specific ethnic background. Titles: Donny's Star (about a black boy); Raquel and Perdido (about a Puerto Rican girl); Teru and the Blue Heron (about a Japanese American boy); Whistling Boy (about an Indian boy); and Pancho's Puppets (about a Mexican American boy).

ESKIMO. CMUSIC. El-J-S. LC 72-75 0987. 12″ LP record $6.98; cassette $7.95.

A collection of important Eskimo legends revolving around the mythical human being who created the world, its people, and the animals typical of the North, such as seals and whales. Because Raven is endowed with human qualities of sensitivity and loneliness, the stories are unusual and highly appealing.

ESKIMOS OF HUDSON BAY AND ALASKA, THE. SCHMAG. El. LC R-55-115. No. R4444: 12″ LP record $8.95.

Authentic Eskimo songs and dances reflect the close relationship between music and everyday life. Includes ceremonial hunting songs, nightly song fests and dances, communal song and story sessions, and a variety of children's games. Recordings and notes by Laura Boulton.

ETHNIC STUDIES. EDR 1973. El-J-S. No. ED1455: 18 cassettes with 4 color filmstrips and work materials.

Covers several ethnic groups. From "Peoples of America" series.

FRENCH AMERICANS. EDR 1973. El-J-S. No. 433.20: 19 min cassette $11.50.

Sixteenth- and seventeenth-century explorers, the Huguenot settlers in New England, Paul Revere, John Jay, Alexander Hamilton, the Marquis de Lafayette, the fur trade, the French and Indian War, the founding of New Orleans, Creoles and Cajuns, Audubon and Dupont de Nemours, and the gift of the Statue of Liberty are all a portion of the French American profile.

GERMANS HAVE HELPED TO BUILD AMERICA. BTC. P-El. 1 cassette with 35 student books $9.95.

History of many German customs which have been assimilated since their immigration to the United States. From "Americans All" series.

IRISH AMERICANS. EDR. J-S. No. 455.12: record. Side A, 14 min; side B, 9 min $11.50.

Topics included are: Irish immigration in colonial times; Charles Carroll of Maryland; Daniel Boone; John Barry, the "Father of the American Navy"; the potato famine and the great migration of 1845-1860; the Irish laborer—a profile; Irish regiments in the Civil War; politics as a way of life; Al Smith—a profile; the union movement; the "fighting Irish"; John L. Sullivan—a profile; Irish American writers; and the election of John F. Kennedy.

IRISH FAIRY TALES. SPA. P-El. No. SAS-5: 2 LP records $13; individually $6.50.

"Very, very Irish" is both the definitive description of, and the ultimate compliment for, this collection of tales. Volume 1: The White Trout, Jamie Freel and the Young Lady, and The Soul Changes. Volume 2: Hudden and Dudden and Donal O'Leary How Cormac MacArt Went to Faery, The Black Horse, and Andrew Coffey.

IRISH HAVE HELPED TO BUILD AMERICA. BTC. P-El. cassette with 35 student books $9.95.

Foods, music, customs, and holidays are featured in portraying the history and customs of the Irish immigration. From "Americans All" series.

ISRAEL. CMUSIC. P-El-J. No. CN119: 12″ LP record $6.98.
Facts about history, language, religion, education, and music are related and performed on the recording and described in accompanying booklet.

ISRAELI FOLK DANCES. CMUSIC. P-El-J. No. DF 331: 12″ LP record with booklet $5.98.
Vigorous, rhythmic dances, songs, and music arranged by Elyakum Shapirra. Included are Mayim-Mayim (Water), Hanoded (Wanderer), and Horas.

ITALIAN AMERICANS. EDR. J-S. No. 455.13: cassette $11.50.
Topics included are: the first explorers—Columbus and Vespucci; Colonial era—Italian artisans and missionaries; the gold rush in California; the Italian winemaking industry; Italian artists help build the Capitol building; the Italian laborer; the rise of "Little Italies"; saints, singers, and sports figures; profiles—Mother Cabrini; Enrico Caruso; Joe DiMaggio; Fiorello LaGuardia—the mayor of New York; and Enrico Fermi.

JEWISH AMERICANS. EDR. J-S. No. 455.16: cassette $11.50.
Topics included are: the world's oldest ethnic minority; background history of the Jews; arrival of first Sephardic Jews in New Amsterdam; tradesmen and craftsmen; Ashkenazic Jews in the mid-1800s; the life of a peddler; Judaism adapts to life in America; the poor and uneducated; Eastern European Jews 1881-1914; life in the sweatshop; reforming the garment industry; Jews in the labor movement; professionals and intellectuals; second-generation Eastern European Jews; Hitler and the final wave of Jewish immigration; and contributions of American Jews to medicine, law, journalism, and the arts.

MINORITIES AND WOMEN IN INSTRUCTIONAL MATERIALS. NEA 1972. S-C-A. No. 385-11716: 17 min cassette $9.
This tape features four principal speakers at the 1972 NEA minorities in textbooks seminar. Each speaker approaches the subject from his or her own group's perspective. Side A: Walter Plotch (Jews), Dr. Shirley McCune (women). Side B: Dr. Chow Loy Tom (Asians), Dr. Charles H. Wesley (Blacks).

MINOR MAJORITY, THE. CSDI. J-S-C-A. No. 407: 51 min cassette $7.95.
The majority of Americans are under 25. Students demand political power commensurate with their numbers, but in this heated discussion during a conference on students and society there is no unanimity about how, or for what, to use it, should they get it. The voices of the students communicate more than the words they speak.

POLISH AMERICANS. EDR. J-S. No. 455.14: cassette $11.50.
Topics included are: the first immigrant ethnics; Jamestown 1608; Polish craftsmen in New Amsterdam; Polish frontiersmen; Jan Sandusky; Revolutionary heroes; Kosciusko and Pulaski—profiles; the flight for freedom—the immigration of 1830-1863; Polish Americans in the Civil War; the flight for life—the immi-

gration of 1970; life in the mines and the cities; the struggle for identity; preserving Polish traditions, language, and religion; the push for assimilation; and Polish sports stars Stan Musial, Ted Kluszewski, Ed Lopat, Carl Yastrzemski, and Bronko Nagurski.

PREJUDICE: THE INVISIBLE WALL. FRSC 1970. J-S-C. LC 70-751801. No. 12001: 12″ LP record 33⅓ rpm $9.33.
People interviewed in Times Square talk about the nature of prejudice; members of a rock band discuss long hair and prejudice; black athletes explain to the press why boycott is a valid protest against discrimination; and students talk about prejudiced and unprejudiced teachers.

THROUGH THEIR EYES—ETHNIC STUDIES. EDR. El-J-S. No. 455.29: 8 cassette cameos on 2 cassettes $23.
Letters, songs, reports, and speeches detailing the personal experiences of typical members of ethnic groups and events of historical significance. Titles: Making It (Italian teenager in U.S.); Teach Me English (Polish immigrant's plea); The Indian and His Land (three speeches by Chief Joseph); Ellis Island (report by H. G. Wells); advice from an Irish Politician (N.Y. State Senator Plunkitt of Tammany Hall); Oleana (the song and its history); Chinese Help Wanted (two labor recruiter's ads, 1860s); and Tenement Living (report by Jacob Riis).

YIDDISH—SHOLEM ALEICHEM. CAED. J-S-C. LC R66-1702. 12″ LP record $6.98.
The fables of the beloved Yiddish author read in English, including A Matter of Advice, Chanukah and Pinochle, Happy Millionaire, It's a Lie, and High School.

Video Cassettes

HUDDLED MASSES, THE. BBCTV/TIMELI. J-S-A. 52 min col. Video $465; rental $100 (available with series).
Alistair Cooke visits ships' holds, Ellis Island, New York's Lower East Side, garment factory sweatshops; all scenes evoking turn-of-the-century immigration. Old photographs of immigrants and their plight contrasts with oil portraits of tycoons. From "America: A Personal History of the United States" series.

IN LIVING COLOR. TIMELI. J-S-A. 12 min col. Video $120; rental $25.
Eddie Albert introduces this film about Walter Washburn, a Black, and Peter Garcia, a Spanish-speaking American, both of whom have felt the sting of discrimination and frustration on their jobs but, having been promoted, look forward with hope. Produced by Parthenon Pictures.

JESUS TRIP, THE—THE SEARCH FOR SPIRITUAL VALUES. BBCTV/TIMELI. S-C-A. 35 min col. Video $300; 16mm $425; rental $45.
In this vivid and absorbing report, cameras penetrate the Jesus Freaks' communes to accurately record the significance and scope of the movement. This heady, fundamentalist Christianity attracts a new breed of Christians who don't

take drugs, don't drink, and don't believe in extramarital sex. In their communes they are seen studying the Bible, praising the Lord, and learning to cope with life.

JUST LIKE YOU. TIMELI. El-J. 6 min col. Video $90; rental $25.

Against a montage of photographic portraits and scenes of daily life from around the nation, a deep concern and sensitivity toward red, black, brown, yellow, and white Americans are projected. The voice of Eugene Osborne Smith narrates this humanistic film expressing the shared hopes and dreams of all people. Produced by Stephen Bosustow.

KALVAK. GPITVL. El-J-S-C. 18 min col. Video $160; rental $15.

Kalvak is an Eskimo woman in her late sixties. Until some 20 years ago, her fame rested solely on her reputation as the finest seamstress on Holman Island in Canada's Northwest Territories. Then a Jesuit priest discovered some of her drawings among her sewing patterns and, supplying her with drawing materials, encouraged her to develop her artistic talent. She has since become increasingly well known among art connoisseurs of the world as the creator of some of the most highly sophisticated and visually articulate drawings to emerge from the world of Eskimo art.

MIGRANT HEALTH. GPITVL. J-S-A. 30 min b&w. 2 inch video tape.

Presents certain insights into the phenomenon of migratory agricultural labor providing a general overview of the subject, the characteristics of the migrant laborer, and the public health implications regarding the migrant and his way of life.

MIGRATION. NET 1973. J-S. No. 11004: 15 min video $125.

Using still photographs, historical film footage, and folk songs, this program depicts the United States as a nation on the move. A documentary sequence probes into some of the reasons for the decline in the population of America's small towns. The possibility of interstellar migration is also examined. From "Life World: 2000" series.

PLACES IN THE NEWS. GPITVL. El-J-S. 20 min lessons $57.50 each.

This award-winning series highlights current world events that have major political, economic, scientific, or cultural significance. The series relates a person or place in the news to the total world situation. And though the lessons deal with extremely current events, the programs may be compared with the weekly "cover story" of the leading national news magazines.

RICH MAN, POOR MAN. BBCTV/TIMELI. J-S. 52 min col. Set video $1,960; 16mm $2,800; rental $275; individually $55.

For centuries man has believed that unlimited progress is an ideal goal, and that our economy, industry, and trade must grow in an endless upward spiral to achieve the greatest good for all. But lately, this traditional and orthodox view is being seriously questioned. This series looks at the consequences of industrial progress in both rich and poor countries.

Study Prints/Pictures/Posters/Graphics

BROTHERHOOD POSTER BULLETIN BOARD. HSPC 1972. El–J. No. BB2032: 12″ × 18″ col posters $3.

An exceptional unit containing full-color posters ready for use on bulletin boards in the halls, libraries, or anywhere else. Also included are examples of finished bulletin boards for easy assembly.

COLORS OF MAN KIT. SVE. No. PAM43–S: kit includes spirit masters, crayons, portfolio, booklet, teacher's guide $22.95.

This kit gives broad-based information for understanding differences in color. Includes: "Colors Around Me"; Teacher's Guide to "Colors"; "Colors Around Me" Spirit Masters; Skin Color Crayons; "Colors Around Us" Portfolio; and "Colors Around Us" Booklets.

IMMIGRATION. DPA. El–J–S. Set of forty col 11″ × 14″ pictures $22.50.

The inscription from Emma Lazarus' poem, "Give me your tired, your poor, your huddled masses yearning to breathe free," epitomizes U.S. policy toward immigration during the nineteenth and early twentieth centuries. This liberal policy attracted more than 20 million strangers to American shores between 1855 and 1934. The series portrays the exodus, the arrival, and the ordeals endured during Americanization

IMMIGRATION IN COLONIAL TIMES. JACK. El–J. SBN 670–39404–1. No. A 10: 10 exhibits, 5 broadsheets, contents brochure $3.95.

Tells of the thousands of Europeans and Africans who voyaged from their native lands to the New World during the American colonial period. Exhibits include a 1732 letter from a Georgia colonist, an indenture, a 1757 account of the slave trade, and a rubbing from a Massachusetts gravestone. By Mary Stetson Clarke.

MAYFLOWER AND THE PILGRIM FATHERS, THE. JACK. El–J. SBN 670–46269–8: 8 exhibits, 5 broadsheets, contents brochure $3.95.

Describes the Pilgrims' voyage on the *Mayflower*, their struggle to establish themselves in the wilderness of the New World, and their influence on America. Exhibits include a feature on the Pilgrims and their England, the first map of New England to be printed in the New World, and the Plymouth patent granted by King James I to the settlers. By Richard Tames.

MIGRANT FARM WORKERS. DPA. S. Set of twenty 11″ × 14″ pictures $11.50.

There are more than one million migrant farm workers. Without roots, leading a nomadic life, following the scorching sun of harvest, performing backbreaking stoop labor, battling pesticides and poverty, they feed America. For what they contribute in the way of health and welfare to this society, they are among the most underpaid Americans.

PIONEERS IN MAN'S WORLD. SSSS. J–S. Twenty-one 11″ × 14″ b&w prints on glossy stock $12.75.

A series of documentary photo aids about the American woman, depicting the vanguard of women who have rebuked tradition by elbowing their way into man-sized jobs. Includes women football players, steeplejacks, construction workers, and carpenters.

Directory of Producers and Distributors

AAPC
Afro-American Publishing Co., Inc.
1727 Indiana Avenue
Chicago, Ill. 60616

ABC
American Broadcasting Company
1330 Avenue of the Americas
New York, N.Y. 10020

ABCTV
(see ABC)

ABF
American Baptist Films
Valley Forge, Pa. 19481

ABFI
Audio-Brandon Films
34 MacQuesten Pkwy So.
Mount Vernon, N.Y. 10550

ACA
Art Council Aids
Box 641
Beverly Hills, Calif. 90213

ACI
ACI Productions
16 W. 46 Street
New York, N.Y. 10036

ADF
Audio-Digest Foundation
(no address available)

ADL
Anti-Defamation League
315 Lexington Avenue
New York, N.Y. 10016

AEVAC
AEVAC, Inc.
1604 Park Avenue
Plainfield, N.J. 07060

AF
Associated Films
600 Madison Avenue
New York, N.Y. 10022

AIM
Association Instructional Materials
866 Third Avenue
New York, N. Y. 10022

AIMS
AIMS Instructional Media Services, Inc.
Box 1010
Hollywood, Calif. 90028

ALCSC
American Library Color Slide Co.
222 W. 23 Street
New York, N.Y. 10011

AMBP
Harold C. Ambosch Prod.
Box 678
Tahoe City, Calif. 95730

AMDOC
American Documentary Films, Inc.
336 W. 84 Street
New York, N.Y. 10024

AMIDON
Pauls Amidon & Assoc., Inc.
1966 Benson Avenue
St. Paul, Minn. 55116

ART
Artisan Productions
Box 1827
Los Angeles, Calif. 90028

AS
Asia Society
112 E. 64 Street
New York, N.Y. 10021

ASAHIA
(see ICF)

ATLAP
Atlantis Productions, Inc.
1252 La Grande Drive
Thousand Oaks, Calif. 91360

AUDIOF
Audio Film Center
2138 E. 75 Street
Mount Vernon, N.Y. 10550

AVED
AV-ED Films
49 N. Main Street
Homer, N.Y. 13077

AVMC
AV Media Craftsman, Inc.
425 Park Avenue South
New York, N.Y. 10016

BAILEY
Bailey Films, Inc.
6509 De Longpre Avenue
Los Angeles, Calif. 90028

BARR
Arthur Barr Productions
1029 N. Allen Avenue
Pasadena, Calif. 91104

BBCTV
British Broadcasting Co.-TV
630 Fifth Avenue
New York, N.Y. 10020

BCB
British Columbia Broadcasting
630 Fifth Avenue
New York, N.Y. 10020

BCMI
BEE Cross Media, Inc.
36 Dogwood Glen
Rochester, N.Y. 14625

BEE
(see BCMI)

BES
BES Bilingual Educational Services
1607 Hope Street
Box 669
South Pasadena, Calif. 91030

BFA
Bailey Educational Media
Box 1795
Santa Monica, Calif. 90404

BHAWK
Blackhawk Films
1235 W. 5 Street
Davenport, Iowa 52805

BIGSUR
Bigsur Recordings
117 Mitchell Blvd.
San Rafael, Calif. 94903

B'NAI B'RITH
B'nai B'rith
1640 Rhode Island Avenue, N.W.
Washington, D.C. 20036

BOWMAR
Bowmar Records
622 Rodier Drive
Glendale, Calif. 91207

BRAN
Brandon Films
221 W. 57 Street
New York, N.Y. 10019

BTC
The Baker & Taylor Company
6 Kirby Avenue
Somerville, N.J. 08876

BUDEK
Herbert E. Budek
P.O. Box 307
Santa Barbara, Calif. 93102

BYU
Brigham Young University
Dept. 9 A-V-Conn
Provo, Utah 84601

CA
(no information available)

CAED
Caedman Records, Inc.
Division Houghton Mifflin Co.
110 Tremont Street
Boston, Mass. 02107

CAF
Current Affairs Films
527 Madison Avenue
New York, N.Y. 10022

CAFM
Cathedral Films, Inc.
2921 W. Alameda Avenue
Burbank, Calif. 91505

CAROUF
Carousel Films, Inc.
1501 Broadway
New York, N.Y. 10036

CBS
Columbia Broadcasting System
485 Madison Avenue
New York, N.Y. 10022

CBSTV
(see CBS)

CCM
CCM Films, Inc.
866 Third Avenue
New York, N.Y. 10022

CCMS
CCM School Materials, Inc.
866 Third Avenue
New York, N.Y. 10022

CDS
Chesterfield Music Shop
12 Warren Street
New York, N.Y. 10007

CEF
Centron Educational Films
1255 Post Street, Suite 625
San Francisco, Calif. 94105

CENTRO
Centron Corp.
P.O. Box 687
1621 9 Street
Lawrence, Kans. 66044

CES
Civic Education Service
1725 K Street N.W., Suite 1009
Washington, D.C. 20006

CF
Churchill Films
662 N. Robertson Blvd.
Los Angeles, Calif. 90069

CFD
Classroom Film Distributors, Inc.
5620 Hollywood Blvd.
Los Angeles, Calif. 90028

CFS
Creative Film Society
14558 Valerino Street
Van Nuys, Calif. 91405

CGJ
Consulate General of Japan
Japanese Embassy
2520 Massachusetts Avenue, N.W.
Washington, D.C. 20008

CGW
Communications Group West
6335 Homewood Avenue
Hollywood, Calif. 90028

CHRONL
Chronicle Productions
364 W. 18 Street
New York, N.Y. 10011

CI
Communications International
22 Oak Drive
New Hyde Park, N.Y. 11040

CIVEDF
Civic Education Service
1725 K Street, N.W.
Washington, D.C. 20006

CLSWP
Classroom World Productions
14 Glenwood Avenue
Raleigh, N.C. 27603

CMSR
CMS Records, Inc.
14 Warren Street
New York, N.Y. 10007

CMUSIC
Children's Music Center, Inc.
5373 W. Pico Blvd.
Los Angeles, Calif. 90019

COMTEC
Instructional Communications Technology
P.O. Box 680
Huntington, N.Y. 11743

CORF
Coronet Films
65 E. South Water Street
Coronet Bldg.
Chicago, Ill. 60601

CREATV
Creative Visuals, Inc.
P.O. Box 1911
Big Spring, Tex. 79720

CSDI
Center for the Study of Democratic Institutions
Box 4068
2056 Eucalyptus Hill Road
Santa Barbara, Calif. 93103

CSMIE
Center for Study of Migrant and Indian Education
Central Washington State College
Ellensburg, Wash. 98926

CURAF
Current Affairs Films
527 Madison Avenue
New York, N.Y. 10022

DANA
(see DP)

DCC
David C. Cook Publishing Company
School Products Division
Elgin, Ill. 60120

DEMCO
DEMCO Educational Corp.
2820 Fordem Avenue
Madison, Wis. 53701

DIS
Robert Disraeli Films
Box 343, Cooper Station
New York, N.Y. 10003

DISNEY
Walt Disney Educational Materials
800 Sonara Avenue
Glendale, Calif. 91201

DOUBLE
Doubleday and Co., Inc.
501 Franklin Avenue
Garden City, N.Y. 11503

DOUBLEDAY MULTIMEDIA
Doubleday Multimedia
Box C-19518
1371 Reynolds Avenue
Irvine, Calif. 92713

DP
Dana Productions
6249 Babcock Avenue
North Hollywood, Calif. 91696

DPA
Documentary Photo Aids
Box 2620
Sarasota, Fla. 33578

EALING
Ealing Corporation
2225 Massachusetts Avenue
Cambridge, Mass. 02140

EAV
Educational Audiovisual
29 Marble Avenue
Pleasantville, N.Y. 10570

EBEC
Encyclopedia Britannica Education Corp.
425 N. Michigan Avenue
Chicago, Ill. 60611

EDC
Educational Dimensions Corp.
25-60 Francis Lewis Blvd.
Flushing, N.Y. 11358

EDDIM
Educational Dimensions Corp.
Box 126
Stamford, Conn. 06904

EDR
Educational Resources Division of Educational Design, Inc.
47 W. 13 Street
New York, N.Y. 10011

EDRECS
Educational Record Sales
157 Chambers Street
New York, N.Y. 10007

EDRS
Educational Reading Services, Inc.
Audiovisual Division
4164 Midland Avenue
Paramus, N.J. 07652

EDS
Educational Services, Inc.
1730 Eye Street, N.W.
Washington, D.C. 20006

EDUCDE
Educational Design
47 W. 13 Street
New York, N.Y. 10011

EE
National Broadcasting Company
(see NBC)

EEM
Educational Enrichment Materials, Inc.
83 East Avenue
Norwalk, Conn. 06851

EFS
Educational Filmstrips
1401 19 Street
Huntsville, Tex. 77340

EGH
Eye-Gate House, Inc.
Subs. of Cenco Instrument Corp.
146-01 Archer Avenue
Jamaica, N.Y. 11435

EH
Educational Horizons
(taken over by EBEC)
3015 Dolores Street
Los Angeles, Calif. 90065

EKC
Eastman Kodak Co.
343 State Street
Rochester, N.Y. 14650

ELKINS
Herbert M. Elkins Co.
10031 Commerce Avenue
Tujunga, Calif. 91042

EMCC
EMC Corporation
Educational Materials Division
180 E. Sixth Street
St. Paul, Minn. 55101

ESP
ESP Discs
156 Fifth Avenue
New York, N.Y. 10010

ETCO
El Teatro Campesino
Box 274
San Juan Bautista, Calif.

FH
Film Heritage
511 E. 84 Street
New York, N.Y. 10028

FI
Films, Inc.
1150 Wilmette Avenue
Wilmette, Ill. 60091

FILMST
Filmstrip Services Ltd.
(no address available)

FISKU
Fisk University
17 Avenue N.
Nashville, Tenn. 37203

FORES
Scott Foresman
1900 E. Lake Avenue
Glenview, Ill. 60025

FP
Friendship Press
475 Riverside Drive
New York, N.Y. 10027

FRC
Film Research Co.
Anthony Lane Studies Building
7401 Wayzata Blvd.
Minneapolis, Minn. 55426

FRITH
Frith Films
Box 424
Carmel Valley, Calif. 93024

FRPR
Friendship Press
475 Riverside Drive
New York, N.Y. 10027

FRSC
Folkways Records
701 Seventh Avenue
New York, N.Y. 10036
(see also SCHMAG/FRSC)

FSR
Folkways/Scholastic Records
50 W. 44 Street
New York, N.Y. 10036

FUTURA
(see MLA)

GA
Guidance Associates
Harcourt, Brace & World
23 Washington Avenue
Pleasantville, N.Y. 10770

GAF
General Aniline and Film Corp.
Audio/Visual Order Dept.
140 W. 51 Street
New York, N.Y. 10020

GATEPI
Gateway Productions, Inc.
Bureau of Audiovisual Services
University of Arizona
Tucson, Ariz. 85721

GPI
Greenwood Press, Inc.
51 Riverside Avenue
Westport, Conn. 06880

GPITVL
Great Plains Instructional TV Library
University of Nebraska
Lincoln, Nebr. 68508

GPN
Great Plains National Films
c/o Don Pedersen
P.O. Box 80669
Lincoln, Nebr. 68501

GREAVES
William Greaves Productions, Inc.
254 W. 54 Street
New York, N.Y. 10019

GROVE
Grove Press
Film Division
214 Mercer Street
New York, N.Y. 10012

HAMMOND
Hammond, Inc.
Educational Division
515 Valley Street
Maplewood, N.J. 07050

HANDEL
(see HFC)

HANDY
Jam Handy Organization
2843 E. Grand Blvd.
Detroit, Mich. 48211

HEARST
Hearst Metrotone News
450 W. 56 Street
New York, N.Y. 10019

HFC
Handel Film Corporation
8730 Sunset Blvd.
West Hollywood, Calif. 90069

HOE
Paul Hoefler Productions
7445 Girard Avenue
P.O. Box 1313
La Jolla, Calif. 92037

HOLCOMB/HOL
Theodore Holcomb
11 E. 90 Street
New York, N.Y. 10028

HRW
Holt, Rinehart & Winston, Inc.
383 Madison Avenue
New York, N.Y. 10017

HSC
Humbolt State College
Arcota, Calif. 95521

HSPC
Hayes School Publishing Co.
321 Pennwood Avenue
Wilkensburg, Pa. 15221

HSTFR
Hour of St. Francis of M Productions
1229 S. Santee Street
Los Angeles, Calif. 90015

HUL
Hulton Press
(no address available)

HUMBLE
Exxon Co. U.S.A.
Box 2180
Houston, Texas 77001

IBC
International Book Corp.
7300 Biscayne Blvd.
Miami, Fla. 33138

IC
Instruction Corporation
1635 N. 55 Street
Paoli, Pa. 19301

ICF
International Communications Films
1371 Reynolds Avenue
Santa Ana, Calif. 92705

IDEAL
Ideal School Supply Co.
11000 S. La Vergre Avenue
Oak Lawn, Ill. 60453

IDI
(see CAFM)

IFB
International Film Bureau
332 S. Michigan Avenue
Chicago, Ill. 60604

IFF
International Film Foundation
475 Fifth Avenue, Suite 916
New York, N.Y. 10017

IMPRL
Imperial Productions, Inc.
Educational Division
Kankakee, Ill. 60901

INSIGHT
Insight
17575 Pacific Coast Highway
Pacific Palisades, Calif. 90272

IQF
Box 326
Wappingers Falls, N.Y. 12590

IU
Indiana University
Audiovisual Center
Bloomington, Ind. 47401

IVAC
International Visual Aids Center
601 Chaussee De Mons
Brussels 7, Belgium

JACK
Jackdaw Kits (see VIKPI)

JOU
Journal Films
909 W. Diversey Parkway
Chicago, Ill. 60614

KETCTV
KETC-TV Channel 9
6996 Millbrook Blvd.
St. Louis, Mo. 63130

KEY
Key Records
Box 46128
Los Angeles, Calif. 90046

KIRK
Louis Kirk Productions
(no address available)

KLEIN
Kleinberg Films
3890 Edgeview Drive
Pasadena, Calif. 91107

KLRNTV
Southwest Texas ETV Council
Box 7158
University Station
Austen, Texas 78715

KPBSTV
San Diego State University and College
San Diego, Calif. 92182

KQED
KQED-TV
525 Fourth Street
San Francisco, Calif. 94107

KR
(see IMPRL)

KRMATV
KRMA-TV
414 Fourteenth Street
Denver, Colo. 80202

LA
Learning Arts
Box 917
Wichita, Kans. 67201

LANSFD
Lansford Publishing Company
P.O. Box 8711
1088 Lincoln Avenue
San Jose, Calif. 95155

LCA
Learning Corporation of America
711 Fifth Avenue
New York, N.Y. 10022

LEART
Learning Arts
P.O. Box 917
Wichita, Kans. 67201

LEPI
Life Educational Productions, Inc.
262 E. 4 Street
St. Paul, Minn. 55101

LES
Irving Lesser Enterprises
Room 1527
250 W. 57 Street
New York, N.Y. 10019

LFR
FLMFR Filmfair Inc.
10900 Ventura Blvd.
Studio City, Calif. 91604

LINE
Line Films
Box 328
Capistrano Beach, Calif. 92624

LLI
Listening Library, Inc.
1 Park Avenue
Greenwich, Conn. 06870

LLL
Look, Listen & Learn, Inc.
825 Third Avenue
Suite 2320
New York, N.Y. 10022

LORIL
P. Lorilland Co.
200 E. 42 Street
New York, N.Y. 10017

LP
Lebran Productions
Manilla, Phillipines

LRC
Learning Resources Center
Virginia State College
Petersburg, Va. 23803

MACMAB
Audio Brandon Films, Inc.
Sub. of Macmillan, Inc.
34 MacQuesten Parkway South
Mt. Vernon, N.Y. 10550

MARSH
Marsh Film Enterprises
7000 Rosewood Drive
Shawnee Mission, Kansas 66208

MARYKN
Maryknoll Land of Free Loan Filmstrips
Maryknoll, N.Y. 10549

MB
Miller-Brody Productions
342 Madison Avenue
New York, N.Y. 10017

MCI
MCI Video Film Productions, Inc.
25 Sylvan Road S.
Westport, Conn. 06880

MFI
CCM Films, Inc. (CCMFI)
866 Third Avenue
New York, N.Y. 10022

MGH
McGraw-Hill Films
330 W. 42 Street
New York, N.Y. 10036

MGM
Metro-Goldwyn-Mayer
1350 Avenue of the Americas
New York, N.Y. 10019

MILLIKEN
Milliken Publishing Co.
611 Olive Street
St. Louis, Mo. 63101

MLA
Modern Learning Aids
Div. of Ward's Natural Science
Box 302
Rochester, N.Y. 14603

MM
(see CHRONL)

MMM
Mass Media Ministries
2116 N. Charles Street
Baltimore, Md. 21218

MMPI
Multi-Media Educational, Inc.
747 Third Avenue
New York, N.Y. 10017

MP
Madison Project
c/o Weston Woods Studios
Weston, Conn. 06880

MPEMC
(see ADL)

MR
Monitor Records
156 Fifth Avenue
New York, N.Y. 10010

MSU
Michigan State University
Audiovisual Center
East Lansing, Mich. 48824

MULMED
Multi-Media Corp.
2530 Kemper Lane
Cincinnati, Ohio 45206

NBC
National Broadcasting Company
30 Rockefeller Center
New York, N.Y. 10020

NBCTV
(see NBC)

NCFP
Northwest Custom Film Processing
University Station
P.O. Box 16
Seattle, Wash. 98105

NEA
National Education Association
1201 Sixteenth Street N
Washington, D.C. 20036

NET
National Educational TV., Inc.
2715 Packard Road
Ann Arbor, Mich. 48104

NEW
Henk Newenhouse, Inc.
1825 Willow Road
Northfield, Ill. 60093

NFBC
National Film Board of Canada
1251 Avenue of the Americas
16th Floor
New York, N.Y. 10020

NFI
Nauman Films, Inc.
Box 232
Custer, S. Dak. 57730

NOF
Northern Films
Box 98
Maine Office Station
Seattle, Wash. 98111

NTREP
(see NTR/NTREP)

NTR/NTREP
National Tape Repository
Stadium Building, Room 348
University of Colorado
Boulder, Colo. 80302

NYCBED
New York City Board of Education
110 Livingston Street
Brooklyn, N.Y. 11201

NYT
New York Times
Office of Educational Activities
229 W. 43 Street
New York, N.Y. 10036

OUSD
A-V Dept. Media Center
Oakland Unified School Dist.
Oakland, Calif.

OXF
Oxford Films, Inc.
1136 N. Las Palmas Avenue
Los Angeles, Calif. 90023

PAN
Pan American Development Foundation
17th and Constitution Avenue N.W.
Washington, D.C. 20006

PATH
Pathway Indian Programs, Inc.
P. O. Box 2231-R
Morristown, N.J. 07960

PAULP
Paulist Productions
Box 1057
Pacific Palisades, Calif. 90272

PCBNM
AV Dept., Board of National Missions
United Presbyterian Church
(no address available)

PEI
Perennial Education, Inc.
1825 Willow Road
Northfield, Ill. 60093

PF
Park Films
228 N. Almont Drive
Beverly Hills, Calif. 90406

PFP
Pyramid Film Producers
Division of Adams Productions
Box 1048
Santa Monica, Calif. 90406

POPSCI
Popular Science Publishing Co.
355 Lexington Avenue
New York, N.Y. 10017

PORTAL
Portal Study Graphics
777 Bridgeway
Sausalito, Calif. 94965

PPC
Pitman Publishing Corp.
6 E. 43 Street
New York, N.Y. 10017

PROTHA
Prothmann Associates, Inc.
2795 Milburn Avenue
Baldwin, N.Y. 11510

PSC
Popular Science Co.
355 Lexington Avenue
New York, N.Y. 10017

QED
QED Productions, Inc.
Box 1608
Burbank, Calif. 91507

RAINAGE
George Rainbied
44 Edgeware Road
London W.2., England

REYP
Stuart Reynolds Productions
9465 Wilshire Blvd.
Beverly Hills, Calif. 90212

RHI
Random House, Inc.
201 E. 50 Street
New York, N.Y. 10022

RMIF
RMI Film Productions, Inc.
701 Westport Road
Kansas City, Mo. 04111

ROBECK
Peter M. Robeck Co., Inc.
230 Park Avenue
New York, N.Y. 10017

ROE
Stuart Roe
1135 S. Sage Court
Sunnyvale, Calif. 94087

RTBL
Roundtable Films, Inc.
321 S. Beverly Drive
Beverly Hills, Calif. 90212

RTOMP
Richard Tompkins
(no address available)

SAN
Sandak, Inc.
180 Harvard Avenue
Stamford, Conn. 06902

SAUDEK
Robert Saudek, Assoc., Inc.
(see IQF)

SBRTC
Southern Baptist Radio-TV Commission
P.O. Box 12157
Fort Worth, Tex. 76116

SCH
Scholastic Book Services
904 Sylvan Avenue
Englewood Cliffs, N.J. 07632

SCHLAT
Warren Schloat Productions, Inc.
Palmer Lane West
Pleasantville, N.Y. 10570

SCHMAG/FRSC
Scholastic Magazines, Inc.
50 W. 44 Street
New York, N.Y. 10036

SCOTT
Scott Education Division
104 Lower Westfield Road
Holyoke, Mass. 01040

SCREEN GEMS
Screen Gems
729 Seventh Avenue
New York, N.Y. 10019

SED
Schott Education Div.
104 Lower Westfield Road
Holyoke, Mass. 01040

SF
Sterling Educational Films
241 E. 34 Street
New York, N.Y. 10016

SHAW
Shaw Productions
619 E. Alvarado Street
Fallbrook, Calif. 92028

SHOSPI
Shoshoni Productions, Inc.
(no address available)

SIGMAT
Sigma Three Productions
(no address available)

SINGER
Singer Sewing Co.
30 Rockefeller Plaza
New York, N.Y. 10020

SM
(no information available)

SMC
Spanish Music Center
127 W. 48 Street
New York, N.Y. 10036

SP
Spencer Productions, Inc.
507 Fifth Avenue
New York, N.Y. 10017

SPA
Spoken Arts
310 North Avenue
New Rochelle, N.Y. 10801

SSSS
Social Studies School Service
10,000 Culver Blvd.
Culver City, Calif. 90230

STAN
Stanton Films
7934 Santa Monica Blvd.
Los Angeles, Calif. 90046

STOC
Standard Oil of California
Public Relations Dept.
225 Bush Street
San Francisco, Calif. 94120

SVE
Society for Visual Education, Inc.
1345 Diversey Parkway
Chicago, Ill. 60614

TA
Troll Associates
(see EDRS)

TAPUNL
Tapes Unlimited
Educational Corp. of America
984 Livernois
Troy, Mich. 48084

TERF
Teaching Resources Films
Station Plaza
Bedford Hills, N.Y. 10507

TEXF
Texture Films, Inc.
Room 200
1600 Broadway
New York, N.Y. 10019

3M/MMAMC
Minnesota Mining and Manufacturing Co.
Medical Film Library
2501 Hudson Road
St. Paul, Minn. 55071

TI
Tweedy Transparencies
208 Hollywood Blvd.
East Orange, N.J. 07018

TIMELI
Time-Life, Inc.
Time & Life Building
Rockefeller Center
New York, N.Y. 10020

TRA
Troll Associates
320 Route 17
Mahwah, N.J. 07430

TRF
Teaching Resources Films
c/o New York Times
2 Kisco Plaza
Mt. Kisco, N.Y. 10549

TWEEDY
(see TI for address)

UC
University of California
2223 Fulton Street
Berkeley, Calif. 94720

UCEMC
(see UC)

UCO
University of Colorado
Bureau of Audiovisual Instruction
Stadium Building
1200 University Avenue
Boulder, Colo. 80302

UCSC
Universal Color Slide Co.
136 W. 52 Street
New York, N.Y. 10017

UEVA
Universal Educational Visual Arts
221 Park Avenue S.
New York, N.Y. 10023

UK
University of Kansas
Audio-Visual Center
Film Rental Service
746 Massachusetts Street
Lawrence, Kans. 66044

UM
University of Michigan
Audiovisual Education Center
416 Fourth Street
Ann Arbor, Michigan 48103

UMAVC
(see UM)

UMINN
University of Minnesota
Motion Picture Production Division
55 Wesbrook Hall
Minneapolis, Minn. 55455

UMM
Urban Media Materials
212 Mineola Avenue
P.O. Box 156
Roslyn Heights, N.Y. 11577

UPMPD
United Presbyterian Motion Pictures Distribution
c/o Association Films
475 Riverside Drive, Room 1204
New York, N.Y. 10027

USC
University of Southern California
Department of Cinema
University Park
Los Angeles, Calif. 90007

USC-ISC
University of South Carolina
Instructional Services Center
Columbia, S.C. 29208

USIA
U.S. Information Agency
1776 Pennsylvania Ave., N.W.
Washington, D.C. 20006

UTEP
University of Texas
El Paso, Texas 79902

UU
University of Utah
Educational Media Center
Milton Bennion Hall 207
Salt Lake City, Utah 84110

UW
United World Films
221 Park Avenue S.
New York, N.Y. 10003

UWASHP
University of Washington Press
1416 N.E. 41 Street
Seattle, Wash. 98105

UWY
University of Wyoming
Audiovisual Services
Laramie, Wyo. 82070

VALIANT
Valiant Industries
172 Walkers Lane
Englewood, N.J. 07631

VEC
Visual Education Consultants, Inc.
Box 52
Madison, Wis. 53701

VEDO
Vedo Films
85 Longview Road
Port Washington, N.Y. 11050

VIGNET
Vignette Films
981 S. Western Avenue
Los Angeles, Calif. 90006

VIKPI
Viking Press, Inc.
625 Madison Avenue
New York, N.Y. 10022

VMI
Visual Materials, Inc.
2549 Middlefield Road
Redwood City, Calif. 94063

WABCTV
(see ABC)

WCAUTV
WCAU-TV
City and Monument Avenues
Philadelphia, Pa. 19131

WCBSTV
(see CBS)

WGBHTV
WGBH Channel 12
WGBH Educational Foundations
125 Western Avenue
Boston, Mass. 02134

WIBLE
Wible Language Institute
24 S. Eight Street
Allentown, Pa. 18105

WILSHH
H. Wilson Corp.
555 W. Taft Drive
South Holland, Ill. 60473

WOLPER
Wolper Productions
8489 W. Third Street
Los Angeles, Calif. 90048

WPES
Western Publishing Educational Service
Division of Western Publishing Co., Inc.
1220 Mound Avenue
Racine, Wis. 53404

WWSI
Weston Woods Studios, Inc.
Weston Conn. 06880

XEROX
Xerox Films
245 Long Hill Road
Middletown, Conn. 06457

YALEDV
Yale University Divinity School
Visual Ed. Service
59 High Street
New Haven, Conn. 06510

Media Indexed by Title

This index provides the reader with an alphabetical listing of all the media and materials titles appearing in *Ethnic American Minorities.* The parenthetical abbreviations used here and their meanings are as follows: (a) audio recordings and audio cassettes, (f) films (16mm), (fs) filmstrips, (p) study prints/pictures/posters/graphics, (sl) slides, (tr) transparencies, and (vc) video cassettes.

Accent on Ethnic America (fs), 251
Adventures of Marco Polo/Genghis Khan and the Mongol Horde (a), 124-125
Afghanistan (f), 92
Africa (tr), 57
Africa: An Introduction (f), 17
Africa, South of the Sahara (a), 61
African ABC (fs), 41
African Art (sl), 55
African Art and Culture (fs), 42
African Heritage (fs), 42
African Past (fs), 42
African Sculpture (p), 69; (sl), 55
African Sculpture—From Private Collections (sl), 55
African Textiles and Decorative Arts (sl), 55
African Village Folktales (a), 61
Africans All (f), 17
Afro-American History (fs), 42; (tr), 57
Afro-American History (In Song and Story) (a), 61
Afro-American Literature: An Overview (fs), 42
Afro-American Studies Materials (sl), 55
Afro-American Thing (f), 18
Afro-Americans Speak for Themselves (fs), 42
Age of Exploration and Discovery—The Spanish (tr), 231
Age of the Buffalo (f), 148
Agriculture and Rural Life (fs), 106
Agricultural Revolution in Mexico (fs), 220-221
Ain't We Got a Right? (f), 17
Alahu Akbar: Faith of Four Hundred Million (f), 92, 242
Alaskan Eskimo Art (sl), 258
Along Sandy Trails (fs), 168-169
America, Home of the Free, Land of the Brave (f), 17
America, Melting Pot: Myth or Reality? (fs), 252
American Family (fs), 251
American Indian (tr), 178
American Indian: A Dispossessed People (fs), 169
American Indian (A Study in Depth) (fs), 169
American Indian—After the White Man Came (f), 149
American Indian and the Jungian Orientation (a), 179

American Indian Art (sl), 176
American Indian Arts and Artifacts (sl), 176
American Indian before Columbus (fs), 169
American Indian—Before the White Man Came (f), 149
American Indian Cultures: Plains and Woodlands (fs), 169-170
American Indian Dances (a), 179-180
American Indian—Harmony and Discord (a), 180
American Indian: History and Leadership, (a), 180
American Indian in Transition (f), 148
American Indian Influence on the United States (f), 148
American Indian Legend (fs), 170
American Indian Mythology (sl), 176
American Indian Myths (Parts 1 and 2) (fs), 170
American Indian-Prehistory (tr), 178
American Indian Series (p), 186
American Indian Speaks (f), 149
American Indian Studio (a), 180
American Indian Tales for Children (a), 180
American Indian Today (fs), 170
American Indian—Western Indians (tr), 178
American Indians (tr), 178
American Indians and How They Really Lived (fs), 170-171
American Indians and Their Education (a), 180
American Indians as Seen by D. H. Lawrence (f), 148-149
American Indians before European Settlement (f), 149
American Indians of the North Pacific Coast (fs), 171
American Indians of the Northeast (fs), 171
American Indians of the Plains (fs), 171; (p), 186
American Indians of the Southwest (fs), 171
American Negro Folk and Work Song Rhythms (a), 61
American Negro Pathfinders (fs), 44
American Negro Sings (f), 17
American Negroes (fs), 44
American Revolution of '63 (f), 17
American Tropical (f), 206-207
Americans: A Nation of Immigrants (f), 243
Americans from Africa: A History with Edgar Toppin (vc), 68
American's Children (fs), 251
America's Old World Background (fs), 252
Amigos Latinos (fs), 221
Anansi the Spider (f), 149
Ancient Africans (f), 14
Ancient American Indian Civilizations (fs), 171-172
Ancient Chinese: An Introduction (f), 92
Ancient Orient: The Far East (f), 92
And Now Miguel (f), 207
And the Meek Shall Inherit the Earth (f), 149-150
Anderson Platoon (f), 18
Angela: Like it Is (f), 18
Anthology of Negro Poets (a), 61
Anthology of North American and Eskimo Music (a), 180
Arab World (a), 258
Arabs and Jews: The Crisis (fs), 252
Architecture of Pluralism (Asian, Black, Chicano, First Americans) (a), 258
Aretha Franklin, Soul Singer (f), 18-19
Around Indian Campfires (a), 180
Arrow to the Sun (f), 150
Art and Architecture of the Near and Middle East (sl), 120-121
Art of Africa (sl), 55-56
Art of Latin America since Independence (sl), 229-230
Art of the Northwest Coast Indian (sl), 177
Arthur Penn Films Little Big Man (vc), 185
Artistic Revolution in Mexico (fs), 221
Arts and Crafts of Mexico (fs), 221
Arts and Crafts of the Southwest Indians (f), 150
Arts in Everyday Life in Japan Series, an Anthropological Study in Depth (fs), 106-107
As Long as the Grass Shall Grow (a), 181
Asia (a), 125; (tr), 123
Asia: A Continental Overview (f), 92-93
Asia—An Introduction (vc), 130
Asia—Climate, Vegetation, Yearly Rainfall (tr), 123
Asia, Folk and Fairy Tales (a), 125
Asia Society (a), 125

Asian American Heritage (vc), 131
Asian Art (sl), 121
Asian Earth (vc), 130
Asian Folk Tales (fs), 107
Asian History—China (tr), 123
Asian World Geography (fs), 107
Asia's Economic Superpower (fs), 107
Asia's First Superpower (fs), 107
Asiatic Civilization (tr), 123
Autobiography of Frederick Douglass (a), 61
Autobiography of Miss Jane Pittman (f), 19
Autumn Comes to the City (f), 243
Avenida de Ingles (vc), 237
Awakening (fs), 221

Ballad of Crowfoot (f), 150
Bangkok—City of the Klongs (fs), 107
Bar Mitzvah (f), 243
Battle of East St. Louis (f), 19
Behind the Names (f), 243
Bernie Casey: Black Artist (f), 19-20
Big Powwow at Gallup (f), 150
Bilingual Adventure Series (fs), 221
Bilingual Animal Tale Series (fs), 221-222
Bilingual Character Series (fs), 222
Bilingual Legend Series (fs), 222
Bilingual Literature Series (fs), 222
Bilingual Primary Series, (fs), 222
Bilingual Stories (fs), 222
Biographies of Outstanding Negro Americans (tr), 58
Birth of a Union (f), 207
Bitter Wind (f), 150
Black ABC's (p), 69
Black Achievers in the North 1790-1860 (f), 20
Black Africa (sl), 56
Black America: The Sounds of History (a), 61
Black America—Yesterday and Today (p), 69
Black American Achievement Posters (p), 69
Black American Civil Rights Leaders (fs), 44
Black American Dream (f), 20; (vc), 68
Black American History (fs), 45
Black American: Past and Present (tr), 58
Black American Wall Posters (p), 69
Black Americans (a), 61-62; (tr), 58
Black Americans: A Historical Portfolio (fs), 56
Black Americans at Work (fs), 45
Black Americans in Government (fs), 45
Black and White: Uptight (f), 20
Black Athletes (f), 20
Black Contributions to American Culture (a), 62
Black Cop (f), 20
Black Dimensions in American Art (f), 20
Black Experience (a), 62; (sl), 56; (tr), 58
Black Experience in Arts (fs), 45
Black Folk Music in America (fs), 45-46
Black Frontier (f), 20-21; (vc), 68
Black Heritage (a), 62
Black Heritage: A History of Afro-Americans (f), 21
Black Heroes of American History (f), 21
Black History (f), 21
Black History: Lost, Stolen, or Strayed (f), 21
Black Leaders of the Twentieth Century (fs), 46
Black Like Me (a), 62
Black Man in America (a), 62
Black Man in the Modern World (sl), 56
Black Man's Struggle (a), 62; (tr), 58
Black Men in Blue (fs), 46
Black Music (fs), 46
Black Music in America: From Then Till Now (f), 21
Black Muslims Speak from America (f), 21-22
Black Pathfinders of Ancient Times (a), 62
Black People in the New South (fs), 46-47
Black Pioneers in American History (Vols. 1 and 2) (a), 63
Black Poems, Black Images (fs), 47
Black Poetry (fs), 47
Black Power: We're Going to Survive America (f), 22
Black Progress: The History of the Afro-American (a), 63
Black Rabbits and the White Rabbits: An Allegory (fs), 47
Black Reconstruction (f), 22
Black Religion (fs), 47
Black Resistance (f), 22

Black Revolution (fs), 47
Black Roots (f), 22
Black Soldiers (f), 22
Black Soldiers and Settlers in the Old West (a), 63-64
Black Views on Race (f), 22-23
Black Wealth (vc), 68
Black World (f), 23
Blacks in Art (a), 63
Blacks in Government and Human Rights (a), 63
Blacks in Music (a), 63
Blacks in Science (a), 63
Bolivar: South American Liberator (f), 207
Booker T. Washington (f), 23
Born Chinese (f), 93; (vc), 130
Boy of the Navajos (f), 148
Boy of the Seminoles (f), 148
Boyhood of George Washington Carver (f), 23
Boys and Girls of Burma (fs), 107
Brentano Foundation Bilingual Film Series (f), 207
Brian's Song (f), 23
Brother John (f), 23
Brotherhood Poster Bulletin Board (p), 263
Bryan Beavers: A Moving Portrait (f), 150
Burma, People of the River (f), 93
Burmese Folk and Traditional Music (a), 125

Cactus Curtain (a), 232-233
California Conflict: Migrant Farm Worker (fs), 252
California's Dawn (Missions, Ranchos, and Americans) (f), 151
Can We Immunize against Prejudice? (f), 243-244
Caribbean, Puerto Rico (fs), 222-223
Carrascolendas (vc), 237
Cave People of the Philippines (f), 93
Central America: A Regional Study (fs), 223
Ceremonial Dances of the Southwest Tribes (f), 151
Chains of Slavery (fs), 47-48
Changing Skylines in Asia (fs), 107-108
Charles Lloyd—Journey Within (f), 23
Cherokee Nation of Oklahoma (fs), 172
Cherokee Trail of Tears (fs), 172
Cheyenne Autumn (f), 151
Chicano (f), 207
Chicano from the Southwest (f), 207
Chicano Posters (p), 238
Chicanos in Transition (vc), 237
Chiefs and Leaders (a), 181
Children of Asia (fs), 108
Children of Australia and the Pacific Islands (p), 131
Children of Courage (a), 258; (fs), 252
Children of the Kibbutz (f), 244
Chile (f), 208
China (tr), 123
China: A Cultural Heritage (p), 131-132
China: A Portrait of the Land (f), 93
China an End to Isolation (f), 93
China and the World (a), 125
China by the Golden Gate (f), 93-84
China, Contrasts and Continuities (fs), 108
China: Economic Development in a Human Context (a), 126
China in Perspective: Roots of Civilization (fs), 108
China in the Modern World (fs), 108
China in the 20th Century—The Two-Headed Dragon (f), 94
China Joins the World (fs), 108
China: Mao Tse-tung's System (vc), 130-131
China Now (fs), 108
China Obsession (a), 126
China: People, Places, and Progress (fs), 108-109
China Problem (a), 126
China Regional Geography Series (fs), 109
China: Teacher's Starter Kit (p), 132
China—The Awakening Giant (f), 94
China—The Past Is Prologue (f), 94
China: The Social Revolution (f), 94
China Today: As Seen through the Eyes of a Typical Chinese Family (fs), 109
China: Twenty Years of Revolution (fs), 110
China under Communism (f), 94-95
China without Poverty (a), 126
China's Industrial Revolution (f), 94
China's New Look (fs), 109
China's Village in Change (f), 94
Chinatown (fs), 109
Chinese American: The Early Immigrants (f), 95
Chinese American: The Twentieth Century (f), 95
Chinese and Japanese Art (fs), 110
Chinese Art (fs), 110

Chinese Arts and Crafts (sl), 121
Chinese Children Next Door (a), 126
Chinese Civilization (tr), 123
Chinese Fairy Tales (a), 126
Chinese Folk Songs (a), 126-127
Chinese Folktales (fs), 110
Chinese Folk Tales, Legends, Proverbs, and Rhymes (a), 127
Chinese in California (vc), 131
Chinese in Dispersion (f), 95
Chinese, Korean, and Japanese Dance (f), 95
Chinese Painting (sl), 121
Chinese Philosophies (tr), 123
Chinese Poems of the Tang and Sung Dynasties (a), 127
Chinese Poetry (fs), 110-111
Chinese Tales (fs), 111
Chiquitin and the Devil: A Puerto Rican Folktale (fs), 223
Choice of Weapons (a), 64
Chosen People (f), 244
Circle of the Sun (f), 151
Citizen Chang (f), 95
Civil Rights Movement: Historic Roots (f), 24
Civil Rights Movement: Mississippi Summer Project (f), 24
Civil Rights Movement: The Angry Voices of Watts (f), 24
Civil Rights Movement: The North (f), 24
Civil Rights Movement: The Personal View (f), 24
Civil Rights Movement: The South (f), 24
Civilizations of the East (fs), 111
Classroom Approaches to the Teaching of Black History and Literature (fs), 48
Cliff Dwellings of the Mesa Verde (sl), 177
Clues to Ancient Indian Life (f), 151
Colombia and Venezuela (f), 208
Color! Color! Color! (f), 244
Color Us Black (f), 24
Colors of Man Kit (p), 263
Communist China (f), 95-96
Como Se Hace Una Pinata (f), 208
Conflict of Cultures (fs), 223
Confucius (f), 96
Consider the Zebra (f), 25
Considerations for the 21st Century (a), 127
Contemporary Afro-American (tr), 58
Contemporary Afro-American Art (fs), 48
Contemporary American Indian Biographies (p), 186
Contemporary Art by Afro-Americans (p), 69
Contemporary Black Artists (sl), 56
Contemporary Black Biographies (p), 69
Contemporary Black Painters and Sculptors (fs), 48; (sl), 56
Conversations in Black (f), 25
Corner (f), 25
Cortez and the Legend (f), 208
Costa Rica (sl), 230
Countee Cullen—The Poetry of Countee Cullen (a), 64
Countries of Southeast Asia—Burma—Malaysia and Thailand (fs), 111
Creation (f), 25
Crisis in Levittown (f), 25
Crunch on Spruce Street (f), 244
Cry, the Beloved Country (f), 25-26
Cuba and the Refugees (fs), 223
Cuba: The Word Is Hope (a), 233
Cuba Today (fs), 223-224
Culinary Art of Japan (f), 96
Culturally Different Learner (fs), 253

Dawn Horse (f), 151-152
Day of Promise (f), 152
Death of Simon Jackson (f), 26
"Decision at Delano" (f), 208
Desert People (f), 152
Differences (f), 244
Discovering American Indian Music (f), 152
Discovering Jazz (f), 26
Discovering the Music of Japan (f), 96
Discovering the Music of Latin America (f), 208
Discovering Today's China (fs), 111
Discrimination in the North 1780-1860 and Black Businessmen and Professionals 1780-1860 (a), 64
Dream Awake (a), 64
Dream Awake—The Black Experience in America (fs), 48
Drop Out Now—Pay Later (f), 245

Ecuador (f), 208-209
Education and Religion (p), 69
Education and the Mexican American (f), 209
El Greco (sl), 230

El Mondo de un Primitivo: Velasquez (f), 209
El Policia (The Policeman) (f), 209
El Sonida y Como se Viaja (f), 209
El Teatro Campesino (f), 209
El Testamento (a), 232
Emancipation—The Aftermath of the Civil War (a), 64
Employment Status of the Negro in America (tr), 58
End of the Trail: The American Plains Indian (f), 152
English for Spanish-Speaking Persons (a), 233
Eskimo (a), 258-259
Eskimo Art (sl), 258
Eskimo Artist Kenojuak (f), 245
Eskimos: A Changing Culture (f), 245
Eskimos of Hudson Bay and Alaska (a), 259
Eskimos of St. Lawrence Island (fs), 253
Ethnic Studies (a), 259
Ethnic Studies: The Peoples of America (fs), 253
Everyday Life in Japan (fs), 111
Everyday Life of the Chinese—Hong Kong (fs), 111
Exile (f), 152
Exploding the Myths of Prejudice (fs), 253
Exploration and Colonization (tr), 231-232
Exploring the Americas and the World—Asia (tr), 123

Fabulas Bilingues (fs), 224
Face of Red China (f), 96
Faces of Chinatown (f), 96
Families Get Angry (f), 26
Families of Mexico and Central America (fs), 224
Family Life in Japan (fs), 111
Family of Central Asia (fs), 112
Famous American Indians (a), 181
Famous Black Americans (p), 70
Famous Negro Leaders (a), 64
Famous Temples of Thailand (f), 96
Fat Black Mack (f), 26
Fayette Mississippi: A Study in Black and White (fs), 48
Fayette Story (f), 26
Felicia (f), 26-27
Felipa: North of the Border (f), 209
Felix Greene's China (vc), 131
Fight for Our Rights (fs), 48-49
First American—Last American (f), 153
First Americans (a), 181; (f) 152; (fs), 172
Five Black Americans and Their Fight for Freedom (fs), 49
Five Chinese Brothers (f), 96-97
Floating Market, Bangkok (f), 97
Folk Music of Japan (a), 127
Folk Songs and Dances (a), 233
Folk Songs and Frederick Douglass (fs), 49
Folk Songs of Israel (fs), 253
Folk Songs of Mexico (a), 233
Folk Songs of the Arab World (fs), 253
Folktales of Ethnic America (fs), 253
Food of Southeast Asia (f), 97
For All My Students (f), 27
Forerunners of Equality (fs), 254
Forgotten American (f), 153
Forgotten Village (f), 209-210
Four Families of Japan (fs), 112
400 Years: Black History in America (fs), 49
Frederick Douglass: House on Cedar Hill (f), 27
Frederick Douglass: Profiles in Courage (f), 27
Free and Slave States (tr), 58
Free at Last (f), 27
French Americans (a), 259
Friendly Game (f), 245
From Upper Room to Crowded Street (fs), 112
Funny Little Woman (fs), 112

Gems from a Rice Paddy (f), 97
George Washington Carver (f), 27
Germans Have Helped Build America (a), 259
Geronimo Jones (f), 153
Ghetto Pillow (f), 245
Ghetto Trap (f), 245
Ghettos of America (fs), 49
Gilberto and the Wind (fs), 224
Glimpse of the Past (f), 153
Go My Son (f), 153
Golden Age of Spain (fs), 224
Grambling College—100 yards to Glory (f), 28
Great African Civilizations in the World (a), 64
Great American Negroes (tr), 58-59
Great Architecture of Japan (sl), 121
Great Depression (a), 65
Great Negroes (p), 70

Growing Up Black (fs), 49-50
Guess Who's Coming to Dinner (f), 28
Guidance . . . Does Color Really Make a Difference? (f), 245-246
Guilty by Reason of Race (f), 97
Guilty One (f), 246
Gwendolyn Brooks—Gwendolyn Brooks Reading Her Poetry (a), 65

Haggadah of Sarajevo (f), 246
Haida (sl), 177
Haida Carver (f), 153
Hands of Maria (f), 153-154
Hanunoo Music from the Philippines (a), 127
Harlem Crusader (f), 210
Harlem in the Twenties (f), 28
Harlem Renaissance and Beyond (fs), 50
Harlem-Renaissance: The Black Poets (f), 28
Harlem Renaissance: The History of the Black in the United States (fs), 50
Harlem—The Making of a Community (f), 28
Harriet Tubman and the Underground Railroad (f), 28
Hasidim (f), 246
Hawaii—Historical and Cultural Features (tr), 124
Hawaii—Polynesia in the U.S.A. (f), 97
Hawaiian Chant, Hula, and Music (a), 127
Hawaiian Island (tr), 124
Hawaiian Music (a), 128
Hawaii's Asian Heritage (f), 97
Hawaii's History: Kingdom to Statehood (f), 97-98
Healer (f), 210
Healing Songs of the American Indians (a), 181
Henry, Boy of the Barrio (f), 210
Heritage in Black (f), 28
Heritage of Afro-American History (fs), 50
Heritage of Slavery (f), 29
Heritage of the Negro (f), 29
Hey Doc (f), 29
Higher Education (f), 29
Hiram Fong (f), 98
Hispanic Cultural Arts (vc), 237
Hispanic Heritage (vc), 237
Hispanic Life in a City (vc), 237
Historical American Indian Biographies (p), 186
Historical Black Biographies (p), 70
History and the Culture of Africa (tr), 59
History of Afro-Americans (tr), 57
History of Black America (fs), 42-43
History of Black America: Firebrands and Freedom Fighters (fs), 43
History of Black America: From Freedom to Disappointment (fs), 43
History of Black America: Hope, Disillusionment and Sacrifice (fs), 43
History of Black America: New Leadership and the Turning Tide (fs), 43
History of Black America: Progress, Depression and Global War (fs), 43
History of Black America: Slavery and Freedom in the English Colonies (fs), 43
History of Black America: The African Past (fs), 44
History of Black Americans (a), 65
History of Japanese Art (sl), 121-122
History of Latin American Art & Architecture (sl), 230
History of the American Negro (fs), 50
History of the Black Man in the United States (fs), 50-51
Hitch (f), 29
Ho Chi Minh (f), 98
Holidays Your Neighbors Celebrate (f), 246
Home (f), 154
Hong Kong—An Historic Port (fs), 112
Hong Kong—Crossroads of the Orient (f), 98
Hopi Indian Arts and Crafts (f), 154
Hopi Indian Village Life (f), 154
Hopi Kachinas (f), 154
Hopi Katcina Songs—And Six Other Songs (a), 181
Hopi Way (f), 154
How Come When It's Thunderin . . . You Don't See the Moon? (f), 29
Huddled Masses (vc), 261
Huddled Masses (Parts 1 and 2) (f), 246-247
Huelga (f), 210
Huey (f), 29

I (Am, Be) Speaking English (f), 30
I Am Joaquin (f), 210
I Am Somebody (f), 30
If There Weren't Any Blacks, You'd Have to Invent Them (f), 30

Ifugao Tribe of the Philippines (fs), 112
Illegals (f), 210-211
Illustrated Black History (p), 70
I'm a Man (f), 30
Images in Black (f), 30
Immigrants in Chains (f), 30
Immigration (f), 247; (fs), 254; (p), 263
Immigration in Colonial Times (p), 263
Immigration: The Dream and the Reality (fs), 254
In Living Color (vc), 261
In Search of a City (f), 157-158
In Search of a Past (f), 30-31
In the Land of Fujisan (fs), 113
India: Crafts and the Craftsman (fs), 98
Indian Agriculture (p), 187
Indian America (f), 154
Indian Arts and Crafts (vc), 185
Indian Boy in Today's World (f), 154-155
Indian Boy of the Southwest (f), 155
Indian Canoes along the Washington Coast (f), 155
Indian Children (a), 181-182
Indian Civil Rights Leaders (Parts 1 and 2) (fs), 172
Indian Conversation (f), 155
Indian Cowboy (f), 155
Indian Creation Myths (a), 182
Indian Cultures of the Americas (fs), 172-173
Indian Family of the California Desert (f), 155
Indian Heritage (fs), 173
Indian Heritage: The Treasure (f), 155-156
Indian House (f), 156
Indian Influences in the United States (f), 156
Indian Land: The Native American Ecologist (f), 156
Indian Life in North America (fs), 173
Indian Life in the Cities (vc), 185
Indian Music of the Canadian Plains (s), 182
Indian Music of the Pacific Northwest Coast (a), 182
Indian Music of the Southwest (a), 182
Indian Musical Instruments (f), 156
Indian Resistance: The Patriot Chiefs (p), 187
Indian Speaks (f), 157
Indian Summer (a), 182
Indian, The Horse and the Buffalo (tr), 179
Indian Tribes (a), 182
Indian Tribes in 1650 (p), 187
Indian Tribes, North America (a), 182
Indian Viewpoints (fs), 173-174
Indian Village Archaeology (fs), 174
Indian Wars (tr), 179
Indian Words from the End of the Trail (fs), 174
Indians (f), 157; (tr), 178
Indians and Settlers (tr), 178
Indians before the White Man (tr), 178
Indians in the Americas (f), 156
Indians of America (fs), 173; (tr), 178
Indians of California: Arrow Making (p), 187
Indians of California: Food (p), 187
Indians of California: Village Life (p), 187
Indians of Early America (f), 156
Indians of North America (tr), 178
Indians of the New World (fs), 173
Indians of the Plains (Indians of North America) (tr), 179
Indians of the Plains—Life in the Past (f), 157
Indians of the Plains—Present Day Life (f), 157
Indians of the Plains—Sun Dance Ceremony (f), 157
Indians of the Southwest (sl), 177; (vc), 185
Indians of the Southwest (Indians of North America) (tr), 179
Indians of the Southwest, Our Land, Our People, U.S.A. Series (f), 157
Indians of the United States (tr), 179
Indians of the United States & Canada (p), 187
Indonesia (fs), 112
Indonesia—A New Nation of Asia (f), 98
Indonesia—The Land and the People (f), 98
Introduction to Japan (fs), 113
Introduction to South Vietnam (fs), 113
Introduction to Soviet Central Asia (fs), 113
Introduction to the Philippines (fs), 113
Irish Americans (a), 259
Irish Fairy Tales (a), 259
Irish Have Helped to Build America (a), 259-260
Ishi in Two Worlds (f), 158

Island in the China Sea (f), 98-99
Island of the Blue Dolphin (An Introduction) (f), 158
Islands of the South Pacific (f), 99
Israel (a), 260
Israel: Making a Land Productive (f), 247
Israeli Folk Dances (a), 260
Italian Americans (a), 260
Italians in America (fs), 254
Ivanhoe Donaldson (f), 31

Jack Johnson (f), 31
Jackie Robinson (f), 31
James Weldon Johnson (f), 31
Japan (fs), 113; (tr), 124
Japan; A Changing Nation (fs), 113-114
Japan—A History of Art (sl), 122
Japan: A Nation of Growing Cities (f) 99
Japan—A Series (a), 128
Japan: A Study of Depth (fs), 114
Japan: An Historical Overview (f), 99
Japan—An Introduction (f), 99
Japan: Asia's Economic Superpower (fs), 114
Japan: Asia's Modern Power (fs), 114
Japan: East Is West (f), 99
Japan: Economic Miracle (fs), 114
Japan: Emergence of a Modern Nation (fs), 114-115
Japan—Harvesting the Land and Sea (f), 100
Japan: Her Voices and People (a), 128
Japan: Miracle in Asia (f), 100
Japan: Old and New (fs), 115
Japan: Pacific Neighbor (f), 100
Japan: Spirit of Lemoto (fs), 115-116
Japan: The Free World in the Far East (a), 128
Japan through American Eyes (a), 128
Japanese American (f), 99-100
Japanese American Relocation 1942 (fs), 115
Japanese Americans (a), 128
Japanese Americans and Chinese Americans (fs), 115
Japanese Americans, Prejudice in America (fs), 115
Japanese Boy—The Story of Taro (f), 100
Japanese Folk Toys (sl), 122
Japanese Haiku (a), 128
Japanese Life (p), 132
Japanese Mountain Family (vc), 131
Japanese Village (f), 100
Japan's Geography—Human and Economic (f), 100
Japan's New Family Patterns (f), 100-101
Jazz: The Music of Black Americans (fs), 51
Jeffries—Johnson 1910 (f), 31
Jesse Owens Returns to Berlin (f), 31
Jesus Trip—The Search for Spiritual Values (vc), 261-262
Jewish Americans (a), 260
Jewish Immigrants to America (fs), 254-255
Jim Thorpe—All American (f), 158
Joe Louis Story (f), 32
John Outerbridge: Black Artist (f), 32
Johnny from Fort Apache (f), 158
Jose Martinez—American (f), 211
Julio Posado del Valle (f), 211
Just Like You (vc), 262
Justice? (f), 32
Justice Thurgood Marshall—Mr. Civil Rights (fs), 51

Kalvak (f), 247; (vc), 262
Kee Begay, Navajo Boy (f), 158
Key Supreme Court Decisions (tr), 59
Kiowa (a), 182-183
Korea, Folk and Classical Music (a), 128
Kwakiutl and Southern B.C. Tribes (sl), 177
Kyudo: Japanese Ceremonial Archery (f), 101

"La Mula No Nacio Arisco" (a), 233
La Raza (fs), 224
Land of Immigrants (f), 247
Langston Hughes, Selected Poetry (a), 65
Langston Hughes, Simple Stories (a), 65
Langston Hughes. The Poetry of Langston Hughes (a), 65
Last Menominee (f), 158
Last Tribes of Mindanao (f), 101
Latin American Cooking (f), 211
Lawless (f), 211
Leading American Negroes (fs), 51
Learn, Baby, Learn (fs), 51
Learning about the Past (f), 159

Learning Tree (f), 32
Legal or Illegal: The Dispossession of of the Indians (fs), 174
Legend of John Henry (f), 32
Legend of the Magic Knives (f), 159
Legends of the Sioux (f), 159
Leopold Sedar Senghor (f), 32
Let's Learn Spanish Songs (a), 233-234
Let's Visit Mexico (a), 234
Let's Visit Spain (a), 234
Life and Words of Martin Luther King, Jr. (a), 65
Life of a Philippine Family (f), 101
Life That Disapperaed (sl), 258
Living in China Today (fs), 116
Living in Harlem (fs), 51
Living in Israel—North to South (fs), 255
Living in Mexico Today (fs), 225
Living in South Vietnam (fs), 116
Loon's Necklace (f), 159
Lorraine Hansberry. A Raisin in the Sun (a), 66
Lorraine Hansberry and Robert Nemiroff—To Be Young, Gifted and Black (a), 65

Madame Butterfly—Puccini (a), 128
Majority Minority (f), 248
Making a Pinata (f), 211
Making of Modern Israel (fs), 255
Malaya, Land of Tin and Rubber (f), 101
Malcolm X (f), 32
Malcolm X Speaks (f), 33
Malcolm X—Struggle for Freedom (f), 33
Man (f), 33
Man Named Charlie Smith (f), 17
Manuel from Puerto Rico (f), 211
Mao Tse-tung (f), 101
Map Reading—Asia (tr), 124
Marco Polo's Travels (f), 101
Maria of the Pueblos (f), 159
Marian Anderson (f), 33
Martin Luther King (f), 33
Martin Luther King: A Man of Peace (f), 33
Martin Luther King: The Man and the March (f), 33
Martin Luther King, Jr. (f), 34; (fs), 52
Martin Luther King, Jr.: From Montgomery to Memphis (f), 34
Masks of Africa (sl), 57
Masks of Japan (sl), 122
Master Prints of Japan—Uniyo-E Hanga (sl), 122
Masuo Ikeda: Printmaker (f), 101-102
Matter with Me (f), 34
Mayflower and the Pilgrim Fathers (p) 263
Meet the Sioux Indian (f), 159
Mexican American (tr), 232
Mexican-American Border Songs (f), 211-212
Mexican-American, It's Culture, It's Heritage (f), 212
Mexican American Speaks (Heritage in Bronze) (f), 212
Mexican-American (Texan) (tr), 232
Mexican American—Viva La Raza (f), 212
Mexican Americans: An Historic Profile (f), 212
Mexican-Americans in Texas History (tr), 232
Mexican-Americans: Invisible Minority (f), 213
Mexican American (Part 2: Minorities Have Made America Great) (fs), 225
Mexican Boy: The Story of Pablo (f), 212
Mexican Ceramics (f), 212-213
Mexican Dancers (f), 213
Mexican Epic (fs), 225
Mexican Folk Dances (a), 234
Mexican Handcraft and Folk Art (f), 213
Mexican Heritage (fs), 225
Mexican Sing Along (Vocal Spanish) (a) 234
Mexicanos of the Southwest (a), 234
Mexicans-Americans; Heritage and Destiny (f), 213
Mexicans Bring Us Rhythms (a), 234
Mexicans in the United States—Education (a), 234
Mexico (p), 238; (sl), 230; (tr), 232
Mexico—A History in Art (sl), 230
Mexico at Work and Play (p), 238
Mexico, Central America & the West Indies Today (p), 238
Mexico, Crafts and Industries (p), 238
Mexico in the 70's Heritage and Progress (f), 214
Mexico in the Twentieth Century (fs), 225-226
Mexico in Transition (fs), 226
Mexico: Its Land and People (fs), 226
Mexico: Its Sounds and People (a), 234

Mexico: Our Dynamic Neighbor (fs), 226
Mexico (Part 1) (f), 213
Mexico (Part 2) Central and Gulf Coast Region (f), 214
Mexico: The Frozen Revolution (Parts 1 and 2) (f), 214
Mexico: The Land and the People (f), 214-215
Mexico's Heritage (f), 214
Mexico' History (f), 214
Mexico's Modern Capital City (sl), 230
Miami's Cuban Community (fs), 226
Mighty Warriors (f), 159-160
Migrant Farm Workers (p), 263
Migrant Health (vc), 262
Migrant Worker (fs), 255
Migration (vc), 262
Mikado (a), 129
Minor Majority (a), 260
Minorities and Majorities (fs), 255-256
Minorities and Women in Instructional Materials (a), 260
Minorities: From Africa, Asia and the Americas (f), 248
Minorities: From Europe (f), 248
Minorities Have Made America Great (fs), 256
Minorities: In the Name of Religion (f), 248
Minorities: Patterns of Change (f), 248
Minorities—USA (fs), 255
Minorities: What's a Minority? (f), 248
Minority Groups—The Development of a Nation (tr), 124
Minority Pioneers: A Western Anthem (f), 248-249
Missing Pages (f), 34
Missions of the Southwest (f), 160,215
Modern American Drama: The Emperor Jones (fs), 52
Modern American Dramas: A Raisin in the Sun (fs), 52
Modern Eastern and Southeastern Asia (fs), 116
Modern Method English Course for Spanish-Speaking People (a), 235
Music and Dance of the Bagobo and Monobo Peoples of Mindanao (f), 102
Music and Dance of the Hill People of the Northern Philippines (f), 102
Music of Asia: Japan/China/Okinawa (a), 129
Music of the American Indians of the Southwest (a), 183
Music of the East (fs), 116
Music of the Pawnee (a), 183
Music of the Plains Apache (a), 183
Music of the Sioux and the Navajo (a), 183
Music, Theatre, and Sports 1885-1929—The World War Era (a), 66
Musical Instruments of the American Indian (sl), 177
My Friend (vc), 185

Nat Turner's Rebellion (fs), 52
Nat Turner's Slave Revolt (p), 70
Nation of Immigrants (fs), 252
National Museum of Anthropology, Mexico (sl), 230-231
Nationalism as a Force in Asia (fs), 117
Native American Painting (fs), 174
Navajo (f), 160
Navajo, A People between Two Worlds (f), 160
Navajo Folklore (fs), 174-175
Navajo Indian (f), 161
Navajo Indian Life (f), 161
Navajo Life (f), 161
Navajo Night Dances (f), 161
Navajo (Parts 1 and 2) (f), 160
Navajo Silversmith (f), 161-162
Navajo: The Last Red Indians (vc), 185
Navajos—Children of the Gods (f), 161
Navajos of the 70's (f), 162
Navajos: Shepherds of the Desert (f), 161
Near and Middle East (sl), 122
Negro-American Citizen (a), 66
Negro and Civil War (tr), 59
Negro and the New Order, 1946-1954 (Negro-American Citizen) (tr), 59
Negro Cowboys (fs), 52
Negro Experience In America (p), 70
Negro Family (tr), 59
Negro from 450 B.C. to 1865 (tr), 59-60
Negro History: 1800-1865 (tr), 60
Negro History: 1865-1919 (tr), 60
Negro History: 1920-1945 (tr), 60
Negro in America (a), 66: (tr), 60
Negro in Post Civil War America (The Afro-American) (tr), 60
Negro Kingdoms of Africa's Golden Age (f), 34
Negro Woman (a), 66
Negroes (fs), 52

Negroes—American Too (Negro American Citizen) (tr), 59
Negroes in America (fs), 52
Nepal Himalayan Kingdom (f), 102
New Age in Japan (f), 102
New Focus on Opportunity (f), 215
New Goals for Black Americans (fs), 52-53
New Japan (fs), 117
New South (f), 34
New World, New Lines Series (a), 235
Nisei: The Pride and the Shame (f), 102
No Jail Can Change Me (f), 35
No Man Is an Island (f), 249
"No More Mananas" (f), 215
Noah (f), 247
Noboby Goes There: Ellis Island (f), 249
Nobody Took the Time (f), 249
Noh Plays (Japanese) (a), 129
Nonviolent Approach to Civil Rights 1925-1963—Militancy and Upheaval 1964-Present (a), 66
North American Indian Legends (f), 162
North American Indian Tribes (tr), 179
North from Mexico (f), 215
North of the Border (f), 215
Northwest American Indian War Dance Contest (f), 162-163
Northwest Coast Indian Traditions Today (A Contemporary Look at Remnants of a Heritage) (fs), 175
Northwest Coast Indians (A Search for the Past) (f), 162
Northwest Indian Art (f), 163
Not with an Empty Quiver (f), 163
Noticias a Fonda (vc), 237
Novel: Ralph Ellison on Work in Progress (f), 35
Nueve Artistas de Puerto Rico (f), 216

Odyssey in Black (vc), 68
Of Black America: Body and Soul, (f), 35
Oh Freedom (f), 35
Oklahoma Land Rush (p), 187
Old Order Amish (f), 249-250
One Special Dog (f), 163
Organization of American States (f), 216
Orient—Peoples of Asian Land (f), 103
Orient: Towards a Better Life (f), 103
Oriental Brushwork (f), 102
Oscar Howe: The Sioux Painter (f), 163
Oscar Robertson (f), 35
Other American Minorities (Parts 1 and 2) (fs), 256
Other 49'ers: White and Chinese in the Early Days of California (fs), 117
Our Country! Too (f), 35-36
Our Family Is Black (fs), 53
Our Immigrant Heritage (f), 250
Our Latin American Neighbors (f), 216
Our Mexican Neighbors (fs), 226-227
Our Proud Land (f), 163
Our Totem Is the Raven (f), 163
Out of the Mainstream (fs), 256
Outstanding American Indians (a), 183
Outstanding Asian Americans (a), 129

Paddle to the Sea (f), 164
Paintings of India (sl), 122
Pancho (f), 216; (fs), 227
Panola (f), 36
Patriot Solders (The Quest for Freedom) (a), 66
Paul Lawrence Dunbar—American Poet (f), 36
Pearl Buck: The Good Earth (fs), 117
Pearl S. Buck (f), 103
People Are Different and Alike (f), 250
People of Japan (fs), 117
People of Malaysia (f), 103
People of Mexico (fs), 227
People of People's China (f), 103
People of the Buffalo (f), 164
People of the Island World (f), 103
People of the Philippines (f), 103
People Uprooted (fs), 44
People's Republic of China (fs), 117-118
Perception/Misperception: China/U.S.A. (fs), 118
Peter La Farge on the Warpath (a), 183
Peter's Chair (f), 36
Philippines: Gateway to the Far East (f), 104
Philippines: Island Republic (f), 104
Philippines: Land and People (f), 104
Physical Geography of Asia (tr), 124

Physical, Social and Economic Geography of Africa (tr), 60
Pioneers in Man's World (p), 263-264
Places in the News (vc), 262
Plains of Yucatan (fs), 227
Poetic Voice of Black Experience (fs), 53
Polish Americans (a) 260-261
Portfolio of Outstanding Americans of Mexican Descent (p), 238
Portfolio of Outstanding Contemporary American Indians (p), 186
Portrait in Black and White (f), 36
Portrait of a Minority, Spanish-Speaking American (fs), 227
Pre-Columbian Art in Latin America (sl), 231
Prejudice: Causes, Consequences, Cures (f), 250
Prejudice: The Invisible Wall (a), 261
Pride and the Shame (vc), 185-186
Primitive Art—The American Indian (sl), 177
Prominentes Chicanos y Chicanas (p), 239
Pueblo Boy (f), 164
Pueblo Heritage (f), 164
Puerto Rican (Parts 1 & 2) (fs), 227
Puerto Rican People (a), 235
Puerto Rican Series (fs), 227-228
Puerto Ricans (a), 235
Puerto Rico (sl), 231
Puerto Rico and the Puerto Ricans (fs), 228
Puerto Rico and the Virgin Islands (tr), 232
Puerto Rico: Awakening Commonwealth (fs), 228
Puerto Rico—Climate for Revolution (f), 216
Puerto Rico Expedition (tr), 232
Puerto Rico: History and Culture (fs), 228
Puerto Rico: Island in the Sun (f), 216
Puerto Rico, Its Past, Present and Promise (f), 216-217
Puerto Rico, "Operation Bootstrap" (f) 217
Puerto Rico—Selecciones Poeticas (a), 235
Puerto Rico: Showcase of America (f), 217
Puerto Rico: Su Pasada, Su Presente y Su Promesa (f), 217
Puerto Rico: The Caribbean Americans (f), 217
Puerto Rico: The Peaceful Revolution (f), 217
Puerto Rico, USA (vc), 238
Puertorriquenos (fs), 225

Que Puerto Rico (f), 217
Quest for Equality (fs), 53

Raisin in the Sun (f), 18
Reconstruction to Disfranchisement, 1860-1900 (Negro American Citizen) (tr), 60
Red China—A Series (f), 104
Red China Diary with Morley Safer (f), 104
Red Hawk's Account of Custer's Last Battle (a), 183
Red Man in Michigan (a), 184
Red, White and Blue and Black (f), 36
Religion and Tradition in Japan (fs), 118
Religious Music of Asia (a), 129
Republic of Indonesia (fs), 118
Reverend Dr. Martin Luther King, Jr. (fs), 53
Rhythms from Africa (vc), 68
Rice (f), 104
Rice in Today's World (f), 104
Rich Man, Poor Man (vc), 262
Richard Wright, Black Boy (a), 67
Right On Be Free (f), 36-37
River People (f), 164
Robert and His Family (fs), 53
Roberta Flack (f), 37
Ron Lyle (f), 37
Rush toward Freedom (fs), 53-54

Sampan Family (f), 104-105
San Francisco (f), 105
Sante Fe and the Trail (f), 217-218
Santillana Bilingual Audio-Visual Program (fs), 228
"Satchmo" by Louis Armstrong (a), 67
Search (p), 70
Seeds of Hate: Examination of Prejudice (fs), 257
Seeing China (fs), 118
Seeing Japan (fs), 118-119
Seeing Mexico (fs), 229
Separate and Unequal (fs), 54
Shadow of the Buffalo (f), 164

Shintoism (f), 105
Siam: The People of Thailand (f), 105
Significance of Malcolm X (f), 37
Silhouettes in Courage (a), 67
Singapore: How it Serves Southeast Asia (fs), 119
Sioux Legends (f), 164-165
Sisibakwat (f), 165
"Siu Mei Wong—Who Shall I Be" (f), 105
Slavery (f), 37
Slavery, Civil War and Reconstruction (a), 67
Slavery in the Americas (tr), 60
Slave's Story: Running a Thousand Miles to Freedom (f), 19
Snowy Day (f), 37
Social Classes in Japan (fs), 119
Social Progress in the Late 1940's —The Eisenhower Years and School Desegregation (a), 67
Soldier Blue (f), 165
Songs and Dances of the Flathead Indians (a), 184
Songs in Spanish for Children (a), 235
Songs of the Seminole Indians of Florida (a), 184
South African Essay: Fruit of Fear (f), 37
South African Essay: One Nation Two Nationalisms (f), 37
South America (a), 235; (f), 218; (sl), 231
South America Today (p), 239
South American War Period (p), 239
South Sea Island Tales Mann Tupou (a), 129
South Vietnam—Key to Southeast Asia's Future (fs), 119-120
Southeast Asia (fs), 119
Southeast Asia Geography (f), 105
Southeast Asia Past and Present (fs), 119
Southeast Indian Families (fs), 175
Southern Appalachia: An Area Left Behind (fs), 257
Southern Asia—Problems of Transition (f), 105
Southwest Indians Arts and Crafts (f), 165
Southwest Indians of Early America (f), 165
Spain and Portugal: Lands and People (f), 218
Spain and Portugal: On the Threshold of Success (f), 218
Spain in the New World: Colonial Life in Mexico (f), 218
Spanish-American War 1898-99 (tr), 232
Spanish-Americans of New Mexico (fs), 229
Spanish Children (f), 218
Spanish Colonial Family of the Southwest (f), 218-219
Spanish Colonial Life (sl), 231
Spanish Community Life (f), 219
Spanish Conquest in the New World (f), 219
Spanish Explorers (f), 219
Spanish Harlem "Mainland Puerto Rico" (fs), 229
Spanish Influences in the United States (f), 219
Spanish Inquisition (p), 239
Spanish Life and Humor (a), 235
Spanish Painting in the Metropolitan Museum (sl), 231
Spanish Songs (a), 235-236
Spanish Stories and Poems (a), 236
Spanish Today (a), 236
Spanish Vocabulary (Cognitive System) (tr), 232
Spanish—Word and Number Games (tr), 232
Sportraits in Ebony (f), 38
Sticks and Stones Will Build a House (f), 165
Still a Brother: Inside the Negro Middle Class (f), 38
Stop Ruining America's Past (f), 165-166
Storm of Strangers (f), 243
Story of America's People (fs), 257
Story of a Three Day Pass (f), 38
Story of Jazz (a), 67
Strangers in Their Own Land: The Blacks (f), 38
Struggle to End Slavery (sl), 57
Sumi Artist (f), 106
Summer of Johnson Holiday—Navajo Boy (f), 166
Sun Dance People (Plains Indians: Their Past and Present) (fs), 175
Suppose They Gave a War and No One Came? (a), 129
Survey of Fifteen Contemporary Afro-American Artists (sl), 57
Survey of Japanese Prints (sl), 121

Tacos and Hamburgers (a), 236
Tahtonka (f), 166
Taiwan (fs), 120
Take a Giant Step (f), 38
Tales from Japan (fs), 120
Tales of China and Tibet (a), 130
Tales of the Plains Indians (fs), 175
Talk with Ho Chi Minh (a), 125
Tall Tales in American Folklore (fs), 257
Tatankaiyotake, Sitting Bull (fs), 175
Telling it Like It Is and How It Ought to Be (f), 38
Tesero de Cuentos de Hadas (fs), 229
Thailand, Land of Rice (f), 106
They Have Overcome (fs), 54
Thinking Seventeen (f), 39
This Is My Country—East Asian Countries (a), 130
Three Black Writers (f), 39
Three Farmers in Mexico (fs), 229
Three Island Women (f), 106
3000 Years of Art in Mexico (sl), 231
Through Their Eyes—Ethnic Studies (a), 261
Tikki Tikki Tembo (fs), 120
Tina, a Girl in Mexico (f), 219
Tlingit (sl), 177
To Be Black (f), 39
To Be Young, Gifted and Black (f), 39
To Feed the Hungry (f), 250
To Sir with Love (f), 39
Tokyo the Fifty-First Volcano (vc), 131
Tomorrow's Yesterday (f), 166
Totems (f), 166
Traditional Songs of Mexico (a), 236
Trail of Tears (f), 166-167; (vc), 186
Trail Ride (f), 167
Treasure (f), 167
Treaties (f), 167
Trial—The City and County of Denver vs. Lauren R. Watson (f), 39
Trial—The First Day (f), 39
Trial—The Second Day (f), 39-40
Trial—The Third Day (f), 40
Trial—The Fourth and Final Day (f), 40
Tribe of the Turquoise Water (f), 167
Tribute to Malcolm X (f), 19
Trouble with Chinatown (f), 106
Two Indians: Red Reflections of Life (f), 167

UNESCO Study Prints (p), 132
Umbrella (fs), 120
Una Prospectiva de Mexico (p), 239
Understanding Contemporary Afro-American Art (fs), 54
Understanding Prejudice (fs), 257
United States Expansion: California (f), 219

Venezuela (f), 220
Victims (f), 250
Vicus (f), 220
Vietnam (a), 130
View from Inside China (a), 125
Viewpoint: Asian—The Tensions of a Non-Western Nation (a), 130
Village Tree (fs), 120
Voice of La Raza (f), 220

W. C. Handy (f), 40
W. E. B. DuBois (a), 67
Walk in My Shoes (f), 40
War in Vietnam (p), 132
War Whoops and Medicine Songs (a), 184
Warriors at Peace (f), 167
Washoe-Peyote Songs (a), 184
Washoe (f), 168
Water Is So Clear That a Blind Man Can See (f), 168
Water People of Hong Kong (f), 106
We Are Indians: American Indian Literature (fs), 176
We Came to America (f), 250
We Learned from the Indians (fs), 176
Weapons of Gordon Parks (f), 41
Wat Color Are You? (f), 250-251
What Is Prejudice? (f), 257
What Is Puerto Rico? (a), 236
Where Has the Warrior Gone? (f), 168
Where Is Prejudice? (f), 251
Whistle for Willie (f), 41; (fs), 54
Who Are the American Jews? (f), 251
Who Is the Enemy? (a), 236-237
Who Needs You? (f), 220
Who Were the Ones? (f), 168
Wilderness Kingdom (fs), 176
William F. Buckley's "Firing Line," the Black Revolution (fs) 55

William from Georgia to Harlem (f), 41
Woodland Indians of Early America (f), 168
World History (tr), 124
World of Julian Bond (f), 41
Yakima Nation (a), 184
Yiddish—Sholem Aleichem (a), 261
Yo Soy Chicano (f), 220
Yoruba Ritual Art (sl), 57
You Dig It (f), 41

Index

This index, covering chapter introductions and media and materials annotations, pulls together broad subject areas which are common to ethnic groups, e.g., Art, Children, Education, Family Life, Music, Religion, and so on. With few exceptions, personal and proper names, for which there is a single citation in the text, are not included. Biographies of two or more persons are listed as "biography (collections)" in the ethnic group entry.

Abernathy, Ralph, 22, 25

Africa
  cultures, 17, 29, 42, 58, 59
  history
    ancient, 29, 34, 42, 59
    contemporary, 3, 64
  land and people, 17, 41, 57
  South Africa, 26, 37
  See also Afro-Americans; Dance; Folktales; Music

African slaves
  in Europe, 3
  in United States, 3, 17, 19, 24, 30, 44

Afro-Americans
  biography (collections), 2, 21, 25, 27, 43, 44, 45, 50, 51, 56, 57, 59, 60, 63, 64, 69, 70
  Civil War, 54, 67, 68
  cowboys (western pioneers), 21, 45, 48, 52, 61, 68
  culture, 18, 29, 36, 38, 39, 42, 50, 62, 67
  emancipation, 3, 4, 19, 22, 29, 42, 43, 70
  modern history, 4, 5, 6, 18, 19, 21, 22, 28, 29, 35, 36
  religion, 47, 60, 62, 69
  self-image, 3, 7, 8, 9, 21, 29, 37, 39, 45, 62
  slavery, 17, 19, 21, 28, 29, 34, 37, 42, 43, 44, 47, 48, 49, 50, 56, 57, 58, 59, 60, 62, 66, 67, 69, 70
  See also Race relations

Agriculture
  Mexico, 220, 226, 227, 229
  United States
    Chinese, 71, 72, 74, 75
    Filipino, 75, 76
    Indian American, 157, 164, 185, 187
    Japanese, 73, 74, 75
    See also Farm workers

Alabama, 17, 31, 34, 46, 56, 66

Alaska, 124, 149, 177

Aldridge, Ira, 60, 63

Allport, Gordon, 54, 257

Anderson, Marian, 33, 56, 60, 63, 70

Archaeology, Indian American, 157, 159, 165, 178

Architecture
  Asian, 72, 109, 111, 120
  Indian American, 156, 165, 177
  Mexican, 213, 214, 237
  Moorish, 190, 224
  Spanish influence, 219, 230

Argentina, 190, 216, 235
Arizona, 165, 166, 167, 126
Armstrong, Louis, 21, 43, 46, 62, 67, 69
Art
  African, 42, 44, 55, 57, 69
  Afro-American, 19, 20, 29, 37, 38, 45, 48, 54, 55, 56, 60, 63, 69
  China, 72, 94, 108, 109, 110, 111, 120, 121, 131
  China, People's Republic of, 104, 116, 118
  Eskimo, 245, 247, 249, 258, 262
  India, 122
  Indonesia, 98
  Japan, 101-102, 106, 110, 111, 114, 120, 121, 122
  Jewish, 242
  Latin American, 230, 231
  Mexican, 208, 213
  Puerto Rican, 211
  Spanish, 231
Arts and Crafts
  Indian American, 148, 150, 153, 154, 159, 160, 161, 163, 165, 166, 167, 169, 170, 171, 174, 176, 177, 178, 179, 185
  Mexican, 213, 221, 230, 231
  Mexican American, 206-207, 213
  Moorish, 190
  Pre-Columbian, 220
  Puerto Rican, 211, 216
Ashmore, Harry S., 125, 127
Asia
  cultures, 92, 103, 106, 107, 111, 116, 117, 118, 123, 124, 130
  U.S. commitment in, 117
  See also China; Japan; Religion
Asian Americans
  biography (collections), 129
  character, 79, 80, 82, 83, 85, 86
  cultural heritage, 103, 109
  self-concept, 84, 85, 86
  See also Education; Immigrants, Immigration; Religion; Youth
Athletes
  Afro-Americans, 20, 31-32, 35, 38, 60, 65, 67
  See also Sports
Aztec culture, 149, 171, 172, 212, 213, 226, 230

Baldwin, James, 39, 62
Banneker, Benjamin, 44, 51, 59, 62, 64, 70
Bethune, Mary McLeod, 44, 46, 51, 59, 66
Bilingual instruction. *See* Education
Black Americans. *See* Afro-Americans
Black Hawk, 178, 180, 181
Black Muslims, 22, 32, 33
Black Panther Party, 21, 29, 39, 55, 66, 68, 70
Black power, 22, 55, 62, 68
Black studies. *See* Ethnic studies
Blacks (Africans). *See* Africa; African slaves
Blacks (American). *See* Afro-Americans
Blacks, U.S. *See* Afro-Americans
Bond, Julian, 22, 41, 70
Bontemps, Arna, 61, 67
Brant, Joseph, 178, 181
Brooke, Edward, 23, 45, 46
Brooks, Gwendolyn, 61, 65, 70
Brown, Claude, 51, 54
Brown, Dr. Dorothy, 51, 54
Brown, H. Rap, 22, 29, 56
Brown, John, 4, 43, 61
Bruce, Louis R., 169, 186
Buck, Pearl S., 103, 117, 126
Buddha. *See* Religion
Bunche, Dr. Ralph, 44, 52, 56, 67, 69
Burma, 93, 107, 111, 116, 121, 125, 132

California, 20, 213, 219, 243, 252
  Alcatraz Indians, 172, 187
  Chinese labor, 72, 94, 96, 117
  "Gold Rush," 72, 95, 223
  history, 150, 151, 158
  Japanese labor, 73, 74
  Los Angeles, 20, 212
    Watts, 24, 26, 38, 49
  restrictive legislation in, 73, 75, 76, 117
Cambodia, 116, 119, 121, 132
Carmichael, Stokely, 20, 22, 23, 29, 44, 68
Carroll, Charles, 2, 259
Carver, George Washington, 23, 27, 44, 45, 51, 52, 59, 70
Castro, Fidel, 198, 229
Catholic religion. *See* Religion
Center for the Study of Democratic Institutions, 233, 237
Central America, 190, 197, 223
Ceremonies (festivals), 246, 247
  Filipino, 101, 112
  Hawaiian, 97

Indian American, 148, 150, 156, 157, 160, 161, 162, 163, 164, 167, 168, 180, 184
Japanese, 113
Mexican, 208, 211
Spanish, 234
See also Recreation
Charles, Ray, 22, 35
Chavez, Cesar, 208, 212, 221, 238
Chicanos. *See* Mexican Americans
Children
Afro-American, 8-9, 30, 36, 49, 53, 54, 69, 251, 252, 258
Asian, 108
Australian, 131
Burmese, 101
Chinese, 95, 96, 97, 120, 126
Filipino, 101
Indian American, 136, 138, 139, 140, 141, 148, 150, 152, 154, 155, 158, 163, 164, 166, 167, 181, 183, 187, 251, 252, 258
Japanese, 100, 120
Jewish, 243
Mexican, 207, 209, 210, 211, 215, 224, 227, 234
Mexican American, 251, 252, 258
Oriental, 251, 252, 258
Pacific Islands, 131
Puerto Rican, 251, 252, 258
Spanish, 218
See also Education; Family life; Music
Chile, 208, 216
China
culture, 92, 103, 111, 131-132
foreign relations, 125, 132
history
modern, 93, 94, 108-109, 111
traditional, 92, 94, 108, 126
U.S. race relations, 118
See also Asia; Communism
China, People's Republic of
culture, 93, 116, 117, 118, 123, 130
economic growth, 95, 118, 123, 126
health care, 94
labor, 96
land and resources, 94, 106
philosophy, 108, 109
religion, 94
See also Art; Communism; Education; Women
Chinese Americans
biography (collections), 95
cultures, 71, 72, 73, 76, 80, 81, 83
ghettos, 94, 95, 96, 105, 106, 109, 131
race prejudice, 117, 118
restrictive legislation, 74, 95, 117
See also Education; Immigrants, Immigration
Chisholm, Shirley, 23, 25, 29, 45, 49, 56
Civil Rights
Afro-Americans (activists biographies), 18, 20, 43, 44, 48, 49, 51
history, 17, 18, 19, 20, 24, 26, 30, 34, 35, 37, 42, 52, 58, 61, 67
legislation, 6, 31, 43, 47, 48, 49
nonviolent programs, 20, 24, 52, 53, 66
Indian Americans, 136, 139, 162, 172
Spanish Americans, 194, 202
Cleaver, Eldridge, 23, 29, 42, 55, 56
Cochise, 176, 178, 180, 181, 186
Collier, John, 138
Colombia, 208, 216
Color, skin, 241, 244, 245, 251, 263
Colorado, 39, 40, 237
Coltrane, John, 22, 46
Comer, Dr. James, 51, 54
Communism, 94, 95, 96, 101, 103, 104, 108, 109, 116, 126, 130, 131
Confucius. *See* Religions
Conyers, John (Rep.), 23, 36
Cosby, Bill, 21, 22, 36
Crazy Horse, 178, 181, 183, 186
Cubans
Cuban Refugee Program, 198
cultural patterns, 221
economic status, 193, 197
Cuffee, Paul, 20, 60, 254
Cullen, Countee, 9, 28, 50, 53, 61, 64, 70
Cuney, Waring, 28, 53

Dance
Afro-American, 18, 35, 37
Bolivian, 208
Chinese, 95, 109, 132
Filipino, 102
Hawaiian, 97, 127
Indian American, 148, 150, 151, 152, 154, 156, 157, 161, 162, 164, 175, 179, 181, 182, 183, 184, 186
Israeli, 260
Japanese, 95, 99
Korean, 95
Mexican, 213, 234, 237

Dance (*Cont.*)
  South American, 235
  Vietnamese, 130
Davis, Angela, 18, 32
Davis, Benjamin O., Jr., 62, 70
Davis, Ossie, 28, 61, 64, 65, 66, 67
Dee, Ruby, 18, 28, 39, 64, 65, 66, 67
Densmore, Dr. Frances, 181, 184
de Soto, Hernando, 194, 219
Discrimination. *See* Race relations
Divine, Father, 28, 56
Dodson, Owen, 48, 64
Douglass, Frederick, 4, 27, 44, 48, 49, 58, 59, 60, 61, 62, 63, 70
Drama
  Afro-American, 18, 19, 30, 38, 45, 48, 52, 65, 66
  Chinese, 109, 131
  Japanese, 99, 128, 129
  Spanish-Speaking American, 209
Drew, Charles, 46, 56, 63, 67, 70
DuBois, W. E. B., 2, 4, 22, 27, 28, 43, 44, 52, 53, 63, 66, 67
Dunbar, Paul Lawrence, 36, 53

Ecuador, 190, 209, 216
Education
  Afro-American, 4, 5, 7, 8, 9, 10, 11, 25, 27, 28, 29, 30, 43, 48, 58, 59, 65, 77, 78, 258
    legislation, 6, 24, 49, 59, 67
  Asian American, 78, 83, 84, 85, 86
  bilingual, 189, 191, 201, 203, 207, 221, 222, 224, 228, 237
  China, People's Republic of, 94, 95, 96, 118, 130, 131
  Chinese American, 77, 78, 202, 204
  Cuban, 197-198
  Filipino American, 78
  Indian American
    bilingual, 138, 139, 140, 141
    European control, 136
    higher, 144, 145, 146
    Mormon Indian Placement Program, 136, 152, 153
    professional organizations, 142, 143
    U.S. control, 137, 158, 160, 164, 180, 185, 258
    See also Language; Missions, Missionaries; Religion
  Indonesian, 118
  Japan, 77
  Japanese American, 74, 77, 78, 83, 128
  Jewish American, 244, 251
  Mexican American, 194, 196, 209, 234, 258
  Polish American, 245
  Prejudice
    instructional materials, 242
    teachers, 261
  Puerto Rican, 196, 227, 228
  Spanish-Speaking American, 191, 201, 204, 232
Ellis Island, 243, 246, 247, 249, 261
Ellison, Ralph, 35, 39
Employment/unemployment, 25, 38, 59
  Afro-American, 58
  Asian American, 78, 79
  Indian American, 158, 161, 185
  Spanish-Speaking American, 144, 145, 147, 148, 163
Eskimos, 241, 245, 249, 253, 258, 262
  See also Art; Women
Ethnic contributions to U.S.
  Afro-American, 21, 23, 27, 28, 35, 40, 42, 51, 52, 55, 57, 58, 61, 62, 63, 65, 67, 68, 248, 256, 257
  Asian American, 86, 130
  Chinese, 72, 73, 74, 248, 251
  European, 250, 252
  Filipino, 76
  German, 256
  Hungarian, 257
  Indian American, 142, 148, 151, 156, 160, 166, 172, 176, 187, 248
  Irish, 256
  Italian, 254, 256, 257
  Japanese, 100, 248, 254
  Jewish, 254, 256, 257
  Mexican American, 212, 213, 215, 224, 248
  Puerto Rican, 228, 248
  Spanish-Speaking American, 256-257
Ethnic studies, 261
  Afro-American, 3, 8-9, 15, 55, 69
  Asian American, 79, 86, 87
Evers, Charles, 26, 48

Family life
  Afro-American, 26, 43, 45, 51, 53, 60, 251
  Asian American, 64
  Central American, 224
  Central Asian, 112

Chinese, 72, 73, 74, 93, 105, 108, 109, 115, 123, 130, 251
Filipino, 76, 93, 101
Indian, 130
Indian American, 136, 138, 140, 148, 154, 155, 160, 161, 163, 165, 166, 167, 168, 175, 185, 187, 251
Indonesian, 98
Italian, 251
Japanese, 75, 100, 111, 114, 115, 117, 131, 132
Jewish, 185
Korean, 80
Mexican American, 194, 207, 224
Puerto Rican, 193, 196
South Vietnamese, 113
Spanish, 218-219
Spanish-Speaking American, 190, 200-201, 216, 251
Thai, 105
White American, 251
Farm workers, Spanish-Speaking American, 193, 208, 209, 210, 211, 214, 219, 220
Filipino American, 76, 81, 82, 83, 210
Fisk University, 4, 34, 57
Flack, Roberta, 32, 37
Folk music. *See* Music, Folk
Folktales. *See* Literature, Folk
Formosa. *See* Taiwan
Franklin, Aretha, 18, 35

Galarza, Ernesto, 232, 238
Garvey, Marcus, 27, 28, 43, 44, 49, 60
Georgia, 34, 41, 166
German Americans, 241, 254, 256, 259
Geronimo, 178, 180, 181, 186
Gibson, Althea, 62, 69
Gregory, Dick, 23, 40
Guatemala, 223, 224

Handy, William Christopher, 40, 63, 70
Hansberry, Lorraine, 18, 39, 46, 52, 65, 66
Harlem (New York City), 28, 41, 49, 50, 51, 60
Puerto Ricans, 210, 229
Harlem Renaissance (Afro-American), 5, 6, 28, 50, 51, 56, 61
Harris, LaDonna, 186
Harris, Patricia, 29, 45
Hawaii, 73, 76, 97, 124
Henson, Matthew, 57, 63
Hiawatha, 181, 182, 186
Holidays. *See* Ceremonies (festivals)
Honduras, 223, 224
Hong Kong, 93, 98, 103, 106, 108, 111, 112, 119
Howard University, 4, 5, 24
Hughes, Langston, 5, 28, 43, 46, 50, 53, 61, 63, 65, 67, 70

Illinois, Chicago, 5, 24, 25
Immigrants, Immigration
Asian American, 71, 72, 78, 79
Chinese, 71, 72, 73, 74, 75, 76, 95, 96, 117
European, 241, 243, 251, 263
Filipino, 75, 76
Japanese, 73, 74, 75, 76, 99
Korean, 76, 80
restrictive legislation, 73, 74, 75, 76, 77, 99-100, 128
Spanish-Speaking American, 189-190, 194, 195, 196-197, 198, 221, 251
India, 92, 98, 107, 111, 122, 130
Indian Americans
biography (collections), 178, 180, 181
culture (many tribes), 133, 136, 137, 138, 139, 141, 149, 155, 157, 159, 161, 162, 167, 169, 170, 171, 172, 173, 175, 176, 178, 179, 180, 181, 182, 183, 184, 186
history
contemporary period, 139, 153, 154, 166, 167, 169, 171, 172, 180
European colonization, 136, 169
Pan Indian period, 139, 162, 174
Pre-Columbian, 135, 151, 153, 169, 171, 172, 178, 181, 187
treaties, legal controls (U.S.), 133, 135, 137, 138, 139, 143, 150, 169, 174, 183, 186
land disputes, 151, 162, 166, 168, 169
Meriam Report, 138
migration from Asia, 149, 152, 156
nature, concept of, 152, 156, 162, 168, 173, 174, 175

Indian Americans (*Cont.*)
reservations, 139, 149, 151, 153, 154, 155, 156, 157, 158, 166, 169, 172, 180, 184, 187
resistance to conquest, 186, 187
self image, 134, 137, 139, 142, 153, 155
tribal areas
Alaskan, 133, 166, 177, 180
Canadian, 150, 151, 153, 157, 159, 164, 166, 167, 168, 170, 171, 173, 177, 179, 186, 187
Eastern Woodlands, 149, 156, 168, 169, 176, 178, 180, 186
Far West, 158, 162, 176, 177, 178
Great Lakes, 168, 176
Great Plains, 148, 149, 152, 156, 157, 159, 160, 162, 164, 166, 169, 170, 171, 172, 173, 174 175, 178, 179, 180, 182, 183, 186
Northwest Coast, 156, 159, 162, 163, 171, 173, 175, 176, 177, 178, 180, 184, 186
Southwestern, 148, 149, 150, 151, 156, 157, 158, 161, 162, 163, 164, 165, 166, 167, 168, 169, 170, 171, 172, 173, 176, 177, 178, 179, 180, 182, 183, 185, 186
urban dwellers, 152, 158, 160, 172, 185
Indonesia, 98, 112, 118, 132
Integration. *See* Race relations
Iran, 121, 122
Iraq, 121
Irish, 241, 243, 254, 256, 259
Israel
agriculture, 244, 247, 254
communal living, 244, 245, 253, 255
culture, 243, 255
Italian Americans, 241, 243, 251, 254, 256, 260

Jackson, Jesse, 20, 68
Jackson, Mahalia, 21, 35
Japan
culture, 76, 77, 99, 111, 112, 113, 114, 115, 117, 118, 119, 120, 122, 124, 128, 132
economic growth, 99, 100, 107, 114, 119, 124, 128
foreign relations, 114, 127, 128
history
modern, 74-75, 77, 99, 100, 102, 113, 114, 118, 124
traditional, 80, 99
land and resources, 100, 114, 117, 131
Japanese Americans
culture, 75, 83, 99
evacuation to war relocation centers 75, 97, 102, 115, 128
Issei, 74, 128
Nisei, 102, 128
See also Immigrants, Immigration
Jazz, 5, 17, 23, 26, 37, 51, 61, 67
Jews, 241, 243
Arab-Jewish relations, 247, 252
culture, 243, 251
European communities, 254, 258, 260
Jewish Americans, 251, 254, 256
See also Education
Johnson, Georgia Douglas, 28, 53
Jones, James Earl, 33, 42, 45, 48, 65
Jones, LeRoi, 9, 20

Katz, William, 48, 56
Kearney, Dennis, 73, 96
Kennedy, John F., 54, 243, 259
Kennedy, Robert F., 66, 153, 208
King, Martin Luther, Jr., 6, 17, 23, 24, 28, 33, 34, 35, 43, 44, 46, 52, 53, 54, 57, 64, 66, 69, 70
Korea, 80, 107, 108, 116
Korean Americans, 76, 80, 83
Ku Klux Klan, 3, 43, 58, 62, 70
Kublai Khan, 101, 124

La Farge, Peter, 181, 183
Labor unions, 73, 255, 259
Afro-American, 4, 30, 43
Filipino, 210
Mexican-American, 195, 207, 208, 210, 212, 221
Language
Asian, 83, 84, 119
China, People's Republic of, 94
English, 84, 199, 211, 215
Hebrew, 243
Indian, 190
Indian American, 135, 137, 138, 140, 141, 170, 171
Japanese, 74, 84
Korean, 80

Spanish, 199, 202, 208, 227, 229, 232, 235
Yiddish, 258
Laos, 116, 119
Latin Americans. *See* Cubans; Mexican Americans; Puerto Ricans; Spanish-Speaking Americans
"Leadbelly," 21, 22
Lincoln, Abraham, 4, 43, 64
Literature
Afro-American, 25, 30, 32, 35, 36, 39, 42, 48, 51, 52, 53, 60, 61, 62, 65, 66, 68, 70
Chinese, 126
Japanese, 120
Jewish, 242
Literature, Folk
Afro-American, 32, 61
Alaskan, 253
Asian, 107, 125
Chinese, 96–97, 110, 111, 127, 130
East Indian, 253
Eskimo, 259
Indian American, 149, 157, 159, 162, 167, 170, 171, 174, 176, 180
Irish, 259
Japanese, 112, 253
Kenyan, 253
Mexican, 253
Puerto Rican, 223, 235, 253
South Sea Island, 129
Spanish American, 229
Yiddish, 261
Lloyd, Charles, 23, 51, 54
Lopez Tijerina, Reies, 221, 239
Louis, Joe, 32, 60, 69

McKay, Claude, 9, 50, 61
McNeil, Claudia, 18, 39, 66
Malaya, 101
See also Malaysia
Malaysia, 103, 107, 111, 119, 131
Malcolm X, 19, 23, 28, 32, 33, 37, 42, 44, 46, 56, 66, 69
Mao Tse-tung, 101, 104, 109, 130–131, 132
Marco Polo, 101, 124–125
Marshall, Thurgood, 43, 45, 51, 62, 63, 69
Massasoit, 178, 180, 181
Melting pot, 1, 137, 189, 243, 247, 252
Meredith, James, 54, 56
Mestizos. *See* Mexican Americans; Spanish-Speaking Americans
Mexican Americans
biography (collections) 238, 239
cultures, 195, 208, 209–210, 211, 212, 213, 221, 224, 225, 227
European heritage, 208, 214, 225, 226
Indian heritage, 213, 214, 226
soldiers, Vietnam, 220
See also Education; Family life; Labor unions
Mexico
biography (collections), 231
cultures, 195, 215, 219, 221, 226, 227, 229
ecology, 230
history, 195, 213, 214, 219, 225, 227, 229, 232, 234
U.S. relations, 195, 213, 223
See also Spanish-Speaking Americans
Migrant Americans, 241, 252, 255, 263
Mindanao. *See* Philippines
Missions, Missionaries, 100, 107
Hawaii, 97
Spanish, 73, 136, 215
Montagu, Ashley, 54, 257
Montalban, Ricardo, 212, 213
Munoz Marin, Luis, 217, 235
Music
African, 17
Afro-American, 21, 25, 37, 40, 45, 46, 51, 60, 61, 63, 66, 68
Arabian, 258
China, People's Republic of, 110, 118
Chinese, 94, 129, 132
Filipino, 102, 107
Hawaiian, 97, 128
Indian American, 152, 156, 159, 180, 182, 183
Indonesian, 98
Israeli, 260
Japanese, 96, 99, 128, 129
Korean, 128
Mexican, 208, 213, 233, 234, 236
Nepalese, 129
Okinawan, 129
Puerto Rican, 217, 228
Spanish (classic), 236
Spanish-Speaking American, 220, 233, 235
Taiwanese, 129
Vietnamese, 130

Music, Folk
  Afro-American, 17, 18, 22, 35, 46, 67
    Spirituals, 17, 32, 33, 49
    See also Jazz
  Arabian, 253
  Burmese, 125
  Chinese, 126, 127
  Eskimo, 259
  Filipino, 127
  Hawaiian, 127
  Indian American, 164, 179, 181, 183, 184
  Israeli, 253
  Japanese, 127
  Korean, 128
  Spanish American, 212, 233
Musical instruments
  Asian, 129
  Indian American, 177
  Japanese, 96
Mythology. *See* Literature, Folk

NAACP (National Association for the Advancement of Colored People), 22, 31, 43, 60, 62, 67
NEA (National Education Association), 258, 260
Negroes. *See* Afro-Americans
New Mexico, 150, 164, 215, 229
New York City, 4, 243, 246, 261
  Chinese in, 72
  Spanish-Speaking Americans in, 196, 203, 220
  See also Harlem
Newton, Huey, 22, 29

Occupational distribution
  Afro-American, 4, 45, 58, 59, 78
  Asian American, 72, 78, 85
Orient. *See* Asia
Osceola, 178, 181, 254
Owens, Jesse, 31, 56, 60

Parks, Gordon, 32, 41, 51, 54, 64, 68
Pellowski, Anne, 127, 180
Peru, 190, 210, 216, 220
Peters, Brock, 61, 67
Philippines, Republic of the, 93, 101, 103, 104, 107, 112, 113, 119, 131
Poetry
  African, 32
  Afro-American, 25, 28, 31, 36, 37, 47, 50, 53, 61, 64, 65, 66, 68, 70
  Chinese, 110, 127
  Japanese, 128
  Puerto Rican, 235
  Spanish, 236
Poitier, Sidney, 18, 23, 28, 70
Polish Americans, 241, 243, 245, 251, 260
Pontiac, 178, 180, 181, 183, 186
Pottery. *See* Arts and Crafts
Powell, Adam Clayton, Jr., 23, 28, 56
Powhatan, 178, 180, 181
Prejudice. *See* Race Relations
Protestant religions. *See* Religion
Puerto Ricans
  cultures, 197, 200, 211, 217, 221, 251
  mainland life, 196–197, 225, 235, 236
  "Operation Bootstrap," 216, 217, 235
  See also New York City
Puerto Rico
  African heritage, 235
  history, 216, 217, 228, 232, 235
  Indian heritage, 235
  Island culture, 228, 232, 236
  Spanish heritage, 223, 235
  U.S. Commonwealth status, 216

Race relations, 242, 244, 246, 248, 250, 256, 257, 261
  Afro-American, 4, 19, 20, 22, 24, 25, 28, 31, 36, 64, 247
  Asian American, 95, 96, 97, 102
  Indian American, 133, 134, 139, 140, 156, 169, 175, 178, 179
  Spanish-Speaking American, 190, 191, 194, 197, 201, 202, 210, 211, 220, 221
  See also Civil Rights; Stereotypes
Race riots, 5, 26, 27, 60
Railroads, construction (U.S.), 72, 95, 103
Randolph, A. Phillip, 43, 44, 46, 56, 60
Recreation
  Asia, 119
  China, 94
  China, People's Republic of, 94, 116
  Hawaii, 97
  Japan, 113

Religion
Amish, 249
Buddhism, 81-82, 99, 100, 102, 111, 118
Catholic, 82, 136, 201
Confucianism, 80-81, 82, 86, 96, 132
Islam, 92, 242
Mormon, 136, 153
Protestant, 82, 136, 201
Shinto, 102, 105, 261
Robinson, Jackie, 23, 31, 44, 69
Rustin, Bayard, 1, 23, 25

Sands, Diana, 18, 61, 63, 66
Sculpture
African, 55, 69
Afro-American, 23, 48, 56, 63
See also Art
Seale, Bobby, 29, 32
Siam. *See* Thailand
Silversmiths. *See* Arts and Crafts
Singapore, 101, 105, 116, 119
Sitting Bull, 175, 178, 181, 183, 186
Smalls, Robert, 51, 59
Smith, Bessie, 21
Soul music. *See* Music, Folk
South America, 190, 197, 216, 218, 239
Southeast Asia, 105, 119
Spain
cultural influence in the New World, 218, 227, 232
explorations, 194, 215, 219, 224, 231
Spanish-American War, 232, 235, 239
Spanish-Speaking Americans, 190, 198, 199, 210, 203, 212, 221, 227, 235
Spirituals. *See* Music, Folk
Sports
Chinese, 109
Hawaiian, 97
Japanese, 101, 128
See also Athletes; Recreation
Stereotypes, 250, 251, 257
African, 17
Afro-American, 1, 17, 21, 24, 30
Asian American, 71, 85
Chinese, 73, 118
Indian American, 134, 135, 154, 176
Spanish American, 190, 191
Stokes, Carl, 23, 46
Strikes. *See* Labor unions

Taiwan, 108, 120, 130
See also China
Tecumseh, 176, 178, 181
Texas
Brownsville, 211
El Paso, 195
Rio Grande City, 211
Texas Republic, 223
Thailand, 97, 105, 106, 107, 111, 116, 121, 125, 130
Toppin, E. A., 20, 68
Transportation
Burma, 93
China, 97, 108
China, People's Republic of, 116
Indonesia, 118
Japanese, 100, 113, 124, 131
Thailand, 107
See also Waterways; Railroads
Truth, Sojourner, 44, 66, 68
Tubman, Harriet, 28, 44, 48, 51, 59, 64, 66, 69
Turner, Nat, 43, 48, 52, 56, 57, 58, 60, 62, 70

"Underground Railroad," 28, 34, 43, 56
Unemployment. *See* Employment
U.S. Armed Forces
Afro-Americans, 4, 5, 18, 36, 43, 46, 47, 56, 58, 64, 66, 70, 132
Mexican Americans, 220

Vazquez, de Coronado, Francisco, 194, 215, 219
Venezuela, 208, 216, 220
Vesey, Denmark, 43, 49
Vespucci, Amerigo, 219, 260
Vietnam, 113, 116, 119, 124, 130, 132

Washington, Booker T., 4, 5, 22, 23, 27, 43, 44, 52, 54, 66, 70
Waterways
Mexico, 214, 238
Southeast Asia, 93, 97, 104-105, 106, 107, 119
Weaver, Robert, 45, 63, 66
Wesley, Dr. Charles H., 2, 260
Wheatley, Phillis, 9, 66, 70

Williams, Daniel H., 63, 69
Wisconsin, Menominee County, 149, 158
Women, 250, 260, 264
  Afro-American, 9, 18, 19, 45, 46, 47, 48, 49, 51, 53, 54, 59, 60, 61, 62, 63, 64, 65, 66, 67, 68, 69
  China, People's Republic of, 94, 118, 132
  Chinese, 72, 74, 96, 106
  Eskimo, 262, 245, 247
  Indian, 148, 153, 155, 160
  Japanese, 74, 94, 118, 132
  Jewish, 263
  Puerto Rican, 196
  Spanish-Speaking American, 201
Wright, Richard, 39, 50, 67
Young, Whitney, 25, 63
Youth, 243, 244, 245, 260
  Afro-American, 3, 5, 6, 7, 8, 9, 24, 25, 26, 27, 29, 30, 34, 39, 41, 46, 49, 53, 79
  Asian American, 79-80, 85, 86, 87
  Chicano, 79
  China, People's Republic of, 118
  Chinese American, 95, 105, 106
  Indian, 207
  Indian American, 134, 136, 167, 185
  Japan, 114
  Japanese American, 75
  Mexican student riots, 214

Zapata, Antonio, 214, 232